"*The Digital Public Square* provides readers with tangible ways to navigate the dilemmas of our technological age in a manner worthy of the gospel. The authors provide scripturally sound approaches to the complex and novel challenges of a digitally connected society. It is a valuable navigational tool for any Christian desiring to engage meaningfully with the unique difficulties ubiquitous in an online world."

—**Katie Frugé**, director of the Center for Cultural Engagement and Christian Life Commission at Baptist General Convention of Texas

"This weighty collection covers vast swaths of surprising ethical boundaries, from the personal tweeting of a Christian intellectual to the local and global digital behaviors mitigating human rights. Each essay simultaneously taught and challenged me in surprising ways."

—**Dru Johnson**, associate professor of biblical and theological studies at The King's College in New York City and author of *Biblical Philosophy: A Hebraic Approach to the Old and New Testaments*

"As Christians engage (and are engaged by) the principalities and powers of the digital public square, they desperately need a critical and constructive public theology to guide that engagement. Readers will be greatly rewarded by this insightful and urgently needed volume."

—**Matthew Kaemingk**, assistant professor of faith and public life and director of the Mouw Institute of Faith and Public Life, Fuller Theological Seminary

"*The Digital Public Square* offers the kind of careful, technically informed, and theologically grounded thinking that is so deeply needed in these conversations. Each contributor helps readers to understand these complex issues and their implications, while the book as a whole serves as a model for how Christians are to engage opaque but consequential matters. I highly recommend this text for anyone seeking to faithfully apply the principles of Scripture in the new digital public square."

—**Klon Kitchen**, senior fellow in national security and defense technology, cybersecurity, artificial intelligence, and robotics at the American Enterprise Institute, and author of *The Current* at the Dispatch

"Almost every question I get from Christians today is, in some way or the other, about technology. This book offers counsel and insight on practical matters of digitized life, from connectivity exhaustion to conspiracy theories to government spying and beyond."

—**Russell Moore**, editor-in-chief at *Christianity Today*

"We live in an age of digital disruption. Town squares—where people once could go debate and persuade neighbors—have given way to rage tweets and social media trolls. But *The Digital Public Square* offers an important look into pressing questions at the intersections of tech and some of the most important parts of life—and how people of faith (and everyone else) should seek to engage this new digital landscape with truth and grace in a way that protects our inalienable rights and promotes human flourishing.

—**Ben Sasse**, United States senator from Nebraska, author of *Them: Why We Hate Each Other—and How to Heal*

THE
DIGITAL
PUBLIC
SQUARE

THE DIGITAL PUBLIC SQUARE

*Christian Ethics
in a Technological Society*

Jason Thacker

EDITOR

B&H
ACADEMIC
BRENTWOOD, TENNESSEE

CONTENTS

Part 3: The Church

PREFACE

Years ago, I was struck by a citation in the late Carl F. H. Henry's *Christian Personal Ethics* about the centrality of love in the Christian ethic. The esteemed evangelical titan quoted German theologian Christoph Ernst Luthardt, saying, "God first loved us is the summary of Christian doctrine. We love Him is the summary of Christian morality."[1] So often in the contemporary church, there is a wedge driven between the study of theology and ethics that hampers the church from engaging some of the most pressing issues of the day as our theology is untethered from ethics and our practice is uprooted from its foundation. Dr. Henry would summarize Luthardt by saying that "[l]ove for another is the whole sum of Christian ethics."[2] This is an apt way to begin a volume on Christian ethics, as so many of the issues we deal with today are not really about bits and bytes, but flesh-and-blood image bearers living in a technological society.

This book is the product of that vision to work toward a Christian ethic for our digital age, one that is rooted in truth and love of neighbor. The title and vision of this book are undoubtably influenced by the late public theologian Richard John Neuhaus and his influential work *The Naked Public Square*, as well as the late Protestant sociologist and theologian Jacques Ellul, who wrote the prescient volume *The Technological Society*. It has been

---

[1] Carl F. H. Henry, *Christian Personal Ethics*, 2nd ed. (Grand Rapids: Baker, 1979), 486, quoting Christoph Ernst Luthardt, *Apologetic Lectures on the Moral Truths of Christianity*, trans. Sophia Taylor (Edinburgh: T&T Clark, 1876), 26.

[2] Henry, 486.

said that we are a product of those who have gone before us, and that will be apparent throughout this work.

There are countless people who made this project possible. First, I want to acknowledge the unending and undeserved support of my wife, who has sacrificed much as I pursued this project and others over the years. Her love and encouragement were key to this project's success. Second, I want to thank each of the contributors for being part of this volume, bringing their expertise to bear on these pressing ethical challenges. Third, I want to thank the entire team at the Ethics and Religious Liberty Commission, including our past president Dr. Russell Moore, who took a flyer on a young guy years ago, and our leadership team, led by Brent Leatherwood. This book would not have been possible without their support and that of Southern Baptists.

Seth Woodley, Alex Ward, and Cameron Hayner all played crucial roles in helping to organize and edit this volume. I am grateful for each of them, especially Seth, who spent long hours alongside me as we finalized the volume. I also want to thank Josh Wester and Daniel Darling for standing beside me and encouraging me to develop these ideas over the years. Their friendship and support are one of the great joys of my life. The entire team at B&H Academic have been a joy to work with—especially my editors Dennis Greeson, Audrey Greeson, Michael McEwen, and Renée Chavez—as well as the leadership of Madison Trammel as publisher. I am also grateful for the continued support of my literary agent, Erik Wolgemuth, and his team at Wolgemuth and Associates.

—Jason Thacker
Chair of Research in Technology Ethics
Director of the Research Institute
Ethics and Religious Liberty Commission
of the Southern Baptist Convention

PART I

Foundations

Simply a Tool?

Toward a Christian Philosophy of Technology and Vision for Navigating the Digital Public Square

Jason Thacker

My family lives just outside a small Tennessee town with a historic downtown district. Like many small towns throughout our nation, we have a downtown square that serves as a hub for our community. In prior generations, these public squares buzzed with energy and served as gathering places. People regularly traveled in from the outskirts of town to shop, eat, bank, gather with their church, and do business. They would also come together for community events and to freely engage with one another. With the rapid growth of suburbs beginning around the mid-twentieth century, many historic downtown public squares were abandoned or fell into disrepute. However, in recent years there has been a renewed interest in revitalizing these historic neighborhoods in many places to provide a place for communities to gather together once again—especially in a digital age that has led to increasing isolation and disconnected communities.

These public gathering places serve as an apt metaphor for a period when much of our daily communication, commerce, and community are facilitated in the digital public square of social media and online connectivity. With the rise of the internet and various social media platforms—such as Facebook, Twitter, and TikTok, and massive online retailers and internet companies like Amazon, Alibaba, and Google—these new digital public squares promised to bring about a vibrant era of connectivity and togetherness across distances, more diverse communities, and more access to information. Many of these initial promises were made in light of oppressive regimes throughout the world that stifled free speech, suppressed human rights, violated religious freedom, and limited access to information to maintain control over other human beings made in the image of God (Gen 1:26–28).

While technology has brought incredible benefits and conveniences into our lives, it also has led to countless unintended consequences and deep ethical challenges that push us to consider how to live out our faith in a technological society. Each day we are bombarded with fake news, misinformation, conspiracy theories, ever-growing polarization, and more information than we could ever hope to process. We regularly face challenges where wisdom and truth are needed, yet faith is not always welcome in the digital public square. In truth, technology has always been used and abused by those who seek to hold on to power and wield it to suppress free expression all around the world. But today, these threats seem more visceral and dangerous to our way of life than ever before.

One of the most challenging ethical issues of our day with technology is centered around the proper role of digital governance and the ethical boundaries of free expression in the digital public square. Many have recently begun to question the role and influence of the technology industry over our public discourse, as well as the responsibilities and roles of individuals, third-party companies, and even the government in digital governance. While much of the dangerous, illegal, and illicit content is rightly moderated, questions remain as to what kinds of ideas or speech are to be welcomed in the digital public square and how we are to maintain a moral order in our secular age as we seek to uphold free expression and religious freedom for all.

As we begin this journey of navigating the digital public square with truth and grace (Eph 4:15), Christians must seek to understand not only the issues at stake but also what is driving them. To do this, we must first slow down enough to ask some of the fundamental questions about what technology is and what it is doing to us. Is technology merely a tool or something that is shaping us all in unique ways, often contrary to our faith? After charting a Christian philosophy of technology, I will shift toward developing a public theology for the digital age built upon the unchanging Word of God and a rich history of church engagement in the public square on the pressing issues of society. With these foundations set, the church can faithfully move forward in addressing the pressing issues of content moderation and digital governance, as the other contributors to this volume write about within a distinctly Christian ethical framework. This chapter will show that technology is much more than simply a tool we use, but something that is truly using us—shaping and forming us in particular ways often contrary to the Christian faith. While we should not uncritically embrace technology, neither should we outright reject the gifts and benefits of these developments. Christians must seek to wisely navigate the challenges of the digital public square as we seek to love God and love others as ourselves (Matt 22:37–39), which is the very core of the Christian ethic. While this chapter and volume will not address every issue in the digital public square, it nevertheless is designed to illustrate the ethical principles and wisdom needed to move forward proclaiming a message of truth and grace amidst an ever-changing technological landscape in the coming years.

A Christian Philosophy of Technology

The late French sociologist and theologian Jacques Ellul, an astute observer of the cultural and moral shifts that took place in the twentieth century due to the rise of modern technology, opened his influential work *The Technological Society* by saying, "No social, human, or spiritual fact is so important as the fact of *technique* in the modern world. And yet no subject is so little understood."[1] These words originally penned in the 1950s

---

[1] Jacques Ellul, *The Technological Society* (New York: Alfred A. Knopf, 1964), 3.

speak directly to the current debates over technology and its proper role in our lives as well as to the complexity of these systems and how they are radically altering our society. Today, technology is often assumed and assimilated rather than examined or questioned regarding its nature and proper role in lives.[2] Ellul wrote his classic work in the midst of his own era's explosion of modern technologies, such as the spread of television to most homes, the rise of many automated systems in homes and factories, and even the earliest beginnings of artificial intelligence (AI) in the West.[3] He prophetically warned of the countless ways that technology was negatively affecting humanity in the pursuit of efficiency and progress, often without any real moral clarity or response. In one of his later works, he claimed that the pursuit of truth used to be what mattered to society, but the "technical means gradually came to dominate the search for truth" as our society sought efficiency over reality and adopted technologies without adequate scrutiny.[4] For Ellul, technology was not merely an isolated tool or instrument as commonly understood in past generations. Instead, it represented a totalizing force in modern life that shapes everything about our lives and society, often toward dehumanizing ends. In his philosophical understanding, technology was not a neutral tool but had a complete reorienting effect on every aspect of human life.

To address many of the pressing ethical questions of our day surrounding the development and use of technology, a firm grasp on the nature of technology must first be established. Without a robust and biblical understanding of the nature of technology, Christians will not be able to see through the veneer of these modern innovations—marketed

---

[2] John Dyer speaks to this lack of questioning the role and nature of technology by saying, "When technology has distracted us to the point that we no longer examine it, it gains the greatest opportunity to enslave us." See John Dyer, *From the Garden to the City: The Redeeming and Corrupting Power of Technology* (Grand Rapids: Kregel, 2011), 28.

[3] For more on the history of AI, see Jason Thacker, *The Age of AI: Artificial Intelligence and the Future of Humanity* (Grand Rapids: Zondervan, 2020), 23–26.

[4] Jacques Ellul, *Presence in the Modern World*, trans. Lisa Richmond (Eugene, OR: Cascade Books, 2016), 41.

as they are with slick slogans, accompanied with promises of a utopian future, and designed to encourage individuals to adopt these tools without adequate reflection on the influence they might exert in their lives. Jacques Ellul's study on the nature and influence of technology can serve as a helpful guide for Christians today as we navigate the contours of our present situation.

What Is Technology?

Ellul, who served as a longtime professor of history and sociology at the University of Bordeaux, was a prolific author of over sixty published works, originally written in French. Trained as a sociologist, he spent most of his life and scholarship exposing the influence of technology on modern human existence, including but not limited to social relationships, political structures, and economic phenomena. Through his study of the prevalence and the transformative nature of technology in modern times, Ellul helped to define a philosophy of technology for both the secular and religious communities of his day as well as to chart a path forward in addressing many of the unforeseen questions and dangers that come alongside the technologies of today. Ellul nevertheless provided a wealth of contributions as he warned readers of many current debates about the nature of technology through his many ethical and theological writings, including his most well-known works, *The Technological Society* and *Propaganda: The Formation of Men's Attitudes.*[5]

The Technological Society was Ellul's first and primary work on the subject where he described his understanding of the ways that technology changes and shapes humanity. Originally published as *La Technique ou l'Enjeu du siècle* in 1954, Ellul sought to provide a "description of the

---

[5] Ellul was not alone in his field. Interested readers can explore other works on the nature of technology such as Lewis Mumford, *Technics and Civilization* (Chicago: University of Chicago Press, 2010); George Grant, *Technology & Justice* (Toronto: Anansi, 1991); and Langdon Winner, *Autonomous Technology: Technics-out-of-Control as a Theme in Political Thought* (Cambridge, MA: MIT Press, 1977).

way in which an autonomous technology is in the process of taking over the traditional values of every society without exception, subverting and suppressing these values to produce at last a monolithic world culture."[6] Ellul preferred the term *technique* to technology because in his view *technique* better described "the *totality of methods rationally arrived at and having absolute efficiency* (for a given stage of development) in *every* field of human activity."[7] To Ellul, technique is an all-encompassing concept that is not simply limited to "machines, technology, or this or that procedure for attaining an end."[8] Ellul saw technique as the integration of machines into our society and argued that technique constructs a certain type of world that the machine needs as it introduces order and drives toward efficiency.[9] But he maintained that machines or the tools themselves are "deeply symptomatic" of technique and "represents the ideal toward which technique strives."[10]

Defining technology is not an easy task, and many words have been penned over the years trying to nail down this complex concept. Some define technology as simply a tool, machine, or instrument that humanity can wield as needed to accomplish our work and shape the world around us.[11] Others, including Ellul, define technology as a totalizing social force

---

[6] See the translator's introduction to the 1964 English edition. Ellul, *The Technological Society*, x.

[7] Ellul, xxv, emphasis original.

[8] Ellul, xxv.

[9] See Ellul, 5. Ellul spoke of this drive to efficiency as *automatism*, which he described as "the one best way" and a technical movement that is "self-directing." Everything in this automatism is measured and calculated mathematically "so that the method which has been decided upon is satisfactory from the rational point of view, and when, from the practical point of view, the method is manifestly the most efficient of all those hitherto employed or those in competition with it, then the technical movement becomes self-directing." See Ellul, 80.

[10] Ellul, 4.

[11] See Mary Tiles and Hans Oberdiek, "Conflicting Visions of Technology" in Robert C. Scharff and Val Dusek, eds., *Philosophy of Technology: The Technological Condition*, Blackwell Philosophy Anthologie 32 (Malden, MA: Wiley Blackwell, 2014), 249–53, for a thorough overview of the instrumentalist position, where they argue that these technological optimists often see "technology as fulfilling the

or culture.[12] This distinction is often defined as a narrow (internalist) or broad (externalist) understanding of technology by scholars like philosopher of technology Doug Hill, who argues that "definitions of technology sometimes carry implications hidden to those not attuned to an argument in progress."[13] Each of these concepts have certain strengths but also concerning elements that do not quite align with the real world of technology.[14]

Most often these narrow or broad approaches to technology are defined as: *technological determinism* and *technological instrumentalism*.[15] Georgetown professor Cal Newport defines technological determinism as the belief that "features and properties of a given technology can drive human behavior and culture in directions that are often unplanned and unforeseen," whereas technological instrumentalism is the belief that "tools are neutral, and what matters in understanding their impact is the cultural context and motivations of the people that develop and use them for specific

---

biblical injunction to 'fill the earth and subdue it, and have dominion over the fish of the sea and over the birds of the air and over every living thing (Gen. 1:28).'" They argue that this dominion view of technology was also promoted by Sir Francis Bacon, who is "regarded by many as the father of modern science and technology."

[12] See Albert Borgmann, *Power Failure: Christianity in the Culture of Technology* (Grand Rapids: Brazos, 2003); Neil Postman, *Technopoly: The Surrender of Culture to Technology* (New York: Vintage Books, 1993); and Ursula M. Franklin, *The Real World of Technology*, CBC Massey Lectures Series (Toronto: House of Anansi, 2004).

[13] Doug Hill, *Not So Fast: Thinking Twice about Technology* (Athens, GA: University of Georgia Press, 2016), 48.

[14] This phrase is borrowed from Franklin, *The Real World of Technology*, 27. She describes this "real world of technology" by stating that she wanted to "discuss technology in terms of living and working in the real world and what this means to people all over the globe," as well as hearken back to C. B. Macpherson's 1965 lecture series where he examined the ideas, dreams, practices, procedures, hopes, and myths of democracy. This holistic view of technology will be examined throughout this chapter.

[15] For a more in-depth treatment of these approaches to technology, see Albert Borgmann, *Technology and the Character of Contemporary Life: A Philosophical Inquiry* (Chicago: University of Chicago Press, 1984, 1987). Borgmann adds a third approach, which he calls a "pluralistic view," and argues for it throughout his work.

purposes."[16] Jacques Ellul argued for a more deterministic approach to technology because he saw technology more broadly than simply isolated tools or machines. To Ellul, technology was a complex system or web of relations that determined the social structure and cultural values.

Technological determinism can also be defined as a reductionistic concept because of the emphasis on the complex systems and structures that shape humanity and the world, rather than emphasizing the ways these tools can be used by humanity for good or ill. According to political theorist Langdon Winner, it was Karl Marx who first applied technological determinism to societal structures, arguing that changes in technology were the primary force behind human social relations and organizational structure, and that human society revolved around technological and economic centers of society.[17] Mary Tiles and Hans Oberdiek describe technological determinism as the "pessimistic" view of technology that is often portrayed as at odds with the "optimistic" view, which they attribute to how many Christians typically see technology as part of the cultural mandate found in Gen 1:28, where technology is simply a value-neutral tool.[18] But as experimental physicist and longtime professor Ursula M. Franklin argues, "Technology is not the sum of the artifacts, of the wheels and hears, of the rails and electronic transmitters. . . . It entails more than its individual

---

[16] Cal Newport, "When Technology Goes Awry," *Communications of the ACM* 63, no. 5 (May 2020), https://cacm.acm.org/magazines/2020/5/244331-when -technology-goes-awry/fulltext.

[17] See Winner, 39. See also Lewis Mumford, *Technics and Civilization* (Chicago: University of Chicago Press, 2010). It should also be noted that this connection between technological determinism and Karl Marx is debated amongst scholars. Winner was the first to establish this connection in his 1977 work *Autonomous Technology.* For a contrary view, see Bruce Bimber, *Three Faces of Technological Determinism* in Merritt Roe Smith and Leo Marx, eds., *Does Technology Drive History? The Dilemma of Technological Determinism* (Cambridge, MA: MIT Press, 1994), 80–100.

[18] See Tiles and Oberdiek, "Conflicting Visions of Technology," in Scharff and Dusek, *Philosophy of Technology,* 253.

material components. Technology involves organization, procedures, symbols, new words, equations, and, most of all, a mindset."[19]

Ellul argued for a view of technology best described as *technological determinism*, which views technology as not merely an instrument or value neutral tool, but rather a movement that captures humanity in its grip and transforms everything in the name of efficiency.[20] Matthew T. Prior summarizes Ellul's position by saying that "technology simply *is*. It is neither good nor bad but nor it is neutral."[21] James Fowler argues that Ellul viewed technology as "but an expression and by-product of the underlying reliance on technique, on the proceduralization whereby everything is organized and managed to function most efficiently, and directed toward the most expedient end of the highest productivity."[22] And to Craig M. Gay, Ellul's view is "hardly surprising" because of the way that technology figures so centrally into the modern project. He states that for Ellul, rationality governs technique because "ours is a society in which taking control of our secular circumstances by means of rational-technical means, methods, procedures, and techniques has become supremely important."[23] This can be seen in our society's ill-fated pursuit of treating every inconvenience as a technical problem to be solved or issue to be mitigated, as illustrated by many modern thinkers like Yuval Noah Harari in his work *Homo Deus: A Brief History of Tomorrow*.[24]

---

[19] Franklin, *The Real World of Technology*, 2–3.

[20] See Jacques Ellul, *Propaganda: The Formation of Men's Attitudes* (New York: Vintage Books, 1973); Jacques Ellul, *The Technological System*, trans. Joachim Neugroschel, Daniel Cérézuelle, and Lisa Richmond (Eugene, OR: Wipf & Stock, 2018); Jacques Ellul, *The Technological Bluff*, trans. Geoffrey Bromiley (Grand Rapids: Eerdmans, 1990).

[21] Matthew T Prior, *Confronting Technology: The Theology of Jacques Ellul* (Eugene, OR: Pickwick, 2020), 6, emphasis original.

[22] James A. Fowler, "A Synopsis and Analysis of the Thought and Writings of Jacques Ellul," Archives of Wheaton College, 2000, https://archives.wheaton.edu/repositories/2/archival_objects/155101.

[23] Craig M. Gay, *Modern Technology and the Human Future: A Christian Appraisal* (Downers Grove, IL: IVP Academic, 2018), 90.

[24] Harari states that "every technical problem has a technical solution" as he argues for a naturalistic understanding of reality and the human condition. See

Technique in Ellul's mind is autonomous, meaning that it seems to take on a kind of agency and fashions a world designed to primarily allow technology itself to thrive, a world that renounced all prior traditions of meaning and understanding.[25] He argued that "technique transforms everything it touches into a machine."[26] Media theorist and cultural critic Neil Postman describes a similar idea saying that "once a technology is admitted, it plays out its hand; it does what is it designed to do."[27] Postman goes on to say that "our task is to understand what that design is—that is to say, when we admit a new technology to the culture, we must do so with our eyes wide open."[28] The totalizing effect of technique on society is the foundation of Ellul's philosophy of technology and provides a salient understanding of our modern world of technology. For Ellul, technique presents a host of ethical and philosophical issues that must be dealt with at the societal level rather than merely at the personal or individual level. Ellul stated, "The ethical problem, that is human behavior, can only be considered in relation to this system, not in relation to some particular technical object or other [because] if technique is a milieu and a system, the ethical problem can only be posed in terms of this global operation. Behavior and particular choices no longer have much significance. What is required is thus a global change in our habits or values, the rediscovery of either an existential ethics or a new ontology."[29]

Postman expands on this idea by stating that this technique "is without a moral center." Postman's technopoly and Ellul's technological society place "efficiency, interest, and economic advance" at the center of society.

Yuval Noaḥ Harari, *Homo Deus: A Brief History of Tomorrow*, Vintage Popular Science (London: Harvill Secker, 2016), 22–23.

[25] See Ellul, *The Technological Society*, 14. This renunciation of all prior traditions of thought and information organization is a line of thought picked up on by Neil Postman in his work *Technopoly*, as well. See chs. 3–4 of Postman, *Technopoly*.

[26] Ellul, *The Technological Society*, 4.

[27] Postman, *Technopoly*, 7.

[28] Postman, 7.

[29] Jacques Ellul, "The Search for Ethics in a Technicist Society," trans. Dominique Gillot and Carl Mitcham, *Morale et Enseignement*, 1983, 7–20.

Humanity is promised "heaven on earth through the conveniences of technological progress."[30]

As a Protestant theologian and a philosopher, Ellul uniquely addressed many of these technological issues facing our society through the lens of his faith as well. He saw that Christianity in particular added an additional layer to the moral evaluation of technical activity by asking the question "is this righteous?" of each attempt to change the modes of production in a given society. In line with the Christian moral tradition, Ellul states "that [just because] something might be useful or profitable to men did not make it right or good," and that these type of shifts in technical activity must also "fit a precise conception of justice before God."[31] Drawing upon the history of thought and technical progress, Ellul pointed out that "technical innovations have always had the same surprising and unwelcome character for men."[32] Here Ellul brought forth an element in the power of technology to shape humanity in ways that are similar to the Christian conception of discipleship—meaning someone who follows Jesus and seeks to align their life with him in every way.[33] Over a long period of time, exposure to these expanded moral horizons of what is possible and the nature of how technology encourages humanity to engage with it will have a transformative effect and shape humanity toward the ends of the technique, by whatever means available. Technologist and theologian John Dyer states that both Ellul and Postman saw that "the more we use technology, the more it mediates to us the value of addressing problems with technological solutions."[34] This meditation of value is an aspect of how technology is constantly shaping individuals and the larger society with each subsequent innovation.

Today, many spaces in our homes are centered around televisions or computer technologies like living areas and personal bedrooms. Even

---

[30] Postman, *Technopoly*, 179.

[31] Ellul, *The Technological Society*, 37.

[32] Ellul, 61.

[33] For more on technology and contemporary issues in discipleship, see chapter 12 of this work by Jacob Shatzer.

[34] Dyer, *From the Garden to the City*, 63.

beds themselves often have some form of technology often incorporated into them with plugs to charge devices within inches of the pillows so that devices are always within an arm's reach. As well, many popular digital assistants such as Amazon's Alexa or Apple's Siri are always at our beck and call. Tristan Harris and other technologists point out many of these transformative effects in the Netflix documentary *The Social Dilemma*, where one expert interviewee states that the question is not if one checks Twitter in the morning after waking, but whether it is before or while you use the bathroom each morning. This concept of technological progress and ubiquity as argued in the 1950s by Ellul was rightfully seen by many as fatalistic or deterministic, often without any hope of renewal. But given the continued transformation of humanity in this technological society up to the present day, many of Ellul's concerns over the power of technology in society are prophetic rather than overreactions to perceived dangers. Many of his predictions have come true and the deleterious effects of technology that he foreshadowed are beginning to show themselves in the daily lives of everyday people and throughout society as a whole. While Ellul's philosophy of technology contains some troubling aspects, including the autonomy of technique and a fatalistic determinism without any real hope of the future, Ellul nevertheless continues to rightfully challenge all of us to think deeper and more broadly about the nature and role of technology today.

A Biblical Vision of Technology

A Christian philosophy of technology is best described as the understanding that technology is not simply an inert tool, and that we interact with it in complex ways. As Dyer puts it, "Both determinism and instrumentalism have elements of truth to them, but we cannot reduce all discussions about technology in either direction." He goes on to say that "People are culpable for their choices, but technology still plays a role in influencing the decisions they make."[35] Verbeek, critiquing a pure instrumentalist view, argues that "Technology has drastically altered culture and human life—and insofar as it

---

[35] Dyer, 86.

can indeed be understood as a neutral means, instrumentalism glosses over the implications of this far too quickly."[36] Computer scientist Derek Schuurman describes this Christian approach to technology as a "value-laden cultural activity in response to God that shapes the natural creation."[37] He states that this view considers that creation itself has not only a structure but also a direction and that "technology is not neutral" because "technological objects are biased toward certain uses, which in turn bias the user in particular ways."[38] But Schuurman also notes that technology is not autonomous—contra Ellul—because "it is an area in which we exercise freedom and responsibility."[39] This value-laden approach to technology recognizes that the designers of these tools embed their personal or corporate values and even worldviews in the structure of these technological artifacts.[40] This view argues that technology has a certain design and use that shapes how one interacts with the world around them, and forms certain structures and systems in our society.

One of the main strengths of Ellul's vision of technique was that he saw past the overly simplistic understandings of technology as an isolated and value-neutral tool. Certain aspects of technological determinism allow us to see through some of the more individualistic understanding in the modern West to the immense societal impact of these monumental technological changes. It can be tempting in this technologically rich society to take a specific technology and isolate it from its context when evaluating its effects, both for good and for ill. Take the popular doorbell cameras like

---

[36] Peter-Paul Verbeek, *What Things Do: Philosophical Reflections on Technology, Agency, and Design* (University Park: Pennsylvania State University Press, 2005), 174–75.

[37] Derek C. Schuurman, *Shaping a Digital World: Faith, Culture and Computer Technology* (Downers Grove, IL: IVP Academic, 2013), 22. For more on the value-laden approach, see Stephen V. Monsma and Calvin Center for Christian Scholarship, eds., *Responsible Technology: A Christian Perspective* (Grand Rapids: Eerdmans, 1986), 24–36.

[38] Schuurman, *Shaping a Digital World.* 15. See also Albert M. Wolters, *Creation Regained: Biblical Basics for a Reformational Worldview,* 2nd ed. (Grand Rapids: Eerdmans, 2005), 49.

[39] Schuurman, *Shaping a Digital World*, 22.

[40] Schuurman, 15. See also Charles C. Adams, "Formation or Deformation: Modern Technology and the Cultural Mandate," *Pro Rege* 25, no. 4 (June 1997): 3.

Ring, for example. It would not be accurate to examine these tools as merely isolated camera technology allowing users to monitor their front porches. There are countless uses of these innovations. A homeowner can see when packages arrive and when they are picked up, which is especially beneficial when online shopping is at all-time highs and many basic needs can be fulfilled through online ordering. One can also see who is at the door before answering, which can be especially useful when someone is home alone or when one simply does not want to speak to the salesman who conveniently overlooked the No Soliciting sign. Homeowners can also check in on their homes when traveling or at work.

Stepping back to view these common technologies through a larger Ellulian perspective can allow one to see that these innovations were developed to meet a need brought about by another modern innovation, that of online shopping.[41] As more and more of a household's needs were being delivered to the front door, innovators sought to accommodate for previous innovations in home goods delivery. These same doorbell technologies also met a growing concern over home safety and neighborhood watch groups. As packages were being delivered, the increased risk of porch thieves rose. These doorbell technologies helped to address the symptomatic issues caused by the original innovation as well as address the fear of homeowners even if they live in relatively safe areas.

Even though he held to a more instrumentalist view of technology, famed philosopher Martin Heidegger observed that tools are tied up within a web of relations.[42] An expanded view of technology in a web of relations

---

[41] It should be noted that Amazon purchased Ring for $1 billion in February 2018 as a way to gain access to the lucrative doorbell technology business that neatly aligns with their primary business of online shopping. See Ali Montag and Sarah Berger, "Amazon Bought 'Shark Tank' Reject Ring Last Year—Here's What the Founder Says about Jeff Bezos," CNBC, February 22, 2019, https://www.cnbc.com/2018/02/27/amazon-buys-ring-a-former-shark-tank-reject.html.

[42] See Martin Heidegger, *Being and Time*, trans. John Macquarrie and Edward S. Robinson (New York: Harper Perennial/Modern Thought, 2008), 67–71. Heidegger argued that the instrumentalist view still held true, even in light of modern technologies like that of a radar station, sawmill, and power plant. Though, he did acknowledge the complex of our relations with technology as stated above.

also fits the Ellulian vision by showing the numerous connections and shifts that occur in a society when a new technology is developed and deployed like that of online shopping, which naturally arose through the advent of the modern internet.

One might question if this movement of technological innovation necessitates a deterministic philosophy of technology or if one could rather see these innovations in light of the biblical mandate to take dominion over the earth as God's image bearers, which Tiles and Oberdiek argue supports an optimistic or instrumentalist view of technology.[43] While Tiles and Oberdiek correctly state that a Christian philosophy of technology is optimistic rather than pessimistic—contra Ellul—the biblical account of technology is much deeper than simply a tool-oriented philosophy. In Genesis 1–2, as God creates everything, it is humanity alone that is created in his likeness and image (Gen 1:26–31). The *imago Dei* serves as the main distinction between humanity and the rest of creation because no other creature or creation is given this status, illustrated in the authority, responsibilities, and abilities that God has given to humanity. Genesis 2:15 speaks of humanity as put in the garden to "work it and watch over it," indicating that God gave his people a job to do and gave them creative abilities to make various tools and technologies like those used to initially maintain the garden itself. Furthermore, humanity is also able to invent new tools for building as seen in God's command to Noah to build an ark to rescue God's people from the flood (Genesis 6–7). Alongside these creative abilities, humanity was kept accountable for how they used these tools to care for and uphold the dignity of all image bearers.

But God's people—affected by the fall and in rebellion against God's design for humanity—began to misuse their image-bearing abilities to create tools and technologies that exacerbated their rebellion and to take advantage of others as seen in the stories of Cain and Abel (Genesis 4) and the Tower of Babel (Genesis 11). Humanity's rebellion is seen in the fact that "nearly

---

See Martin Heidegger, *Basic Writings: From "Being and Time" (1927) to "The Task of Thinking" (1964)*, ed. David Farrell Krell (New York: Harper Perennial Modern Thought, 2008), 312–13.

[43] See Tiles and Oberdiek in Scharff and Dusek, *Philosophy of Technology*, 249.

every tool available to us enables us to perpetuate the myth that we can live apart from dependence upon God."[44] God's people choose to reject his call to ultimately love him and to love their neighbor (Matt 22:37–39), refusing to uphold the dignity and worth of a fellow image bearer. As Dyer explains, "In our sin we attempt to live independent of our need for God and others, but God originally designed humans to function in a deeply interdependent way that reflects the tri-personhood of God."[45] While after the fall we see humanity still able to make tools and technologies, it is clear that humanity ultimately seeks to love themselves first and exploit their neighbors for their own glory rather than use these tools to love God and love others (Genesis 4). Through the examples of Cain in Genesis 4 and of the entire world, save for Noah, in Genesis 6–7, one can see how the nature of innovation and toolmaking coupled with a rebellious humanity and broken society can lead to widespread shifts in culture and begin to build out the web of relations that is far more complex than that of a singular instrument.

It is naïve, then, to look at technology as a mere tool, rather than to the widespread influence that comes alongside its use, including the push toward certain inherent goals set in the design of the tools themselves. Theologian and ethicist Jacob Shatzer summarizes the influence and disciple-making aspect of technology by reframing the popular adage, "When you have a hammer, everything looks like a nail," as, "When you've got a smartphone with a camera, everything looks like a status update."[46] Through this riff, Shatzer illustrates that technology is more than simply a useful tool but something that expands our moral horizons and something that shapes how we see the world around us, including our fellow image bearers. He states that "each tool pushes us toward the goal that the tool is best made for" and that we must be "aware of this, unless we think that our goals in life will always align with the goals that tools were made for."[47]

---

[44] Dyer, *From the Garden to the City*, 71.

[45] Dyer, 45.

[46] Jacob Shatzer, *Transhumanism and the Image of God: Today's Technology and the Future of Christian Discipleship* (Downers Grove, IL: IVP Academic, 2019), 7.

[47] Shatzer, 7.

But while technological determinism has its merits and reveals the fuller impact of technology on individuals and the society at large, it fails to address the biblical understanding of the creator and creature distinction, including the moral accountability and agency we maintain as creature before our Creator. It also misses that technology is no more autonomous than other non-image-bearing parts of creation. A Christian philosophy of technology displays the riches of humanity as the sole bearer of God's image and also a creature with full moral accountability and agency before God for how we love God and love our neighbor as ourselves (Matt 22:37–39). It can be easily overlooked with concepts of autonomous technology and the technological imperative that humanity is responsible and accountable to God not only for how we use these instruments in creation, but also for the systems and structures these instruments contribute to in the formation of society. As God's sole image bearers, humanity plays a unique role not only in how we create technologies but also in how we love and care for those around us as we seek to structure society in a way that honors the value of every human being, no matter their position, status, race, sex, religion, or background.

In the translator's note to the first English edition of *The Technological Society* in 1964, John Wilkinson quotes Ernst Jünger saying that "technology is the real metaphysic of the twentieth century."[48] To some, this overarching conception of technology might seem at odds with the way many people approach technology today as merely a tool that can be used for good or ill. It is far too easy to isolate particular technologies and allow a myopic view of technology to drive the moral and social questions posed by technology today, especially in the digital public square. This new stage of history has led some to become so intoxicated with the promises of technology that they miss the negative effects on human development and culture

---

[48] Ellul, *The Technological Society*, ix. A similar sentiment has been echoed in recent years by theologian and ethicist Brent Waters as he describes the role of technology in society. He states that "technology is ontology of late modernity," meaning that "we cannot define who we are or express what we aspire to become in the absence of technology." See Waters, *This Mortal Flesh*, 15–17.

making. On the opposite side of the spectrum, others focus so much on the negative effects that they miss that God gave his children the abilities to create and use technology in ways that honor him and love our fellow image bearers.

A Christian philosophy of technology seeks to balance these two views by providing a framework of agency and accountability, alongside expanding our view of technology to see the larger social effects of these tools. Often technology's influence on our society and the march toward progress has led some to believe that through technology, humanity will ultimately usher in a new era of a society. This striving is often encapsulated in the dreams of a technological utopia, where the ills and brokenness of this world are solvable if we had the right technology at hand.[49] These dreams in some ways are understandable given the immense progress over the last seventy years in computer technology and how nearly every aspect of our lives is tied in some way to modern marvels of human creativity and ingenuity. But often beneath the surface of the utopian dreams of technological progress is the reality that technology is constantly shaping and molding us and society—both for good and for ill. The power and disciple-making aspects of technology have naturally led to a growing interest and study of technology by both secular and Christian communities. But given the ubiquity of technology, the reality is that everyone in our communities is being shaped in this technological society. The question is, How are we being formed, and to what end? Christians must ask then whether these technologies are transforming us to be more like Christ or if we are ultimately being conformed to the likeness of this world instead (Rom 12:2).

---

[49] Futurist Yuval Noah Harari claims that humanity has already overcome the main three issues of the world: war, famine, and plague. Now that humanity has overcome these perennial issues, we may set our sights on overcoming death itself and ultimately become gods in our own right. See Yuval Noah Harari, *Homo Deus: A Brief History of Tomorrow*, Vintage Popular Science (London: Harvill Secker, 2016); Yuval N. Harari, *21 Lessons for the 21st Century* (New York: Spiegel & Grau, 2018).

Toward a Public Theology for a Digital Age

Recently, I read an insightful article by Shira Ovide of the *New York Times* on the splintering of the internet and the complexities surrounding digital governance around the world.[50] She writes about how most countries around the world have their own car safety regulations and tax codes, but currently there is widespread debate over how online expression should be governed. She highlights how technology companies—many based in the Western world—are essentially governing speech and free expression online, which leads to major controversies and dissension as many countries want to retain that power for themselves.

One of the most salient points she makes in the piece concerns the promises of how technology was going to usher in a new world order. She writes, "The utopian idea of the internet was that it would help tear down national boundaries, but technology watchers have been warning for decades that it could instead build those barriers even higher." Not only are those barriers being built higher around the world, but technological power is also being exerted by powerful governments and leaders to control and manipulate people created in God's very image.[51] Over the last few years, we have even seen numerous companies shut down the internet to quell protests and dissension among their own people, like that in Iran, Belarus, China, and Cuba. These stories represent a much larger question that is being debated about how technology companies like Meta, Twitter, and many others should do business around the world, especially in areas where there is significant disagreement over the basic freedoms we enjoy in America. But even in the United States, we have significant differences and major disagreements on the role of the government and third-party technology companies concerning issues like content moderation, free expression, and online governance. These complexities and differences are present even

---

[50] Shira Ovide, "The Internet Is Splintering," *New York Times*, February 17, 2021, https://www.nytimes.com/2021/02/17/technology/the-internet-is-splintering.html.

[51] For more on the widespread use of technology to suppress human rights and free expression around the world, see chapter 11 by Olivia Enos in this work.

though we have some level of a shared culture and agreement on many basic human freedoms—even though that agreement seems to be fraying with each passing day.

Technology policy expert Klon Kitchen, who serves at the American Enterprise Institute as a Resident Fellow, wrote a brilliant essay at *National Affairs* about the realities we face in this technological age. He states that "all governments must [now] acknowledge and adapt to the fact that they no longer wield exclusive power and influence on the global stage."[52] The rise of a technology industry operating transnationally with enormous power over public discourse presents a unique challenge to our society but also an opportunity for Christians to engage with these companies as we have historically done with governments, standing for human dignity and religious freedom around the world. The Christian church has a rich heritage of public theology and navigating church/state relations, drawn in large part directly from the scriptural calling to honor the leaders God has placed in charge, hold the government accountable to their calling to stand for justice, and honor the God-given freedoms of all as created in God's image (Rom 13:1–6). While the rise of these transnational entities in the digital age may present unique challenges on issues like online governance, it also presents a unique opportunity for Christians to engage the technology industry with a robust public theology built upon an unchanging understanding of human dignity and freedom derived from Scripture. It is far too easy in our technological society to see other human beings as simply problems to be solved or as pawns in the pursuit of power. But a Christian understanding of humanity and the nature of society is rooted in the dignity of all people that transcends our national allegiances and even the technological order itself we spoke of earlier.

As Christians engage on these important ethical issues, we must do so from a position of principled pluralism—recognizing the inherent dignity

---

[52] Klon Kitchen, "The New Superpowers: How and Why the Tech Industry Is Shaping the International System," *National Affairs*, no. 49 (Fall 2021), https://nationalaffairs.com/the-new-superpowers-how-and-why-the-tech-industry-is-shaping-the-international-system.

of all people and with a clear moral vision of a common good grounded in God's Word.[53] Grounded in these two truths, we can model for our society how to have these debates from a convictional, yet grace-filled perspective. In a society that prizes efficiency, speed, and at times public contempt for our political and social "enemies," we should seek to prioritize the dignity of all, including those who disagree with us on these important issues. We can do so by recognizing that our battle is not against flesh and blood but against the cosmic powers of darkness (Eph 6:12). That means that we engage from a position of hope and grace, knowing that we are to seek the right changes in the right way (Rom 3:8).

A second and vital requirement is understanding the basic tenets of the debates at hand, rather than simply dropping into these complex debates or speaking to issues without a full understanding of the gravity of the situation. Just as we seek to gain insight and expertise in other areas of life—especially engagement with government—to honestly engage, we must do the same with the technology industry and the complex issues they face doing business around the world. This is one of the many reasons this volume consists of two corresponding chapters speaking to the domestic and international issues of technology policy as well as a host of important issues in the digital public square. It does not serve well the message of the gospel, much less our society, to engage on issues without knowledge or awareness of the issues at stake, even if our society seems to reward hot-takes on social media over true action oriented toward lasting change. Even with the immense complexity of these debates, one thing is clear: the dignity of our neighbor is at stake around the world, especially under repressive authoritarian regimes. We must keep that truth central in this debate over digital governance. Even though these issues may at times seem to be simply about tweets, posts, and even the contours of content moderation, these are simply expressions of how human beings, created in God's image, are able to communicate, express themselves, and do life in an ever-increasing digital society.

---

[53] For an expanded discussion of this approach, see chapter 10 where this model is applied to the rise of conspiracy theories and misinformation in the digital public square.

Charting a Path Forward

This volume is designed to speak to the complexities of these various issues from the richness of the Christian theological and ethical traditions. While there are many ways for Christians to think about the issues presented here, each author helps us see the complexities of these issues, while also pointing out where Christians may disagree on the best approach. Part 1 focuses on a foundational understanding of technology, the public square, and the technology policy landscape. First, Bryan Baise helps us see some of the contemporary shifts in how we think about the public square today and how technology is altering how we organize our society. Next, Nathan Leamer and Patricia Shaw offer readers a snapshot of the landscape of technology policy from both an American perspective and a global perspective—namely highlighting the European, British, and Australian approaches to these pressing issues in the digital public square, ranging from telecom law and government agencies to calls for AI ethics and digital privacy. Lastly, David French helps set the stage for the remaining chapters by speaking to the various legal and policy debates over online governance that transcend many of the partisan talking points of the day.

In part 2, each contributor takes on a major facet of digital governance and content moderation. Attentive readers will see that this section mirrors many of the community guidelines of major technology companies that function as the governing documents of content moderation on these platforms. The goal here is to tease out how Christians might engage these major aspects of moderation and raise concerns about how these policies may be ill-defined or dangerously applied in the digital public square. First, Joshua Wester casts a compelling vision for religious freedom and free expression in the digital age, which is often missing from many of the conversations surrounding digital governance today.

Two complementary chapters follow focused on the meteoric rise of hate speech and hate crimes online—often focused on the socially contentious issues of sexuality and gender. Brooke Medina addresses the confusion over defining hate speech today while modeling an ethic of dignity for all, especially with the concerning trends of hate crimes orchestrated in and through digital means. Christiana Kiefer and Jeremy Tedesco write about how we are increasingly seeing the historic understandings of sexuality and gender labeled as hate speech under overly broad content moderation policies. They argue that these policies need to transcend the mores of the day and be tethered to a robust application of First Amendment doctrine while recognizing that this same doctrine is also routinely extended to these companies themselves in how they set their moderation and content policies for their platforms. Next, Bonnie Kristian helps readers understand the complexities of banning pornography online and offers a vision for Christian engagement in combatting this dehumanizing industry's grip on our society. I then write on the concerning rise of conspiracy theories, fake news, and misinformation in the age of social media and how these issues transcend the digital technologies of the day before offering a vision for public policy grounding in standing for truth in an increasingly pluralistic society. Lastly in this section, Olivia Enos writes about how authoritarian regimes around the world are utilizing these powerful tools and suppressing human rights in the pursuit of power and control over their people. She highlights the oppressive nature of surveillance technologies, especially in countries like China, North Korea, and others.

In part 3, Keith Plummer and Jacob Shatzer offer complementary chapters on how the church goes about ministry in the digital age. Plummer focuses on how the church communicates with the outside world and the ways that our digital witness reflects the truths we proclaim as believers in Jesus Christ. Shatzer highlights the need for rich discipleship in the digital age, where we are often tempted to segment our lives into the real and the digital. He challenges readers to see how technology is shaping us in specific and deleterious ways before challenging the church to take a more holistic view of discipleship in the twenty-first century.

The overall goal of this volume is to contribute to the ongoing conversations about the role of technology in our society while casting a vision for a holistic Christian engagement on these pressing issues in the digital public square. While there are common threads amongst the various contributions, readers will notice that there are wide-ranging views on how best to navigate these complex challenges in light of the Christian ethic. This is by design, as to model an epistemic humility that should mark the Christian life as well as our engagement with all in the digital public square. The church and the broader society are facing what at times seems to be daunting challenges that are endlessly complex, but it is our prayer and hope that the following chapters model a rich engagement on these issues—one grounded in hope and truth, not driven by the polemics of the day but a peace that surpasses all understanding (Phil 4:7).

2

Once More, with Tweeting?

Bracketing a Public Square from the Perils of Notoriety

Bryan Baise

For the better part of a decade, I've taught a class at my Christian college called "Religion in the Public Square."[1] The course material serves as what might be described as a broad history about Christian and non-Christian political thought. The first half explores concepts and categories showing how Christians throughout history have engaged with the wider society. From the role of law and authority to civil disobedience, students begin to develop a vocabulary necessary to distinguish faithful service to Christ and kingdom from more recent and fanciful alternatives of platforms and public praise. The class provides a theological grammar, paired with unique issues from the current moment. This balance of history with recent

---

[1] Elements of this chapter were originally presented at the Ethics and Religious Liberty Commission Research Institute National Meeting in 2019, where I attended as a featured speaker. Reused with permission.

innovations fosters an environment for fascinating discussion when it's not eight o'clock in the morning. Alongside teaching this class, I've developed a habit of jotting down remarks about course content, student engagement, and if certain topics or issues gain purchase. As I began to investigate my scribbles and visuals, I noticed a consistent pattern of questions and concerns from students: technology's influence on *everything we talk about in the class.* This was almost entirely absent from my required reading, assignments, and classroom discussion. Technological intrusion in the public square was the elephant in the room, and I wasn't talking about it.

What is a public square in a digital age? How do we live out our "good deposit" (2 Tim 1:14) in public, in a space where technology has irreversibly shifted the meanings of our words? How do we advocate for, say, justice in a technological society? There are dangers to even posing this kind of question. Perhaps we would need a provisional answer to the first part: How do we advocate for justice? Yet even this kind of framing becomes difficult. How do you advocate? And furthermore, what justice is one advocating? Banana republics secure justice but do so despotically. The answers seem neither obvious nor simple. Maybe the latter end of this question will serve us better: fighting for justice in a *technological* society. The qualifier does provide some context but invites additional inquiry. In what sense would a society become sufficiently "technological," and to what ends is it directed? Perhaps these questions do not need an exact answer to address the issues before us.

And yet our current context demands clarity of thought and conviction, and given the stakes, one should be *crystal clear* about what "faith," "public square," and "technology" mean. But specificity does not always render clarity. You may know exactly which turns to make to arrive at a destination, but that does not mean you have the awareness to adjust directions if a traffic jam forces alternative routes. The map on your phone can automatically reroute, but operating in the public square does not allow for the same kind of quick redirect.

Instead of a road map, where every twist and turn has a clear dictate, one might consider the following discussion like a kind of land survey where boundaries are discovered and the shape of the land becomes known. Once aware of the contours and potential problem cases within its margins, you can consider proper action. A quick glance at social media reveals technology's outsized sway in shaping public discourse. Whether the scope narrowed onto race and justice, immigration, "big tech," or something else, the effect of technology on these topics casts a large shadow. Yet those social media channels are often in the spaces that think least about how theological conviction shapes not merely *what* but also *how* we deliberate in these matters. Let's be honest: the exchange—inside and outside confessional contexts—has left much to be desired. The Christian faith should carry significant weight when exploring concepts and categories often discussed but seldom defined. Christianity does have something to say about who people are, how they are ordered to live in society, and toward what kinds of goods they should direct their activities. Moreover, it should teach us how we shape these desires, actions, and political movements toward a common good, where shared pursuits render peace and order.

Technology fractures this shared activity where "engagement" takes new forms and "dialogue" becomes something wholly different. A crisis of epistemology is often first a crisis of etymology. To chart some path forward there must be clarity of concepts. What is meant by "public" in a public square? To what ends are these public actions directed? If there is something prior to a public square, it seems important to consider. Presented in this chapter are provisional offerings for a path forward in navigating these difficult waters.

A Naked Public Square?

In 1984 Richard John Neuhaus published a work titled *The Naked Public Square*. The thesis, well-known to many today, describes the divorce of religion from society and how this disconnect placed strains on religious citizens. More importantly for our purposes, Neuhaus notes the burgeoning chasm is perilous for democracy. The rise of the Moral Majority in the 1980s, writes Neuhaus, "kicked a tripwire alerting us to a pervasive contradiction in our culture and politics. We insist that we are a democratic society, yet we have in recent decades systematically excluded from policy consideration the operative values of the American people, values that are overwhelmingly grounded in religious belief."[2] Neuhaus's work inspired a generation of theologians, ethicists, and political activists to recognize that Janus-faced offerings of political engagement meant nonreligious citizens stood free to bring assumptions into the public square whereas religious citizens were hindered, all because misplaced views of church-state affairs persisted. As a result, the public square is "naked," stripped of its longstanding belief that religious invocations are rightly part of deliberative democracy.

Insofar as we can look back at present events with clear eyes, the inference that Neuhaus was wrong or too glum does not make sense of the data. We *have* seen a kind of naked public square, established long before Neuhaus (the French *laïcité* being just one example, and most assuredly a kind of implicit establishment of this notion is present in the twenty-first century). But the window amid Neuhaus's writing in 1986 and the early twenty-first century spoke with a different voice. Herein lies Moral Majority politics, transcendent language and appeals following 9/11, and untold examples from Family Values Coalitions in the 2004 presidential election. All these suggest Neuhaus was right *in the main*. His idea that faith plays a serious role in the public square was laudable. Present examples demonstrate his thesis. Yet the advent of technological expansions means paths for securing deliberative democracy have shifted. Smoke-filled rooms where deals are debated and settled find their actions across text message and teleconference.

A Virtual Public Square

The advent of social media has adjusted what we now consider a "public square." Social media has disrupted our beliefs and societal rhythms. To reflect on the shape of a public square if the promises of coming to consensus seems grim feels like a fool's errand. After all, the growing sense among society is we are not merely disagreeing about the contours of a public square; we are not seeing the same world as our neighbors. How can we find agreements to move forward when we can't seem to agree on basic

---

[2] Richard John Neuhaus, *The Naked Public Square: Religion and Democracy in America* (Grand Rapids: Eerdmans, 1984), 37.

fabrics of reality? This frightening reality is present in Netflix's documentary *The Social Dilemma*. Released in 2020, the film highlights all the ways social media is curating not merely your interests, friends, or news, but *you*. Your entire reality is being shaped by this medium. Roger McNamee, an early investor in Facebook, puts it this way: "The way to think about it is as 2.5 billion Truman Shows. Each person has their own reality with their own facts. Over time the false sense that everyone agrees with you because everyone in your news feed sounds just like you."[3]

Recent decades have weakened the depth of public order,[4] and as the downslope continues apace, those interested in forming a common good in a world of Truman Shows must recognize the path back has a different route.[5] A growing body of data suggests a yearning for harmony despite difference, but it takes discerning ears to block out the noise of slacktivism where engagement takes the form of profile picture changes or hashtags. This impulse for consensus is good and should be praised as a central feature of democracy. We often call such ideas "pluralism," a term designating the pursuit for consensus despite deep difference so society can provide space where ideas vie for public approval and majority. In one sense this is true: the concept of pluralism in contemporary society pervades and surrounds the public square.

Yet, in a desire for securing peace, order, and consensus, the mechanics of today's pluralism fall well short of its chosen end. For society to flourish,

---

[3] *The Social Dilemma*, directed by Jeff Orlowski, Exposure Labs, Netflix, 2020.

[4] It is worth noting that some scholars have questioned whether society in the West was ever really ordered toward good ends; perhaps it was doomed from the start. This is, at least in part, the argument of Patrick Deneen in *Why Liberalism Failed*. In recent years there have been more insidious versions. I don't wish to contend with this latter group for prudential reasons; it seems to have little import to discuss matters with individuals that view disagreement as complicity, or nuance as coterminous with nefarious. While charity demands an extension of goodwill, prudence might demand only a *listening* ear.

[5] "Truman Shows" is a reference to the 1998 film *The Truman Show* starring Jim Carrey where everything in Truman Burbank's life is part of a massive TV set. Everything that takes place in Truman's life is orchestrated by the producer of the show and captured on hidden cameras.

says pluralism, we must make sure disparities are limited and that structures of public thought have clearly defined boundaries, resulting in narrow consensus. Disputes are inevitable but they need not destroy. If the contours of public thought can be decided *before* dialogue even begins, all the better. Thus, a feigned olive branch is presented with the promise of peace provided terms are accepted *prior* to debate. But this sense of pluralism, where difference is cancer instead of remedy, is precisely where it fails, for it takes lack of camaraderie as a *problem* to be solved. Convictional difference between deliberative agents entering and leaving the public square becomes *angst*, a strain that must be resolved before the goods of society can be ordered.[6] This fiery digital furnace of reflection has extended the meaning of a *public* square from merely "public" to now "virtual" being included in the term. In doing so, this extension has brought new challenges for the public square and makes consensus a near impossibility.

Current technological mediums only exacerbate the ideological disparity and offer a platform for the loudest voices to stand as exemplars. Social media drives unity at the expense of sober judgment and in doing so mirrors the insidious rehearsals of today's pluralism; it delimits prospects offered as true and right and fractures consensus at the start. By pressing for consensus, driven by technological platforms, essential categories necessary to ensure a public square's own flourishing become flattened: reason, mutual exchange, honesty, and more. Likeness is not sameness,[7] and as Edmund Burke once wrote, "those who attempt to level never equalize."[8]

For a public square worth its name to rise from the doldrums of its current form, there must be a reappraisal of the project. It is beyond my ability in this chapter to fully describe a path forward; legal and political scholars

---

[6] For more on this, see Oliver O'Donovan, "Reflections on Pluralism," *Princeton Seminary Bulletin* 29 (2008): 54–66.

[7] See Robert Spaemann's reflections on recognition, difference, and personhood. Robert Spaemann, *Persons: The Difference Between 'Someone' and 'Something': Oxford Studies in Theological Ethics* (Oxford: Oxford University Press, 1996), 180–96.

[8] Edmund Burke, *Revolutionary Writings: Reflections on the Revolution in France and the First Letter on a Regicide Peace* (Cambridge, UK: Cambridge University Press, 2014), 50.

have done laudable work on this topic for years.[9] And yet we can say a few things about charting a road less traveled. One step in the right direction provides an account of pluralism where private is not merely understood as the opposite of public.[10] As we have seen above, the shape of pluralism today is on perceived malignant effects of private conviction on public life. But this misnomer feigns integrity by presuming "private" *always harms* "public" goods. Instead, we might respond by suggesting that private convictions do not harm but rather fill out and direct a public square toward ordered ends and common good. It might gesture a conclusion suggesting the current contours of a public square *harm* a common good because it does not allow for charity, and even incentivizes the opposite.[11] When a public square is expanded to include the rhythms of social media, a distrust of another agent's motives almost inevitably arrives and totalizes the space.[12] When purposes are assumed or read with nefarious intent, what Yuval Levin describes as "the durable forms of our common life" becomes increasingly difficult to uphold.[13]

The public square we now inherit looks something like what we have described above. This leaves us with a tantalizing question: How are we as Christians to act in these spaces? If we cannot disentangle the public square from its technological and social media grapples, what hope do we have to secure those durable forms and stabilize for ourselves and the next generation? Perhaps, as hinted already, the key is less in the details. Now aware of the prospects and perils of the current moments, we might see a way

---

[9] One example would be John Inazu, *Confident Pluralism: Surviving and Thriving through Deep Difference* (Chicago: University of Chicago Press, 2016).

[10] For more on this, see O'Donovan, "Reflections." Also see part 2 of Hannah Arendt, *The Human Condition* (Chicago: University of Chicago Press, 1958).

[11] Jean Bethke Elshtain is worth reading on charity and Augustinian "politics" in *Augustine and the Limits of Politics*, 36–47.

[12] For more on the totalizing of suspicion, see Oliver O'Donovan, *The Desire of the Nations: Rediscovering the Roots of Political Theology* (Cambridge, UK: Cambridge University Press, 2008), 6–20.

[13] Yuval Levin, *A Time to Build: From Family and Community to Congress and the Campus, How Recommitting to Our Institutions Can Revive the American Dream* (New York: Basic Books, 2020), 31.

forward to engage the public square. Let us return to the image of the land survey. If what we have described here is an accurate account of the current boundaries, shape, and even topography of the public square, we might consider the next piece of this a consideration for *how we live* in the land. It does little good to build a house on a piece of land unaware of what is underneath; better to build knowing full well what lies beneath the soil and the necessary tools for the project.

Public Faith and a Faith of Publicity

As Christians consider engaging in the broader boundaries of the public square, it is important to consider what shape a public faith might take in the twenty-first century. It seems most helpful movements of history happen because of at least two factors: retrieval and recasting. The former operates from a desire to stabilize current measures of the moment with the wisdom of the past. For Christians, public engagement becomes informed by *all features* of Christianity leading up to their time and place. It means trusting a fourth-century bishop in a North African province has something to say about twenty-first-century society. Retrieval does not merely take the past and transfer it to the present; rather, retrieval asks carefully: How can previous theological axioms be deployed *now* to ensure faithful Christian witness?

Retrieval stabilizes the Christian in an era fraught with instability from technology. It suggests the uncertainty so prevalent today is, in fact, *not unique.* This recognition assists in our response to current predicaments by suggesting their origins are of the same kind: restless hearts searching for an end to its agitation. "History doesn't repeat itself," quipped Mark Twain, "but it often rhymes."[14] This simple distinction, small though it may seem, offers a pathway on how to apply Christian truths to our current context. Here is where the notion of recasting might arise. There are unique issues, concepts, and categories that must be addressed, and copy-and-pasting

---

[14] This quote is often attributed to Mark Twain even though there is substantial debate as to if he actually said it.

ancient responses into the current context simply will not do. Recasting takes what has been given to us through retrieval and asks, "How do we properly deploy theological clarity for the present age?"

Perhaps no simple solution arrives and thus requires *waiting.* Yet such a posture serves us well in a social media age where answers, demanded sooner than wisdom might allow, require a window of time where one simply says nothing. Indeed, the capacity to patiently consider how to answer is worth more in weight than a tweet or post fired off in quick response. Here we learn what it means for Christians in a social media age to have a *public faith.* It does not mean having the answers right as someone demands them. A public faith acknowledges Christians should feel compelled to give an account of their faith in this newfangled public square, but we can do so slowly and deliberately and in doing so model a hope-filled posture that embodies the already and not yet of our eschatology. Being careful to speak clearly means recognizing the intermixed reality we find ourselves in and exercising prudence with our words, our tweets, and our rejection of flattening complex situations into digestible social media bytes. A public faith is a prudent faith. Prudence is more than mere patience; it resists thoughtlessness and reckless actions. Prudence, what has been described as the "charioteer" for all other virtues, guides human actions.[15] Prudence is where we see the world aright and make decisions with reality. A public faith renders its judgments *when* they should and not a moment sooner.

Current technological challenges often ensure even the most careful voices are shut out of public debate, considered "unreasonable" or "bigoted" because of their confessional accounts or beliefs. It would be unwise and naive to pretend as if the posture of a public faith will somehow lead to a wider engagement with society and the current cultural kingmakers. Indeed, it may take us in the opposite path, toward marginalization instead of Congress or the golden paths of podcast and platforming offers. It is true a kind of totalized suspicion is prevalent in current political discourse, and no doubt citizens of religious beliefs have received more of this distrust than their counterparts. A reasonable person could respond to such measures

---

[15] Thomas Aquinas, *Summa Theologiae*, II–II, 47.

with a posture of ideological defense. After all, who among us does not wish to protect what we love? It is understandable, given the moment, that one might feel pressed into a protective disposition through tough words and the rallying of troops. We might call this a *faith of publicity*. A faith of publicity, unlike a public faith, has been catechized by a social media age. It suggests the Christian faith must clearly and *quickly* separate itself from its ideological rivals; that it must speak *clearly* in the measure of a moment instead of considering that clarity often arrives not by quick response but rather through careful and prudential responses. A faith of publicity suggests if we do not say something, if we do not tweet something, how will the world know what Christians believe? More to the point, if *I* do not say something, who will?

Notice in this posture how much a sense of *anxiety* perpetuates. If, as we said earlier, the cunning form of pluralism is driven by anxiety, what compels those who might prefer this kind of response? Perhaps they will respond to the present difficulties, but their anxiety will often cause them to find sharp words for both those who find the faith antagonistic *and* those faithful Christians who might not be willing to respond just yet. This engenders our well-meaning but sometimes misguided Christian to often situate themselves as the only one who will faithfully stand in the gap. While a well-trodden path, such attitudes produce as many adversaries as allies, often boldly displaying a long list of enemies as a badge of honor. "Look, Lord, see how many people I have upset in your name!"

And yet wisdom suggests resistance to this enticement; to shortening paths of reflective judgment by locating enemies and identifying cobelligerents. After all, the book of Proverbs tells us to both answer a fool according to his folly *and* answer *not* a fool according to his folly (Prov 26:4–5). Wisdom may dictate the former or the latter. If the latter is implemented it must be done carefully and with great concern, for if the bonds of society are to survive despite variance, *persuasion* must hold its boundaries and Christians must adopt a different kind of posture than what a faith of publicity suggests. Courage, for example, shines brightest not when confused with brashness but rather as prudence, charity, and persuasion mark its field. A public square is best served when those within its borders persuade with their words *and* disposition. Courage is far removed from bellicose blustering, yet this is precisely what a faith of publicity encourages. "This is what the LORD says," wrote Jeremiah, "Stand by the roadways and look. Ask about the ancient paths, 'Which is the way to what is good?' Then take it and find rest for yourselves" (Jer 6:16). The alternative to the measure of the moment is not weak-kneed retreat but reframing *how* and *to what end* persuading occurs.

"Christianity does not simply project its hopes for public life upon the world by force of its will," Charles Mathewes writes.[16] Indeed, a vital part of Christian political engagement in these new spaces will be persuasion. Convinced the state is not lord over any man's conscience, we appeal to those in power.[17] By delimiting the malady of pluralism and defending what it means to be faithfully Christian in a contested age by retrieval and recasting, the persuasive and prophetic in the public square are given space to flourish.[18] Shaping the political imagination in the public square includes both tasks.

At issue with the expansion of what it means for a public square to be public is the creeping decline of life beyond the political. A piece of the task of Christian faith in this new public square is invoking margins on the

---

[16] Charles T. Mathewes, *A Theology of Public Life* (Cambridge, UK: Cambridge University Press, 2008), 309.

[17] Paul Ramsey's reflections in *Who Speaks for the Church?* are worth mentioning on this point. While his overall conclusions might lead in a different direction than I would endorse, his admonitions are still worthy of attention. See Paul Ramsey, *Who Speaks for the Church? A Critique of the 1966 Geneva Convention on Church and Society* (Nashville: Abingdon, 1967), 147–49.

[18] "Public square" has a wider view than "political" but here it is limited to the political. Obviously, you can debate the morality of abortion with a friend over lunch or in the offices of Congress; the same goes for the prophetic. Pluralism as understood today seems to have no problem with this kind of public deliberation. And yet, when it comes to legislative and political measures, the boundaries and norms change. The contour of this separation is in part the legacy of John Rawls and precisely why Katrina Forrester's thesis that we remain within the shadow of Rawls's political philosophy rings true. See Katrina Forrester, *In the Shadow of Justice: Postwar Liberalism and the Remaking of Political Philosophy* (Princeton, NJ: Princeton University Press, 2019).

political ethos of a people. In doing so, we suggest to those bound up in the moment that the goods of societal life are discovered beyond the political. This image invites a wider view of the public square and begins to hem the boundaries those foxes of social media and technology seek to destroy. The public nature of faith requires *attentiveness* toward the current dilemmas; it does not require *anathematizing* those agents with whom one finds sincere but serious disagreement. A public faith suggests, with words and actions, technology unencumbered hampers pursuits of a common good. It suggests we distinguish between disagreement and denouncement. Sometimes the slightest of distinctions is the difference between a public faith and faith of publicity; between faithfully ensuring the use of social media instead of social media's use of you. As the many technological platforms only grow in their reach, Christians will be tempted to succumb to the spirits of the age, driven by political commitments or common good. A public faith, insofar as it is able, speaks prophetically for the latter where publicity speaks with an eye toward a platform. Public faith makes room for prophetic indictments that do not collapse into impatient denouncements for sake of platform and publicity.

In her excellent book *Prophecy without Contempt*, Cathleen Kaveny attempts to situate the prophetic in the American political mind. She notes that often prophecy functions like a "legal indictment" and those using it frequently

> chastise their own people for fundamental violations of the basic social compact, which they frequently present as divinely sanctioned and supported. The rhetoric of the jeremiad, therefore cannot but condemn; that is the core social function. At the same time, it is extremely important that its contemporary practitioners of the jeremiad resist the urge to condemn those whom they condemn. . . . In the heated battles of the American public square, it is all too tempting for practitioners of prophetic rhetoric to let their condemnation mutate into contempt. They—we—must resist this temptation. In an increasingly pluralistic liberal democracy, prophetic condemnation of deep social evils can be justified on occasion, although such

rhetoric never comes without ancillary costs. Citizens rightly call each other to account for violations of our most fundamental commitments as a people. Contempt, however, is a different matter entirely. To treat one's political interlocutors as vile or worthless is to risk undermining their equal status as participants in our political community. It is to treat them as unworthy citizens of citizenship, as people who are "pruned" from our common political endeavor.[19]

Notice anger has a focus: those who violated an important social compact. Where technology fails to correctly shape a public square is exactly at these inflexion points; the opening for persuasion in those spaces to devolve into contempt is high, where one can safely view "enemies" as *outside* the gates only. Included in indictment, says Kaveny, must be individuals found derelict *inside one's own community as well*; but this should never carry over into contempt. When technology catechizes the rhetorical spaces of a public square, you become susceptible to confusing condemnation with contempt.

And yet Kaveny's counsel aligns with a Christian public ethic of speaking truth to power and reminding those who uphold such laws, customs, and institutions their sins are before the Lord, and he will repay wrath to his foes and retribution to his enemies (Isaiah 59). So we work with an eye on the immediate horizon and the one to come, ensuring earthly establishments are exercising proper judgments and securing *right order* so all within her walls might flourish (Jeremiah 29). It suggests that patience with one's denouncements is better than the rush to draw lines and declare enemies. While the latter may very well *simplify*, it does not always *clarify*. A public faith will walk in the new public square with patience instead of posturing.

Securing temporary peace and order is part of the task of Christian faithfulness in the public square. It should defend and form the spaces necessary for concern of both *temporary* and *eternal* things. In other words, the fruits of securing a public square, at least in part, are so those within her reach might consider a greater peace that has no abiding city here. If so, the

---

[19] Cathleen Kaveny, *Prophecy without Contempt* (Boston: Harvard University Press, 2016), preface.

path of persuasion over platform, public faith over publicity, matters. Here, the persuasive meets the prophetic and censure does not render contempt. It is, after all, God's kindness that leads to repentance (Rom 2:4).

Conclusion

Alongside the questions explored in this chapter, a posture can arise that might hinder our inquiry. Eager to "contend for the faith that was once for all delivered to the saints" (Jude v. 3), a methodology in Christian thought frequently suggests the following: the aptitude of one ideology to uncover significant failures in another ideology demonstrates the preeminence of the former to the latter. In other words, because one belief system shows the failure of another belief system, you should therefore prefer the first and disbelieve the second. A simple formula, borne from good intentions no doubt. But such paradigms confuse more than clarify. They present the essence of Christian faith as ensuring a person's beliefs are right; your worldview is found in proper assembly of ideas. So long as one can systematically demonstrate the paucity of alternative options, the truth of Christian faith is secured, safe in the arms of the experts.

Yet this posture often empties itself of the vital force in Christian belief: our deepest longings and desires are not secured by merely expressing a proper and systematic formulation of ideas. We, as James K. A. Smith has so eloquently stated, "are lovers first and foremost."[20] Augustine, writing around 1,600 years before Smith, presented the same posture when he wrote *pondus meum amor meus*: "my weight is my love."[21] It is not enough to demonstrate why alternative explanations for justice and pluralism fail; there must be some positive expression of *why* our invitation accords with creation and human experience. In a search for answers, the posture we take matters and the principles we defend are critical. But in doing so we should

---

[20] James K. A. Smith, *You Are What You Love: The Spiritual Power of Habit* (Grand Rapids: Brazos, 2016), 12.

[21] Augustine, *Confessions*, 13.9.10.

be careful to present the road less traveled in a way that *compels.* Goodness, truth, beauty, and a life of virtue draw; let us not be the reason for retreat.

This is not an easy task in an age that demands exactitude as quickly as it demands contempt. In these moments how do we ensure we are not the reason for easy dismissal? Perhaps that fourth-century bishop from North Africa has something to say to us as he reflects on his own journey in coming to Christ. In the *Confessions,* Augustine reflected on his life, friendships, and those whom God providentially placed in his path. After carefully surveying all that had occurred, he wrote, "You are present, liberating us from miserable errors, and you put us on your way, bringing comfort and saying: 'Run, I will carry you, and I will see you through to the end, and there I will carry you (Isa 46:4).'" A little over a decade later, as Rome was being sacked by the Visigoths and the Roman Empire was falling, Augustine returned to this theme. What might the bishop of Hippo say to twenty-first-century Christians concerned about the social media age and the effects it has on the public square? He would remind us of the good news declared to us in Christ. As he wrote in *City of God,*

> It is this Good which we are commanded to love with our whole heart, with our whole mind, and with all our strength. It is toward this Good that we should be led by those who love us, and toward this Good we should lead those whom we love. In this way, we fulfill the commandments on which depend the whole Law and the Prophets: "Thou shalt love the Lord Thy God with thy whole heart, and thy whole soul, and with thy whole mind"; and "Thou shalt love thy neighbor as thyself." For, in order that a man might learn how to love himself, a standard was set to regulate all his actions on which his happiness depends. For, to love one's own self is nothing but to wish to be happy, and the standard is union with God. When, therefore, a person who knows how to love himself is bidden to love his neighbor as himself, is he not, in effect, commanded to persuade others, as far as he can, to love God?[22]

---

[22] Augustine, *City of God,* X.3.

We who find ourselves needing to build houses within these borders are beginning to see how this land survey of the public square has uncovered questions and concerns for us. Let us take our cue from this bishop of Hippo, who always had his eye on two horizons: the one under his feet and the one to come. When we mistake the present horizon as more pressing than the coming horizon, we will feel hard pressed to respond irascibly. If we mistake the coming horizon as *displacing* the current predicaments, we misunderstand what it means to be a people set apart but not *separated*. In this present age we must give an account for our hope, demonstrate our happiness in God is settled, and persuade others to join us in this new hope kept in heaven. We seek to persuade and invite them into a reclamation project. This invitation does not so easily submit itself to the categories of the common age or to technological specificity. Instead, we persuade those around us to enlarge their view of the world and the one who made it.

Technology may demand from us certain prescribed paths demonstrating this hope, asking us to quicken our path to sober judgments and quick responses. Perhaps a feature of Christian witness in a social media era should be those who are, as James implores us, "quick to listen, slow to speak, and slow to anger" (Jas 1:19). The nature of the public square today suggests that we all must conform to its image and speak like it demands. The challenge for faithful Christians in this age is to kindly reject its invitation to do so and, instead, demonstrate to a watching world that we are being conformed to a different kind of image, and he has told us to be wise as serpents and as innocent as doves (Matt 10:16). He calls us to keep our eyes on the coming horizon where he will make all things new. He calls us to live a public faith.

3

The Wild West of Tech Policy

A Convergence of Optimism and Pessimism in the United States

Nathan Leamer

Technology is a central part of daily life. It has dramatically transformed how Americans participate in the economy and communicate with one another. Through increased internet connectivity and innovation, there are unprecedented opportunities for individual advancement and education, as well as kickstarting political movements and economic revolutions empowering communities to flourish.

However, this radical transformation has also given rise to tangible concerns and fears for many Americans previously left unconsidered: consternation about personal privacy for individuals and their children; questions about the power of Silicon Valley tech giants and the degradation of discourse on social media; fears that traditional values might soon be considered tomorrow's hate speech; and longer-term worries about the dignity of work in the face of automation and increased reliance on artificial intelligence.

It is for both the opportunities and concerns raised by emerging technology that it has become such a prominent issue in the United States—including throughout Washington, DC, and state capitals across the country. According to a recent Pew Survey, "56% of Americans think major technology companies should be regulated more than they are now, and 68% believe these firms have too much power and influence in the economy."[1] This is but one 2021 data point of a continuing trend over the past several years of a bipartisan cynicism about the reach, power, and influence of technology in the life of citizens. With this increased skepticism have come calls for greater scrutiny and transparency. Critics of the technopoly have focused on whether the current regulatory and legal framework in the United States is sufficient for protecting consumers, creating economic opportunity, and safeguarding free expression.[2]

Further, the rate at which policy discussions are changing increases as technology advances. Unlike discussions of energy or foreign policy that may have decades of strategy behind them, discussion about technology can become outdated in a matter of years or months, creating a rapidly changing landscape for policymakers. This dynamic environment creates opportunity—there is not the need to "rewrite" all of technology policy—while also providing intense instability in the face of rapid change.

However, it is impossible to ignore the importance of the decisions being made by legislators. As former UK prime minister Tony Blair aptly explained, "The first politicians who master this tech revolution and shape it for the public goodwill determine what the next century will look like. Rapid developments in technologies such as gene-editing and Artificial

---

[1] Emily Vogels, "56% of Americans support more regulation of major technology companies," Pew Research, July 20, 2021, https://www.pewresearch.org/fact-tank/2021/07/20/56-of-americans-support-more-regulation-of-major-technology-companies/.

[2] Neil Postman coined the term *technopoly* to describe the all-encompassing power of technology over society and drive toward efficiency in every aspect of life. Postman states, "Every technology is both a burden and a blessing; not either-or, but this-and-that." Neil Postman, *Technopoly: The Surrender of Culture to Technology* (New York: Vintage Books, 1993), 5.

Intelligence, as well as the quest for potential ground-breaking leaps forward in nuclear fission and quantum computing, will provoke significant changes to our economies, societies and politics."[3] In many respects, policymakers are struggling to learn a new language, forced to respond to both the benefits and consequences of the rapid changes as they occur.[4]

Complicating this process, tech policy is not just one concept or subset of issues. Rather it includes a host of topics that, like the internet, are constructed in a way that complicates and raises stakes for all involved. As the longtime cryptographer and public policy lecturer at Harvard University Bruce Schneier made clear, "Technology is now deeply intertwined with policy. We're building complex socio-technical systems at all levels of our society. Software constrains behaviour with an efficiency that no law can match. It's all changing fast; technology is literally creating the world we all live in, and policymakers can't keep up. Getting it wrong has become increasingly catastrophic. Surviving the future depends on bringing technologists and policymakers together."[5]

It takes time for government institutions and bureaucracies to adapt to the technological shift that has brought forth these unprecedented cultural changes. This complicated, nuanced process of technology policy is even tedious for those at the forefront of decision-making. Former Office of Management and Budget (OMB) cloud policy lead Bill Hunt remarked, "There's a lot of stages, there's a lot of steps. Moreover, when you're dealing

---

[3] Tony Blair, "The Next Great Debate Will Be about the Role of Tech in Society and Government," *TechCrunch*, March 10, 2019, https://techcrunch.com/2019/03/10/the-next-great-debate-will-be-about-the-role-of-tech-in-society-and-government/.

[4] For some humorous exchanges between members of Congress and the CEOs of technology companies, see Avi Selk, "'There's So Many Different Things!': How Technology Baffled an Elderly Congress in 2018," *Washington Post*, January 2, 2019, https://www.washingtonpost.com/lifestyle/style/theres-so-many-different-things-how-technology-baffled-an-elderly-congress-in-2018/2019/01/02/f583f368-ffe0-11e8-83c0-b06139e540e5_story.html.

[5] Bruce Schneier, "We Must Bridge the Gap Between Technology and Policymaking. Our Future Depends on It," World Economic Forum, November 12, 2019, https://www.weforum.org/agenda/2019/11/we-must-bridge-the-gap-between-technology-and-policy-our-future-depends-on-it/.

with policy at the federal level, there's a lot of large players, there's a lot of major stakeholders who have a lot of vested interest in these things."[6] These curious political dynamics and complications are part and parcel of tech policy discourse, especially in the West.

Given the ubiquity of technology and its power over our society, Christians should strive to develop an understanding of tech policy that goes beyond commenting on a Facebook post or impulsively responding to a Twitter thread. This will shape how Christians communicate and engage in the world going forward. Christians ought to seek to understand and shape the policies that will determine how religious activity is moderated on social media platforms, the ways that cryptocurrencies could create new economic opportunities for marginalized communities, or the ways that privacy and security are essential for global mission work. In these and a host of other areas, Christians should understand that the decisions made by and about Meta (Facebook), Twitter, Google, Apple and others have massive ramifications well beyond the digital public space because of the deeply intertwined nature of technology in our lives.

Discerning Technology: A Complicated but Important Aspect of Our Lives

In her book *Why Science and Faith Need Each Other*, Elaine Howard Ecklund echoes the importance of engaging in these policy debates by exploring the shared virtues between science and faith. Those values include "curiosity, doubt, humility, creativity, healing, awe, shalom, and gratitude."[7] While engaging in technology policy is not the same as being a scientist or doctor, it does require Christians to utilize those same values in evaluating debates around technology. Christians should seek to create a coherent paradigm

---

[6] Aaron Boyd, "Why It's So Hard to Write Federal Technology Policy," Nextgov, September 24, 2019, https://www.nextgov.com/policy/2019/09/why-its-so-hard-write-federal-technology-policy/160100/.

[7] Elaine Howard Ecklund, *Why Science and Faith Need Each Other* (Grand Rapids: Baker, 2020), 21.

that builds toward an actively engaged public discourse about the role of technology in our personal lives and throughout society.

As one example, the virtue of humility should cause us to be cautious in advancing any single, quick, simple program as the solution to concerns about technology. When the political heat is turned up, many are tempted to rush to a simple solution, an easy-to-remember slogan, or an authoritative body to solve it. However, as is often the case, it is necessary to evaluate all the tools in the toolbox, whether in Silicon Valley or on Capitol Hill, to solve the problem at hand. As former Federal Trade Commission (FTC) chief technology officer Neil Chilson writes, "Government solutions are not the only solutions. There are usually multiple competing solutions—many different answers to the problem. Such fixes could include innovative new technologies or business models. But they could also include non-commercial solutions such as evolving norms, manners, or customs."[8]

One of the ways Christians can help to shape technology policy is through recognizing the various spheres of influence they have in their own lives. Writing eloquently about the importance of vocation in the Christian life, philosopher Cornelius Plantinga says that "we all have a certain range in which our will is effective. We all have a particular sphere over which we 'have our say.'" This approach has been a guiding light for many Christian public policy professionals currently engaged in all discussions about the future of American laws, regulations, and culture. As Plantinga points out, "God uses national, intermediate, and local government to keep order and protect freedom—not an easy balance."[9]

While Christians often associate those shared connections with traditional policy issues like international policy or tax policy, technology's deep connection to our lives creates similar reasons for this multilayered approach. Christians should think through the long-term consequences, not only about how these policies will shape the nation, but also about how

---

[8] Neil Chilson, *Getting Out of Control: Emergent Leadership in a Complex World* (Potomac, MD: New Degree Press, 2021), 174–75.

[9] Cornelius Plantinga Jr., *Engaging God's Word: A Reformed Vision of Faith, Learning, And Living* (Grand Rapids: Eerdmans, 2002), 107.

they will impact those spheres closer to home: churches, ministries, local communities, and religiously affiliated institutions.

In my own career, I have been able to see how this multilayered approach can be effective and the ways the debates have moved from niche projects to central platform planks. The mainstreaming of tech policy was something I did not expect when beginning my career in Washington, DC, back in 2011 as a Congressional legislative aid. At the time, I was a young junior Hill staffer embarking on a journey to be a public policy professional. While my friends and contemporaries were embarking on careers in more traditional topics like taxes, budgets, immigration, and foreign policy, I found myself drawn to the debates around internet policy and innovation. I continued that trajectory to a senior fellow position at a DC-based think tank and a policy advisory to the chairman of the Federal Communications Commission (FCC).

A decade ago, technology and innovation policy was a relatively niche subject that few in DC were pursuing. Plenty of lawyers, technologists, and engineers were engaged, but there were fewer Hill staffers, political operatives, and policy advocates. This is not to say I was a pioneer, like John Perry Barlow,[10] for there have been many incredibly talented scholars, technologists, and policymakers who had been doing work for years. But it was not, at the time, an overly saturated market for young individuals who wanted to build a vocation. This was especially true of Christians who were engaged in these discussions. In a sense, as Silicon Valley was economically booming and transforming our lives, DC was being forced to adjust to this market deficiency in public policy.

Washington, DC, and Tech: A Complicated Relationship

After the 2020 election, Public Citizen, a DC-based nonprofit, released a report on lobbying expenditures and found that the largest tech firms

---

[10] See Cindy Cohn, "John Perry Barlow, Internet Pioneer, 1947–2018," EFF .org, February 7, 2018, https://www.eff.org/deeplinks/2018/02/john-perry-barlow -internet-pioneer-1947-2018.

spent a combined "$124 million in lobbying and campaign contributions—breaking its own records from past election cycles."[11] In the span of twenty years, some of these companies had gone from relatively small players to some of the largest companies in the world. These companies recognize that there is a lack of understanding on tech policy debates even as the decision for regulation and legislation rests with Congressional members and federal agencies. Yet even as companies such as Google and Amazon spend record amounts on lobbying efforts and advocacy campaigns to engage public policymakers, there is still a shortage of tech policy expertise on Capitol Hill. The tech policy literacy gap is real and can make legislating and rulemaking extremely tedious and frustrating. This lack of understanding has been on display every time there is a Congressional hearing featuring a tech company CEO or social media personalities.[12]

It has now become a tradition among tech policy reporters, especially on Twitter, to note how many senators and members of Congress (regardless of political party) ask questions or make statements that betray their lack of sophisticated understanding of technological progress. This was epitomized by Sen. Ted Stevens (R-AK) describing the internet as "a series of tubes" in 2018,[13] but has continued with elected leaders from both parties asking basic questions, such as how free platforms make money,[14] asking for help

---

[11] Jane Chung, *Big Tech, Big Cash: Washington's New Power Players*, Public Citizen, March 2021, https://mkus3lurbh3lbztg254fzode-wpengine.netdna-ssl.com /wp-content/uploads/Big-Tech-Big-Cash-Washingtons-New-Power-Players.pdf.

[12] See Joe Perticone, "Pro-Trump Vloggers Diamond and Silk Testified Before Congress and It Got out of Hand Fast," *Business Insider*, April 26, 2018, https:// www.businessinsider.com/diamond-and-silk-testimony-before-congress-got-out-of -hand-fast-2018-4.

[13] Alex Gangitano, "Flashback Friday: 'A Series of Tubes,'" Roll Call, February 16, 2018, https://www.rollcall.com/2018/02/16/flashback-friday-a-series-of-tubes/.

[14] See Emily Stewart, "Lawmakers Seem Confused about What Facebook Does—And How to Fix It," Vox, April 10, 2018, https://www.vox.com/policy -and-politics/2018/4/10/17222062/mark-zuckerberg-testimony-graham-facebook -regulations.

with sending emails,[15] or even for help finding their interviews online.[16] There is often a temptation to point out the ignorance on display by some of these elected officials, but these hearings and statements also demonstrate a disconnect between the conversations in Silicon Valley and those that most Americans (elected and unelected) are having at home and in their communities.

The tech policy literacy gap marks much of the current discourse. Technologists, Silicon Valley CEOs, and other think-tank scholars are speaking one language with precise terminology, context, and experience; while many others, including members of Congress and the wider public, are on the outside looking in. As *New York Times* tech writer Shira Ovide articulates, "tech companies are built around software that is designed not to be understood by outsiders."[17] This is a real barrier that makes discernment, Congressional oversight, and public discourse difficult to carry forward.

Problems, both perceived and real, can exist. But cutting through the noise and speaking on the same terms is a truly Herculean task. As numerous recent polling demonstrates, many involved in the tech policy debate—politicians, communications experts, and others—have struggled to communicate to those outside their circles, both decision-makers and constituents.[18] This should lead Christians, especially Christian policy makers, to work toward enhancing tech literacy and improving the lines of communication with those outside the policy bubble. This will require humility

---

[15] See Sean Burch, "GOP Congressman Asks Google CEO Sundhar Pichai Why His Campaign Emails Always Go to Spam," Yahoo, July 29, 2020, https://www.yahoo.com/now/gop-congressman-asks-google-ceo-201746634.html.

[16] See Jack Crowe, "Dem. Rep. Accused Google of 'Overusing Conservative News Organizations' in Search Results," *National Review*, December 11, 2018, https://www.nationalreview.com/news/steve-cohen-accuses-google-of-overusing-conservative-news-organizations-in-search-results/.

[17] Shira Ovide, "Congress Doesn't Get Big Tech," *New York Times,* July 29, 2020, https://www.nytimes.com/2020/07/29/technology/congress-big-tech.html.

[18] See Knight Foundation, "The Future of Tech Policy: American Views," https://knightfoundation.org/wp-content/uploads/2020/03/Gallup-Knight-Report-Techlash-Americas-Growing-Concern-with-Major-Tech-Companies-Final.pdf.

on the part of experts to translate their work into a language that is understandable rather than hiding behind jargon-heavy or obtuse discourse. The goal should be to encourage more, not less, of the public to participate in a literate way in the debate.

This void between those who understand and those who do not is a real barrier for productive public discernment. If elected officials and their constituents are so far behind on this process, there is an important opportunity for Christians to step up and raise the level of discourse. Christians have a rich understanding of the complexities of this world grounded in our theology and ideological framework. We should extend that grace to others working through complicated questions that do not always have easy answers.

In 2016 *Wired* magazine security writer Kim Zetter expounded upon this knowledge-gap problem, bemoaning that "politicians on Capitol Hill have plenty of staff to advise them on the legal aspects of policy issues, but, oddly, they have a dearth of advisers who can serve up unbiased analysis about the critical science and technology issues they legislate."[19] This observation is also supported by a 2020 New America Foundation study titled the "Congressional Brain Drain," which found "Most staff who manage policy portfolios in Congress have only one or two years of Hill experience. That is, roughly one-third of legislative staffers have not yet served the duration of a single Congress."[20] Even sitting Congressman Ted Lieu (D-CA), one of a handful of members with a computer science degree, explained in a 2019 *Bloomberg* interview, "There is a large skills gap in Congress in terms of people who have had training in technology. . . . You see the same phenomenon among staff where many do not have technical degrees, whether

---

[19] Kim Zetter, "Of Course Congress Is Clueless about Tech—It Killed Its Tutor," *Wired*, April 21, 2016, https://www.wired.com/2016/04/office-technology-assessment-congress-clueless-tech-killed-tutor/.

[20] Alexander C. Furnas and Timothy M. LaPira, "Congressional Brain Drain: Legislative Capacity in the 21st Century," New America Foundation, September 8, 2020, https://www.newamerica.org/political-reform/reports/congressional-brain-drain/.

it's engineering or science. It causes a lack of information and understanding when legislation does appear."[21]

This knowledge gap also puts the legislative branch at an incredible disadvantage when conducting oversight and accountability on thorny questions regarding technology. As American Enterprise Institute scholar Kevin Kosar notes, "Our national legislature is constantly trying to catch up with presidents and their agencies, who make policy via regulations, executive orders, and the like. Congress, quite simply, is overwhelmed."[22] This imbalance may explain why so much of the heavy lifting on issues like privacy and competition are being deliberated by independent federal agencies like the Federal Communications Commissions, Federal Trade Commission, and the Department of Commerce, who are filled with a bureaucracy of experts and experienced professionals.

However, recently, there are new initiatives attempting to correct this imbalance. Two nonpartisan, nonprofit organizations called Tech Congress and the Aspen Tech Policy Hub are working to improve tech literacy on Capitol Hill. These organizations are stepping up to create opportunities on Capitol Hill for technology professionals and experts to more actively participate in the legislative process. As Tech Congress explains on their site, "We place computer scientists, engineers, and other technologists to serve as technology policy advisors to Members of Congress."[23] The Aspen Tech Policy Hub has a different approach, "modeled after tech incubators like Y Combinator, we take STEM experts, teach them the policy process through fellowship and executive education programs, and encourage them to develop outside-the-box solutions to society's problems."[24]

While taking different approaches, both projects are working to enable policymakers to benefit from their expertise as their teams deliberate on

---

[21] "Capitol Hill's STEM Skills Gap Targeted by Tech Fellowships," Bloomberg Law, September 5, 2019, https://news.bloomberglaw.com/tech-and-telecom-law/capitol-hills-stem-skills-gap-targeted-by-tech-fellowships.

[22] Kevin Kosar, "Our Overwhelmed Congress," LegBranch, December 7, 2020, https://www.legbranch.org/our-overwhelmed-congress/.

[23] TechCongress, https://www.techcongress.io/about-us.

[24] Aspen Tech Hub, https://www.aspentechpolicyhub.org/.

these complicated questions. Improving these resources will benefit the quality of understanding a member of Congress can have as they prepare for a hearing, markup, or vote. But it will also, hopefully, improve communication and the education of constituents trying to learn more about these issues at home.

Bipartisanship: The Only Way Forward

Unlike other policy debates where the political lines have existed for years or decades, discernment around technology does not always break down along traditional party lines. The nature of tech policy often brings together unique political alliances in pursuit of a common goal. At the beginning of 2021, the Information Technology and Innovation Foundation, a well-respected nonpartisan think tank based in Washington, DC, released their report titled "The Year Ahead: Twenty-Four Ways Congress and the Biden Administration Can Advance Good Tech Policy in 2021."[25] The recommendations are noteworthy in how they are congruent with current discussions on Capitol Hill and the bipartisan nature of the whole agenda. This focus on bipartisanship is not a one-off instance from a single organization. When evaluating past tech policy initiatives, whether over intellectual property in the internet age, efforts to enact e-mail privacy rules, or concerns over anti-trust and competition policy, fascinating alliances and bipartisanship are a central theme.

A key legislative example of tech bipartisanship revolves around Congress's response to the leaks by former CIA staffer Edward Snowden. In late May 2013, the *Guardian* and the *Washington Post* initially reported the groundbreaking Snowden revelations. The reports detailed troves of classified and secret documentation that shed light on the massive surveillance apparatus of the United States government. These controversial reports

---

[25] Robert Atkinson and Daniel Castro, "The Year Ahead: Twenty-Four Ways Congress and the Biden Administration Can Advance Good Tech Policy in 2021," ITIF, January 4, 2021, https://itif.org/publications/2021/01/04/year-ahead-twenty -four-ways-congress-and-biden-administration-can-advance.

showed the American public explicit detail about the National Security Administration's bulk data collection under the Patriot Act and several other questionable practices.

This kicked off a years-long debate over surveillance policy in the United States, specifically the laws passed in the aftermath of the attacks on September 11, 2001. It also opened a serious dialogue among privacy activists, lawmakers, and technologists about the implications of American surveillance policies and procedures. Several raised concerns about the surveillance techniques employed during the proliferation of communications networks and platforms. The debate over the future of these surveillance programs was fierce and heated, and it created strange alliances with politicians not usually seen as co-belligerents. There were some conservatives and progressives who joined together in support of surveillance reform, while others argued in support of the position of the intelligence community.[26]

One of the strongest leaders for surveillance reform was in fact the original author of the Patriot Act, Rep. Jim Sensenbrenner (R-WI). He claimed, "We have to make a balance between security and civil liberties. And the reason the intelligence community has gotten itself into such trouble is they apparently do not see why civil liberties have got to be protected."[27] While he did not call for the outright repeal of the Patriot Act, his introspection about how sections of the law had been abused was a refreshing change of pace in Washington. Rare enough is it for politicians to admit a wrong, even more rare to have the humility to admit something they authored and led did not go as they planned.[28] It also required him to criticize the same intelligence community he had worked with over the previous decade. However,

---

[26] See Editorial Board, "Rep. Jim Sensenbrenner's Quest to Rein in the NSA," *Milwaukee Journal Sentinel,* November 2, 2013, https://archive.jsonline.com /news/opinion/rep-jim-sensenbrenners-quest-to-rein-in-the-nsa-b99132667z1 -230291471.html/.

[27] "Rep. Jim Sensenbrenner's Quest to Rein in the NSA," *Milwaukee Journal Sentinel.*

[28] Jim Sensenbrenner, House of Representatives, June 6, 2013, https://www .scribd.com/doc/146169288/Sensenbrenner-Letter-to-Attorney-General-Eric -Holder-RE-NSA-and-Verizon.

after recognizing the policy's shortcomings, he joined with other legislators from across the aisle to improve it. Rep. Sensenbrenner collaborated with Sen. Patrick Leahy (D-VT) to bring together an emergent bipartisan coalition to rein in what they perceived to be an unaccountable surveillance system. After several efforts, including close votes in the House and procedural gamesmanship in the Senate, the bipartisan first step to reevaluate our surveillance state crossed the finish line.

On June 2, 2015, Congress passed the bipartisan USA Freedom Act, which rolled back several provisions in Section 215 of the Patriot Act.[29] It enacted new restrictions on the bulk collection of telecommunication metadata of US citizens by intelligence agencies such as the National Security Agency. However, there is still a great debate in the United States, particularly within the tech community, about whether other sections of the Patriot Act and intelligence community authorities should be curtailed. Yet the USA Freedom Act does stand as a helpful example about how bipartisanship is an essential ingredient to building effective coalitions to make meaningful technology policy change.

Pre-Internet to Now

Often the debates over technology and innovation are shaped by legal, cultural, and economic frameworks developed years before the advent of the internet. These frameworks take laws that were created even before AOL CDs were sent to households across the country and apply them to current challenges.[30]

One example of this challenge is the constant debate over the Fourth Amendment—which prohibits unreasonable searches and seizures—and

---

[29] This bill passed the House on May 13, 2015 (338–88), and passed the Senate on June 2, 2015 (67–32).

[30] See Alex Byers, "Disconnect: Old Laws vs. New Tech," Politico, October 21, 2014, https://www.politico.com/story/2014/10/washington-dc-technology-112091; Rebecca J. Rosen, "The Thorny Combination of Old Laws and New Tech," *Atlantic,* November 10, 2011, https://www.theatlantic.com/technology/archive/2011/11/the-thorny-combination-of-old-laws-and-new-tech/248111/.

how it applies to our internet age. Is an email the same as a personal letter? A letter is physical and located in a specific space, but when a user sends an email, that data does not reside in one state or even one nation. How should the courts and policymakers think through the ramifications? We also saw this dynamic when ridesharing apps like Uber and Lyft transformed transportations in cities across the country. The regulatory framework and insurance practices for taxis and other transportation companies were developed in a pre-internet world. As ridesharing became a prominent part of transportation options, new scrutiny emerged.

Competing corporate interests and other critics are lobbying policy makers and municipal leaders to evaluate whether these ridesharing innovations are a net positive or if new regulations should be developed and adopted in the name of safety or other concerns. This approach was manifested in a 2014 NPR article that described "Uber's strategy with that well-known saying: It is better to ask forgiveness than permission."[31]

The ramifications of ridesharing apps and other innovations in the "gig economy" go far beyond the road. As increasing numbers of people gain flexible employment and find easier ways to shop or travel, a debate over the future of work has arisen. Do these apps provide good economic opportunities for those who choose to pursue alternative career paths or an additional revenue stream, or do they lock individuals into careers with stunted opportunities?

Many states, especially in the wake of the 2020 California Ballot Proposition 22, have been wrestling with the question of whether Uber and Lyft drivers are employees or independent contractors.[32] This distinction is

---

[31] Aarti Shahani, "As Uber Expands, It Asks Cities for Forgiveness Instead of Permission," NPR, December 26, 2014, https://www.npr.org/sections/alltech considered/2014/12/26/373087290/as-uber-expands-it-asks-cities-for-forgivness -instead-of-permission.

[32] Proposition 22 was a ballot initiative in California that passed with 59 percent of the vote granting an exception to app-based transportation and delivery companies from providing a full suite of employee benefits (and providing other protections), allowing them to classify their drivers as independent contractors rather than employees. For more see Kate Conger, "Uber and Lyft Drivers in

one that state and federal policy makers, as well as the rest of the tech industry, are thinking about because of how it could have major effects on the rest of the US economy. Adam Jackson, CEO of Braintrust and TechCrunch contributor, explains this challenge succinctly by noting "where tech has succeeded in creating hundreds of thousands of independent contractor positions, it also has to lead the way in reimagining how we may treat them and reward them for their work."[33]

Applying policy frameworks for a future of tech innovation is even more unsettled when thinking about the implications of artificial intelligence (AI) and the future of work. Politicians such as former Democratic presidential candidate Andrew Yang made a concern about the employment implications of these innovations a central plank of his platform. A *New York Times* article describes Yang's belief "that automation and advanced artificial intelligence will soon make millions of jobs obsolete—yours, mine, those of our accountants and radiologists and grocery store cashiers. He says America needs to take radical steps to prevent Great Depression–level unemployment and a total societal meltdown."[34] On the other hand, there have been other more optimistic predictions such as a 2021 MIT paper titled "Artificial Intelligence and the Future of Work," which downplayed the rise of robots and instead painted a more optimistic picture, asserting, "AI will enable new industries to emerge, creating more new jobs than are lost to the technology."[35]

California Will Remain Contractors," November 4, 2020, https://www.nytimes .com/2020/11/04/technology/california-uber-lyft-prop-22.html.

[33] Adam Jackson, "Tech Must Radically Rethink How It Treats Its Independent Contractors," TechCrunch, September 22, 2020, https://techcrunch.com/2020/09 /22/tech-must-radically-rethink-how-it-treats-independent-contractors/.

[34] Kevin Roose, "His 2020 Campaign Message: The Robots Are Coming," *New York Times*, February 10, 2018, https://www.nytimes.com/2018/02/10/technology /his-2020-campaign-message-the-robots-are-coming.html.

[35] Thomas Malone, Daniela Rus, Robert Laubacher, "Artificial Intelligence and the Future of Work," Massachusetts Institute of Technology, December 17, 2020, https://workofthefuture.mit.edu/research-post/artificial-intelligence-and-the -future-of-work/.

Christian theology has a deeply developed theology of work and vocation that would be valuable to the discussion around technology, automation, and vocation, particularly discussions over labor disputes brought on by ridesharing apps.[36] As ethicist Jason Thacker has written, our work is not the result of sin but something we were created by God to do to reflect him.[37] He states that these types of conversations are key for the church to engage in today because we often build "our lives around our work and [we] let it define who we are, as opposed to letting God define who we are and being reminded that our world is meant to reflect God."[38] As our society is seeing rapid changes in the workforce through the use of automation and other forms of technology, we need to thoughtfully engage these pressing issues, evaluating the many ways our lives are being transformed with the adoption of automation and artificial intelligence in the workplace.

Encryption: Security for Missions and Ministry

In the aftermath of the 2016 San Bernardino terrorist attack, there was an intense and important national debate about the value of encryption and device access. Essentially, encryption "is the process of converting or scrambling data and information into an unreadable, encoded version that can only be read with authorized access to the decryption key. Encryption is a widely used security tool that can prevent the interception of sensitive data, either while stored in files or while in transit across networks."[39] This technology is embedded within many devices, protocols, and services, often

---

[36] For more on a theology of work, see Timothy Keller and Katherine Leary Alsdorf, *Every Good Endeavor: Connecting Your Work to God's Work* (New York: Penguin, 2012), Sebastian Traeger and Greg Gilbert, *The Gospel at Work: How the Gospel Gives New Purpose and Meaning to Our Jobs* (Grand Rapids: Zondervan, 2018), and Gene Edward Veith, *God at Work: Your Christian Vocation in All of Life* (Wheaton, IL: Crossway Books, 2002).

[37] See Jason Thacker, *The Age of AI: Artificial Intelligence and the Future of Humanity* (Grand Rapids: Zondervan, 2020), 101–2.

[38] Thacker, 118.

[39] "What Is Encryption?" Cisco, https://www.cisco.com/c/en/us/products/security/encryption-explained.html.

without users noticing.[40] The debate focused on whether encryption should be absolute or if there should be mandated backdoors to allow government access in certain unique circumstances, such as the terrorist attack and the government's attempt to prevent another.

Specifically, the debate hinged on Apple's refusal to grant law enforcement access to the phone of the dead terrorist from the San Bernardino attack. The process of accessing his phone would require Apple to "break" the number code to unlock the phone in question.[41] While the desire to "catch the bad guys" is understandable and the government's goal of preventing further violence was noble, it was not as simple as just unlocking a single phone. Weakened encryption makes citizens vulnerable to government snooping, hackers, and other unwanted prying eyes. Encryption is an essential security measure necessary to safeguard our financial system and communications networks.[42] If the United States were to change its encryption framework, there are a number of unintended consequences that would reshape our experience on the internet.

To understand the concerns, Christians should look at a country where Apple was less concerned with upholding encryption. Recent reports from the *New York Times* reveal that in China, Apple has created weaknesses that specifically enable the Chinese Communist Party to circumvent encryption protections or gain backdoor access to private communications of Chinese citizens.[43] This is a very real threat for Chinese journalists, political activists, and religious minorities (including Christians and Uyghur Muslims) who

---

[40] See Namrata Maheshwari and Raman Jit Singh Chima, "Why Encryption Is Important: 10 Facts to Counter the Myths," AccessNow, August 31, 2021, https://www.accessnow.org/why-encryption-is-important/.

[41] See Tim Cook, "Message to Our Customers," Apple, February 16, 2016, https://www.apple.com/customer-letter/.

[42] See Will Cathcat, "Encryption Has Never Been More Essential or Threatened," *Wired,* April 5, 2021, https://www.wired.com/story/opinion-encryption-has-never-been-more-essential-or-threatened/.

[43] See Jack Nicas, Raymond Zhong, and Daisuke Wakabayashi, "Censorship, Surveillance and Profits: A Hard Bargain for Apple in China," *New York Times*, May 17, 2021, https://www.nytimes.com/2021/05/17/technology/apple-china-censorship-data.html.

are being persecuted and could potentially be caught up in government surveillance efforts.

Christians should recognize that debates about encryption are complicated and that decisions to decrypt information could have unaccounted-for ramifications. At the same time, Christians should make clear to their elected leaders the importance of this issue for them. We should work to clarify to our representatives in Congress the concerns that come with companies being so willing to work with an authoritarian regime such as China, especially considering how these surveillance technologies are weaponized in the persecution of Uyghurs; Christian pastors such as Wang Ti, who is currently imprisoned for leading a congregation; and democracy activists in Hong Kong.[44]

Though it is a complicated discussion, Christians must not cede the digital public square to companies or lobbyists. Rather, we must recognize that the legal frameworks developed by policymakers will have an effect on our communities as well as those to whom we are called to minister.[45] Though difficult and complex, Christians must wrestle with these thorny issues and clearly articulate a Christian vision for the development and use of technology, including issues of surveillance.

Technology and the Stock Market: A Case Study in Interconnection

In 2021, we saw how structures established in the real world can be significantly challenged or experience upheaval by the harnessing of technology. Nowhere was this more poignantly clarified than with meme stocks and their creative, destructive nature on Wall Street. A meme stock is a particular kind of stock that has gained viral attention on social media platforms among the retail investor community. A company's stock would become

---

[44] See AP News, "China Sentences Protestant Pastor to 9 Years for Subversion," December 30, 2019, https://apnews.com/article/381d2f040b3f610d624b04f9af2dd3f9.

[45] For more on the legal and policy debates in the digital public square, see chapter 5 from lawyer David French.

popular, similar to a meme, and online investors would artificially push up the price of the stock. Because of the onslaught of coordinated engagement, the stock would become highly volatile and unstable because it was "traded mostly by retail investors in search of the next big thing and with little regard for valuation models or the business's underlying fundamentals."[46]

Throughout January, online retail investors and day traders, most of whom were organizing through the r/wallstreetbets subreddit and private Discord channels,[47] coordinated a short squeeze of the meme stock GameStop (NYSE:GME), the American video game retailer. The intrepid day traders fancied themselves as activists and a continuation of the Occupy Wall Street movement standing up to the corporate "suits" on Wall Street. These investors primarily used the aptly named retail commission-free investment app Robinhood to place their trades and operate their financial revolution.

This sudden manipulation of the market by millions of traders through social media platforms caused significant financial consequences for specific hedge funds and major losses for short sellers. On January 28, at its zenith the squeeze caused GameStop's stock to reach a pre-market value price of over $483 per share, which was almost thirty times the $17.25 valuation from the beginning of the year. Over the next month the price went down dramatically. After it was all said and done, the short squeeze had created and largely destroyed $27 billion in market value,[48] with many retail investors who were caught up in the excitement losing large sums.[49] In the immediate

---

[46] Derek Horstmeyer and Valerie Meyer, "Meme Stocks and Systematic Risk," CFA Institute, August 9, 2021, https://blogs.cfainstitute.org/investor/2021/08/09/meme-stocks-and-systematic-risk/.

[47] See Tom Warren, "Discord Has Turned into a Virtual Trade Floor with Memes, Stonks, and Chaos," The Verge, January 28, 2021, https://www.theverge.com/2021/1/28/22253892/discord-wallstreetbets-server-virtual-trade-floor-reddit.

[48] See Matt Phillips, Gillian Friedman, and Taylor Lorenz, "Plunging GameStop Stock Tests the Will of Investors to Stick with the Ride," New York Times, February 2, 2021, https://www.nytimes.com/2021/02/02/business/gamestop-investors-plunging-shares.html.

[49] See Matt Phillips, "Recast as 'Stimmies,' Federal Relief Checks Drive a Stock Buying Spree," New York Times, March 21, 2021, https://www.nytimes.com/2021/03/21/business/stimulus-check-stock-market.html.

aftermath of the short squeeze, there was rapid reaction from the SEC, the House Financial Services, and Senate Banking Committees, all stepping up their oversight duties. They organized hearings and investigations into the role of social media platforms, and whether this was a precursor to a radical restructuring of investing rules and disclosures.

Policy makers and regulators were busy scrutinizing whether Robinhood had proper consumer protections or if social media platforms like Reddit were being misused to enable illegal market manipulation. Federal policy makers continue to grapple with the confluence of these two separate spheres, the heavily regulated world of trading on Wall Street and the wild west on subreddits and Discord channels. This is a microcosm of the challenge before policy makers. It is a difficult balancing act requiring an approach that enables innovation to connect people to unprecedented opportunities while also ensuring proper consumer protections.

What Is Section 230? That Notorious Little Law

Content moderation has become a central battlefield in tech policy conversations within both Republican and Democratic circles. Yet it is important to summarize how Section 230 of the 1996 Communications Decency Act has governed the public discourse on the internet since the law's passage.[50] Section 230 states that "No provider or user of an interactive computer service shall be treated as the publisher or speaker of any information provided by another information content provider" (47 U.S.C. § 230). The law governs the large ecosystem of social media platforms, any website with a comment section, and a plethora of other online spaces.

The law came to fruition through the bipartisan work of Chris Cox, a former Republican US Representative from California and then US Representative Ron Wyden, a Democrat who crafted Section 230 of the Communications Decency Act. This statute governs "the allocation of liability for online torts and crimes among internet content creators, platforms,

---

[50] See Jeff Kosseff, *The Twenty-Six Words That Created the Internet* (New York: Cornell Press, 2019).

and service providers. The statute's fundamental principle is that content creators should be liable for any illegal content they create. Internet platforms are generally protected from liability for third-party content, unless they are complicit in the development of illegal content, in which case the statute offers them no protection."[51]

Or as the Congress Research Service articulates, the law "broadly protects operators of 'interactive computer services' from liability for publishing, removing, or restricting access to another's content."[52] Over the past several years, some Democrats have argued the law allows platforms to get away with too little moderation on their sites, particularly when it comes to hate speech or misinformation. On the other side of the political aisle, many Republicans argue the law allows platforms to do too much moderating, enabling tech companies to act as unfair gatekeepers.

This debate hit a crescendo in 2020 when both major presidential candidates called for its repeal, yet for very different reasons. Then president Donald Trump claimed tech companies were hiding behind Section 230 to enable bias and censorship of conservative speech. Then-presidential candidate Joe Biden believed the law allowed social media companies too much leeway in not taking down more misinformation or potentially unsavory speech. The debate was not solved during the election and the fight over those twenty-six words continues, with dozens of proposed fixes, and potential legislative solutions introduced by both Democrats and Republicans.

Christians and religious institutions should be paying close attention to this discourse. It is true that the worldview of Silicon Valley is different on several issues that are important to Christians. On one hand, Senator Ben Sasse of Nebraska has raised the concern that deeply held religious beliefs, such as the sanctity of life, could one day be seen as hate speech

---

[51] Christopher Cox, "The Origins and Original Intent of Section 230 of the Communications Decency Act," *University of Richmond Journal of Law and Technology*, August 27, 2020, https://jolt.richmond.edu/2020/08/27/the-origins -and-original-intent-of-section-230-of-the-communications-decency-act/.

[52] Jason Gallo and Clare Y. Cho, "Social Media: Misinformation and Content Moderation Issues for Congress," January 27, 2020, https://crsreports.congress.gov /product/pdf/R/R46662.

and run afoul of content moderation decisions.[53] And we are already seeing some signs of this today, where deeply held religious beliefs on sexuality and gender are being suppressed as hate speech.[54] However, on the other hand, there could be real unintended consequences to changes to state and federal law that could degrade the internet experience and limit the ability of free expression on internet platforms.[55] As this debate continues, it is important to see how potential outcomes will affect our communities, even as we also look holistically at how the conversation around other internet gatekeepers can inform the dialogue.

Explaining the Stack

Tech policy in the United States is not governed by one statute or regulated by one federal agency. There is no "Digital Bill of Rights" or Ministry of Tech. The American framework is more akin to a puzzle with different rules, guidance, practices, and procedures that fit together into a (hopefully) coherent and holistic understanding of the internet ecosystem.

A popular analogy considers the internet as a stack with different layers. This is most effectively explained by tech blogger Ben Thompson, who describes the top of the stack as the platforms that users publish through directly and engage with on a daily basis. These platforms include Yelp, Reddit, Facebook, Twitter, TikTok, YouTube, and other social networks. This layer is "about broadcasting—reaching as many people as possible—and while you may have the right to say anything you want, there is no right to be heard."[56] It is the level of the stack that is most relevant to the Section 230 discussion.

---

[53] See Ben Sasse, "Pro-Life Speech Is Not Hate Speech," April 10, 2019, https://www.sasse.senate.gov/public/index.cfm/2019/4/sasse-pro-life-speech-is-not-hate-speech.

[54] For more on these issues, see chapter 8 from Jeremy Tedesco and Christiana Kiefer.

[55] For more on these unintended consequences, see chapter 5 from David French.

[56] Ben Thompson, "A Framework for Moderation," Stratechery, August 9, 2019, https://stratechery.com/2019/a-framework-for-moderation/.

Further down the stack are internet infrastructure and web-hosting companies such as Cloudflare, GoDaddy, or Amazon Web Services (AWS). These entities ostensibly allow websites to function (such as providing cloud hosting) or shield websites from Distributed Denial-of-Service (DDoS) attacks and other vulnerabilities. While they are not user-facing, they have on occasion made very public moderation decisions. At this level Ben Thompson explains there are no explicit rules defining these moderation decisions: "The difference between an infrastructure company and a customer-facing platform is that the former is not accountable to end users in any way."[57]

The most notable example of how this distinction plays out is from August 2017 when Cloudflare's CEO Matthew Prince unilaterally decided to pull service from the alt-right website the Daily Stormer after they were instrumental in planning the infamous neo-Nazi demonstration in Charlottesville, Virginia.[58] As Prince explains in a *Wall Street Journal* column, he decided it was no longer in Cloudflare's interests to service this client, so he pulled the plug.[59] There was no rule or law preventing him. Cloudflare found that the Daily Stormer was in breach of his company's Terms of Service and decided to act accordingly. At the time of his column, Matthew Prince openly wrestled with his decision, explaining, "I continue to worry about this power and the potential precedent being set. The reality of today's internet is that if you are publishing anything even remotely controversial, your site will get cyberattacked. Without a massive global network similar to Cloudflare's, it is nearly impossible to withstand the barrage."[60]

Considering there are a multitude of other web infrastructure companies, it is possible that a site like the Daily Stormer, which was effectively canceled by Cloudflare, could take their business elsewhere. But Prince's central challenge is still worth considering: "a few private companies have

---

[57] Thompson, "A Framework for Moderation."

[58] See Matthew Prince, "Why We Terminated Daily Stormer," Cloudflare, August 16, 2017, https://blog.cloudflare.com/why-we-terminated-daily-stormer/.

[59] See Matthew Prince, "Was I Right to Pull the Plug on a Nazi Website?" August 22, 2017, https://www.wsj.com/articles/was-i-right-to-pull-the-plug-on-a-nazi-website-1503440771.

[60] Prince, "Was I Right to Pull the Plug on a Nazi Website?"

effectively become the gatekeepers to the public square—the blogs and social media that serve as today's soapboxes and pamphlets. If a handful of tech executives decide to block you from their services, your content effectively can't be on the internet."[61]

At this level of the stack, beyond a Terms of Service agreement between vendor and client, there is no regulatory framework to curtail these decisions. It is not a Section 230 question or even a question of common carriage as experienced by internet providers. *Wired* columnist Molly Wood explores this conundrum in a 2020 article titled "We Need to Talk about Cloud Neutrality."[62] Wood says that different entities in the internet ecosystem have plenty of oversight and regulatory rules of the road, yet: "[web] infrastructure is solely owned by a handful of companies with hardly any oversight. The potential for abuse is huge, whether it's through trade-secret snooping or the outright blocking, slowing, or hampering of transmission. No one seems to be thinking about what could happen if these behemoths decide it's against their interests to have all these barnacles on their flanks."[63]

Wood acknowledges it is unclear how this type of regulatory framework should look, but she does note that this layer presents different challenges for consideration when thinking about a framework for industry standards and potential questions of regulatory oversight. Thompson looks at this same potential concern and lands a bit differently: "I ultimately reject the idea that publishing on the Internet is a right that must be guaranteed by third parties. Stand on the street corner all you like, at least your terrible ideas will be limited by the physical world. The Internet, though, with its inherent ability to broadcast and congregate globally, is a fundamentally more dangerous medium that is by-and-large facilitated by third parties who have rights of their own."[64] Both Wood and Thompson demonstrate how there are lessons to be learned when thinking about governance related

---

[61] Prince, "Was I Right to Pull the Plug on a Nazi Website?"

[62] See Molly Wood, "We Need to Talk about 'Cloud Neutrality,'" *Wired*, February 10, 2020, https://www.wired.com/story/we-need-to-talk-about-cloud-neutrality/.

[63] Wood, "We Need to Talk about 'Cloud Neutrality.'"

[64] Thompson, "A Framework for Moderation."

to platforms. Looking throughout the internet ecosystem can reveal standards that could help inform the overall direction of discourse.

At the bottom of the stack are telecommunication companies otherwise known as internet service providers (ISPs), which enable users to access the internet. Generally, these ISPs are the cable, wireless, and satellite companies that enable entities (individuals and corporations) to access the internet. From the dial-up era to the high-speed internet that allows social media posts to go viral, ISPs are the backbone of the internet. While debates and discussions about how corporate interests could alter the experience of users is relatively new—particularly because of recent incidents further up the stack—the debate about net neutrality, which directly relates to the question of what regulatory framework should govern internet service providers, has been going on for almost two decades.

The Never-Ending Saga of Net Neutrality

Gallons of ink have been spilled and many billable hours for lobbyists and lawyers have been allocated all because of net neutrality. This policy battle offers a prescient lesson for ongoing and future technology policy debates. When political zeitgeist and activist fervor takes over a complicated policy debate without carefully considering the complexities of internet networks and administrative law, a longstanding framework that both promotes innovation and protects consumers cannot be attained.

First coined in 2003 by Columbia University professor Tim Wu,[65] the term *net neutrality* refers to the principle that ISPs must treat all internet traffic, all bits and bytes, equally "regardless of its content or sender."[66] Over the course of the 2000s, this idea became a central rallying point for internet activists, concerned that broadband providers would someday use their

---

[65] See Tim Wu, "Network Neutrality, Broadband Discrimination," Columbia Law, 2003, https://web.archive.org/web/20140424062409/http:/www.jthtl.org /content/articles/V2I1/JTHTLv2i1_Wu.PDF.

[66] Daniel Lyons, "Net Neutrality: A Primer, American Enterprise Institute," *AEIdeas* (blog) November 28, 2017, https://www.aei.org/technology-and-innovation /telecommunications/net-neutrality-a-primer/.

market power to block access of competitors or degrade certain sites they do not approve of.

The impetus for this was based on a few limited occasions where internet providers, such as Madison River Communications in 2005, temporarily blocked ports used for Voice over Internet Protocol (VoIP) services. The incident was resolved, and as Ben Thompson notes, "no other ISP has tried to do the same; the reasoning is straightforward: foreclosing a service that competes with an ISP's own service is a clear antitrust violation. In other words, there are already regulations in place to deal with this behavior, and the limited evidence we have suggests it works."[67] Relying on antitrust enforcement at the Federal Trade Commission, technological advancement that would improve internet speeds or resiliency, as well as market forces was not enough for a cadre of online activists who rallied around the concept. In 2008, Democratic presidential candidate Barack Obama embraced the cause, making "net neutrality a campaign promise, vowing to achieve it through the FCC."[68]

Beyond activists calling for net neutrality, Silicon Valley giants also engaged in advocacy for net neutrality. As University of Nebraska law scholar Gus Hurwitz says, net neutrality is "just the latest example of a fight between bilateral media oligopolists. 'Big content' and 'big distribution' have always fought over how to split the rents they extract from consumers, users have always distrusted distributors, and content providers have always used this to their advantage. From this perspective, the net neutrality rules are pure rent seeking by a content/edge industry as a way to hinder potential industrial competitors."[69]

Without legislation from Congress, all eyes turned to the Federal Communications Commission to designate internet service as a Title II

---

[67] Ben Thompson, "Pro-Neutrality, Anti-Title II," *Stratechery*, November 28, 2017, https://stratechery.com/2017/pro-neutrality-anti-title-ii/.

[68] Peter Suderman, "Internet Cop," *Reason*, March 2011, https://reason.com /2011/02/08/internet-cop/.

[69] Gus Hurwitz, "Volokh Conspiracy: One law professor's overview of the confusing net neutrality debate," *Washington Post*, November 28, 2017, https://www .washingtonpost.com/news/volokh-conspiracy/wp/2017/11/28/one-law-professors -overview-of-the-confusing-net-neutrality-debate/.

service, thereby regulating broadband providers as a public utility-style. This finally occurred in 2015 when the FCC, along partisan lines, established a rule, the Open Internet Order, prohibiting broadband providers from blocking, throttling content, or from paid prioritization of online traffic. This order also established broadband providers as common carriers under Title II of the 1934 Communications Act, subjecting these providers to the regulatory framework written to govern the old wireline telephone network.

Professor Hurwitz argues the core issue at stake is a debate over "ex ante or ex post" framework for regulation. He goes on to illustrate the primary argument opposing Title II, by noting that "the likelihood of harmful conduct is small, where it happens existing legal frameworks are likely sufficient to address it, the political economy of consumer concern about and outrage over discriminatory practices will serve as a substantial check on problematic ISP conduct, and where nonneutral practices are implemented it will be because there are significant gains to trade that will ultimately benefit consumers."[70]

Opponents of Open Internet Order have also highlighted the economic case against strict net neutrality rules, focusing on decreased investment.[71] Others have also observed that inherent to network management is the need to prioritize data, especially in the case of more sophisticated networks. The telecom blogger Morris Lore opined that future 5G networks are not compatible with the definitions of net neutrality because through prioritization they can be turned "into a multi-lane highway, minus the hassle of building lots of separate physical lanes. Ideally, one of these lanes could be conjured up when needed, providing superior bandwidth, lower latency or other guarantees denied those cruising along the same road."[72] This technological

---

[70] Hurwitz, "Volokh Conspiracy."

[71] See Randy May, "Broadband Investment Slowed by $5.6 Billion Since Open Internet Order," Free State Foundation, May 2017, http://freestatefoundation .blogspot.com/2017/05/broadband-investment-slowed-by-56.html.

[72] Morris Lore, "Joe Biden's Net Neutrality Threat to 5G," Light Reading, July 12, 2021, https://www.lightreading.com/5g/joe-bidens-net-neutrality-threat-to-5g /a/d-id/770800.

innovation could essentially solve the concerns many had during the age of slower speeds.

In 2017, the FCC, under Republican control, repealed the Open Internet Order, establishing a lighter touch approach under a Title I framework. Although CNN initially ran a headline claiming the change would mean the "End of the Internet as We Know It"[73] and many activists predicted the internet would load one word at a time, there was no cataclysmic change. If an anticompetitive action like the 2005 Madison River incident occurs, there would still be a process to adjudicate that harm. In the days, weeks, and months after the rule change went into effect, it became clear that no internet user's experience was altered, and no website or platform's performance was degraded. The hysteria subsided and the political discourse moved on to the next trending topic of the moment.

Yet the presidential election of 2020 ushered in a political sea change, and part of that change was a turnover of the FCC. There is every indication the agency will again restart a proceeding to undo the 2017 order and reinstate some sort of net neutrality regime. As the FCC begins a new back-and-forth over this policy debate, it has created a politically volatile environment ensnaring other layers of the internet stack into the tech political ping-pong match that began over net neutrality. This political dynamic was presciently predicted in a 2009 paper by internet scholars Berin Szoka and Adam Thierer, who argue that "unless we find a way to achieve 'Digital Détente,' the consequences of this increasing regulatory brinkmanship will be 'mutually assured destruction' (MAD) for industry and consumers."[74]

A vital lesson of net neutrality is clear beyond the question of broadband regulation. As these debates go on for years, without long-lasting pragmatic solutions and bipartisan agreement, the regulatory uncertainty can

---

[73] Joe Concha, "CNN Headline Declares the End of the Internet as We Know It," The Hill, December 14, 2017, https://thehill.com/homenews/media/364959 -cnn-headline-declares-end-of-the-internet-as-we-know-it-after-net-neutrality.

[74] Berin Szoka and Adam Thierer, "Net Neutrality, Slippery Slopes & High-Tech Mutually Assured Destruction," The Progress and Freedom Foundation, *Progress Snapshot* 5, no. 11 (October 2009): 1, http://www.pff.org/issues-pubs/ps /2009/pdf/ps5.11-net-neutrality-MAD-policy.pdf.

trap consumers and companies in a regulatory purgatory, while also setting up a political quagmire that will ensnare other industries and interests at the platform, infrastructure, or access levels of the stack.

Conclusion: A Charge for Christians

As these political debates continue, it is imperative for all voters, policy makers, and advocates to step back and see how these different threads fit together into a more holistic understanding of the internet ecosystem. Developing a deeper understanding of how these different facets of the tech policy conversation connect to one another will have a profound effect on how we seek to navigate these issues in the digital public square that affect all our communities.

It can be tempting at times, given the weightiness of the issues before us in the digital public square, to impulsively jump on the cause of the day or latest hashtag, but Christians must do the necessary homework to see how the layers of the internet stack fit together and to understand the contours of these important issues.

Amid a raging public discourse on these difficult and nuanced topics, the Christian understanding of discernment is an essential element of our social engagement. Our approach should reflect the psalmist's request for God to "Teach me good judgment and discernment, for I rely on your commands" (Ps 119:66). By being the people that James 1:19 calls us to be, we can be quick to listen and slow to speak as we learn about these emerging technologies and seek to chart a path of faithful engagement in technology policy. We can speak into these issues at the local, state, and federal levels that are shaping both today's society and tomorrow's. Cultivating the virtue of epistemic humility to realize what we do not know and be willing to admit when we err is vital to a thriving public discourse on these issues. But we also need to muster the confidence to participate in the public conversation as we seek to live out our faith in an increasingly secular public square that often relegates our faith to simply a private matter.[75]

---

[75] For more on the public nature of faith, see chapter 2 by Bryan Baise.

As one daily engaged in these thorny and complex subjects, there is currently a dearth of thoughtful engagement from many different constituencies, including people of faith. Finding new ways to engage in the digital public square and to model our faith will bring an invaluable perspective and serve our communities well. But this type of vision will take all of us, including technologists, policy makers, ethicists, theologians, pastors, business leaders, and even parents, to chart a new path of Christian engagement in the digital public square. We must be able to articulate how our faith informs every aspect of our lives and how these issues connect to the historic beliefs of the church on human dignity, justice, and the good of our communities.

Our rich historical texts that have shaped nations and public discourse for generations can be valuable for today, articulating a uniquely Christian paradigm that can productively shape or instruct the cultural and political conversations of these technological changes. With these deliberations occurring now, Christians should strive to be at the forefront of public dialogue, and not be found sitting on the sidelines waiting for others to steer the discourse.

4

The Global Digital Marketplace

Engaging International Technology Policy from a Christian Perspective

Patricia Shaw

We live in a fallen world. To many, morality seems subjective and relative. While some argue that there is no objective standard for moral absolutes, the world is searching for a consensus on ethical principles that guide our development of technology (particularly AI) in the digital ecosystem. But consensus on what? The rights and wrongs of digitization.

The loss of a shared moral vision has had a profound effect on the outcomes and consequences of the technology we create and use today. We have seen this most dramatically in how both data and information have been framed. Distorted online advertisements (so-called dark ads[1]) have impacted how people and populations have been profiled and manipulated,

---

[1] See Electoral Reform Society, "21st Century Electoral Laws," accessed October 1, 2021, https://www.electoral-reform.org.uk/campaigns/upgrading-our-democracy/21st-century-electoral-laws/.

with their behaviors predicted, creating economies of action,[2] ultimately resulting (this is not an exhaustive list) in interference with digital political campaigning. This among other online harms is what the United Kingdom's Online Safety bill and the European Union's Digital Services Act are seeking to address. In the UK, there has been a call for greater transparency in digital political campaigning and a call for electoral reform.[3] In March 2021, the UK's Information Commissioner's Office issued revised guidance on political campaigning, including campaigning in the online world.[4] These are just a few of the measures that have resulted out of the distorting effects of the digital world around us.

But without a set of fixed moral values to anchor us as a society, we remain unconscious to the potential benefits or harms of our actions or inactions toward ourselves, people groups, populations, and our planet.

Shareholder Capitalism to Stakeholder Capitalism

In 2020, the World Economic Forum created a revised Davos Manifesto titled "The Universal Purpose of a Company in the Fourth Industrial

---

[2] See Shoshana Zuboff, *The Age of Surveillance Capitalism* (London: Profile Books, 2019), 292–98.

[3] See Electoral Commission, "Transparency in digital campaigning: response to Cabinet Office technical consultation on digital imprints," last updated October 14, 2020, accessed October 1, 2021, https://www.electoralcommission.org.uk/who-we-are-and-what-we-do/changing-electoral-law/transparent-digital-campaigning/transparency-digital-campaigning-response-cabinet-office-technical-consultation-digital-imprints.

[4] See UK Information Commissioners Office, "Guide to Data Protection," accessed October 1, 2021, https://ico.org.uk/for-organisations/guide-to-data-protection/key-dp-themes/guidance-for-the-use-of-personal-data-in-political-campaigning-1/ and UK Information Commissioners Office, "Blog: Supporting UK Democracy Through Data Protection with New Political Campaign Guidance," accessed October 1, 2021, https://ico.org.uk/about-the-ico/news-and-events/news-and-blogs/2021/03/supporting-uk-democracy-through-data-protection-with-new-political-campaigning-guidance/.

Revolution."[5] In 1973 it called for management to serve society to "assume the role as trustee of the material universe for future generations."[6] In 2020, it had called for management to invoke stakeholder capitalism: a more holistic understanding of their guardianship role reflecting stakeholder responsibility; respecting human rights (particularly in employment and supply chains); ensuring the safe, ethical use of data; acting as a steward of the environment; and using technology to improve people's well-being.[7] All in all, it called for them to act for the betterment of our shared global future, not just to be an economic unit generating wealth. In short, digital ethics.

While there has been significant growth in the number of AI principles, guidelines, and requirements, calling for greater understanding of the ethical and societal risks associated with AI,[8] very few specifically call out the wider issues of digitization and how it is shaping our societies.

Digital ethics considers the "broader social, economic, and cultural background against which digital innovation is happening" and considers its impacts.[9] In some discourses, digital ethics is further broken down into

---

[5] Klaus Schwab, "Davos Manifesto 2020," World Economic Forum, December 2, 2019, https://www.weforum.org/agenda/2019/12/davos-manifesto-2020-the-universal-purpose-of-a-company-in-the-fourth-industrial-revolution.

[6] Klaus Schwab, "Davos Manifesto 1973: A Code of Ethics for Business Leaders," World Economic Forum, December 2, 2019, https://www.weforum.org/agenda/2019/12/davos-manifesto-1973-a-code-of-ethics-for-business-leaders/.

[7] See Klaus Schwab, "Why We Need the Davos Manifesto for a Better Kind of Capitalism," World Economic Forum, December 1, 2019, https://www.weforum.org/agenda/2019/12/why-we-need-the-davos-manifesto-for-better-kind-of-capitalism/.

[8] For a few examples from corporations, governments, and the church, see Google's AI principles (https://ai.google/principles/), the European Commission's approach to AI (https://digital-strategy.ec.europa.eu/en/policies/european-approach-artificial-intelligence), the United States's National AI strategy (https://www.ai.gov), the Rome Call for AI Ethics (https://www.romecall.org), and the Evangelical Statement of Principles on AI led by the Ethics and Religious Liberty Commission of the Southern Baptist Convention (https://erlc.com/ai).

[9] As defined by Charlotte de Broglie, "We Need to Talk about Digital Ethics," OECD, accessed October 1, 2021, https://www.oecd.org/science/we-need-to-talk-about-digital-ethics.htm.

segments: the ethics of big data, AI, algorithms, and image recognition that encompass aspects of privacy as well as power and the purpose in work (i.e., man versus machine). Overlapping with these concepts are other ethical spheres such as medical ethics, media ethics, information ethics, technical ethics, and social ethics, which includes issues such as justice, human dignity, democracy, and environmental sustainability.[10]

Digital ethics, particularly when conceived in the terms of corporate digital responsibility—a set of practices and behaviors that help an organization use data and digital technologies in ways that are perceived as socially, economically, and environmentally responsible—brings us back to a necessary precondition of it being applied: governmental- and organizational-level change (i.e., from the top down), which in turn is dependent on greater stakeholder engagement, not apathy.[11] Greater, more meaningful and informed civic engagement of the stakeholders from all walks of life (i.e., individuals and groups, citizens, employees, or consumers, impacted by influencing outcomes) need to participate in this newfound stakeholder capitalism to ensure digital ethics also works from the bottom up.

Digital Human Rights

An increasing recognition of how technology is shaping how we understand human rights has resulted in a quest for tools to operationalize digital ethics, and a call for digital human rights.[12] As the United Nations secretary-general António Guterres stated in 2020:

---

[10] See Corporate Digital Responsibility, "Exploring CDR and Digital Ethics," accessed October 1, 2021, https://corporatedigitalresponsibility.co.uk/f/exploring-cdr-and-digital-ethics?blogcategory=Digital+Ethics.

[11] See Corporate Digital Responsibility, accessed October 1, 2021, https://corporatedigitalresponsibility.co.uk/.

[12] See Office of the Secretary-General's Envoy on Technology, United Nations, accessed October 1, 2021, https://www.un.org/techenvoy/content/digital-human-rights; United Nations, "Digital Human Rights Summary," accessed October 1, 2021,

Digital technology is shaping history. But there is also the sense that it is running away with us. Where will it take us? Will our dignity and rights be enhanced or diminished? Will our societies become more equal or less equal? Will we become more, or less, secure and safe? The answers to these questions depend on our ability to work together across disciplines and actors, across nations and political divides. We have a collective responsibility to give direction to these technologies so that we maximize benefits and curtail unintended consequences and malicious use.[13]

Across the global landscape there is in some quarters a call for voluntary self-regulation, while in other quarters more mandatory rules are being pursued. The latter is the case for the European Union (EU). Policy makers who once thought we were part of an AI race and that we had to "move fast and break things" aimed at economic gains from disruptive innovation are now part of an AI regulation race. Whether this is intended to be a race to the top, on who gets to hold the moral high ground first, or it is a rather elaborate and costly power play for control of AI markets, only time will tell. What it is not is a race to the bottom. The mantra of the self-regulatory approach may just well be dead given that the "look how well we have managed AI for ourselves without regulation" has ended in some very public disasters, undermining trust in this technology, let alone the real-life consequences to the people impacted by these systems such as COMPAS,[14]

---

https://www.un.org/techenvoy/sites/www.un.org.techenvoy/files/general/Digital _Human_Rights_Summary_PDF.pdf.

[13] "Report of the Secretary-General: Roadmap for Digital Cooperation," United Nations, June 2020, https://www.un.org/en/content/digital-cooperation -roadmap/assets/pdf/Roadmap_for_Digital_Cooperation_EN.pdf.

[14] See Jeff Larson, Surya Mattu, Lauren Kirchner, and Julia Angwin, "How We Analyzed the COMPAS Recidivism Algorithm," May 23, 2016, https://www .propublica.org/article/how-we-analyzed-the-compas-recidivism-algorithm.

Cambridge Analytica,[15] Amazon HR AI,[16] Dutch SyRi,[17] and Deliveroo worker rating system.[18]

With human rights impacts by AI and digital technologies being increasingly seen, the human rights framework is being interpreted as a quasi-moral code that has gained consensus across the globe. The Universal Declaration of Human Rights was established following the Second World War and sought to invoke four basic freedoms: the freedom of speech, the freedom of religion, the freedom from fear, and the freedom from want.[19] Although areligious, some commentators suggest that it reflects a Western or a secular understanding of the Judeo-Christian tradition.[20] As French philosopher Jacques Maritain wrote in his text *On the Philosophy of Human Rights*, which he sent from Rome in June 1947, "No declaration of human rights will ever be exhaustive and final. It will ever go

---

[15] See Issie Lapowsky, "How Cambridge Analytica Sparked the Great Privacy Awakening," *Wired*, March 17, 2019, https://www.wired.com/story/cambridge -analytica-facebook-privacy-awakening/.

[16] See Jeffrey Dastin, "Amazon scraps secret AI recruiting tool that showed bias against women," Reuters, October 10, 2018, https://www.reuters.com/article /us-amazon-com-jobs-automation-insight-idUSKCN1MK08G.

[17] See News & Analysis, "The SyRI case: a landmark ruling for benefits claimants around the world," Privacy International, February 24, 2020, https:// privacyinternational.org/news-analysis/3363/syri-case-landmark-ruling-benefits -claimants-around-world.

[18] See Jonathan Keane, "Deliveroo Rating Algorithm Was Unfair to Riders, Italian Court Rules," *Forbes*, January 5, 2021, https://www.forbes.com/sites /jonathankeane/2021/01/05/italian-court-finds-deliveroo-rating-algorithm-was -unfair-to-riders/.

[19] See United Nations General Assembly, "Universal Declaration of Human Rights" (General Assembly resolution 217 A), proclaimed in Paris on December 10, 1948, https://www.un.org/en/about-us/universal-declaration-of-human-rights; Dania Akkad, "Human Rights: The Universal Declaration vs the Cairo Declaration," *LSE Middle East Centre Blog*, December 10, 2012, https://blogs.lse.ac.uk/mec /2012/12/10/1569/.

[20] See David Littman, "Universal Human Rights and Human Rights in Islam," *Midstream*, February/March 1999, https://www.dhimmitude.org/archive/universal _islam.html.

hand-in-hand with the state of moral consciousness and civilization at a given moment in history."[21]

What is now being recognized in the UN Roadmap for Digital Cooperation—which addresses how the international community can better harness opportunities and address challenges brought about by digital technologies—is that human rights exist in the world both offline *and* online.[22] On the one hand, digital technologies and the online world can be used to connect and unite people in collective action. They can provide greater accessibility to information, and greater transparency to wrongdoing, and can be used to advocate, exercise, and defend rights. On the other hand, digital technologies and the online world can be used to distract, disconnect, and divide people. Unlawful images, identity artifacts, and other surreptitious information are bought and sold on the dark web.[23] People's activities are tracked (if not also their geolocation, app permissions permitting). Digital technologies are being permitted (through anonymization, conscious consent or wide interpretations of legitimate interest) to make inferences about individuals and households based on their online behaviors and metadata activity. People can be distilled to data variables, features, and characteristics in one big data primordial soup, categorized in preparation to be commoditized. The information harvested about people can be further optimized to predict future behaviors and used against individuals and people groups to manufacture economies of action and in some cases behavioral modification.[24]

---

[21] Jacques Maritain, "On the Philosophy of Human Rights," in UNESCO, ed., *Human Rights: Comments and Interpretations: A Symposium* (London: Allan Wingate,1949), 74.

[22] See "Report of the Secretary-General Roadmap for Digital Cooperation," June 2020, pages 14, 26, and 30, https://www.un.org/en/content/digital-cooperation-roadmap/assets/pdf/Roadmap_for_Digital_Cooperation_EN.pdf.

[23] The dark web refers to a part of the internet that is not searchable or accessible to everyday users, requiring special software or authorization to access.

[24] See Zuboff, *The Age of Surveillance Capitalism*. Economies of action refers to the use of real-time information to analyze behaviors and the use of machine intervention in the state of play in the real online world to modify behaviors in real time.

The non-legally binding Universal Declaration of Human Rights was signed and ratified by over 150 countries in the pre-digital era and has influenced or been adopted into most national constitutions or laws. Is now the time for an evaluation of human rights in the digital age?[25]

The New Normal

No conversation, or chapter on digital policy would be complete without mentioning the effects of the global COVID-19 pandemic on digitization and ethics of technology. In short, digitization accelerated it, and at great speed. Overnight, businesses went from largely office- and paper-based operations with face-to-face meetings, to remote-based work environments. This sudden change brought a new and greater requirement for cloud-based digital storage with secure access and control mechanisms, greater use of digital identification, and multifactor authentication. New concerns about data protection and confidentiality arose due to device sharing in families, processes were digitized, digital signatures were deployed for signing contracts, and a plethora of video call platforms (such as Zoom and Microsoft Teams) and communications channels emerged to cut across the geographical divide. The pandemic also heightened concerns about the effects of these technologies on the environment given their enormous energy usage.

This rapid digital transformation in a time of crisis meant that society had little time to process the practical, ethical, and legal benefits and risks associated with such digitization. Much has been spoken of the economic detriment of the pandemic, often compared to times of war. Transitioning into this technological revolution was something being "done to" people and populations as it was deemed essential for the ongoing operations of governments, health-care providers, and businesses across the world in solidarity combatting the COVID-19 virus.

---

[25] See Eileen Donahoe, "Human Rights in the Digital Age," *Just Security*, December 23, 2014, https://www.justsecurity.org/18651/human-rights-digital-age/.

New ways of working and new digital businesses arose in this period. Digital platforms are now the key to new value chains as a new global marketplace for digital goods and services unfolds,[26] provided you have access to the digital. Words like "digital exclusion" became more well-known, and many nations around the world struggled to find the right balance between protecting people's right to health against the encroachment on freedoms of movement, assembly, expression, privacy, and nondiscrimination caused by self-imposed and/or government-stipulated coronavirus confinement. Suddenly, not only did the impact of the pandemic itself become very real, but it brought to the fore the power that digital platforms (and their impact on competition and traditional marketplaces and shops) and digital technologies (such as covid tracker and tracer tools) could wield.[27] The asymmetry of power wielded by seemingly omnipresent and unobtrusive technologies (if left unchallenged and unchecked without appropriate accountability, governance, transparency, or oversight) may alter how we see ourselves and our neighbors as image bearers of God.[28] Being able to invoke governance over the digital in such a way that it engages with citizens in a meaningful way requires a new kind of participation with citizens: *digital citizenship*. Digital citizens are those with digital skills, awareness, and understanding. This is a theme that we will see become more entrenched as we enter the digital decade leading up to 2030.

Representation Matters

Proactive leadership, participatory engagement, and participatory governance will be necessary in the digital sphere to ensure that Christian

---

[26] See Klaus Henning, "Artificial Intelligence Is a Gamechanger of the Way of Living and Working," in *The 4th Industrial Revolution from an Ethical Perspective*, ed. Timo Plutschinski (Amersfoort, Utrecht: NL, 2022), 30, 35.

[27] See "Technology Governance in a Time of Crisis," Human Technology Foundation, June 2020, https://www.itechlaw.org/sites/default/files/Final%20Report_ENGLISH.pdf.

[28] See Jeremy Peckham, "The Ethical Implications of 4IR," in Plutschinski, *The 4th Industrial Revolution from an Ethical Perspective*, 26.

perspectives are brought to bear among the voices of the heard and the previously unheard. Representations from the faith community concerning the impact and harm to personhood and society, inappropriate bias, and at worst discrimination and exclusion of segments of society, will be essential.

Christians standing up and providing direction—being able to add their unique perspective on what it means to be a human made in the image of God—will help abate the unintended and negative impacts on society in this generation and into the next. This is not just calling out religious rights and freedoms but contextualizing what it means to be truly human in a hybrid (online and offline) world.[29]

Hybrid Life

The Onlife Initiative, a one-year project funded by the European Commission to study the deployment of ICTs and its effects on the human condition, highlighted (1) the blurring lines between reality and virtuality; (2) the blurring of distinctions between human, machine, and nature; (3) the reversal from information scarcity to information abundance; and (4) the shift of primacy of standalone things, properties, and binary relations, to the primacy of interactions, processes, and networks. It is amid this complexity that we see both positive and negative changes.[30]

Subtle and sometimes not so recognizably, the digital world incrementally impacts us all. It has implications on our "data" selves (the digital twin of our information held in the digital domain). There are implications for the custodianship and control of all data about or concerning us, representing us, our actual or inferred views and behaviors. This also includes questions about our privacy in the home, in the workplace, and/or in public, our movements and locations. These implications extend to our thought-life as

---

[29] For more on how technology has segmented our lives, see chapters 12 and 13 on the church's witness and the nature of discipleship in the digital age.

[30] See Luciano Floridi, *The Onlife Manifesto: Being Human in a Hyperconnected Era*, Springer Open Access (2015), https://link.springer.com/book/10.1007%2F978 -3-319-04093-6.

well—intruded upon with images, information, and content (moderated or not on our behalf) available 24/7/365 that can steal our attention, our joy, our peace, our patience, and perhaps even our love and ability for self-control. How people interact with others, institutions, and technology will likely change.

Technology may not impact us equitably, as some are being more impacted due to belonging to a minority group, a protected class, or a particular geolocation and/or political situation.[31] We are all, however, humans; and whether we interact with the digital world or actively choose not to participate in it, technology will ultimately impact us all. Therefore, engaging with the digital requires a greater level of intentionality to safeguard human well-being, human autonomy, human agency, and we must be mindful of our moral responsibility and moral accountability to God and to one another.

Our Shared Digital Future

Many current digital policy initiatives look a decade ahead to 2030. The UK's Digital Catapult produced the Digital Future Index 2021–2022 (DFI).[32] The Digital Catapult DFI measured averaged country performance across the fields of AI, immersive technologies, blockchain, internet of things, and infrastructure based on six pillars: (1) talent, (2) innovation and commercial ventures, (3) infrastructure, (4) research, (5) operating environment, and (6) development. According to the DFI, the United States, China, and the United Kingdom ranked first, second, and third in the world. Other global leaders ranked next in the following order: South Korea, Japan, Israel, Canada, Germany, Australia, and Singapore.

The Digital Catapult DFI also identified the top three emerging technology trends that will transform business next:

---

[31] This can include access to digital services, increased technology use due to family situations, and more.

[32] See "Digital Future Index 2021-2022," Digital Catapult, September 20, 2021, https://www.digicatapult.org.uk/news-and-insights/publication/digital-future-index-2021-2022.

- **Digital twins** (i.e., the digital representation in virtual models and performance data of a physical object) to reduce the impact of supply chain shocks
- **The rise of the metaverse**, including spatial computing (i.e., the use of space around you to act as a three-dimensional user interface) and augmented reality cloud (i.e., user-centered contextual digital content overlaid over a physical object delivered through headsets, phones, glasses, etc.)
- **Remote and autonomous machines** with better accuracy, reliability, and security

You may be thinking right now that the future looks quite bright, or you may be fearing a future dystopia. Either way, what is clear is that digital transformation is happening right before our eyes, and at pace. Governments, businesses, and civil society are responding with proclamations, promises, policies, and plans to help us navigate these unchartered waters.

Digital Policy from around the World

Digital policy is contingent on four things: AI (or other emerging technologies that use and/or process data), data, infrastructure, and connectivity. It is these core cross-cutting themes we will see repeatedly in international policy. While many countries across the globe are developing digital policies, for the purposes of this chapter, I have focused on three economic areas: Australia, the European Union, and the UK, to demonstrate the convergence and dissension seen among global policy making right now.

Australia

Digital Policy

In December 2019, the Australian Human Rights Commission set its own technology policy agenda with proposals for "safeguarding human rights and encouraging accessible, equal and accountable use of new technology in Australia."[33] The aim was to create technology within the human rights framework. Australia was nailing its colors to the mast by ensuring emerging digital technologies were human centered, promoted fairness, and were accessible by all.

The Australian government's Digital Economy Strategy states it wants Australia to have a leading digital economy and society by 2030.[34] Key features of that plan are digital skills, AI, enhancing government service delivery, investment incentives, Small and Medium Sized Enterprise (SME) digitization, emerging aviation technology, data, and cybersecurity, safety, and trust.

AI

Australia's AI Action Plan, published on June 18, 2021, is a key feature of the Australian government's Digital Economy Strategy.[35] The AI Action plan identified four areas of focus:

- adoption of AI to create jobs and boost productivity
- growing and attracting AI talent and expertise
- using AI to solve national challenges and benefit all Australians
- ensuring AI technologies are responsible, inclusive, and reflect Australian values

Data

Australia is set to deliver its first National Data Strategy over the period 2021 to 2025,[36] but it is expected to cover use, custodianship, and sharing and

---

[33] Australian Human Rights Commission, "Human Rights and Technology Discussion Paper," December 2019, https://tech.humanrights.gov.au/sites/default/files/inline-files/TechRights2019_DiscussionPaper_Summary.pdf.

[34] See Australian Government, Digital Economy Strategy, accessed October 1, 2021, https://digitaleconomy.pmc.gov.au/.

[35] See Australian Government, "An Action Plan for Artificial Intelligence," June 18, 2021, https://www.industry.gov.au/news/an-action-plan-for-artificial-intelligence-in-australia.

[36] See Australian Government, Data and Digital Economy Factsheet, accessed October 1, 2021, https://digitaleconomy.pmc.gov.au/fact-sheets/data-and-digital-economy.

security of public and private data sets to improve outcomes for Australians. The Australia government plans to increase consumer awareness and empower consumers to use and control their data for personal benefit. The government hopes to increase place-based decision making for Australian businesses; plans to build data competence, capability, and maturity within the Australian Public Service; and intends to create government data stores so that the data can be used for community benefit.

Infrastructure and Connectivity

Australia has already completed a program of ubiquitous access to high-speed wholesale broadband for retail service providers with the plan that this should be rolled out to households and businesses across the country. Furthermore, the government has pledged a Universal Service Guarantee (USG) that all premises in Australia should have access to baseline broadband services. While trials of 5G for business appear to have commenced through the Australian 5G Innovation Initiative, it is the regional connectivity program that will create investment in 5G for so-called place-based telecommunications infrastructure across rural and remote Australian communities, particularly to indigenous communities. By 2030, all Australians are to have access to and be able to use effectively high-speed internet services.

European Union

Policies are being developed across the world but none more comprehensive than that of the European Union (EU). It all started in 2015 when the European Commission launched its initiative to create a Digital Single Market across the EU with its six building blocks related to digital service used by European consumers and citizens.

Figure 1: EU Digital Single Market Building Block

Building block One:	**E-commerce and online platforms** aimed at improving cross border trade and harmonizing rules on online services. Chiefly recognizing cross-border portability of digital content and prohibiting unjustified geo blocking.
Building block Two:	**E-government services** aimed at encouraging best government practice across Europe, increasing cooperation and interoperability between member state national public services.
Building block Three:	**Data and AI** aimed at easing movement of data across Europe while also harmonizing data governance practices. This has resulted in the GDPR and the yet-to-be-finalized Privacy Directive.
Building block Four:	**Security** aimed at strengthening EU cybersecurity, which resulted in the implementation of the directive on network information security, the EU Security Union,[37] and EU Cyber Security Strategy.[38]
Building block Five:	**Consumer protection in the digital era** aimed at strengthening consumer protection and enforcement concerning digital services.
Building block Six:	**Electronic communications networks and services** aimed at harmonizing services provided via electronic communications networks such as ISPs and telephony.

[37] See European Commission, Digital Priorities 2019-2024, https://ec.europa.eu/info/strategy/priorities-2019-2024/promoting-our-european-way-life/european-security-union_en.

[38] See European Commission, Press Release: "New EU Cybersecurity Strategy and new rules to make physical and digital critical entities more resilient," December 16, 2020, https://ec.europa.eu/commission/presscorner/detail/en/ip_20_2391.

Human-Centric AI Built on Trust

Against this backdrop, we saw the appointment of the EU High Level Expert Group on AI (AIHLEG) by the European Commission in June 2018 as part of "Shaping Europe's Digital Future." Here we start to see the bigger digital policy challenge for the EU unfold. Although the AIHLEG was established to support the implementation of the European strategy on AI, AI does indeed form a key component in how we see, experience, and access the digital world. It was through the work of the AIHLEG that the EU recognized the need to evaluate the ethical, legal, and societal implications, as well as the socioeconomic challenges of AI.

During its mandate the AIHLEG delivered: (1) a definition of AI,[39] (2) ethics guidelines for trustworthy AI,[40] (3) policy and investment recommendations for trustworthy AI,[41] (4) an assessment list for trustworthy AI (ALTAI),[42] and (5) sectoral considerations on the policy and investment recommendations.[43]

Most fundamentally it distilled seven ethical guidelines that are requirements for AI to be deemed "trustworthy":

---

[39] See Independent High Level Expert Group on Artificial Intelligence, "A Definition of AI: Main Capabilities and Disciplines," December 2019, https://www.aepd.es/sites/default/files/2019-12/ai-definition.pdf.

[40] See European Commission, "Ethics Guidelines for Trustworthy AI," accessed October 1, 2021, https://wayback.archive-it.org/12090/20210728013426/https://digital-strategy.ec.europa.eu/en/library/ethics-guidelines-trustworthy-ai.

[41] See European Commission, "Policy and Investment Recommendations for Trustworthy Artificial Intelligence," accessed October 1, 2021, https://wayback.archive-it.org/12090/20210728103937/https://digital-strategy.ec.europa.eu/en/library/policy-and-investment-recommendations-trustworthy-artificial-intelligence.

[42] See European Commission, "Assessment List for Trustworthy Artificial Intelligence (ALTAI) for Self-Assessment," accessed April 19, 2021 https://digital-strategy.ec.europa.eu/en/library/assessment-list-trustworthy-artificial-intelligence-altai-self-assessment.

[43] See Jola Dervishaj, "AI HLEG—Sectoral Considerations on Policy and Investment Recommendations for Trustworthy AI," European Commission, July 23, 2020, https://futurium.ec.europa.eu/en/european-ai-alliance/document/ai-hleg-sectoral-considerations-policy-and-investment-recommendations-trustworthy-ai.

1. human agency and oversight
2. technical robustness and safety
3. privacy and data governance
4. transparency
5. diversity, non-discrimination, and fairness
6. environmental and societal well-being
7. accountability

Before the COVID-19 pandemic, the EU had begun an initial coordination plan on AI in 2018,[44] a white paper on AI published in February 2020,[45] and a Commission Report on safety and liability implications of AI, the Internet of Things, and robotics, also in February 2020.[46] After a short disruption due to the pandemic, the EU's journey of a European approach to AI really got underway.

The publications of both the European Commission's Communication and their Coordinated Plan for AI 2021 Review occurred in April 2021.[47] The results of prior EU consultation produced a proposal for a Regulation on Machinery Products and a proposal for a Regulation on AI (hereafter the

---

[44] See European Commission, "Coordinated Plan on Artificial Intelligence," December 7, 2018, https://knowledge4policy.ec.europa.eu/publication/coordinated -plan-artificial-intelligence-com2018-795-final_en.

[45] See European Commission, "White Paper: On Artificial Intelligence—A European Approach to Excellence and Trust," February 19, 2020, https://ec.europa .eu/info/sites/default/files/commission-white-paper-artificial-intelligence-feb2020 _en.pdf.

[46] See European Commission, "Report on Safety and Liability Implications of Artificial Intelligence, the Internet of Things and Robotics," February 19, 2020, https://eur-lex.europa.eu/legal-content/EN/TXT/HTML/?uri=CELEX:52020 DC0064&from=en.

[47] See European Commission, "Communication on Fostering a European Approach to Artificial Intelligence," April 21, 2001, https://digital-strategy.ec .europa.eu/en/library/communication-fostering-european-approach-artificial -intelligence; European Commission, "Coordinated Plan on Artificial Intelligence 2021 Review," April 21, 2021, https://digital-strategy.ec.europa.eu/en/library /coordinated-plan-artificial-intelligence-2021-review.

EU AI Act) to bring AI in line with the seven key ethical requirements, with the attempt at harmonizing regulatory approaches across Europe.[48]

While the move to regulate AI in a manner befitting of the populations it is meant to serve is welcome, at the time of writing concerns have been raised as to the cost of compliance and the disproportionate burden this might play for start-ups and SMEs in contrast to more established AI players.

Although the European Data Protection Board and European Data Protection Supervisor welcome AI-specific regulation, in a joint statement in June 2021, they raised concerns about the lack of an international dimension to the EU AI Act proposal. They fear it could create a risk of circumvention due to reliance on high-risk applications operated by "third countries" (any country outside the EU) or international organizations.[49]

A Digital Ecosystem for a Digital Decade

AI is just one part of the digital ecosystem that the EU is seeking to create in the next digital decade. Growth in the use of digital technologies led the European Commission to publish its vision for Europe's digital transformation on March 9, 2021. This plan seeks to put in place four key tenets to practice in the decade leading up to 2030: (1) skills, (2) secure and sustainable digital infrastructures, (3) digital transformation of businesses, and (4) digitization of public services. This is intended to shape: (1) digital society, (2) advanced digital technologies, (3) international cooperation in digital, and (4) the digital economy.

---

[48] See European Commission, "Proposal for a Regulation of the European Parliament and of the Council on machinery products," April 21, 2021, https://ec.europa.eu/docsroom/documents/45508; "Proposal for a Regulation of the European Parliament and of the Council Laying Down Harmonised Rules on Artificial Intelligence," accessed October 1, 2021, https://eur-lex.europa.eu/legal-content/EN/TXT/?qid=1623335154975&uri=CELEX%3A52021PC0206.

[49] See "EDPB-EDPS Joint Opinion 5/2021 on the Proposal for a Regulation of the European Parliament and of the Council Laying Down Harmonised Rules on Artificial Intelligence (Artificial Intelligence Act)," June 18, 2021, https://edpb.europa.eu/system/files/2021-06/edpb-edps_joint_opinion_ai_regulation_en.pdf.

- **Digital Society:** bringing into focus cybersecurity, digital inclusion, digital public services and environments, green digital sector, language technologies, media and digital culture, next-generation internet, and online privacy and safety
- **Advanced Digital Technologies:** bringing into focus advanced computing, advanced digital technologies, AI, Data and cloud computing, and Internet of Things (IoT)
- **International Cooperation:** international relations to protect European values
- **Digital Economy:** understanding the need for increasing digital skills among consumers, citizens, and workforce; supporting industry by creating digital innovation hubs; supporting connectivity as the EU wants to become the most connected continent by 2030; and increasing the prominence of the role online platforms and e-commerce businesses have to play to create a truly online marketplace that is accessible, safe, and without unjustified barriers

Figure 2: EU Digital Facts

- Over 1 million EU businesses sell goods or digital services via online platforms.[50]
- Ninety percent of professional roles require a basic level of digital knowledge; 42 percent of Europeans lack basic digital skills, including 37 percent of those in the workforce.[51]
- Digital technologies account for 8–10 percent of our energy consumption and 2–4 percent of our greenhouse gas emissions.[52]

---

[50] See European Commission, "Online Platforms and E-Commerce," accessed October 1, 2021, https://digital-strategy.ec.europa.eu/en/policies/online-platforms-and-e-commerce.

[51] See European Commission, "Digital Skills," accessed October 1, 2021, https://digital-strategy.ec.europa.eu/en/policies/digital-skills.

[52] See European Commission, "Green Digital Sector," accessed October 1, 2021, https://digital-strategy.ec.europa.eu/en/policies/green-digital.

- If 40 percent of the workforce works digitally from home for two days a week, we can reduce CO_2 emissions by 5.2 million tons.[53]
- The EU has co-funded the LUMI supercomputer in Finland, which is capable (at its peak) of a combined power the equivalent of 1.5 million laptops (550 petaflops). If those laptops were stacked on top of each other, a tower twenty-three kilometers high would be formed.[54]
- A new Cybersecurity Competence Centre will be located in Bucharest, Romania.[55]

To affirm European values in the digital world and to make Europe "fit for the Digital Age," the Commission in December 2020 responded with both the EU Digital Services Act and the EU Digital Markets Act. The aim of the Digital Services Act is to create a safe and accountable online environment, whereas the Digital Markets Act is to ensure fair and open digital markets.

These two new proposed laws came shortly after a very public conversation between Thierry Breton (European commissioner for the Internal Market) and Mark Zuckerberg (CEO of Meta/Facebook) in May 2020 about the roles and responsibilities of online platforms.[56] Most notably, Mr. Breton criticized attempts at self-regulation and made it clear to Mr. Zuckerberg that Facebook was to adapt to Europe's standards (and not the

---

[53] See European Commission, "Green Digital Sector."

[54] See European Commission, "Advanced Computing," accessed October 1, 2021, https://digital-strategy.ec.europa.eu/en/policies/advanced-computing.

[55] See European Commission, "The European Cybersecurity Competence Centre and Network is now ready to take off," June 28, 2021, https://digital -strategy.ec.europa.eu/en/news/european-cybersecurity-competence-centre-and -network-now-ready-take.

[56] See "Debate: Mark Zuckerberg and Thierry Breton," May 18, 2020, broadcast and hosted by CERRE, The Centre on Regulation in Europe, https://cerre.eu /news/debate-mark-zuckerberg-thierry-breton/.

other way round), and by suggesting that if things did not change, the EU would have no choice but to regulate online platforms.

Data, Data, and More Data

Digital policy cannot be considered in isolation. It goes hand in glove with data, hence the notable importance of the EU's data strategy,[57] which came into being on February 19, 2020.[58]

Key elements of the EU's data strategy include the following:

- **A single market for data:** free flow of data across sectors, with respect of data protection legislation.
- **Overcoming barriers to data sharing**, by implementing technical infrastructure, legal rules, and ethical guidelines.
- **Promotion of the sector-specific data spaces**, including health data, financial data, and personal data spaces. Most pertinent is the facilitation of access to and reuse of sensitive data such as health or social welfare data for scientific research purposes and allowing people to make their data available for the "common good" so researchers can innovate for the benefit of society.
- **Ensuring EU autonomy** in supplying European cloud services.
- **Empowering people** to have a greater say over who can access the data they generate, including data generated from IoT devices.

This data policy has led to a plethora of proposed new laws surrounding data, data governance, and data sharing or flows. These include the EU Data Governance Act (DGA),[59] a proposed new Data Act (yet to be seen),

---

[57] See European Commission, "A European Strategy for Data," accessed October 1, 2021, https://digital-strategy.ec.europa.eu/en/policies/strategy-data.

[58] See European Commission, "Communication from the commission to the European Parliament, the Council, the European Economic and Social Committee and the Committee of the regions," February 19, 2020, https://eur-lex.europa.eu/legal-content/EN/TXT/HTML/?uri=CELEX:52020DC0066&from=EN.

[59] See European Commission, "Regulation of the European Parliament and of The Council on European data governance (Data Governance Act),"

the Open Data Directive,[60] and regulation on the free flow of non-personal data in EU.[61] All these legislative measures are aimed to create a single market for data to complement the digital policy.

Infrastructure: In the Cloud and on the Edge

Scalable infrastructure is going to be vital to any digital policy to be able to process the large volumes of data that European citizens, consumers, and businesses are likely to generate.

The term *cloud computing* may bring to mind masses of server racks contained within high-security, controlled-access data center compounds that are bomb-proof, fire-proof, flood-proof, and with back-up generators and off-site disaster recovery duplicate servers and facilities to boot. However, it is envisaged that by as early as 2025 the current trends of centralized data processing within data centers will be reversed, with 80 percent likely to be processed on localized, decentralized, smart devices.[62] This is known as edge computing.

But amidst this change in technological infrastructure, there is also a desire by the EU to increase its data sovereignty (i.e., keeping European data within Europe). This has led to the call for more European data spaces, and a European marketplace for cloud services, perhaps even acting as a single portal to European cloud services that are compliant with European standards and best practices on cloud use in storage. In October 2020 this led to twenty-five member states signing a joint declaration to create a "European Cloud."[63]

November 25, 2020, https://eur-lex.europa.eu/legal-content/EN/TXT/PDF/?uri =CELEX:52020PC0767&from=EN.

[60] See "Directive (EU) 2019/1024 of the European Parliament and of the Council," June 20, 2019, https://eur-lex.europa.eu/legal-content/EN/TXT/HTML /?uri=CELEX:32019L1024&from=EN.

[61] See "Regulation (EU) 2018/1807 of the European Parliament and of the Council," November 14, 2018, https://eur-lex.europa.eu/legal-content/EN/TXT /HTML/?uri=CELEX:32018R1807&from=EN.

[62] See European Commission, "SCloud Computing," accessed October 1, 2021, https://digital-strategy.ec.europa.eu/en/policies/cloud-computing.

[63] European Commission, "Commission Welcomes Member States' Declaration on EU Cloud Federation," October 15, 2020, https://digital-strategy.ec.europa.eu /en/news/commission-welcomes-member-states-declaration-eu-cloud-federation.

Connectivity

Of course, having state-of-the-art next-generation internet infrastructure is useless if one cannot connect to it. To that end, the EU wants every European household to have access to high-speed internet coverage by 2025 and gigabyte connectivity by 2030.[64] The EU has sought to address barriers to connectivity, such as bandwidth and payload to carry the larger data demands, through additional support to wireless 5G networks, and through eliminating charges by electronic communication networks associated with roaming and data use.

The introduction of the European Electronic Communications Code (EECC),[65] in an attempt to modernize the telecommunications framework, is intended to enhance consumer choice and incentivize operators to invest in higher speed networks. Member states had until December 21, 2020, to transpose the EECC into national legislation. However, as of September 2021, eighteen of the EU's member states had still not fully transposed the code into their national law.

United Kingdom

The Union of the United Kingdom

The United Kingdom is made up of England, Scotland, Wales, and Northern Ireland. Each has its own delegated authority and devolved administration. While the UK often produces policy as a singular unit, the separation from Europe (known as "Brexit") has seemingly put a strain on internal relations. Devolved administrations have the power to set policy agendas for themselves. Digital policy seems to be one area where other parts of the UK have sought to create their own paths, in some cases ahead of England's published wider UK strategy.

---

[64] See European Commission, "Connectivity," accessed October 1, 2021, https://digital-strategy.ec.europa.eu/en/policies/connectivity.

[65] See European Electronic Communications Code, accessed October 1, 2021, https://eur-lex.europa.eu/legal-content/EN/TXT/PDF/?uri=CELEX:32018L1972.

For example, Scotland launched its "Digital Strategy for Scotland" on March 11, 2021, with three key themes: people and place, a strong digital economy, and digital government and services that embrace the opportunities of data.[66] The themes of connectivity, digital inclusion, and digital skills seem consistent with other union policies.

The "Digital Strategy for Wales" was set on March 23, 2021, and stated how it intended to use digital, data, and technology to improve the lives of people in Wales.[67] Like others, the policy appears to be centered around digital skills, improving public services, connectivity, data, collaboration, and digital inclusion "where everyone would be equipped with skills and confidence to engage in a digital world."

The Digital Agenda in a Post-Brexit World

Since the UK has exited the EU, the sentiment is that it has the opportunity now to set its "own global path for digital regulation,"[68] which the UK set out in July 2021. The UK is on a pro-innovation and pro-growth journey.

The UK has tried to set itself apart as one of the safest and securest places to do business in the world, hence we have seen the introduction of proposed legislation combatting "online harms" now referred to as the draft Online Safety Bill.[69] Furthermore, the UK has also introduced the Age-Appropriate Design Code (AADC) to protect children while they interact

---

[66] See Scottish Government, "Launch of New Digital Strategy for Scotland," March 11, 2021, https://blogs.gov.scot/digital/2021/03/11/launch-of-new-digital-strategy-for-scotland/.

[67] See Welsh Government, "Digital Strategy for Wales," March 23, 2021, https://gov.wales/digital-strategy-wales-html.

[68] UK Government, "Digital Regulation: Driving growth and unlocking innovation," July 6, 2021, https://www.gov.uk/government/publications/digital-regulation-driving-growth-and-unlocking-innovation/digital-regulation-driving-growth-and-unlocking-innovation#our-digital-regulation-principles.

[69] See UK Government, "Draft Online Safety Bill," May 12, 2021, https://www.gov.uk/government/publications/draft-online-safety-bill.

with their connected devices and the online world.[70] Both the draft Online Safety Bill and AADC have one thing in common: the focus on protection from harm.

The three key objectives of the recent UK Digital Policy paper have been to:

1. drive growth, promote competition and innovation;
2. ensure digital growth and innovation does not harm citizens or businesses; and
3. shape the digital economy such that it protects fundamental rights and freedoms and promotes a flourishing and democratic society.

However, throughout the globe we have already acknowledged that the COVID-19 pandemic has acted as an enzyme for all things digital. This can also be seen in the UK's DCMS top 10 tech priorities to build back better, safer, and stronger post-pandemic. These priorities include sharing data, AI, infrastructure, connectivity themes chiefly among the need for digital education, upskilling and re-skilling, awareness raising, economic growth, sustainability, having a competitive edge, and showing leadership.[71]

The United Kingdom is calling for proportionate regulation and potentially deregulation. It intends to use its range of regulatory tools and is not ruling out self-regulation or non-regulatory tools, such as industry-led technical standards that can be amended in a more agile technologically responsive way and have the benefit of global expertise and best practice.

Features of regulation to drive growth call for personal data empowerment through greater data portability; governance and oversight and accountability; transparency concerning the use of advanced data analytics

---

[70] See UK Information Commissioners Office, "Introduction to the Age Appropriate Design Code," accessed October 1, 2021, https://ico.org.uk/for-organisations/guide-to-data-protection/ico-codes-of-practice/age-appropriate-design-code/.

[71] See UK Department for Digital Culture Media and Sport, "Our 10 Tech Priorities," accessed October 1, 2021, https://dcms.shorthandstories.com/Our-Ten-Tech-Priorities/index.html.

and algorithms; and conversely recognizing how fragile and open to disruption digital services are, how data and digital services are global in nature, and the critical role of digital infrastructure and networks.[72]

The UK's "regulatory" approach to digital seems to be in three pillars:

1. **Pro-competition** establishing a new Digital Markets Unit that sits within the Competition and Markets Authority.[73] This unit is intended to respond to competition concerns of online platforms and digital advertising (so called AdTech).

2. **Reevaluating the existing data protection regime**, involving better facilitation of data sharing for data-driven technologies such as AI and automated decision making, removing barriers, opening up greater opportunities for data portability, and creating public, economic, and social benefit for all. Again, trustworthiness and consumer confidence appear to be key.

3. **A duty of care on online companies to keep their users safe**, while defending freedom of expression. Aimed at social media, websites, and apps that host user-generated content, these services will now become arbiters of content, tasked with obligations that will require them to remove and limit the spread of illegal content, disinformation, and misinformation.

Data

Data is fundamental to any digital strategy. England published its National Data Strategy on September 9, 2020, which was subject to a period of public consultation. It published its response on May 18, 2021, with a clear way

---

[72] See UK Government, "Digital Regulation Driving Growth and Unlocking Innovation," July 6, 2021, https://www.gov.uk/government/publications/digital-regulation-driving-growth-and-unlocking-innovation/digital-regulation-driving-growth-and-unlocking-innovation#fn:25.

[73] See UK Government, "Digital Markets Unit," accessed October 1, 2021, https://www.gov.uk/government/collections/digital-markets-unit.

forward for a National Data Strategy Framework.[74] On September 19, 2021, the UK government published a public consultation proposing reforms to the UK's data protection laws. The paper, "Data: A New Direction,"[75] suggests a deviation from what has become the global gold standard for the protection of personal data: General Data Protection Regulation (GDPR). This all to create a pro-growth, pro-innovation data protection regime.

AI

The UK's Department for Digital, Culture, Media and Sport (DCMS) published the National AI Strategy on September 22, 2021; whereas Scotland's AI Strategy Steering Committee in conjunction with the Scottish AI Alliance had published Scotland's AI Strategy six months earlier in March 2021. Scotland calls for trustworthy, ethical, and inclusive AI, placing people at its heart.[76] England's National AI Strategy has a ten-year plan calling for investment in an AI ecosystem to create an AI superpower; support for the transition to an AI-enabled economy benefiting all sectors and regions, and about getting governance right to protect the public and fundamental values.

Among the promises of better data, better cyber-physical security, innovation, compute capacity, better international engagement (in particular US-UK cooperation in AI research and development), there are potential plans for utilizing AI-driven technologies in health and social care through the NHS AI Lab, a Ministry of Defence AI Strategy, and consulting on intellectual property right ownership for AI (i.e., should AI ever be an inventor).

AI governance and AI regulation create certainty for business, while more investment in education and user awareness raises up the next generation of

---

[74] See UK Government, "Government Response to the consultation on the National Data Strategy," May 18, 2021, https://www.gov.uk/government /consultations/uk-national-data-strategy-nds-consultation/outcome/government -response-to-the-consultation-on-the-national-data-strategy#executive-summary.

[75] UK Government, "Data: A New Direction," September 10, 2021, https:// www.gov.uk/government/consultations/data-a-new-direction.

[76] See "Scotland's AI Strategy," March 2021, https://www.scotlandaistrategy .com/.

employees and entrepreneurs. Benefits to all sectors and regions aid growth, employment, and leveled-up economic prosperity. What is clearer with this plan as opposed to other AI strategies is the call for greater diversity in the workforce, which creates a more diverse, equitable AI ecosystem given that a greater breadth of perspectives has been considered.

Key Observations

Technological Advancement

Cross-cutting themes common to each of these digital policies range from economic growth and job creation to improving the lives of the citizens of the nations they serve. Most policy is pro-innovation and does not want to be seen to be innovation stifling for risk of putting up barriers to business. Most want to be first movers, to show international leadership, to create a competitive edge, and in some cases to secure digital and/or data sovereignty.

To do that requires (as the policies themselves point out) investment (from both the private and public sector), an increase in local research and development, and more availability of data, hubs, sandboxes, and the like to stimulate entrepreneurship and enterprise. There also must be improved education in STE(E)M subjects for both the next generation of workers as well as for upskilling existing workers and digital skills for users and civil servants in government.[77] Reeducation or transferring skillsets mid-career is being encouraged. Digital awareness is required for informed use to avoid exploitation of the public and designed to empower.

As data and technology can be borderless, factors outside the control and jurisdiction of one country or economic block will be at play. Cooperation, collaboration, and coordination with other global partners are key for any country looking to affect what and how digital technologies

---

[77] STEM and its alternative acronyms, STEEM and STEAM, stand for Science, Technology, Engineering, (Ethics/Applied Ethics), and Maths; see also UK Government, "Digital Leadership Course," February 24, 2021, https://www.gov.uk /guidance/digital-leadership-course.

impact their citizens. International relations will be key to preserving values in the design, development, and deployment of these often data-driven technologies. Some policies recognize digital exclusion (the power of the digital to exclude and to leave swaths of society behind) and therefore have emphasized digital inclusion and eradicating the digital divide.[78] Other policies seek to embed the same sentiment but by including it in a leveling-up agenda, where all lives gain benefits from the digital economy, all parts of a nation and its regions receive economic benefit from this digital age.

Despite demonstrating some consideration for the societal impacts of the digital, fundamentally, the policies are about technological progress of application agnostic technologies through greater data availability. In my view, it is not always a case of technological advancement no matter the cost. There clearly is a cost to someone—usually those who can least afford it—and it depends on how much society will bear it, adapt, and let it be normalized.

Data Empowerment: The Promise and Perils

What is clear is that data is important, if not vital, to the proper functioning of this digital policy. Data—when used in data-driven technologies—is perceived to produce benefits for citizens and businesses in many ways, such as to improve health care, create safer and cleaner transport systems, reduce the costs of public services, improve sustainability and energy efficiency,[79] and create more jobs at a time when the future of work is uncertain.

Informed consent, data portability, and data spaces may indeed give personal empowerment, but they lack one small thing—an understanding of not just application domain, but also of personal context and bias.

---

[78] See Office of National Statistics, "Exploring the UK's digital divide," March 4, 2019, https://www.ons.gov.uk/peoplepopulationandcommunity/householdchar acteristics/homeinternetandsocialmediausage/articles/exploringtheuksdigitaldivide /2019-03-04.

[79] See European Commission, "A European Strategy for Data," accessed October 1, 2021, https://digital-strategy.ec.europa.eu/en/policies/strategy-data.

Some commentators would argue that this has come too late. Data-driven technologies can reduce humans to a mere set of characteristics, behaviors, features, and variables—our digital twins. Businesses and governments have been keen to develop and adopt AI and digital technologies and platforms at pace without real foresight for the perils of data.

Data can corroborate perceived facts to validate whether something is true or not. But data can also be both the source and cause of bias. Data can be the source of bias because we live in a biased world, where certain inequities have long existed in society. Not all data is perfectly representative but can often be incomplete and incomprehensive. As well, it can be time sensitive (relevant only to a specific time frame) and time bound (data changes over time and will only ever be as accurate up to the point changes).

Data can also be the cause of bias in that poor or incomplete data understanding and analysis—whether accuracy, aggregation, collection, curation, evaluation, selection, measurement, and validation (this list is not exhaustive)—can result in unintended consequences.[80] Practices such as prediction of protected characteristics,[81] and anonymization of personal data to avoid direct discrimination are rife.[82] On this basis alone, some might be led to believe that the EU's General Data Protection Regulation is not fit for purpose when it comes to AI (and new law is needed) or that protection of personal data is an inhibitor to innovation, because of the additional hurdles

---

[80] See Ninareh Mehrabi et al., "A Survey on Bias in Machine Learning," accessed October 1, 2021, https://arxiv.org/pdf/1908.09635.pdf.

[81] Facial recognition technology can be used to identify political orientation. See Michal Kosinski, "Facial recognition technology can expose political orientation from naturalistic facial images," *Scientific Reports,* January 11, 2021, https://doi.org/10.1038/s41598-020-79310-1. See also Bob Yirka, "AI algorithm over 70% accurate at guessing a person's political orientation," Tech Xplore, January 14, 2021, https://techxplore.com/news/2021-01-ai-algorithm-accurate-person-political.html.

[82] Anonymous job applications can abate some initial discriminatory barriers but often postpones that discrimination to later stages of the process. Anonymization should not be regarded as a universal remedy to prevent discrimination. Ulf Rinne, "Anonymous job applications and hiring discrimination." World of Labor, accessed October 1, 2021, https://wol.iza.org/articles/anonymous-job-applications-and-hiring-discrimination/long.

required to obtain more sensitive accurate information about a person (and that deregulation is necessary). Data alone is not the sole component of blame. How data is interpreted (whether by humans or by algorithm) to produce inference or insight and models on which autonomous and semi-autonomous systems are built highlights perhaps an even greater, less easily tackled problem: humanity.

People have their own culture, are diverse and inclusive (or not), and have been conditioned by upbringing, social context, and geopolitical factors associated with where in the world they grew up or live. People are complex. Whether it is people in the data or people in the making of the model or algorithm or machine or business leadership, complexity exists. When people create amazingly complex machines, it will inevitably contain echoes of the person. To that end, humanity can no longer ignore bias—our own human bias—that contributes to the technologies we are creating, contributing to, or consuming. Data clearly communicates part of who we are: our behavior, our preferences, our credentials (such as date of birth, where we live, what we have achieved through our educational and work attainments), the state of our health, and even our political and religious beliefs.

Greater data sharing and portability, so called data empowerment, could, with appropriate safeguards, be beneficial. If we are not careful, it could undermine our privacy, our autonomy, and other human rights, with disempowering effect.[83]

Trustworthiness

Trustworthiness is about being relied upon as someone who is honest and truthful. Trust is something that occurs in a relationship between people. But what it is, in whom it is placed, and why it is that we are being asked to trust, goes to the root of digital policy making.

---

[83] One only must look to authoritarian regimes that use a social credit rating system, such as the Chinese Communist Party, to see the disempowering effects of an all-knowing government.

Policy makers are asking for trust not to rest in the AI artifact or digital technology itself (although safety and reliability would be important preconditions to use), but in the legal person, institution, or entity and its organizational structures that design, develop, and deploy AI- and data-driven technologies. We are being asked to put our trust in their governance—the conduct of those who run these organizations. Trust leads to confidence to use, and use leads to adoption.

For trust to be gained, governments and organizations need to demonstrate effective and meaningful governance and oversight with clear lines of humans taking responsibility and being held accountable. This calls for process and decision transparency; nominated persons for accountability and redress; assurance of cyber and physical security; assurance that humans remain in the decision-making seat, retain autonomy, and preserve their privacy; and trust that follows through into fair and just outcomes.

There is a growing call for standardization. Whether it goes by the name "best practices," "codes of practice" or "codes of conduct," some kind of blanket *standard* concerning interoperability, ethical data use/reuse, ethical design, or understanding ethical and societal impacts and risks associated with deploying digital or other emerging technologies is sought by government and businesses alike. To some this may provide certainty and guidance; to others it may be a way of creating more flexible "soft law" that can easily adapt to new technological challenges. These are all laudable aims and should be standard good business practice.

The cynic in me, however, realizes that the overarching policy is not really about trust but about user adoption. User adoption leads to scalability and economic growth, which further leads to investment, improvement, innovation, digital expansion, and job creation, which with continued good practice leads to good reputation and further adoption. It creates a "virtuous cycle" feedback loop (or a vicious circle, depending on how you look at it). We do not have to look back too far in human history to see that no government, organization, or human is ever beyond reproach, nor can they ever be completely relied upon. Caution, critique, and safeguards should always be applied. Complete trustworthiness can only ever be found in God, as one who is wholly faithful, reliable, and truthful (Ps 86:15; Prov 30:5; John 14:6).

The Digital Markets Power Play

A story that is not so clearly communicated on the pages of these digital policies is about the power play. Not the transformative power of digitization, not the consumer and citizen empowerment through meaningful informed choice, nor the legitimate use of data to create ecosystem and cultural change. It is the legitimization of the gain, use, and re-use of data to fuel limitation of market channels, digital platforms, and coerce digital markets by dominant actors to control competition.

Opportunities for informed consent can appear deliberately like inconvenient script. Data altruism and donations of data can be used for the common good, but massive amounts of data are still fundamentally required to fuel the technology. Many people likely lack the ability, knowledge, time, or desire to fully understand what they would be agreeing to in many of the cases, which can be interpreted as people reinforcing their desire for the online service, the app, and its benefits, without due care for their data or privacy, because of their behavior. This has been used to justify the notion that privacy is dead.

A concentration of digital services through platform economies, and a ready and willing audience and supply chain, without scrutiny or checks and balances, can soon make perceived digital or data empowerment turn to market domination and manipulation: concentrating power. This is where some competition and anti-trust authorities are starting to step into so as to level up the power and protect both businesses and consumers from harm.[84]

It is important to always see the bigger picture of digital technologies and how and why they operate in the social context of the markets they operate in to encourage entrepreneurship and play a part of ecosystem change, one small change at a time.[85]

---

[84] The Competition and Market's Authority launched a Digital Markets Taskforce in March 2020 because it identified that powerful digital firms could pose a risk to competition: https://www.gov.uk/cma-cases/digital-markets-taskforce.

[85] See Jason Furman, "The Furman Review: Unlocking Digital Competition," March 2019, https://assets.publishing.service.gov.uk/government/uploads/system

Autonomy

Most policies recognize the need to respect fundamental human rights in the context of digital products and services, but because we have not yet seen the full scope of the ramifications that digital services and digital markets have or will have on those rights, we do not fully know what the corresponding responsibilities of the digital operators, providers, and users ought to be to preserve those rights.

While autonomy (in terms of the power to decide and act without interference) is singled out as a fundamental right and ethical principle, the criteria for good decision-making is less so. Free and unfettered discussion, freedom of conscience regarding what you think and believe, having access to unfiltered and non-curated content so that people can apply their own critical thinking to inform and discuss decisions, and providing skills to help people conduct their own critical thinking to their decision-making do not appear front and center on the list. Digital skills, yes. Cognitive skills, no.

People may have the power to decide, but with information overload due to the abundance of data clouding and confusing our judgment, it makes sense to want to have tools to assist us in making decisions, like a calculator for doing math. However, if the functional ability to make decisions or critically assess information for its truth, validity, falsehood, obfuscation, and gaps is slowly left to become redundant—because human (and perhaps even moral) agency has been effectively granted to autonomous and semi-autonomous algorithmic systems underlying the digital—then decision-making and the ability to differentiate between right and wrong may itself soon become a lost art. It is therefore vital to keep critical thinking as well as autonomy high up on the digital skills agenda.

/uploads/attachment_data/file/785547/unlocking_digital_competition_furman _review_web.pdf.

2030

Many of the digital policies we have seen refer to 2030 as the golden age by which digital policy transformation will have occurred. While there is no doubt that the 2020s are going to be an important decade that will have a profound impact on all of us as a society, I am not convinced that there is anything more crucial in this span of time than a ten-year action plan or business outlook. The consistency among nations may arguably stem from countries trying to align with the United Nation's 17 Sustainable Development Goals (SDGs) for the 2030 Agenda for Sustainable Development that were adopted by world leaders in September 2015 and came into force on January 1, 2016.[86] The aim of the SDGs is to "mobilize efforts to end all forms of poverty, fight inequalities and tackle climate change, while ensuring that no one is left behind." They are intended to transform our world for good: aiming for an end to poverty, freedom from hunger, healthy lives, quality education, gender equality, clean water and sanitation, decent work, care for creation, and peace and access to justice for all, among many other goals. As Christians we, too, should be genuinely aiming for some of these goals that align with our fundamental beliefs about God and humanity as well as using technology to achieve them.

Change within the "digital decade" will undoubtedly occur very quickly, but I suspect that as it was with the invention of the Gutenberg press in and around 1440 (which not only transformed communication and the spread of printed copies of the Bible but also led to even greater levels of literacy), it will take decades for us to realize the true impacts—both the intended and the unintended—of the digital age's ability to benefit and to harm.

Our involvement in digital policy cannot be merely about doing good but engaging in it *with* God and *for* God, calling for a better kind of digital literacy that helps people navigate for themselves what it means to be truly human in a digital age.

---

[86] The United Nations Sustainable Development Agenda, accessed October 1, 2021, https://www.un.org/sustainabledevelopment/development-agenda-retired/.

Why Is This Important to Christians?

Christians do not have to be Luddite about advancements of technology, but the Bible does require us not to be futile in our thinking and to seek and apply wisdom (Prov 4:6–7). It requires little observation to see that digital interactions are changing our lives and humanity around us. Digital and data-driven technologies have a social dimension that impacts fundamental human rights such as privacy (both in public and in our own homes due to connected devices), freedom of speech, and freedom of conscience. Among these rights are protection against other harms including manipulation, exploitation, loss of control, and a sense of powerlessness caused by automated decisions.

Whether it's the pace of life in a digital society where we jump from video call to video call; clickbait keeping us distracted on a device; the ease with which we accept cookies, privacy policies, online terms, and conditions to save time and inconvenience; or the frictionless way we can fall into a lifestyle of consumption, it would be difficult to counteract the argument that humanity is not being changed by the digital.[87]

As Christians, we believe in the creator God, who created us in his very image (Gen 1:26). We have therefore been bestowed with responsibilities to represent him in all aspects of life that we cannot ignore. We each have a role bestowed on us to be good stewards of this planet and its inhabitants, and to defend truth and freedom for all to live in accordance with their deeply held beliefs. Furthermore, Jesus left us with a mandate not only to love God but to love our neighbor as ourselves, as well as a lived example of servant leadership (Luke 10:27; John 13:15).

With most digital policies decreeing that their country is going to be a digital or AI or data leader, it appears that there might be a lacuna of leadership, particularly regarding how this affects people and planet, individuals, relationships, communities, and societies. Our role then is to get involved

---

[87] For more on how technology is shaping each of us, see chapter 12 by Jacob Shatzer.

and to affect the ecosystem change we want to see out of a motivation of love of God and neighbor.

We are called to defend the defenseless and stand up for the powerless (see Ps 82:3–4). When we see people being exploited and manipulated online and/or deceived by fake news and dis- or misinformation that further fuels distrust, we must not simply stand by and watch.[88] Nor can we remain idle and unbothered when we see people unjustly discriminated against; when we see societies divided and democracies undermined; when we see families excluded from society because they cannot afford the devices, or the connectivity, or do not have "data" to be able to use the internet for schooling; or when we see the unbanked or underbanked unable to pay for goods and services digitally, because they do not have access to an online payment account.

In our lifetimes we must act justly, love mercy, and walk humbly with our God (Mic 6:8) to be a people that seek justice, truth, and righteousness. We must consider our greatest legacy to be that of protecting future generations (Psalm 78). Where there is injustice or the potential for harm to people and planet, we have been given ears to hear and *listen up*; we have been given a voice and mouth to *speak up*; and we have fingers and hands to write and *reach out*; we have feet and legs to *stand up*.

Conclusion

The strategies, plans, and roadmaps for digital policy discussed in this chapter are laudable aims, particularly where they seek to protect, preserve, and manifest the fundamental rights of people in the digital public square. Scraping beneath the surface of these policies, you get a sense that protecting humanity or acting for the benefit of all for the common good in the digital world may not be the sole aim of bringing us into the digital age.

With the striving toward global leadership and digital or data sovereignty, there is a sense that this might be more about economic prosperity

---

[88] For more on misinformation, see chapter 10 by Jason Thacker.

than first disclosed. Financial rewards are not in and of themselves a bad goal, provided it is not the sole real ambition here of thrusting humanity into a digital world. Economic enrichment must not and should not supersede human welfare and dignity. It should not make us lose our sense of humanity. Instead, it should facilitate collaborative peaceful human leadership, human-to-human relationship, a human-centric culture and a human-centric society.

What lessons can be learned from digital policy? There is a need for all of us to stand up, engage with policy makers about these issues, for businesses to lead by example, to help create best practices, and to help make better laws and instruments that safeguard people and planet whether in our own jurisdictions or in and through multi-jurisdictional agencies.

All of us can choose how to act, but all will either act or omit to act, and each will be held accountable for the consequences of their actions and omissions. Each person should simply play their own part in accordance with the gifts and talents God has bestowed upon them in the places and times where God has chosen for them to live and have their being. Having opened the chapter with the Davos Manifesto of 2020, I would like to draw attention to Jesus's own vision from two millennia ago concerning his Spirit-anointed ministry, which I believe provides a compelling vision for social engagement today.

In Luke 4:1–40, Jesus traveled to his hometown of Nazareth and read from Isaiah 61. As he read, he stated that he had been anointed by the Holy Spirit to preach good news to the poor, to proclaim freedom for the prisoners, to recover sight for the blind, and to release those held captive and oppressed.

Jesus's words involve us too in respect of digital policy. We can and should carry on his work throughout the digital public square. If God has given you skills and talents to work in policy and government affairs in respect of digital policy, use them wisely to transform lives, relationships, culture, society, and leadership:

1. **Transforming lives:** where the digital world and its dark practices are used to oppress and thus we are needed as salt and light

2. **Transforming relationships:** where technology is available that could change how we interact with other humans or with machines and with God

3. **Transforming culture:** where technology may foster isolation, exclusion, and individualism to always provide hope that there is a good God and because of this to show love, to care about our community and our society, and to be inclusive

4. **Transforming society:** to want to see the need for ecosystem change in society for the better, being a voice, influencing change, and making change for good happen

5. **Transforming leadership:**[89] to fill the leadership dearth by being better leaders, with strength of conviction and with vision; to lead by example; to be truthful, honest, open and kind; to have servant hearts and be humble; to treat others as you would want to be treated yourself; to listen and respond with respect and gentleness and to stand up for those who cannot stand for themselves

---

[89] Special thanks to Rev. Nicky Gumbel of Holy Trinity Church, Brompton, London, who provided fantastic insight from Isaiah 61 in his "Spirit-Powered Living," Day 268 of the Bible in One Year (BIOY) daily devotional app (classic version), https://bibleinoneyear.org/en/classic/268/. Reverend Gumbel's insight coincides with how we should live as Spirit-empowered Christians in the digital marketplace. The One Year® is a registered trademark of Tyndale House Publishers.

5

Can the Government Save Us from Ourselves?

The Legal Complexities of Free Speech and Content Moderation

David French

It somehow feels appropriate that the modern history of free speech online began with a series of alleged, anonymous lies. They happened on October 23 and October 25, 1994, with an old internet company called Prodigy. What passed for the "internet" in the early 1990s was mainly accessed through three companies: America Online, CompuServe, and Prodigy. Each service was similar. You would install the software on your computer—often from a disc you got in the mail—and then you would dial in to the service from a telephone modem that would render people unable to call you on your home phone. Once online, you would wait for a moment, as the images slowly populated your screen. And then, "Voila!" you were "online."

For those of us who spent high school and college in truly offline worlds, the advent of services like Prodigy was a wonder. Real-time baseball box scores? Are you kidding me? News you could access with just a click of the mouse? And then there were these entirely new things called "chat rooms" and "bulletin boards." Using a simple interface, you could talk in real time to people across the country. You can guess what happened next. Acting at the speed of human depravity, chat rooms and bulletin boards quickly became cesspools and often even hunting grounds for sexual predators. Prodigy, however, wanted to be clean. Since its founding, it had defined itself as a family network. So it exercised what one court called "editorial control" (now called "moderation") over the messages placed online. Prodigy's intent was clear: "We make no apology for pursuing a value system that reflects the culture of the millions of American families we aspire to serve. Certainly, no responsible newspaper does less when it chooses the type of advertising it publishes, the letters it prints, the degree of nudity and unsupported gossip its editors tolerate."[1]

And that brings us back to October 1994. On its "Money Talk" bulletin board, an anonymous user claimed that the initial public offering of stock by a company called Solomon Page Ltd. was a "major criminal fraud" and "100% criminal fraud." The user also said that Daniel Porush, the president of an investment banking firm called Stratton Oakmont, was "soon to be proven criminal" and that there was a "cult of brokers who either lie for a living or get fired."[2] In other words, the rhetoric looked like an average day of venting on Twitter, in which anonymous accounts spill wild accusations into the public square as a matter of course.

At the time, Prodigy worked much like Twitter, Facebook, and other social media companies work today. Users posted content without pre-screening, but the combination of software (which filtered out bad language) and human moderators acted as a failsafe to delete or filter out content that violated the company's rules and policies. Stratton Oakmont and Porush

---

[1] Stratton Oakmont, Inc. v. Prodigy Services Company, 1995 WL 323710 (N.Y. Sup. May 24, 1995).

[2] *Stratton Oakmont, Inc.*

were understandably upset at the anonymous accusation, and they filed suit against Prodigy. They claimed that since Prodigy moderated its content, it was a "publisher" of the allegedly false, anonymous posts in the same way that a newspaper is a publisher of its news stories or its op-eds.

Prodigy disagreed, arguing that it was a mere passive distributor of content, more like a library or a bookstore than a newspaper. It cited a recent case filed against its rival CompuServe where a federal court had dismissed a defamation lawsuit against the service on the grounds that it had little ability to moderate content and no opportunity to review content before it was posted. Therefore, it was more like a library than a newspaper. The CompuServe court said: "A computerized database is the functional equivalent of a more traditional news vendor, and the inconsistent application of a lower standard of liability to an electronic news distributor such as CompuServe than that which is applied to a public library, bookstore, or newsstand would impose an undue burden on the free flow of information."[3]

Prodigy, however, was a bit different. According to the court in Prodigy's case, "By actively utilizing technology and manpower to delete notes from its computer bulletin boards on the basis of offensiveness and 'bad taste,' for example, Prodigy is clearly making decisions as to content." This, the court said, was the equivalent of "editorial control" and Prodigy could be liable for its users' unlawful speech.[4] Amidst this explosion of communication technology and the ability for users to post content online, legal challenges to free speech and content moderation exploded, necessitating a hard look at the rise of content moderation in the modern era, who is responsible for user-generated content, and who sets the standards for online conduct. This chapter will examine the legal and ethical complexities of free speech and content moderation, including various proposals for regulating this industry given its outsized influence over the digital public square. Ultimately, we all must take responsibility for the state of affairs online, as governments will not be able to save us from ourselves.

---

[3] Cubby, Inc. v. CompuServe Inc. 776 F.Supp. 135 (S.D.N.Y. 1991).
[4] *Stratton Oakmont, Inc.*

The Communications Decency Act and the Modern Internet

The court in Prodigy's case hit the emerging internet world like an earthquake. Here was a technology that allowed more people the ability to speak in the public square than any technology in human history, but if internet companies moderating that content could be liable for their users' speech, then the internet as it was emerging would come to a screeching halt. To put it in plain English, the only way to be certain that you would not be liable for users' speech would be to exercise essentially no control over what they post. Sadly, we already knew exactly what that would lead to—an avalanche of truly terrible content, including pornography, predation, and harassment. Trying to prevent that content from reaching readers would, however, make you liable for everything on the site.

This all-or-nothing free-speech regime was facially deeply problematic. It had no real offline analogue. For example, think of a classroom. Virtually every teacher in America "moderates" classroom discussion. They might cut off students if they go off topic. They might prohibit personal insults or profanity. They might limit the length of discussions so that students cannot filibuster an entire class. But that moderation does not suddenly transform student speech into the teacher's speech. The student's speech only becomes the teacher's speech when the teacher works with the student to create, say, an essay or an article. Or consider a different example. Across the United States city councils and school boards place strict limits on public engagement even at open meetings. They'll sharply limit the length of time that any given member of the public may speak. They'll limit the topics they can address. They'll even limit whether members of the public can engage in verbally abusive conduct. But not one of those limits transforms the public's speech into the school board's or city council's speech.

Taken together, the Prodigy and CompuServe cases represented a sharp departure from the culture and legal tradition of American free speech. The all-or-nothing approach risked creating competing spaces of virtually unspeakable online obscenity and depravity versus tightly controlled environments where only a select, vetted few were free to speak. So, in 1996

Congress stepped in. It passed the Communications Decency Act (CDA), and—in one stroke—tried both to tame the worst parts of the internet while granting ordinary citizens access to public platforms at a scale never seen before in human history. Only one of those goals was achieved. The decency provisions of the law were primarily aimed at preventing minors from gaining access to the internet's worst content. In particular, the act imposed criminal penalties on anyone who "knowingly (A) uses an interactive computer service to send to a specific person or persons under 18 years of age, or (B) uses any interactive computer service to display in a manner available to a person under 18 years of age, any comment, request, suggestion, proposal, image, or other communication that, in context, depicts or describes, in terms patently offensive as measured by contemporary community standards, sexual or excretory activities or organs."[5]

Free speech advocates immediately challenged this provision in court, and in a 1997 case called *Reno v. ACLU* the Supreme Court ruled unanimously that the decency provisions violated the First Amendment. According to the court, the combination of the vagueness of phrases like "patently offensive" and the criminalization of misconduct meant that the act would chill the expression of speech that the Constitution protects. The CDA, the court noted, suppresses "a large amount of speech that adults have a constitutional right to send and receive. . . . [Its] breadth is wholly unprecedented." And thus efforts to regulate internet pornography received an early, fatal blow.[6]

But another, unchallenged provision of the CDA survived, and it transformed our world. Whereas the Supreme Court sharply limited the power of the government to censor free speech online, Section 230 directly and intentionally enabled *private* censorship.[7] The government couldn't mandate that sites exclude pornography, for example, but private companies could set up their sites according to their own rules, and they could do so

---

[5] As cited in Reno v. American Civil Liberties Union, 521 U.S. 844 (1997).

[6] *Reno,* 521 U.S. 844.

[7] Section 230 was coauthored by then representative Chris Cox, a California Republican, and then representative Ron Wyden, an Oregon Democrat.

without being sued. This was accomplished by two key provisions of the law. First, it declared that "No provider or user of an interactive computer service shall be treated as the publisher or speaker of any information provided by another information content provider."[8] This means that my comment on a friend's Facebook page is my comment, not Facebook's. My Yelp review of a local Mexican restaurant is my review, not Yelp's.

This provision by itself helped clarify the law, but it does nothing to specifically empower websites to cleanse their platforms of problematic content. So, the statute went further. It said internet providers can "restrict access to or availability of material that the provider or user considers to be obscene, lewd, lascivious, filthy, excessively violent, harassing, or otherwise objectionable" without being held liable for user content.[9] This provision does not require any form of neutrality. It places the judgment of obscenity, lewdness, and so forth squarely in the hands of the provider. It permits censorship of content the "provider considers" objectionable. In other words, if Facebook and Instagram want to ban nudity, they can. If Twitter wants to permit nudity, it can.[10] If any site wants to ban profanity or racial slurs, they can, and they can do so without becoming liable for users' posts. Again, this law brought online speech rules into harmony with offline speech traditions.

My experience on Facebook could match my experience in a classroom or my experience in a convention hall. The private entity sets the rules, and I can choose whether to comply or not with the rules. The result of this law was nothing short of a free speech explosion. Commercially savvy companies created spaces—including comments sections in newspapers and message boards on social media apps—that permitted enough freedom for robust debate but restricted the kind of content that repels the mass market. This is the internet we know—where we feel entitled to post our own public commentary about virtually any aspect of our lives, whether it's a movie

---

[8] 47 U.S.C. Section 230.

[9] 47 U.S.C. Section 230.

[10] For more on the debate over banning pornography, see chapter 9 written by Bonnie Kristian.

review or commentary about election outcomes. We spend our online lives in private spaces governed by private rules, and we've grown accustomed to considerable freedom governed by a few guardrails.

Freedom of Speech, Private Platforms, and Content Moderation

In fact, it's the lure of that freedom that has helped suck us online. Ordinary citizens now have the ability to reach more people with their private thoughts than at any point in the entire history of the human race. Even a short generation ago, we could speak but there were profound limits on the reach of our words. Walk into a public park, and we could say virtually anything we wanted, but our audience was limited to those in earshot. Did you want to speak to a broader public? Try submitting an op-ed or letter to the editor. The media could print it, or not; there was nothing you could do to force your way onto their pages. Virtually the only way to guarantee your voice would be heard was to pay to play. Take out an ad, but ads were expensive, especially the larger, more visible ones. But now? Set your Facebook privacy settings to public, start posting on Reddit, start tweeting, or start dancing on TikTok, and you've got hope of virality where your voice has the opportunity to be heard by people around the world in an instant. At the very least, you know more people can and will see what you say than if you were in the park shouting at the top of your lungs. This access to public platforms is now embedded into our culture. It's part of our way of life. A generation of children has been raised in a world where they can say virtually everything they think, and someone, somewhere, can see it online. It's easy to think of all this access not as a privilege but as a right. Except it's not.

And therein lies the root of some of the most contentious public controversies of our time. It's easy to forget that phrases like "my Facebook page" or "my Twitter feed" or "my TikTok channel" are simply and fundamentally wrong. "My Facebook page" is Meta's page. "My Twitter feed" is Twitter's. "My TikTok channel" is TikTok's. These social media platforms are letting me use their virtual property and their platform for the cost—not of money—but of my personal information, which they use to make billions of dollars through advertising revenue.[11]

Now, here's the next complication. This confusion about ownership is taking place at the exact same time that American polarization and division are escalating to dangerous levels. While there is a valid causation/correlation debate as to the role of social media in American division, it is indisputable that American polarization was escalating even before the growth of social media. The result is that Americans do not just fight on the internet; they fight *about* the internet. Broadly speaking, those on the ideological right and left are developing different priorities based on their distinctly different cultural realities. The Left tends to want social media companies to regulate speech more than they do. Even though every major social media platform maintains speech policies that regulate a broad range of expression, critics on the left maintain that the companies can and should do more. They believe free speech online is a bit too free. They want Meta and Twitter to clamp down more on misinformation.[12] They seek to regulate "hate speech"[13] (a term notoriously difficult to define) and see the prevalence of conspiracy theories as mortal threats to public health, social peace, and even American democracy itself.

And while the Left hopes to persuade Silicon Valley to crack down on "hate speech" and misinformation, it's also appealing to the government for greater regulations, including for rules that could hold social media companies responsible for the harms caused by their users' speech.

---

[11] This concept is called "surveillance capitalism" by Harvard Law professor Shoshana Zuboff. For more on online advertising and data collection, see Shoshana Zuboff, *The Age of Surveillance Capitalism: The Fight for a Human Future at the New Frontier of Power* (New York: PublicAffairs, 2019).

[12] Misinformation refers to a broad category of false or misleading information that often spreads *unintentionally*, while disinformation refers to the *intentional* dissemination of false information by moral actors. For more on these topics, see chapter 10 by Jason Thacker.

[13] For more on the nature of hate speech and free expression, see chapters 7 and 8.

The Right has both an opposite and identical instinct. The opposite argument is the demand that social media companies regulate speech less. They often want fewer regulations governing hate speech and misinformation, and they vigorously protest cancellations and suspensions even of fringe figures, arguing that social media companies are well down the slippery slope to banning even the most mainstream of conservative figures and ideas, especially conservative religious ideas. This leads the Right to its identical approach. Just as the Left hopes to persuade Silicon Valley but is determined to turn to the government if tech companies fail to meet their demands, the Right is similarly seeking government intervention. At the time of writing, states like Texas and Florida have already passed statutes designed to limit corporate control over public speech on their platforms with more likely to follow suit in the coming years barring federal legislation.[14]

Regulating "Big Tech"?

Republican senators like Missouri's Josh Hawley proposed legislation in 2019 that would require large social media companies to prove that moderation policies are not "designed to negatively affect a political party, political candidate, or political viewpoint" and that its moderation does not "disproportionately restrict or promote access to, or the availability of, information from a political party, political candidate, or political viewpoint" before it can receive protection from liability for user content.[15]

---

[14] See Office of the Texas Governor, "Governor Abbott Signs Law Protecting Texans from Wrongful Social Media Censorship," September 9, 2021, https://gov .texas.gov/news/post/governor-abbott-signs-law-protecting-texans-from-wrongful -social-media-censorship; Office of the Florida Governor, "Governor Ron DeSantis Signs Bill to Stop the Censorship of Floridians by Big Tech," May 24, 2021, https://www.flgov.com/2021/05/24/governor-ron-desantis-signs-bill-to-stop-the -censorship-of-floridians-by-big-tech/.

[15] See the Ending Support for Internet Censorship Act, located at: https:// www.hawley.senate.gov/sites/default/files/2019-06/Ending-Support-Internet -Censorship-Act-Bill-Text.pdf.

Why do the two sides desire such different moderation policies? The left-wing idealist would say that Blue America is more committed to truth and tolerance than the right. The right-wing idealist would say Red America is more committed to speech and debate than the left. The cynic says that the competing positions are more easily explained since they are grounded in the will to power, in the eternal temptation of "free speech for me, but not for thee." Silicon Valley corporations are overwhelmingly staffed and controlled by individuals on the left side of the political spectrum, thus it simply makes sense that left-wing Americans would have greater confidence in the moderation decisions made by those who broadly share their values. Conversely, it makes sense that right-wing Americans would have little to no confidence in moderation decisions made by individuals who profoundly disagree with their ideology and worldview. The complicator for both sides is the legal reality that no matter one's degree of trust in Silicon Valley, each of the corporate giants that make up "Big Tech" are private actors who possess their own free speech rights. They're composed of private individuals who can express their own values through the products they make and the rules they set.

This brings us back to the Communications Decency Act, the First Amendment, and the Supreme Court. If anything, Supreme Court jurisprudence has grown more protective of corporate free speech rights since *Reno v. ACLU* was decided in 1997. As a result, those who seek to regulate the free speech choices of private corporations have fewer legal tools at their disposal. Moreover, corporate free speech rights are at their apex when they engage in the political and religious arena. Corporate political speech is specifically protected by a case called *Citizens United v. Federal Election Commission* (2010).[16] Corporate religious free exercise is specifically protected by a case called *Burwell v. Hobby Lobby* (2014).[17] Moreover, some of the strongest doctrines in all of constitutional law protect private citizens from so-called compelled speech (i.e., being forced to broadcast or proclaim views they despise).

---

[16] Citizens United v. Federal Election Comm'n, 558 U.S. 310 (2010).

[17] Burwell v. Hobby Lobby Stores, Inc., 573 U.S. 682 (2014).

In light of this precedent, recent laws attempting to regulate Big Tech's moderation of political speech were blocked in court in Florida and in Texas (both laws were blocked in 2021).[18] As much as the public may distrust the tech titans and the moderation regimes they oversee, constitutional law does not yet permit their replacement by government power, and expansion of government power to swallow existing First Amendment precedent is highly likely to do more harm than good.

Virtually every American citizen who longs for a Democratic administration to reform social media would have grave concerns about a Republican president at the helm. The same principles apply to Republican citizens. They have serious concerns about Democratic control. Given the dramatically competing goals of Republican and Democratic regulators, the expansion of government power over social media would only increase the stakes of America's political contexts—creating a contest for control not just over the government, but over our nation's primary means of communication as well.

Common Carriers and Public Utilities

There are those who answer this conundrum of competing proposals for regulating the technology industry by arguing that social media companies have grown so powerful that they function as the government. In other words, the challenge of social media moderation should be solved by the First Amendment itself. Treat social media companies as government entities, and you do not have to worry about which president holds power. The First Amendment will protect everyone, and all viewpoints will have neutral access to the (digital) public square.

This argument is loosely rooted in actual case law. In a 1946 case called *Marsh v. Alabama*, the Supreme Court protected the First Amendment

---

[18] See Benjamin Din, "Federal Judge Blocks Florida's Social Media Law," *Politico*, June 30, 2021; James Pollard, "Federal Judge Blocks Texas Law That Would Stop Social Media Firms from Banning Users for a 'Viewpoint,'" *Texas Tribune*, December 1, 2021.

rights of a Jehovah's Witness who was passing out religious literature on the sidewalk of a "company town." Company towns are largely extinct, but there was a period in American history where workers sometimes lived in towns constructed and owned by their employers. These private towns essentially mimicked all the functions of normal towns. As the Supreme Court explained in *Marsh*, the town (called "Chickasaw") shared "all the characteristics of any other American town." The property was owned by the Gulf Shipbuilding corporation and consisted "of residential buildings, streets, a system of sewers, a sewage disposal plant, and a 'business block' on which business places are situated." Moreover, the company even paid for law enforcement. As the court explained, "A deputy of the Mobile County Sheriff, paid by the company, serves as the town's policeman."[19] In other words, the corporation essentially stood in the shoes of the state and cooperated with the state to perform state functions. Yet what is the "state function" of even the largest of social media companies?

In 2019 conservative media company Prager University (PragerU) sued YouTube and YouTube's parent company Google after a number of its videos had been placed in a "restricted mode," which limits the reach of videos. It also "demonetized" some of PragerU's videos, an action that blocks third parties from advertising on the videos. PragerU argued that YouTube and Google performed a public function by hosting a vast amount of speech online, but the Ninth Circuit Court of Appeals rejected PragerU's argument, explaining, "It is true that a private entity may be deemed a state actor when it conducts a public function, but the relevant function 'must be both traditionally and exclusively governmental.'"[20] (A private prison fulfills a traditional and exclusive governmental function, for example.) Yet in 2019, in a case called *Manhattan Community Access Corp. v. Halleck*, the Supreme Court held that "merely hosting speech by others is not a traditional, exclusive public function and does not alone transform private entities into state

---

[19] Marsh v. Alabama, 326 U.S. 501 (1946).

[20] Prager University v. Google LLC, et al., case no. 18-15712 (9th cir. Feb. 26, 2020).

actors subject to First Amendment constraints."[21] This rationale intuitively makes sense. Movie theaters host speech by others, yet they're not deemed to be state actors, even if a movie theater company has vast reach. Private convention centers and private arenas host private speech. Private schools and colleges host private speech. None of those actions transforms a private company into an arm of the government.

Moreover, social conservatives in particular should think long and hard about whether they would even *want* social media companies to be treated like the government. As much as conservatives may dislike the perceived bias of social media moderation decisions, one cannot forget that pornography is protected speech according to longstanding First Amendment precedent.[22] Treating Facebook like the government and restricting Facebook's moderation decisions to match First Amendment requirements would likely contribute to an explosion of pornography on social media.

Other conservative legal thinkers have floated ideas such as treating large social media companies like "common carriers." A common carrier is a category of company that holds itself out to the public as transporting goods and some forms of information. FedEx is an example of a common carrier. So is AT&T. Common carriers by their nature tend to use means of interstate transport to precisely deliver goods or information to specific customers. Common carriers are subject to a degree of regulation that can inhibit their ability to refuse to service customers. Yet there is a substantial difference between a phone call on an AT&T phone or a FedEx package and a public Facebook post. Facebook posts, tweets, and TikTok videos are far more like public letters to the editor—or public forms of entertainment—than the private messages carried by package companies. When our ability to communicate to the public was limited to literal letters to the editor or op-ed submissions that editors were free to accept or reject, were those newspapers common carriers? To compare my public rant about the latest Marvel movie or about the president's foreign policy to a FedEx package

---

[21] Manhattan Community Access Corp. v. Halleck, 587 U.S. ___ (2019).

[22] For more on this debate, see chapter 9 written by Bonnie Kristian.

containing a present for my aunt is to completely distort the definition of the term "common carrier."

Time and again, you see the same challenge. A nation that is often rightly frustrated by the negative effects of social media has trouble grasping legal solutions to problems created by private choices.[23] If you undermine the First Amendment by removing autonomy from social media companies, you not only risk the political bias inherent in government control, but you also risk undermining the autonomy of all private American institutions. Additionally, if you use novel First Amendment arguments to limit social media moderation, you risk further polluting the public square with pornography and truly hateful expression. The First Amendment protects a broad range of speech, and if Facebook or Twitter is required to publish posts that they find repugnant, then our online space will grow even more toxic.

Trusting in Antitrust

Can nothing be done? A number of conservatives and progressives have raised the possibility of using antitrust laws to "break up" Big Tech. Antitrust law is a powerful governmental tool that can be used to break up monopolistic companies or to inhibit or prohibit "anticompetitive" business practices such as price fixing or group boycotts. Progressives have tended to aim at Big Tech's market share and economic power rather than its ideology, believing that the size and power of the nation's largest tech companies harm consumers and inhibits competition. Conservatives share many of these concerns, but they have also argued for the punitive use of antitrust law. If they cannot control Big Tech, then at least they can punish major corporations when they use their market power to discriminate against disfavored voices.[24] It is true that antitrust law is a viable means of breaking

---

[23] For a deeper look at some of the negative effects of social media and the challenge of discipleship today, see chapter 12 by Jacob Shatzer.

[24] See Evan Halper, "How Conservative Anger at Big Tech Pushed the GOP into Bernie Sanders' Corner," *Los Angeles Times*, May 6, 2021.

up monopolies, of requiring them to "spin off" parts of their operation. Perhaps one of the most famous examples of an antitrust action leading to the breakup of an immense corporation was the 1982 consent decree that required AT&T to split its Bell Operating Companies into a collection of different "Baby Bells," smaller corporations that were regionally based.

The antitrust approach, however, suffers from a number of problems. First, if the government wields antitrust lawsuits as a weapon to punish companies for making moderation decisions it dislikes, then it will likely violate the First Amendment. Antitrust law is designed to address problems created by anticompetitive practices and commercial monopolies, not to make sure that companies make politically approved decisions. Second, the monopoly that many conservatives are most concerned about is the Left's *ideological* monopoly in Silicon Valley, not the market share of any given tech company. Requiring Meta to spin off Instagram or WhatsApp, for example, would not do anything to change the overall ideological makeup of the workforce, nor its content moderation decisions.

Third, there's the stubborn reality that most social media companies are not monopolies in the traditional sense. There is ample competition. Yes, the competitors are all big companies themselves, but market share changes rapidly. Consider TikTok, who "had a 1157.76% increase in its global user-base between Jan 2018 and July 2020; the US saw a 787.86% user growth rate in the same period." Moreover, "TikTok has been downloaded 3 billion times and was the most downloaded non-game app in the first 6 months of 2021, hitting 383 million installs from January to June 2021 alone." It took TikTok slightly over four years to reach that level of market penetration.[25] Facebook and Instagram compete with TikTok and Snapchat and Twitter and Reddit and YouTube (and Telegram and Pinterest and Quora, the list goes on). They're all big. They all have immense reach. They all compete with each other. The more interesting antitrust analysis applies to Google, being the dominant search engine, and portions of Amazon's business, particularly its dominant position in book and e-book sales. But even then,

---

[25] Brian Dean, "TikTok User Statistics (2021)," Backlinko, January 5, 2022, https://backlinko.com/tiktok-users.

antitrust cases are immensely challenging, often lengthy, and frequently overtaken by new and unanticipated developments in the industry.

Personal Responsibility in the Digital Public Square

The information revolution is changing American (and world) culture every bit as thoroughly as the industrial revolution before it. Quite simply, there is no going back, and while there are perhaps *some* legal ways to blunt the hardest edges of our new online world, there is little way to avoid what a tech company executive told me in 2018. "Our technology," she said, "exposes who we really are." It puts human nature on full blast. It exposes who we are, yes, but it also changes us—just like other technological leaps have changed the basic rhythms of our lives.[26] And now we know. There was a time when we did not. There was a time when you would hand a new phone to your child and you had no idea what Facebook or Instagram would do to their friendships, their self-image, or their mental health.

In fact, it's easy to remember the sheer idealism that accompanied the explosive growth of information technology. There were the heady days of the early Arab Spring in 2011—before jihadist voices grew too prominent—where Twitter celebrated the use of its platform by revolutionaries in the streets. I can remember first opening a Facebook account and the sheer delight of connecting with friends I had not seen or talked to in years. Even now, I take for granted technology's blessings. Because of it I remain in daily contact with the men I served with in Iraq. Instant communication has helped preserve our bond. That same instant communication preserves my bond with friends from college and law school. I know instantly when a friend or an acquaintance is sick. We can instantly provide money or order food for a family in need.

Each of these blessings is real. But sadly, the negative effects of these technologies are real as well. Young girls suffer from body-image issues and profound anxiety as they see a constant parade of filtered and curated images

---

[26] For more on technology and how it is shaping us as humans, see chapter 1, written by Jason Thacker, and chapter 12, written by Jacob Shatzer.

of beautiful celebrities and "influencers." The same technology that shows me images of a disaster in real time and provides me with links to donate to relief agencies is the technology that also helps create disasters by sharing inflammatory lies and conspiracy theories until people lose their moral compass in online rabbit holes they cannot seem to escape. So we turn to the companies and beg for the best of the product, and not the worst. We turn to government and plead for it to regulate the worst and liberate the best. Yet, at the end of the day, there is no substitute for our own choices—the ways in which we choose to use (or not use) the historically unprecedented capacity to connect with other humans.

There's no substitute for self-discipline. There's no substitute for wise parenting. This means monitoring and controlling your own internet and social media use, as well as the internet and social media use of your children. It means intentionally seeking reliable sources of information rather than consuming the content the algorithm feeds you. It means teaching your children about the uses and abuses of the internet and training them to seek out the best and shun the worst. None of this is easy. All of it is necessary. Yes, there are creative ways to perhaps smooth out the hardest edges of the online world. Regulations aimed at actual illegality are most promising and it is vital to exert moral and market pressure on corporations to choose those products that have best moderated the most dangerous content or have platforms or algorithms that promote or enhance better forms of content.

Freedom of expression is both a blessing and a responsibility. The blessing of online freedom and the responsibility of that freedom remind me of John Adams's famous words regarding the profound liberty protected by the United States Constitution. "Our Constitution was made only for a moral and religious People," he said. "It is wholly inadequate to the government of any other."[27] Our Constitution protects our internet, and thus we'll define what Big Tech means. There is no government that can save us from ourselves.

---

[27] "From John Adams to Massachusetts Militia, 11 October 1798," *Founders Online,* National Archives, https://founders.archives.gov/documents/Adams/99-02 -02-3102.

PART II

Issues

6

Free to Believe?

The Case for Religious Freedom and Free Expression in the Digital Age

Joshua B. Wester

It might seem strange at first, but for Christians much of the conversation about the role of religious freedom and free expression in the digital age revolves around the Great Commission. Matthew 28:16–20 captures the scene where Jesus gathered with his disciples sometime after his resurrection and commissioned them to go into the world and make disciples "of all nations." With those instructions, Jesus gave his people a mission to teach and proclaim the message of the Christian faith across the globe.

Though not an original disciple of Jesus, the apostle Paul was perhaps the single most important missionary in the history of the Christian church. His missionary journeys spanned thousands of miles and took the gospel to new places across the Roman Empire.[1] As he traveled, he preached and made converts, planted new churches, and raised up leaders to guide the young congregations he helped establish. His efforts gave rise

---

[1] For an extensive and interesting look at Paul's life and missionary journeys, see N. T. Wright, *Paul: A Biography* (New York: HarperOne, 2018).

to the Christian church in the West, and the impact of his missionary work is still felt today.

Paul's approach to his missionary work can helpfully inform an evangelical perspective on the emerging digital age, which has brought forth new questions and challenges concerning Christians and various digital technologies, especially in the public square. The book of Acts clearly demonstrates that Paul relied on the Holy Spirit to guide him (13:4), his missionary partners to assist him (16:1–5), and the broader church to support him (28:14) as he worked to proclaim Christ among the nations. But in addition, he also relied on various tools and resources to accomplish his impressive missionary endeavors. Paul traveled by land and sea, availing himself of the famous Roman roadways and maritime technology of his day to traverse the Mediterranean and beyond. He frequently authored letters to his companions in ministry and the churches he established or assisted, utilizing the written word to exercise his apostleship and extend the reach of his ministry. (Approximately one-third of the New Testament consists of Paul's letters.) More than once, he appealed to the laws of Rome and his rights as a citizen after encountering trouble in the course of his missionary work (16:37; 22:25).

This chapter will explore the role of religious liberty and free expression in our increasingly online world from an evangelical perspective. First, we'll establish why these issues matter to Christians by considering the importance, potential, and challenges of utilizing digital technologies to advance and fulfill the Great Commission. Second, we'll consider why these freedoms should matter to all people by exploring the critical role of religious freedom and freedom of speech for establishing flourishing human communities. Third, we'll review emerging challenges to public discourse in the digital public square by exploring two recent events as case studies. The chapter will conclude with a call for Christians to work toward the preservation of religious liberty and free expression across various digital platforms as more and more of our lives and interactions become concentrated online.[2]

---

[2] A note for the reader: This chapter does not provide a legal or public policy framework for addressing issues of online censorship. It is instead a reflection from

Christians and Technology

In my lifetime, there is no innovation that rivals the internet in terms of its world-shaping influence. Though the advent of the internet is technically dated to the mid-twentieth century, it was the emergence of the World Wide Web during the final decade of the century that slowly ushered online connectivity into the rhythms of our daily lives.[3] According to the United Nation's International Telecommunications Union (ITU), as of late 2021 roughly 4.9 billion people, or 63 percent of the global population, now have access to the internet.[4] Over the next decade, that number is expected to continue to rise rapidly through domestic and international efforts aimed at ensuring internet access is available almost everywhere in the world.

For Christians, what happens with the internet matters because of the Great Commission.[5] Christians have worked for nearly 2,000 years to fulfill this mandate by taking the message of the gospel to every nation— literally to "every nation, tribe, people, and language" (Rev 7:9). To

---

an ethicist and public theologian on the critical importance of establishing and safeguarding robust protections for religious freedom and free expression across various digital platforms. For a legal and policy framework, see the previous chapter by David French.

[3] See Aja Romano, "The World Wide Web—Not the Internet—Turns 30 Years Old," Vox, March 2019, https://www.vox.com/2019/3/12/18260709/30th-anniversary-world-wide-web-google-doodle-history.

[4] Despite the staggering number of people with internet access today, nearly 3 billion people have still never used the internet. Notably, according to the same report many of "these 'digitally excluded' face formidable challenges including poverty, illiteracy, limited access to electricity, and lack of digital skills and awareness." "2.9 billion people still offline," ITU, November 2021, https://www.itu.int/en/mediacentre/Pages/PR-2021-11-29-FactsFigures.aspx.

[5] This is not to say Christians' interest in this subject is merely pragmatic. Christians certainly defend the merits of religious freedom and free expression for their own sakes, which will be discussed in the next section of this chapter. However, the internet's potential to further the Great Commission presents an urgent and compelling reason for Christians to endeavor to protect these freedoms across digital platforms.

accomplish this extraordinary task, generations of Christians have followed the lead of the apostle Paul in availing themselves of various tools to enhance and further these missionary endeavors. Early Christians did this by adopting the codex—the precursor to books—in place of the scroll around the second century to preserve, reproduce, and disseminate their Holy Scriptures.[6] Similarly, many centuries later, Christians would adopt another innovative communications tool to advance the work of the gospel: the printing press.

Before Johannes Gutenberg's (c.1400–1468) revolutionary invention in the fifteenth century, the reproduction of books and documents was performed manually. It was a tedious and labor-intense process that required skill, precision, and extended amounts of time. Almost overnight, the printing press revolutionized the nature of written communication. Whereas a monk or scribe was estimated to produce four to five hand-copied pages per day, which would take two to three years to complete a copy of the Bible, a single press could yield up to 3,600 pages per day.[7] A generation after Gutenberg, Martin Luther, the famed leader of the Protestant Reformation, utilized the printing press to great effect, seeking to awaken European Christians to a theological and ecclesial crisis.

Luther wielded the printing press as a powerful tool through which he produced an incredible volume of books and pamphlets, including a translation of the Bible into German, which were then made accessible to the masses. These efforts helped spark a movement to oppose and remedy the ills of the Roman Catholic Church that ultimately culminated in the inauguration of the Protestant tradition. As one scholar noted, apart from Luther's use of the printing press "the Reformation could not have occurred as it did."[8]

---

[6] For more on this topic, see Larry W. Hurtado, *The Earliest Christian Artifacts: Manuscripts and Christian Origins* (Grand Rapids: Eerdmans, 2006).

[7] See Armin Siedlecki and Perry Brown, "Preacher and Printers," Christian History Institute, 2016, https://christianhistoryinstitute.org/magazine/article/urban-reformation-preachers-and-printers.

[8] For more on Luther's use of the printing press to ignite and sustain the Reformation, see Andrew Pettegree, *Brand Luther: How an Unheralded Monk*

Christians and Rights

The printing press serves as a helpful analog in thinking about the digital age. Today, it is not uncommon to hear a few common objections whenever Christians discuss the idea of rights and liberties. Usually, these objections appeal to the nature of Christian faith to argue that Christians should not defend intrusions upon our freedoms. "Jesus laid his rights and privileges aside" or "Christians are called to deny themselves" are frequent refrains in this line of reasoning. It would be a mistake to simply dismiss these critiques. Indeed, there are times when Scripture clearly instructs Christians not to pursue a rightful claim for the sake of the gospel. Paul specifically gave this admonition in his first letter to the Corinthians where he instructed that it is better to suffer wrongdoing than press a lawsuit against a fellow Christian (1 Cor 6:1–8). But is such a prohibition rightly applied to seeking protection for religious expression or free speech online?

At first glance one might reason that since Christians are not *required* to use the internet or digital technology it is just as well for believers to simply accept whatever limits or restrictions are set in place across various digital platforms. But as the West continues to secularize, such a proposal is highly impractical. More importantly, such acquiescence is almost certainly not rooted in biblical conviction.[9] Paul's teaching about lawsuits in 1 Cor 6:1–8 directly addresses the issue of not bringing reproach upon the gospel message, and his reasoning is rather straightforward. Believers are supposed to dwell in unity. But should they be unable to do so, such matters should be resolved within the church rather than bringing conflicts among brothers before secular authorities. There is no reason,

---

Turned His Small Town into a Center of Publishing, Made Himself the Most Famous Man in Europe—and Started the Protestant Reformation (New York: Penguin, 2016), 11.

[9] For a recent treatment of the rationale for Christians to defend robust protections for religious and civil liberties from an evangelical perspective, see Andrew T. Walker, *Liberty for All: Defending Everyone's Religious Freedom in a Pluralistic Age* (Grand Rapids: Brazos, 2021).

however, to assume Paul would have given similar counsel to Christians who had been instructed or commanded not to share the message of Jesus. In fact, this very scene plays out with Peter and the other apostles in the book of Acts.

As the earliest Christians were proclaiming the message of Jesus in the months following his ascension, their ministry began to draw a significant following as thousands of people believed the gospel and joined the church. Not surprisingly this displeased those in authority, who determined to arrest the men leading what appeared to be a schismatic movement. Bringing Peter and the apostles before them, they asked, "Didn't we strictly order you not to teach in this name?" To this question the apostles replied, "We must obey God rather than people. . . . We are witnesses of these things [the resurrection and ascension of Jesus]" (Acts 5:27–32). Above all else, those who walked with Jesus during his earthly ministry and were commissioned by him to take his gospel into all the world were determined to let nothing stand in their way of obeying Jesus and fulfilling the Great Commission.

Returning to the printing press, remember that Luther used this tool to launch the Protestant Reformation. Though he hoped his work would lead to reform within the Roman Catholic Church, it ultimately led to renewal efforts outside of the church of Rome and later, if indirectly, within the Roman Catholic Church itself. But consider for a moment the consequences and how history would have been different had Christians like Luther successfully been barred by ecclesial or civil authorities from accessing such technology. Simply put, without access to the printing press, there would have been no Protestant Reformation. The same would likely be true had Luther's words and those of other Reformation leaders been successfully censored prior to publication.[10] And beyond the significant differ-

---

[10] To be clear, extensive efforts *were* made to suppress Luther's writings including having them burned. For a recent and compelling treatment of Luther's complicated and tumultuous life and ministry, see Lyndal Roper, *Martin Luther: Renegade and Prophet* (New York: Random House, 2016). For a broader history of the Protestant Reformation, see Diarmaid MacCulloch, *The Reformation: A History* (New York: Penguin Books, 2005).

ences between the Catholic and Protestant traditions, this thought exercise can also be applied to the Bible itself. What if Christians were barred from accessing such technology to reproduce copies of the Scriptures? What if the Scriptures being copied were subject to external review and approval before publication today?

Censorship and the Great Commission

Clearly, the rules governing how Christians use technology are of great consequence for the health of the church and the progress of the Great Commission. This is hardly limited to the printing press. In the modern age, Christians have made use of all manner of technological innovations to propagate the gospel. This includes such things as the use of aircraft and medicine to pioneer new pathways for international missions. It also includes the adoption of new mediums like radio and television to broadcast sermons and Bible teaching to audiences around the world, such as how the evangelist Billy Graham helped to pioneer the use of broadcast technology for his rallies.[11] More recently, it has included digital innovations such as websites, social media channels, video streaming platforms, podcasts, and even virtual meeting applications like Zoom. Through these various platforms, Christians can reach people with the gospel message, coordinate ministry efforts, provide training and instruction, and even gather virtually with people in various parts of the world. Where once the gospel was inaccessible to an unreached people group until a missionary was finally able to make physical contact, thanks to the internet it is now possible for such peoples to have access to the gospel by merely going online.

Imagine then the consequences of significant restrictions being placed upon the use of these various technologies for religious purposes. Indeed,

---

[11] For more on Billy Graham's use of technology, see Benjamin B. Phillips, "Preaching beyond the Stadium: Billy Graham's Use of Technology for Evangelism." ERLC, January 23, 2019, https://erlc.com/resource-library/articles/preaching -beyond-the-stadium-billy-grahams-use-of-technology-for-evangelism/.

the results of severe restrictions would strike a devastating blow to various Christian endeavors, with global missions suffering a particularly unfortunate setback as a critical mass of the world's population is connecting to the internet. Until recently the internet has served as a broad and open terrain for the dissemination of all kinds of information. Apart from truly dangerous or criminal content, the internet was essentially a freewheeling digital marketplace of ideas. But in recent years the ground has begun to shift. Whether from internal activism or outside pressure, various digital platforms have begun to exercise greater oversight of their users and the content produced and shared via their platforms. While not all such efforts are cause for concern, it is incumbent upon Christians to ensure that such oversight and moderation does not adversely affect their ability to use these technologies to exercise their faith or advance the Great Commission. After all, God calls all Christians to "make disciples," which includes teaching the fullness of the biblical ethic even in the face of social pressure to do otherwise.

Lest this appear to be needless fearmongering, consider the potential challenges such restrictions may pose in light of this limited review of the scope of digital technologies Christians employ today: websites require hosting to remain online, email requires a digital service provider, social media is platform dependent, apps are likewise subject to host approval, and virtual meetings and streaming services are subject to regulation. Even the text messages we send and word processors we utilize are subject to terms of use. This is not to imply that each of the various companies operating these platforms intends to restrict their use for religious purposes. Instead, it is meant to demonstrate the necessity of securing and maintaining robust protections for religious freedom and freedom of expression in the digital age.

Christians are under a mandate from Jesus to see the gospel proclaimed across the globe. In the modern world, digital technology is almost inextricably linked to the fulfillment of that mandate. For Christians, concern for fulfilling the Great Commission necessarily entails concern for the rules governing the accessibility and use of digital technologies. This is why Christians must work to safeguard religious expression and free speech across a broad range of digital mediums.

Religious Freedom, Free Speech, and Human Flourishing

Let's now turn our attention to why every person should support broad protections for free expression. For most Americans, the ideals of religious freedom and freedom of speech are quite familiar. They are enshrined into our nation's laws via the First Amendment to the Constitution, which reads in part, "Congress shall make no law respecting an establishment of religion, or prohibiting the free exercise thereof; or abridging the freedom of speech."[12] But to be sure, it is not merely their esteemed place at the head of the Bill of Rights that makes these freedoms more memorable than most secured by the Constitution. Instead, it is the significance of these rights in our own lives that makes them both memorable and crucial.

Freedom of Religion

Religious freedom is critical for human flourishing because it preserves for all people the right to decide for themselves the things they hold as sacred.[13] As natural law philosopher Robert P. George has observed, "religious freedom means . . . we have the right to ponder life's origins, meaning, and purpose; to explore the deepest questions about human nature, dignity, and destiny; to decide what is to be believed and not to be believed; and, within the limits of justice for all, to comply with what we conscientiously judge to be our religious obligations, and to do so openly, peacefully, and without fear."[14] Human beings are rational creatures, and as such our minds are drawn toward questions of metaphysics. We seek answers to questions about

---

[12] "Constitution of the United States," Library of Congress, https://constitution.congress.gov/constitution/.

[13] For an excellent and recent treatment of religious liberty in the United States from a Christian perspective, see Luke Goodrich, *Free to Believe: The Battle over Religious Liberty in America* (Colorado Springs: Multnomah, 2019).

[14] Robert P. George, "Religious Freedom & Why It Matters: Working in the Spirit of John Leland," *Touchstone*, 2014, https://www.touchstonemag.com/archives/article.php?id=27-03-022-f.

human origins (where did we come from?), our identities (who are we?), meaning of life (what are we here for?), morality (how should we live?), and destiny (where are we going?). When robustly implemented, religious freedom ensures that every person has both the space to consider these and other questions about ultimate reality and the right to meaningfully live in concert with his or her deepest beliefs.

Despite frequent claims to the contrary, religious freedom is not special pleading.[15] Though it enjoys broad support among Christians, it is not exclusively a Christian doctrine. Nor is religious freedom exclusively a religious doctrine. Properly conceived, religious freedom does not seek to privilege any religion or set of beliefs over against any others. Likewise, it does not seek to establish religion by means of civil laws. In other words, religious freedom protects the rights of the atheist just as securely as it protects the rights of the devoutly religious person. As Professor George argues, "It is therefore essential that freedom of religion include the right to hold any belief or none at all; to change one's beliefs and religious affiliation; to bear witness to one's beliefs in public as well as private, corporately as well as individually; and to act on one's religiously inspired convictions about justice and the common good in carrying out the duties of citizenship." Further, he contends, "it is vital that religious liberty's full protections be extended to those whose answers to life's deepest questions reject belief in the transcendent."[16] This is consistent with Article 18 of the Universal Declaration of Human Rights (UDHR), which insists, "Everyone has the right to freedom of thought, conscience and religion; this right includes freedom to change his religion or belief, and freedom, either alone or in community with others and in public or private, to manifest his religion or belief in teaching, practice, worship and observance."[17]

---

[15] Nor do laws supporting religious freedom give "license to discriminate" or act as a cover for bigotry. See, for example, Andrew T. Walker, "4 Reasons Why Religious Liberty Laws Don't Discriminate," *TGC*, April 2016, https://www.thegospelcoalition .org/article/three-reasons-why-religious-liberty-laws-dont-discriminate/.

[16] George, "Religious Freedom & Why It Matters."

[17] "Universal Declaration of Human Rights," United Nations, https://www.un .org/en/about-us/universal-declaration-of-human-rights.

In practice, religious freedom allows individuals to determine and exercise their faith individually and corporately, publicly and privately. At the same time, religious freedom also protects individuals from any manner of state-sanctioned coercion to adopt or adhere to religious beliefs or practices. It is a vital tool in cultivating a flourishing society because it ensures that the beliefs individuals hold at the core of their beings are respected as they seek to live in harmony with those beliefs within their communities. Many arguments can be marshalled in support of religious freedom, but we will focus here on two.

Human Dignity

Religious freedom should enjoy universal support because of its respect for the nature of the human person. Whether it rests upon religious or rational grounds, arguments in support of human rights center upon human dignity.[18] Consider these words from the Second Vatican Council's *Declaration on Religious Freedom*:

> A sense of the dignity of the human person has been impressing itself more and more deeply on the consciousness of contemporary man . . . and the demand is increasingly made that men should act on their own judgment, enjoying and making use of a responsible freedom, not driven by coercion but motivated by a sense of duty. The demand is likewise made that constitutional limits should be set to the powers of government, in order that there may be no encroachment on the rightful freedom of the person and of associations. This demand for freedom in human society chiefly regards

---

[18] Christians ground their beliefs about human dignity in the doctrine of the *imago Dei*—the belief that all human beings are created in the image and likeness of God and thus have intrinsic and inalienable dignity (Gen 1:26–27). Jason Thacker provides a helpful discussion of the application of this doctrine to issues related to technology in *The Age of AI: Artificial Intelligence and the Future of Humanity* (Grand Rapids: Zondervan, 2020), 17–20, 46–49.

the quest for the values proper to the human spirit. It regards, in the first place, the free exercise of religion in society.[19]

By our nature, human beings have agency and rational capacity. Together, our minds and bodies are equipped to receive and analyze information, make informed decisions, and take deliberate action. Of course, this includes quotidian acts such as performing household chores, engaging in conversation, accomplishing work-related tasks, and countless other daily activities. But as reflected above, it also includes much more significant exercises such as forming communities, raising families, and considering questions about ultimate reality such as seeking answers to the nature and purpose of our existence.

Respecting human dignity requires the preservation of freedom for every person to act based upon their beliefs, desires, and best judgments.[20] Note again that grounding religious freedom in the dignity of the human person transcends any specific religious beliefs or faith commitments. As the preamble to the UDHR—a document eschewing any specific religious or cultural beliefs—states, "recognition of the inherent dignity and of the equal and inalienable rights of all members of the human family is the foundation of freedom, justice and peace in the world."[21] From whatever standpoint, it is apparent that honoring the dignity of others requires respecting their right to make their own judgments about things sacred and

---

[19] This argument is set forth in *Dignitatis humanea*, approved on December 7, 1965. "DIGNITATIS HUMANAE," The Vatican, https://www.vatican.va/archive /hist_councils/ii_vatican_council/documents/vat-ii_decl_19651207_dignitatis -humanae_en.html.

[20] This does not give license to perpetrate injustice under the guise of faith. Religious freedom does not constitute an unbridled endorsement of any conceivable act. Instead, it promotes broad protections for individuals to live in accordance with their beliefs, drawing boundaries for such only where it inappropriately infringes on the rights and liberties of others. For a historical overview that gives definition to religious freedom in the Christian tradition, see Robert Louis Wilken, *Liberty in the Things of God: The Christian Origins of Religious Freedom* (New Haven, CT: Yale University Press, 2019).

[21] "Universal Declaration of Human Rights," United Nations, https://www.un .org/en/about-us/universal-declaration-of-human-rights.

transcendent. Conversely, failing to allow for such constitutes a violation of that person's dignity.

The Nature of Faith

Religious freedom should also enjoy broad support because of the nature of faith itself.[22] For faith to be genuine, it cannot be coerced. Similarly, genuine faith cannot be destroyed by obstruction or persecution. Because of the nature of faith, it is of no use for governments to seek to impose religion upon citizens nor to deny citizens the right to practice religion as fits their understanding. Indeed, such endeavors never achieve desirable outcomes.[23] As the preamble to the UDHR asserts, throughout world history "disregard and contempt for human rights have resulted in barbarous acts which have outraged the conscience of mankind."[24] Religious freedom is both vital and necessary because true faith will always find expression—even in the face of oppression and persecution. Our deepest beliefs reside at the core of our beings (Prov 4:23). They are not ancillary to our identities but part of the very fabric of our lives.

My own Baptist tradition has supported religious freedom since its inception on these very grounds. It is because of the nature of faith that Baptists oppose any manner of coercion or government intervention in matters of religion. As the Baptist Faith and Message (2000) puts it:

> The gospel of Christ contemplates spiritual means alone for the pursuit of its ends. The state has no right to impose penalties for religious opinions of any kind. The state has no right to impose taxes for the support of any form of religion. A free church in a free state is the Christian ideal, and this implies the right of free and unhindered access to God on the part of all men, and the right

---

[22] Though this is technically a theological argument, based on its reasoning it should also gain significant purchase with atheists and secularists alike.

[23] Cf. Noel D. Johnson and Mark Koyama, *Persecution and Toleration: The Long Road to Religious Freedom* (New York: Cambridge University Press, 2019).

[24] "Universal Declaration of Human Rights," United Nations, https://www.un .org/en/about-us/universal-declaration-of-human-rights.

to form and propagate opinions in the sphere of religion without interference by the civil power.[25]

Those words are significant because Baptists—as a movement birthed amid intense persecution—speak to the need for religious liberty with historical credibility. From the early seventeenth century through the American Revolution, Baptists in England and North America endured fines, public beatings, and imprisonments for practicing their faith. The outcome of that experience only strengthened their resolve to fight against religious oppression and to promote religious freedom.[26] And though their primary rationale was spiritual, it was also practical. As the early Baptist layman Leonard Busher—whose own pastor, Thomas Helwys, was imprisoned for leading a Baptist congregation in defiance of the king—wrote, "as kings and bishops cannot command the wind, so they cannot command faith. . . . You may force men to church against their consciences, but they will believe as they did afore."[27] Busher's words, first penned in 1614, still ring true today. Religious freedom not only upholds the dignity of the human person but reflects the nature of faith itself. For both reasons, it is critical that religious exercise remain protected.

Freedom of Speech

The arguments in support of free expression—freedom of speech in particular—are naturally bolstered by the preceding discussion about religious freedom. For this reason, we will not dwell too deeply in defense of

---

[25] From article 17, "Religious Liberty," The Baptist Faith and Message 2000, https://bfm.sbc.net/bfm2000/#xvii-religious-liberty.

[26] In a famous speech delivered on the steps of the United States Capitol in 1920, the legendary Baptist pastor George W. Truett affirmed, "Baptists have one consistent record concerning liberty throughout all their long and eventful history. They have never been a party to oppression of conscience. They have forever been the unwavering champions of liberty, both religious and civil." George W. Truett, "Baptists and Religious Liberty," *Baptist History and Heritage* 33.1 (1998): 66–85.

[27] Leon McBeth, *A Sourcebook for Baptist Heritage* (Nashville: Broadman, 1990), 73.

free speech here. Still, it is worth underscoring the *value* of free speech. Consider whether there is any benefit if a person is unhindered in believing as they see fit but prohibited in expressing those beliefs. To deny such a right is to trample upon the dignity of the individual and to deny the potential value of his or her contribution to the broader community. In his famous work *On Liberty*, the English philosopher John Stuart Mill put forward a remarkably strong defense of free speech making just this case. As Mill argued:

> The peculiar evil of silencing the expression of opinion is, that it is robbing the human race; posterity as well as the existing generation; those who dissent from the opinion, still more than those who hold it. If the opinion is right, they are deprived of the opportunity of exchanging error for truth: if wrong, they lose, what is almost as great a benefit, the clearer perception and livelier impression of truth, produced by its collision with error.[28]

Mill likewise grounded his arguments in the dignity of the human person. As he rightly asserted, to respect the dignity of all persons it is necessary to allow them to freely share their opinions, even those rightly deemed distasteful or unpopular, so long as their speech does not cause actual harm to others. In other words, "If all mankind minus one were of one opinion, and only one person were of the contrary opinion, mankind would be no more justified in silencing that one person than he, if he had the power, would be justified in silencing mankind."[29]

There is little to debate about the legitimacy of speech that expresses popular views on a given subject. Indeed, such views rarely risk the perils of censorship. Free speech exists to protect minority opinions. As Mill

---

[28] John Stuart Mill, *On Liberty, Utilitarianism, and Other Essays* (Oxford, UK: Oxford University Press, 2015), 19.

[29] It's worth noting that Mill's "harm principle" is narrowly construed. According to Mill's principle, only speech that can be directly shown to result in the actual infringement upon the rights of another individual would be restricted. John Stuart Mill, *On Liberty, Utilitarianism, and Other Essays* (Oxford, UK: Oxford University Press, 2015), 19.

pointed out, minority opinions are of great value to the human community. Imagine, for example, a world that had successfully repressed the ideas of Galileo or Copernicus, Martin Luther or Martin Luther King Jr., or Peter and the apostle Paul. The fact that significant efforts were made to silence these voices only demonstrates the point. Free speech is vital for human flourishing—for the sake of human dignity, as well as truth, progress, and innovation. If human beings have the dignity of personhood, they must be afforded the right to form their own views and freely express those thoughts or beliefs without the threat of state-sanctioned censorship or harassment.

The Challenge of the Digital Age

For religious freedom and free expression, the great challenge of the digital age is the movement of the traditional public square into private hands. While the internet itself may remain open to all, the digital platforms through which public discourse is now mediated online are owned by private companies. In recent years, many questions have arisen concerning the actions of these nascent technological marketplaces and social media companies to regulate content on their platforms. These questions include concerns about the stifling of free speech; the role of government in regulating private corporations like Amazon, Meta, and Twitter; and the extent to which such companies are free to determine and enforce these policies on their own. In the United States, the robust protections afforded by the First Amendment are a vital bulwark in protecting religious exercise and free speech, but they only serve to protect these freedoms from government intrusion.[30] A public square in private hands raises significant questions about censorship, free speech, and religious expression. To better assess these issues, let us consider two recent events that garnered much attention as case studies on threats to religion and free expression in the digital age.

---

[30] For more on First Amendment doctrine and its connection to the digital public square, see chapter 8.

Amazon Delists Ryan Anderson's Book on Transgenderism[31]

In late February 2021, conservative scholar and president of the Ethics and Public Policy Center, Ryan T. Anderson, received an online message from a would-be reader that his book *When Harry Became Sally: Responding to the Transgender Moment* was no longer available for purchase on Amazon.com.[32] The book had been pulled by Amazon, without any prior notification to the author or publisher, for violating Amazon's offensive content policy (though Amazon would not clarify the reason for the move for several days). Days later, after considerable public outcry, the company released a statement about the book being removed from the marketplace. Amazon said it reserved the right not to sell certain products that violated its content guidelines. The statement claimed, "All retailers make decisions about what selection they choose to offer and we do not take selection decisions lightly."[33] According to Amazon's content guidelines for books, they "don't sell certain content including content that we determine is hate speech, promotes the abuse or sexual exploitation of children, contains pornography, glorifies rape or pedophilia, advocates terrorism, or other material we deem inappropriate or offensive."[34] It is worth noting the open-ended nature of this policy and its application in this instance.

Anderson's work challenged the premises of transgender ideology and highlighted uncomfortable realities about the mental, emotional, and relational difficulties people who identify as transgender often face. When the

---

[31] A version of this section was adapted with permission from an article co-authored with Jason Thacker for the Ethics and Religious Liberty Commission, "Should Amazon be able to ban books?" https://erlc.com/resource-library/articles/should-amazon-be-able-to-ban-books/.

[32] Ryan T. Anderson, *When Harry Became Sally: Responding to the Transgender Moment* (New York: Encounter Books, 2019).

[33] Jeffrey A. Trachtenberg, "Amazon Faces Questions about the Removal of Book by Conservative Author," *WSJ*, February 2021, https://www.wsj.com/articles/republican-senators-send-letter-to-jeff-bezos-asking-why-amazon-pulled-book-by-conservative-author-11614212331.

[34] "Content Guidelines for Books," Amazon.com, accessed December 15, 2021, https://www.amazon.com/gp/help/customer/display.html?nodeId=201995150.

book was originally removed by Amazon, search results recommended other works on transgenderism but from a very different ideological perspective, including a work written specifically as a rebuttal to Anderson's book. As of this writing, more than a year later, *When Harry Became Sally* has yet to be relisted. This clear example of censorship is deeply unfortunate, because in his book, Anderson thoughtfully responds to many questions that have arisen out of the transgender movement and offers a scientific, philosophical, and ethical treatment of trans ideology's inherent redefinition of human nature and repudiation of biological realities about sex and gender. In an essay about Amazon's action to remove the book, Anderson noted that the book was praised by "the former psychiatrist-in-chief at Johns Hopkins Hospital, a longtime psychology professor at NYU, a professor of medical ethics at Columbia Medical School, a professor of psychological and brain sciences at Boston University, a professor of neurobiology at the University of Utah, a distinguished professor at Harvard Law School, an eminent legal philosopher at Oxford, and a professor of jurisprudence at Princeton."[35]

Amazon's removal of Anderson's book from its marketplace does not appear to involve issues of free speech under the First Amendment.[36] But even so, the removal of a popular book under this overly broad—and easily abused—"inappropriate or offensive" policy is deeply distressing. Clearly, Anderson's work was censored because of the views it expressed about human sexuality—views that are in lockstep with the beliefs of millions of Christians, Jews, Muslims, and others in the United States. Digital content moderation or removal often leads immediately to claims that a person's freedom of speech or even freedom of religion is being violated. However, such appeals fail to recognize that the First Amendment specifically protects individuals from

---

[35] Ryan T. Anderson, "When Amazon Erased My Book," First Things, February 2021, https://www.firstthings.com/web-exclusives/2021/02/when-amazon-erased -my-book.

[36] Nor does Anderson's case specifically involve religious discrimination. As he has made clear, his arguments were based in philosophy, reason, and empirical data, rather than religion. It's also worth noting the book is currently sold by other online retailers, such as Barnes and Noble, independent bookstores, and through his publisher's website.

the overreaching hands of government, not from content policies of private companies. Still, there is no doubt that Amazon sought to wield its influence to shape public opinion on a crucial cultural and policy concern by silencing dissenting voices. Given Amazon's enormous size and market share, such actions could potentially result in inquiries about antitrust or lead to federal oversight, which may override Amazon's ability to set its own content policies.

Private company or not, Amazon was wrong to remove Anderson's book from the marketplace. Not only did the company violate its own stated policy of including content it deems objectionable, but it did so to deny users access to a countervailing argument to its preferred ideology of human sexuality. No one needs to be protected from a robust and informed public debate. As Alan Jacobs responded, "Amazon clearly believe[s] there is only one reason to read a book. You read a book because you agree with it and want it to confirm what you already believe."[37] If the rise of the digital age brings forth a future where only certain "acceptable" ideas will be tolerated, then the future is bleak indeed.

At this point it seems unlikely that Amazon will restore the book to the marketplace. But regardless of this particular outcome, it is clear we are living in a new era of human history—one where powerful and often unrivaled technology companies wield enormous amounts of power over our public discourse. For Christians, the proper response is not fear or panic but to work to maintain an open digital public square. We can engage these pressing concerns with confidence, knowing that while our beliefs may not always be popular or fashionable, they nevertheless correspond to reality and lead to human flourishing.

Twitter Bans Donald Trump

In early January 2021,[38] Twitter suspended the forty-fifth president of the United States, Donald Trump, from its platform for violating the company's

---

[37] Alan Jacobs, "Damnatio memoriae," *Snakes and Ladders*, https://blog.ayjay .org/damnatio-memoriae/.

[38] A version of this section was adapted with permission from an article co-authored with Jason Thacker for the Ethics and Religious Liberty Commission,

stated community policies related to inciting violence and spreading false information.[39] The suspension was announced two days after the attack on the United States Capitol on Wednesday, January 6, following a rally on the National Mall hosted by the president and his key supporters. The protest, which culminated in significant violence and rioting, was organized in response to the congressional certification of the results of the 2020 presidential election.

As the Associated Press reported at the time, "Twitter has long given Trump and other world leaders broad exemptions from its rules against personal attacks, hate speech and other behaviors."[40] But following the election in November 2020, many of President Trump's tweets were labeled for promoting conspiracy theories alleging election fraud and the stealing of votes as well as encouraging violence. Twitter utilized these warning and fact-check labels to inform the public of the potential misinformation, while the content remained available online due to the compelling public interest of having direct access to communication from the president of the United States.

But as the Capitol Police and National Guard were clearing the Capitol Building once the protests and rioting were quelled, Twitter disabled the president's account temporarily and deleted certain tweets deemed as encouraging further violence.[41] The temporary suspension also came with a warning that continued violation of Twitter's policies might lead to a

---

"Understanding Twitter suspensions and the need for consistent policies," https://erlc.com/resource-library/articles/understanding-twitter-suspensions-and-the-need-for-consistent-policies/.

[39] See Twitter, "Permanent suspension of @realDonaldTrump," Twitter, January 2021, https://blog.twitter.com/en_us/topics/company/2020/suspension.

[40] Tali Arbel, "Twitter bans Trump, citing risk of violent incitement," Associated Press, January 2021, https://apnews.com/article/election-2020-donald-trump-media-michael-flynn-social-media-f41b11060d7703e3a3136ddb5eefa055.

[41] See Bobby Allyn, "Twitter Locks Trump's Account, Warns of 'Permanent Suspension' If Violations Continue," NPR, January 2021, https://www.npr.org/sections/congress-electoral-college-tally-live-updates/2021/01/06/954190994/twitter-locks-trumps-account-warns-of-permanent-suspension-if-violations-continue.

permanent ban from the platform. The account was reenabled on Thursday, January 7. But due to continued policy violations by the president, his account @RealDonaldTrump was permanently suspended the next evening.

Many prominent technology critics, including several lawmakers, journalists, and public figures, had long called for social media platforms to take a firmer stance on President Trump's violations of their content policies. But until January 2021, Twitter and other social media platforms, such as Meta (Facebook), allowed the president to continue posting due to the compelling public interest surrounding his speech given the gravity and responsibilities of the Oval Office. But after repeated violations of these policies, including the violent attack on the US Capitol during an official congressional session, Twitter took the unprecedented step of permanently suspending the president's personal account.[42]

While some celebrated the decision, many others have since questioned the wisdom and timing of the suspension. Indeed, the potential ramifications of banning the sitting president of the United States from using an online platform are uniquely difficult to fathom. Again, much of the concern lies in the fact that these social media platforms have become ubiquitous in our society. In our digital age, social media sites now represent a primary vehicle of communication. Twitter, for example, serves as a news platform for many users and is a significant conduit of real-time information, including the live reporting that took place during the assault on the Capitol on January 6.

Every social media platform has its own set of community standards, policies, or rules to govern user activity. The implementation of community policies and content moderation is actually encouraged by Section 230 of the 1996 Communication Decency Act—a bipartisan piece of legislation designed to *promote* the growth of the still-emerging internet in the

---

[42] The official suspension only applied to @RealDonaldTrump, and not official White House accounts such as @POTUS or @WhiteHouse. However, because Twitter does not allow users with banned accounts to operate alternate accounts, some tweets were also removed from @POTUS after the president chose to post to that account following his suspension.

mid-1990s.[43] Section 230 gives internet companies a liability shield for online user content—meaning *users,* and not the platforms themselves, are responsible for the content of posts—in exchange for enacting "good faith" measures to remove objectionable content and make the internet a safer place for our society.

Online content moderation is a difficult and thorny ethical issue. Such cases are beyond the scope of the First Amendment because online communication is mediated via private companies. But because social media has become a massive and integral part of our lives, the rules governing online speech and expression are of great consequence for the health of our society. To be sure, an internet or social media platform without any type of moderation or rules would quickly devolve into a dangerous environment filled with misinformation, and interminable unfiltered or illegal content. Even with such rules, it is undeniable that social media has been utilized in ways leading to real-world harm. However, in the case of this particular suspension, Twitter believed that a line had been crossed when President Trump's speech endangered members of the public as well as law enforcement officers and elected officials by inciting physical violence and destruction. In response, Twitter determined the threat of further violence and physical harm outweighed the compelling public interest, which is the rationale they had used previously to justify the president's account remaining active and his posted content remaining online even in violation of its policies.

As news of the suspension broke, many rightfully questioned how this type of action by a social media giant could also be used to silence views outside of the mainstream such as those of conservative Christians. This is a legitimate concern based on the unequal and often controversial application of content moderation by various digital platforms. Undoubtedly, action of this kind opens the door for further censorship. The most alarming element is not the suspension of the president itself, but the inconsistency of Twitter's policy enforcement across the board. While the company is within its rights to enforce suspensions due to policy violations, Twitter had also

---

[43] For more on Section 230 and other US technology policy issues, see chapter 3 by Nathan Leamer and chapter 5 by David French.

allowed posts from accounts representing authoritarian leaders around the world, such as from Chinese and Iranian governments, that clearly violate the same policies used to ban the president's account.[44] The oppressive and authoritarian regimes promoted by these accounts incite and perpetrate devastating violence and human rights abuses beyond anything we've witnessed firsthand in the United States.[45]

For example, in China, over one million Uyghur Muslims have been detained, persecuted, and even sterilized in "reeducation camps." But social media platforms often turned a blind eye to these atrocities. Deceptive tweets from Chinese officials have often failed to be restricted, or labeled as potential misinformation, yet nearly every tweet by President Trump between the November 2020 election and his permanent suspension on January 8, 2021, had been labeled with warnings about misinformation. However reasonable or necessary Twitter's decision in this instance may have been, its inconsistency in content moderation is harmful to our social fabric, which is sustained by ideals like trust and equality. It is impossible to maintain public trust while overlooking such egregious violations or selectively enforcing the company's own rules.

Moral courage and responsibility require the equal application and enforcement of these policies. Taking difficult but necessary action is only meaningful if such actions are carried out consistently. If leaders at Twitter felt compelled to curtail the president's speech in the name of public safety, it is only right that they follow suit by banning the accounts of other known offenders, including officials within the Chinese Communist Party—the single greatest human rights abusers on the planet.

---

[44] Since banning President Trump's account, Twitter began to take some action to restrict or ban certain accounts after intense criticism. See, for example, this permanent ban on an account linked to Iran's supreme leader, Ayatollah Ali Khamenei. Dustin Jones, "Twitter Bans Account Linked to Iran's Supreme Leader," January 2021, https://www.npr.org/2021/01/22/959736537/twitter-bans-account-linked -to-irans-supreme-leader.

[45] For more on the authoritarian abuses of technology, see chapter 11 by Olivia Enos.

The Future of the Public Square

The two examples presented here helpfully demonstrate the challenges that lie ahead for free expression and religious freedom in the public square. Christians are especially wise to be vigilant about matters related to censorship in this current moment. Because technology companies are not technically bound by the rules of the First Amendment, it is critical for Christians and other advocates of free expression to act to entreat these independent entities: (1) to recognize the immense power they hold as mediators of public discourse; and (2) to protect and promote the free and open exchange of ideas across their various platforms. While these companies should certainly act to curtail speech that directly threatens or elicits physical harm,[46] it is likewise vital that these new gatekeepers of the public square ensure actors and ideas of all kinds are able to be robustly represented and debated across various digital platforms.

These two examples also demonstrate how easily large technology companies could become enforcers of moral and cultural orthodoxies. Whether it is religious or ethical views a given company may find objectionable, or the political or ideological views it may determine to oppose, the possibility of having giant private corporations silence or stifle dissenting views and voices is of the deepest concern for the future of our society. The answer to such concerns is indeed complicated. Certainly, the preferred remedy is for private companies to independently commit to carefully and consistently enact broad measures to protect all kinds of speech and viewpoints. Less desirable alternatives include government intervention to regulate the policies of various technology-based companies, or the continued balkanization of public life as alternate platforms proliferate to address issues of religious or ideological censorship among extant companies. Christians will doubtless find a means of thriving despite any limitations imposed upon religious expression or free speech in the digital age—indeed Jesus promised as much when he committed to build his

---

[46] For an expanded discussion on physical violence and hate crimes, see chapter 7 by Brooke Medina.

church (Matt 16:18). However, insofar as Christians can influence policies on these matters, they should unapologetically speak in defense of robust protections for religious freedom and free expression, not merely for their own sake but for the good of all.

Conclusion

As we stare into a digital future, evangelicals like me have enormous cause for optimism. At the same time, we also have serious reasons for concern. Already, the internet and other digital technologies have served to advance the cause of the gospel and further efforts to fulfill the Great Commission in ways unimaginable only a few decades ago. At the same time, there is good reason to be concerned about hostility manifesting toward certain religious, moral, and political actors and viewpoints from leading platforms in the tech industry. If anything, opposition to religious viewpoints and restrictions upon specific types of speech should only galvanize evangelicals and others to act with urgency to see these concerns addressed and remedied. Free speech benefits everyone, as does religious freedom. They are vital tools for cultivating flourishing communities. If the internet is to remain a digital public square, it will only remain such if the online marketplace of ideas remains open to all.

7

Defining the Limits of Hate Speech and Violence

Dignity, Truth, and Speech in the Digital Public Square

Brooke Medina

Members of society, regardless of age, are more digitally connected than ever before. Decades from now, digital migrants—those who lived in a world during the advent of the internet—will no longer exist. The now ubiquitous reliance on digital tools and mediums for business and entertainment have driven a wedge among those who embrace the rapid dominance of tech and those who view it as a necessary evil. Living during this exciting but often complex period in history brings its own set of challenges, not the least of which is the question of how to conduct oneself in the digital square. Questions surrounding what should and should not be allowed on an online platform quickly become messy and complicated as one tries to find some semblance of coherence in a digitally complex ecosystem.

This is most clearly seen in the debate over free speech and censorship. What is deemed as problematic speech, including hate speech, is shaped by cultural norms and governments alike. It is every bit as informed by mores as it is by law. With the advent of the printing press in 1440, speech became increasingly democratized, and, as a result, in some cases, a threat to the status quo. Eric Berkowitz, writing in *Dangerous Ideas*, notes that "once printing gave all strata of society access to words and images, modern censorship began in earnest."[1] Following the Protestant Reformation, which began with Martin Luther's historically defiant act of publishing his *95 Theses,* the Roman Catholic Church, under Pope Paul IV, published the first ever *Index of Forbidden Books.*[2] With the proliferation of information and opinion, the question of what types of speech should be tolerated within the public square has been hotly debated.

For Christians, the tension between the beautiful but imperfect reality we live in and the hopeful anticipation of future restoration offers us an invitation when considering the challenges of speech in the digital public square. There exists an opportunity for believers to exercise wisdom in the still-evolving digital landscape by creating and advocating for policy solutions that are rooted in a desire to honor the dignity of all while safeguarding the rights and responsibilities that come with free expression.

Our Bifurcated Lives

One of the primary concerns about life online is that the historically relied-upon accountability structures inherent in face-to-face interactions are often missing. Customs and visual cues that govern in-person exchanges serve as a natural feedback loop and reward system for us, but in a landscape that is typically devoid of such normative guardrails, others will naturally emerge to guide these on-screen interactions. We know that in-person engagements

---

[1] Eric Berkowitz, *Dangerous Ideas: A Brief History of Censorship in the West, From the Ancients to Fake News* (Boston: Beacon, 2021), 11.

[2] *Index of Forbidden Books, 1559.* http://www.freespeechhistory.com/timeline/1559-the-index-of-forbidden-books/.

have the capacity to quickly reap consequences and benefits that can affect our careers, relationships, and reputations. As a result, we often self-censor so as to interact with others in an appropriate manner. But what happens when these helpful guardrails are not present?

The emergence of hate-speech policies and legislation across the public and private sectors were created with the intention of establishing rules of engagement and instituting punitive measures for those who violated them. Particularly within the governmental sphere, these rules can be an attempt to cater to a constituency/class that legislators and bureaucrats view as warranting protected status. Although the United States protects online speech from government intrusion (barring a few exceptions, such as libel and fraud), many other countries are less liberal with their speech protections. Yet, even where the government refuses to interfere with speech, private entities are free to do so.[3]

This freedom has led to large American tech companies, universities, and social media platforms creating their own hate-speech policies within their terms of service or community standards. In some cases, the goal of such policies has been to create a safe, welcoming environment for individuals to be a part of an online community where they can freely discuss virtually any topic. In other instances, such policies have served to isolate and marginalize the voices of individuals who do not share the same ideological values as the company whose platform they are using.

Because the digital public square is often the first touchpoint many of us have with new brands, institutions, communities, and ideas, reasonable rules of conduct are expected, and in many cases, welcome. Although many online interactions are mundane and harmless, the degree of degradation some are subjected to has resulted in growing calls for regulation and policy reforms to create a safer, tamer internet. The goal of creating online spaces where people are shielded from the most egregious verbal attacks, able to log off each day with their dignity still intact, is a good one.

Yet many questions remain: Whose job is it to police politeness and propriety online? How will they devise rules and arbitrate accusations? How do we

---

[3] For more on this discussion, see chapter 6 by Joshua B. Wester.

resolve the naturally occurring tensions between one person's free expression and another's offense? A growing tide of illiberalism has been building across the West, and history has shown that authoritarianism and speech restrictions go hand in hand. This sobering reality should be enough to make anyone approach questions of defining the limits of online hate speech and violence with humility. The internet has often been likened to the Wild West in that it is devoid of the stabilizing norms and societal expectations that accompany most civilized in-person interactions. The "thick" civil society that has long governed our exchanges with other individuals does not automatically transfer to the digital world where people have the liberty of anonymity and the freedom of mocking, jeering, and lying about others with carte blanche.

There's no denying the internet's Wild West persona has created conditions that have made it difficult and painful for many. According to a 2021 Pew research survey, 41 percent of American adults say they've experienced online harassment, with 25 percent stating they've been subjected to more severe forms of harassment, such as physical threats, sexual harassment, and stalking.[4] Women in particular view online harassment as a problem.[5] The Pew research found that women are three times more likely than men to experience sexual harassment online, whereas men are more likely than women to have said they experienced other forms of harassment, such as "offensive name or having someone trying to purposefully embarrass them."

The gender disparities in online harassment were made clear in a controlled study conducted by the University of Maryland's Electrical Engineering and Computer Department. Researchers found that "users with female names received on average one hundred 'malicious private messages,' which the study defined as 'sexually explicit or threatening language,' for every four received by male users. User gender had a 'significant impact' on the number of malicious private messages sent."[6] Sexual harassment and

---

[4] Emily A. Vogels, "The State of Online Harassment," Pew Research, January 2021, https://www.pewresearch.org/internet/2021/01/13/the-state-of-online-harassment/.

[5] Vogels, "The State of Online Harassment."

[6] Danielle Keats Citron, *Hate Crimes in Cyberspace* (Boston: Harvard University Press, 2014), 14.

its role in hate speech policies should not be overlooked, as the humiliation and embarrassment that often accompany such speech affects an individual's willingness to engage with others in both the in-person and digital public squares.[7] So long as humans exercise domain over the digital public square, it will be a place vulnerable to corruption. Yet, even so, there are opportunities to create life-giving interactions, and it is that belief that should inform an approach to creating hate speech policies.

In 1880, Abraham Kuyper, a Dutch theologian and politician, said, "There is not a square inch in the whole domain of our human existence over which Christ, who is Sovereign over all, does not cry, Mine!"[8] God's all-encompassing sovereignty also includes the digital tools and platforms we use today. Wisdom, as well as love for our neighbor, implores us to find ways to bring truth, goodness, and beauty to our world, of which the digital landscape is a part. This means understanding how policies, including those related to speech, affect our online interactions with each other. Christians ought to adopt a spirit of grace and truth (Eph 4:15) as we communicate to a world hungry for both. Ultimately, a decision to thoughtfully consider and construct online speech policies is an invitation to celebrate human dignity and explore how to love our digital neighbors well. The words of the prophet Jeremiah carry relevance for us today: "But seek the welfare of the city where I have sent you" (Jer 29:7 ESV). This verse provides an opportunity to consider what seeking the welfare of our neighbors in the digital public square looks like.

Around-the-clock social media use in an increasingly isolated society, where more individuals live alone, and fewer spend time in physical workplaces with others, has fostered the conditions for a new landscape of engagement to emerge. Although there are discernible generational differences when it comes to how we interact, work, and socialize online, across

---

[7] See Marjan Nadim and Audun Fladmoe, "Silencing Women? Gender and Online Harassment," July 30, 2019, https://journals.sagepub.com/doi/full/10.1177/0894439319865518.

[8] Roger Henderson, "Kuyper's Inch," Pro Rege, March 2008, https://digitalcollections.dordt.edu/cgi/viewcontent.cgi?article=1380&context=pro_rege#:~:text=There%20is%20not%20a%20square%20inch%20in%20the%20whole%20domain,course%2C%20in%20the%20Dutch%20language.

the spectrum there is little debate that the norms of the internet are much more laissez-faire than face-to-face exchanges. The perception is that our words, likes, and retweets cost us less than if we were to attack or endorse the same statements in the "real" world. The ease and swiftness one person can engage with another, often absent the useful in-person social norms of decorum and deference, makes self-restraint all the more valuable.

The time we spend online is *real* time and the people we are engaging with are real people. What we do behind the screen *is* part of the real world, and the costs associated with it are real. As our platforms and apps have become more sophisticated and integral to our twenty-first-century conception of community, demands for social media reforms have increased. The calls for policing online behavior take on a variety of shapes, ranging from removing the visibility of how many "likes" a post garners to outright government regulation at the state and federal levels.

Psychological Effects of Online Living

Despite the First Amendment's protections, private enterprises, including publicly funded universities, can levy their own speech codes. The term "safe spaces" has worked its way into academic parlance as higher education has sought to lead the way to define hate speech as broadly as possible. Born out of a desire to provide emotional protection to individuals, particularly those battling mental health challenges, private institutions, including social media companies and colleges, have sought to accommodate their customers and consumers' desire for safety.

Unfortunately, whether attending college in-person or online, the excessive attempts to mitigate emotional turmoil might have a counterproductive effect as an individual's psychological coping tools atrophy and they are no longer expected to exert agency. This deprives a person of the opportunity to learn how to navigate life's inevitable hurts. Authors Greg Lukianoff and Jonathan Haidt have chronicled the alarming rise in mental health and suicide cases among teenagers and young adults. One of the latest ways in which speech is being threatened is through the "medicalization" of censorship where "the rationale for speech codes and speaker disinvitations [is] becoming medicalized," with students claiming "certain kinds of speech . . . interfered with their *ability to function*."[9] The rise in mental health challenges, particularly among Gen Z—those born between 1997 and 2012—is of unique concern given their ubiquitous use of social media and the ongoing research related to psychological harms levied by a life lived online. Between 2004 and 2019 there was a 10 percent increase in girls aged twelve to seventeen who said they had experienced a major depressive episode in the past year, increasing the overall percentage of the sample group from 13 to 23 percent.[10]

In addition—or in tandem—to these concerning statistics are the questions surrounding the long-term impact of the COVID-19 pandemic and government-mandated shutdowns on the mental health of young people. These effects will continue to materialize over the next decade, but early reports paint an excruciatingly grim picture of mental health among the public as a whole and youth in particular. A 2021 Kaiser Family Foundation report found that 56 percent of young adults experienced symptoms of anxiety or depressive disorder during the pandemic. Contrast that to those over sixty-five years, which stood at 29 percent. Without a doubt, online bullying and harassment is contributing to the rise in mental health challenges.[11]

The Subjectivity of Hate Speech

Defining the limits of online hate speech and violence is a titan-sized task. However, for those who have been, or will be, subjected to cruel, even

---

[9] Greg Lukianoff, Adam Goldstein, and Ryne Weiss, "Catching Up with 'Coddling' Part Three: 'Right-on-Left' Censorship Is Still a Thing on Campus," *The Eternally Radical Idea*, August 18, 2020, https://www.thefire.org/catching-up-with-coddling-part-three-right-on-left-censorship-is-still-a-thing-on-campus/.

[10] Greg Lukianoff and Jonathan Haidt, "'Coddling' the Afterword Part 1: Gen Z's Mental Health Continues to Deteriorate," *The Eternally Radical Idea*, September 16, 2021, https://www.thefire.org/coddling-the-afterword-part-1-gen-zs-mental-health-continues-to-deteriorate/, fig. 141.

[11] See Steven A. Sumner, Brock Ferguson, Brian Bason, "Association of Online Risk Factors with Subsequent Youth Suicide-Related Behaviors in the US," JAMA Network, September 20, 2021, https://jamanetwork.com/journals/jamanetworkopen/fullarticle/2784337.

criminal treatment online, as well as those who have been deplatformed, ostracized, or otherwise penalized for speaking their unpopular opinions that challenge mainstream thought on a given subject, it is an essential task.

The spectrum of what constitutes "hate speech" online is incredibly broad and often subjective. On some social media platforms, simply using a person's biological pronouns when referring to them is deemed hate speech.[12] Yet on the other end of this spectrum are individuals who have been subjected to horrifying and humiliating lies or attacks related to their character, sexuality, ethics, and more. When digital companies and private organizations blur the lines, rolling everything a person might deem unpleasant into an overly broad category of hate speech, we stand to do real damage to those who need and deserve swift support in fighting off their harassers.

A needlessly nebulous definition of hate speech can also preclude meaningful debate in the digital public square because individuals will choose to self-censor rather than violate the vague terms of service a company has laid out. They view the risk of being locked out of their account, which they might use to conduct business or household management tasks, as greater than their contributions to a debate. The costs relative to the benefits of mistakenly violating an ambiguous policy simply are not worth it for many, and so instead of the digital public square becoming richer and more representative, it becomes more censored and homogenous. An ever-expanding view of what constitutes hate speech also erodes trust in a company's ability to adjudicate fairly, because oftentimes the rules are not applied evenly across the political or ideological spectrum or are updated so often that an individual cannot keep up.

In the face of unfairly applied speech policies, some will argue for an uncensored digital public square. During, and in the wake of, the 2016 and 2020 US presidential elections, the demand for "free speech" social media platforms shot up, resulting in companies like Gab, Rumble, and Truth Social entering the market. These platforms were a reaction to Big Tech's seemingly uneven and heavy-handed applications of their speech policies

---

[12] For some examples, see Jason Thacker, "Where Do We Draw the Line on Hate Speech?" ERLC, August 9, 2021, https://erlc.com/resource-library/articles /where-do-we-draw-the-line-on-hate-speech/.

and other terms of service. Many in the public perceived the deplatforming of President Trump from Twitter and Facebook as politically motivated and the equivalent of the industry putting its digital thumb on the scale. Not only did this spur an exodus of users from these platforms, but it also led to calls for legal action, increasingly summarized in the phrase "Break up Big Tech." The legal tools for punishing or breaking up Big Tech include reforming or repealing Section 230 and expanding antitrust law.

As has been explained elsewhere in this book, Section 230 is a protection built into the Communications Decency Act (CDA) of 1996. It is "one of the most valuable tools for protecting freedom of expression and innovation on the Internet," according to the Electronic Frontier Foundation.[13] In its current application, Section 230 is "perhaps the most influential law to protect the kind of innovation that has allowed the Internet to thrive since 1996."[14] In practice, Section 230 provides immunity for platforms, preventing them from being held legally liable for content posted by its users. Absent such a protection, most online companies, from YouTube and Amazon to small startup media outlets, could be held liable for content published on their site, risking drawn-out legal battles. This would inevitably lead to more online censorship, as companies would feel the need to extensively police speech on their sites to avoid lawsuits. The internet would be far less free and open as a result.

For over four decades, antitrust law, the other oft-cited legal tool for making tech companies behave more like government agencies than private companies, has relied on the "consumer welfare standard" when determining whether it is appropriate to "break up" an entity. Judge Robert Bork has long been viewed as the leading legal voice on the consumer welfare standard as applied in antitrust law since the 1960s. In his hallmark book *The Antitrust Paradox,* he writes, "The only goal that should guide interpretation of the antitrust laws is the welfare of consumers. Departures from that standard destroy the consistency and predictability of the law; run counter

---

[13] CDA230: The Most Important Law Protecting Internet Speech, https://www.eff.org/issues/cda230.

[14] CDA230: The Most Important Law Protecting Internet Speech.

to the legislative intent, as that intent is conventionally derived; and damage the integrity of the judicial process by involving the courts in grossly political choices for which neither the statutes nor any other acceptable source provide any guidance."[15]

The consumer welfare principle has sustained numerous attacks by modern antitrust advocates, who argue for courts to consider a company's competitors as interested parties, as well as give credence to political actors who may disagree with a burgeoning tech company's policies or application of its policies. Experts warn that "weaponizing antitrust for broader socioeconomic purposes would fundamentally alter the primary goal of antitrust and seek to address the increasing calls to move away from the consumer welfare standard and to use antitrust as a tool for unrelated concerns."[16]

Politicians on both sides of the aisle continue to call for Section 230 repeals and reforms, as well as a broader interpretation of antitrust law. However, they typically do so for reasons at odds with one another. There are those on the political left who would like to see social media and other tech companies clamp down more severely on types of speech they deem harmful, whereas some on the political right believe these companies should be treated like public utilities, requiring them to forego private censorship in favor of a more laissez-faire approach to speech. Legal tools, like those mentioned above, should not be the preferred recourse for Americans interacting in the digital public square. Standing between the legal maneuvers called for by politically motivated actors and private companies, should be a thick and dense ecosystem of civil society that creates a hospitable environment for culture, inquiry, and business to take place. Yet that is not a reason for private institutions and companies to turn a blind eye to the men, women, and children who have been subjected to dehumanizing speech. An internet free of government intervention relies on other mitigation measures to function.

---

[15] Robert H. Bork, *The Antitrust Paradox: A Policy at War with Itself: With a New Introduction and Foreword* (New York: Bork Publishing, 2021), 405.

[16] Ashley Baker, "Statement for the Record on Antitrust, Digital Ad Markets, and the Rule of Law," Alliance on Antitrust, September 15, 2020, https://www.allianceonantitrust.org/blog/7nkf4035eu5zdc83ftr0f4etvj7a0e.

Speech versus Violence

Defining the limits of online hate speech and violence is much more nuanced and expansive than many realize, and how such policies are crafted will affect the public in weighty ways. It is important that we approach this issue with humility and wisdom. The pressure for both private companies and the federal government to enact protections against hate speech is real. There are men, women, and children who have been egregiously wronged online and made a target of hateful and grotesque rhetoric. As well, there have been threats of doxxing—the exposing of identifiable details of an individual, such as where they live or work—loss of livelihood,[17] and violence. Heartbreakingly, some have even taken their own lives, such as the tragic story of Mallory Grossman, because of the sense of hopelessness and dejection they felt due to a lack of recourse.[18]

But there is, in fact, hope of course correction as many companies look to create a more hospitable environment on their platform. As Eric Berkowitz writes in his book *Dangerous Ideas,* "The First Amendment bars the government from censoring most speech of private citizens, but it also allows private companies to enforce their own speech restrictions."[19] Berkowitz goes on to say that "it appears what some call the Wild Wild Web may already be taming somewhat, even without legislative action," due in no small part to the actions taken by social media companies. Yet, how should companies structure these actions so they do not mistakenly inhibit important debates and the exchange of information from taking place in the digital public square, while still providing effective protection for those legitimately wronged by others?

---

[17] See Ted Rall, "Free Speech Has Consequences, but Should Firing Be One?" *Wall Street Journal*, September 30, 2021, https://www.wsj.com/articles/free-speech-consequences-firing-political-democrat-republican-cancel-culture-11633033545?mod=Searchresults_pos4&page=1.

[18] See Justin Zaremba, "The Tragic Suicide of 12-year-old Mallory Grossman: A Timeline," NJ, May 15, 2019, https://www.nj.com/morris/2017/08/timeline_mallory_grossman_death.html.

[19] Berkowitz, *Dangerous Ideas*, 228.

Discerning the degrees of hate speech and the ideological conflicts surrounding how speech policies are created must be approached with preference for freedom *and* care for those subjected to degrading speech. It does not need to be one at the expense of the other. It's important to understand the line of distinction between the most egregious forms of hate speech and harassment, which threaten bodily harm and immediate danger, and that of undignified treatment that is emotionally hurtful. Although neither should be defended, it is clear there are degrees of separation between the cruel gravity of the former and the painful, albeit transient, annoyance of the latter.

Although some speech might be deemed hateful, either broadly among the public or narrowly among a particular demographic, it should not be treated the same as a hate crime, which often involves violence and is motivated by hatred for a person or group based on race, religion, ethnicity, gender, or other grounds. The Department of Justice (DOJ) defines hate crimes as "crimes committed on the basis of the victim's perceived or actual race, color, religion, national origin, sexual orientation, gender, gender identity, or disability."[20] The DOJ elaborates on what types of crime are most often accompanied by racial animus: "The 'crime' in hate crime is often a violent crime, such as assault, murder, arson, vandalism, or threats to commit such crimes. It may also cover conspiring or asking another person to commit such crimes, even if the crime was never carried out."[21]

When it comes to casting a vision for dignity, truth, and speech in the digital public square, the first order of business must be distinguishing the free speech rights afforded to Americans by the First Amendment of the United States Constitution and the rights of private entities to govern their businesses and institutions as they see fit. For much of her history, the United States has been a stalwart defender of speech, disallowing government interference into the sacred realm of words. Even the most offensive of speech, including racist, xenophobic, anti-religious, and sexually derisive speech, receives impunity from the government.

---

[20] Department of Justice, "Learn About Hate Crimes," https://www.justice.gov/hatecrimes/learn-about-hate-crimes.

[21] Department of Justice, "Learn About Hate Crimes."

This essential protection from government punishment, however, does not prohibit private companies and institutions such as churches, schools, and media outlets from levying their own speech codes and conduct policies. Many private Christian schools rightfully forbid certain types of speech that it deems unbecoming of good character and gospel witness. Workplaces and universities also enforce such restrictions. Churches have the right to forbid hate-filled messages from being spoken from their pulpits. Social media companies currently have legal latitude to set ground rules on their platforms and forbid certain types of speech they deem antithetical to their company values.

This freedom to create speech policies in the private sector means that companies and institutions are tasked with the responsibility to thoughtfully consider if, and how, they will define hate speech. Beginning any such policy discussion with a preference for freedom is crucial if a company or platform is going to facilitate robust conversations and reward honest, open inquiry. This means applying a least-restrictive-means approach to speech and avoiding too broad a definition of hate speech and violence (e.g., *Silence is violence* and other such highly subjective mantras).

Content Moderation in the Digital Public Square

Yet even the complexity of navigating consumer and employee expectations and demands within the United States is precarious. Hate speech policies that are overly broad run the risk of inviting so many violation complaints that a company will be required to either hire more staff to meet the demand or walk back restrictions. In addition, catering to one user might risk alienating another if terms of service, including speech policies, are not clearly laid out and fairly applied. We should want to make the internet a safe place for individuals while not heavy-handedly quelling speech. Content moderation traditionally is defined as "the process through which platforms make decisions about what content can and cannot be on their sites, based on their own Terms of Service, 'community standards,' or other rules. This process typically relies upon a system of community policing, whereby users of a given service report or 'flag' content that they believe violates the rules. The content then enters a moderation queue, and a human moderator determines whether or not it violates the rules."[22] An appeal, if an option, can take an extended amount of time and effort, eating up even more employee and user time.

Given the extraordinarily large number of individuals using a social site at any given time, the volume of flagged content can be enormous. As a result, content filters are built utilizing artificial intelligence to assist in the process. However, far from perfect, these filters lack the human ability to contextualize content, thereby sweeping away important posts pertaining to human rights violations or campaigns denouncing sexually exploitative practices, because of triggers built into the tool. Policing speech is messy and difficult, and companies should only levy speech codes that they are willing to enforce fairly and defend.

The American government's preference for unrestrained free speech, even the variety deemed hateful by most, is not shared in many parts of the world. Even a number of our allied countries, like Germany, Canada, and the United Kingdom, do not take a deferential approach to free speech. Instead, their governments weigh such speech against other interests, like Holocaust denial or words that cause distress for a protected group. This is to say nothing of the more authoritarian nations, like China and Russia, which make no attempt to hide their hostility toward free speech. Even our own history is riddled with moments where we compromised our commitment to free speech, which are outlined in the next section.

Despite the freedom and latitude American tech companies and private institutions have when it comes to establishing and enforcing their hate speech policies, "U.S.-based companies such as Facebook, Twitter, and YouTube [voluntarily] look to U.S. regulations to underpin their policies."[23] Designations like the State Department's Foreign Terrorist Organizations are often applied (imperfectly in many cases) to a tech companies' speech policy matrix. Some companies, in an effort to conduct business in global markets, will comply

---

[22] Jillian C. York, "Caught in the Net: The Impact of 'Extremist' Speech Regulations on Human Rights Content," EFF, May 30, 2019, https://www.eff.org/wp/caught-net-impact-extremist-speech-regulations-human-rights-content.

[23] York, "Caught in the Net."

with an illiberal nation's laws. The cost-benefit analysis of an American company playing by an authoritarian regime's speech or privacy policies to enter their markets is fraught with hazards, but companies intent on expansion are willing to take it on, hopeful for a significant return on investment.[24]

Even so, successful CEOs of multinational corporations are not likely to have a rosy picture of world dynamics and are often aware of the competing values that inevitably play into their ability to do business. Testifying before a House subcommittee in July 2020, Facebook CEO Mark Zuckerberg said, "We believe in values—democracy, competition, inclusion, and free expression—that the American economy was built on . . . but there's no guarantee our values will win out. For example, China is building its own version of the Internet focused on very different ideas, and they are exporting their vision to other countries."[25]

The demands authoritarian regimes place on American companies often include the suppression of speech and a disregard for user privacy. These "pay to play" tactics throw a complicated variable into discussions of social media speech policies and are part of the broader conversation surrounding corporate governance in a global economy.

Policing Speech

How American companies conduct business internationally, and the speech policies they do or do not enforce, is a tenuous dance and will remain so for the foreseeable future. Over the decades, particularly in the early twentieth century, the United States has experienced waves of illiberalism, an intolerance for dissenting viewpoints. Albeit limited in scope, these instances serve as cautionary tales, reminding us that even in a nation with a robust

---

[24] For more on the international aspects of technology policy and the rise of digital authoritarian regimes, see chapter 4 by Patricia Shaw and chapter 11 by Olivia Enos.

[25] Testimony of Mark Zuckerberg before the House Subcommittee on Antitrust, Commercial, and Administrative Law, July 29, 2020, https://docs.house.gov/meetings/JU/JU05/20200729/110883/HHRG-116-JU05-Wstate-ZuckerbergM-20200729.pdf.

Bill of Rights that includes free speech guarantees, its citizenry must be vigilant to guard against government encroachment, from the municipal to the federal levels.

Even during the United States's fledgling founding, the Sedition Act of 1798 was designed to silence Republican opposition to the Federalists, threatening "deportation, fine, or imprisonment" of "anyone publishing false, scandalous, or malicious writing."[26] This was signed into law by President John Adams and opposed by future presidents Thomas Jefferson and James Madison. However, it was a wildly unpopular piece of legislation and expired before the Supreme Court had an opportunity to weigh in.

In the early part of the twentieth century, during World War I, numerous states across the US passed criminal syndicalism laws designed, in part, to restrict communism's influence by punishing and imprisoning those who espoused pro-communism, pro-union speech. The First Amendment was made subservient to the fears of communism's harmful effects. As a result, there was "a shared feeling that the prosecution of radical elements within society was necessary, appellate courts at the state level and federal courts generally upheld criminal syndicalism laws, even at the expense of individual rights."[27]

In a course correction of the speech policing during the 1910s and '20s, courts began to step away from adjudicating offensive, hateful speech. This resurgence of broad speech rights was clearly seen in *Brandenburg v. Ohio* (1969), which offered a new matrix for determining when the government was permitted to punish speech. *Brandenburg v. Ohio* is a case that involved Clarence Brandenburg, a leader in the Ku Klux Klan. The state of Ohio convicted Brandenburg under an Ohio syndicalism law, which made it illegal to advocate for "crime, sabotage, violence, or unlawful methods of terrorism as a means of accomplishing industrial or political reform."[28] The Supreme Court pushed back on the Ohio statute, stating that Brandenburg's speech

---

[26] Historical Highlights: The Sedition Act of 1798, https://history.house .gov/Historical-Highlights/1700s/The-Sedition-Act-of-1798/.

[27] Dale Mineshima-Lowe, "Criminal Syndicalism Laws," *The First Amendment Encyclopedia*, https://www.mtsu.edu/first-amendment/article/942/criminal-syndical ism-laws.

[28] Brandenburg v. Ohio, Oyez, https://www.oyez.org/cases/1968/492.

was protected by the First Amendment unless it met two conditions, known as the "Imminent Lawless Action Test." These are the two conditions:

1. It is directed at inciting imminent, lawless action.
2. Is likely to incite or produce such action. If this level of scrutiny cannot be met, then the speech is permitted.

Barring the satisfaction of these two conditions, speech is left to defend itself in the public square and rise or fall on the hearer's acceptance or dismissal of it. The federal government made clear that if offensive, hateful speech could not pass the Imminent Lawless Action test, its role was to remain silent.

Before the internet became a primary means of communicating with others not physically proximate to an individual, landline telephones were one of the most ubiquitous means of distance communication. Despite the Supreme Court's Imminent Lawless Action test, the government nonetheless looked for new ways to regulate speech in this emerging communications landscape.

Free Speech in a Digital Age

According to Kim Holmes, former executive vice president of the Heritage Foundation, "In 1992 Congress directed the National Telecommunications and Information Administration to examine the role of telecommunications in disseminating hate speech as an incitement to hatred and violence. In 1993 the National Telecommunications and Information Administration issued a report titled 'The Role of Telecommunications in Hate Crime,' in which it argued that a 'climate' of hate can be seen as an inducement to violence."[29] Although unsuccessful, Holmes suggests that these sorts of attempts served to move the Overton window (i.e., the range of policies that are politically acceptable to the majority of people at a given time) on the conversation surrounding what hate speech is in the court of public opinion.

---

[29] Kim Holmes, "The Origins of 'Hate Speech,'" The Heritage Foundation, October 22, 2018, https://www.heritage.org/civil-society/commentary/the-origins -hate-speech.

Today, who and what are censored in the digital public square are often determined by platform gatekeepers, particularly social media companies. In the United States, the protections afforded by the First Amendment mean that market forces and private institutions are where most discussions surrounding censorship, hate speech, and free expression occur. Authoritarian regimes take the role of censorship upon themselves, making the stakes much higher for its citizens, who are subjected to threats of fines and imprisonment, rather than the market's recourse, which gravitates toward less restrictive means, such as heated public debate, at best, and deplatforming, at worst. The internet of the twenty-first century is an ecosystem, where an interaction or piece of information on one platform or site often bleeds over into another, creating a climate and environment that reflects the health of its individual parts. The state of our digital public square is a barometer of the state of our societal values, vision, and health.

Historically, societal mores and laws evolved over decades and centuries. The common law had time to permeate the lives and consciousness of the public. It was, in effect, common knowledge before it was ever common law. Today's "common law," however, is shaped in a matter of months, or even weeks. As a result, the social norms of today are often fickle and unproven. How institutions and individuals define hate speech stands to become society's de facto law, enshrined by lengthy terms of service agreements.

The domestic and international pressure is palpable, and competing interests jockey for dominance over how hate speech is defined. Yet at the center of these debates are individual human beings, created in the image of God, deserving of fair treatment. How social media companies and other private institutions structure their online speech policies has real implications on their lives.

In 1994, over a period of 100 days, Hutu civilians and soldiers across Rwanda slaughtered over 800,000 Tutsis. As Eric Berkowitz explains, "If the slaughter had a soundtrack, it came from Radio Television Libre des Milles Collines (RTLM), a Hutu radio station that played anti-Tutsi hate music, punctuated with broadcasts calling for a 'final war' to 'exterminate the cockroaches,' even going so far as to broadcast the names and addresses of Tutsi victims."[30] The United States, although capable of jamming the RTLM radio signal, did not. The clear and imminent danger the Tutsis faced is a tragic and horrifying instance that drives home the power that hate speech has to foment violent action when left unchecked.

The questions surrounding whether such speech should be censored, and by whom, are ethically clear in terms of prioritizing the saving of innocent lives. However, the complexities surrounding national sovereignty and second- and third-order effects as it pertains to one government setting a precedent of passing their territorial lines to protect innocent civilians must be faced. Undoubtedly, the role of policymakers and leaders will require that they evaluate their decisions from a variety of angles, to lessen the likelihood of unintended consequences, even as they pursue justice on behalf of the innocent. Thus, a first step in constructing a speech policy that has staying power and fair application is to define the distinction between speech that calls for physical acts of violence and speech that expresses contempt. The tragedy in Rwanda could have been, at the very least, minimized, and lives saved, if there had been a willingness by our government and other actors to jam the radio signals and quell the murderous clarion calls.

Unfortunately, an overly broad definition of hate speech, which is aimed at alleviating discomfort rather than preventing crimes, leads to a broad-brush approach. The inevitable result is that otherwise innocuous voices risk being deplatformed rather than giving offended users the agency to electively "block" them on their own terms. Additionally, this unfortunately means that individuals who dissent from evolving cultural norms related to gender and sexuality or challenge emerging theories related to race, class, and religious dynamics are often subjected to censorship for speaking an opinion that was often mainstream even as little as a few years ago. The wide spectrum of which words and sentiments can fall into the basket of hate speech in present times should not be lost on decision makers. A preference for freedom, with a clear red line distinguishing between calls for immediate physical danger of an individual or group with other types of speech, should be paramount.

---

[30] Berkowitz, *Dangerous Ideas*, 199.

Kim Holmes notes that, over the years, hate speech in the public square went from meaning words that incited physical violence to a preoccupation with "utterances, gestures, conduct, or writing that they deemed prejudicial against a protected individual or group."[31] This approach to hate speech all but assures a perpetual stream of complaints and witch hunts, taking up a company's valuable time that it could otherwise devote to investigating legitimate claims of incendiary hate speech.

A private imminent lawless action test that more narrowly defines hate speech as speech that calls for physical harm to a person or group, or which proves libelous, should be the standard by which companies and other private institutions craft and enforce their speech codes. Should companies and institutions move beyond this, they would be wise to divert more funds and technology into training and deploying their staff to field the influx of complaints and create a fair and swift appeals process. Absent such mechanisms, they will lose public trust, which is often difficult to regain.

The degree of separation many perceive their online behavior to have from their "real" life—including the layer of anonymity some individuals create by masking their identity online—has limited the normative and customary restraints that come with face-to-face interactions where we are threatened with tangible and immediate consequences for our words.

Is there a way to create an online system of accountability that avoids the excesses of scorched-earth, reactionary speech policies and a laissez-faire, libertine approach to online interactions? Speech codes serve the public best when they are tethered to a vision of dignity and truth rather than a reactive tool that is merely designed to respond to circumstances ad hoc. Most modern speech codes in both the public and private sector have been reactionary in nature, adding new parameters with little consideration of such a code's sustainability.

Whether it is a government reacting to politically unfavorable opposition or a private company responding to a real or perceived need from a consumer base, a speech code that is solely crafted as a response to a problem rather than cast as a vision for civil dialogue will often miss the opportunity

---

[31] Holmes, "The Origins of 'Hate Speech.'"

to lay a solid foundation that can be defended in the long term, especially when subjected to national or international scrutiny. It is first and foremost an individual's responsibility to engage in the digital public square in a way that honors the dignity of others. Teaching this truth should be a priority for leaders who have the privilege of discipling others. In addition to teaching this, there should be accountability systems in place, wherein individuals subjected to derision by others are not left to fend for themselves. They deserve mediation, which will require that leaders and community members not turn a blind eye to their mistreatment online.

However, as has been argued, there should be recourse within the digital public square for those who are subjected to bullying, libelous claims, and threats of physical harm. Companies and private institutions must set the parameters for what they will allow on their platforms and ensure they have the systems and staff in place to do so. Empowering individuals with the ability to block and/or file a complaint of inappropriate behavior, particularly in the face of libel or harassment, is of the utmost importance. The most egregious speech, including threats of violence, should be taken seriously, dealt with swiftly, and reported to law enforcement as necessary.

The digital public square will continue to see its share of hate and injustice. Yet Christians have the opportunity, and the responsibility, to use online public spaces as mediums for reconciliation, redemption, and the dissemination of the good news. If they are in positions of influence, they also must take the opportunity given them to advocate for and design wise speech policies that honor the dignity of each person. We cannot flee from the problems found in the digital public square. Rather, we should engage thoughtfully, providing a vision that protects the innocent and celebrates diversity of opinion.

8

Content Moderation and Suppressing Speech

Are There Limits on Talking about Sexuality and Gender Online?

Jeremy D. Tedesco and Christiana Kiefer

The answer to this chapter's subtitle is straightforward: yes, technology companies are adopting and enforcing content moderation policies that threaten the freedom of Christians to express their views on sex, marriage, the immutability of biological sex, and a host of other consequential social issues. But what are Christians to do about it? What is our role and responsibility in a pluralistic society? Christians must understand that in the digital age, guaranteeing freedom of speech in the digital public square is vital to advancing the gospel and preserving the voice of faith in public discourse.[1] There are certain institutions—ranging from education and media to business and the non-profit sector—that are increasingly deploying their

---

[1] For more on religious freedom and Christian mission, see chapter 6 by Joshua B. Wester.

political and economic power to censor or deplatform those who stand against an increasingly intolerant secular orthodoxy that views Christianity and other faiths—especially Christian teachings on human dignity and sexuality—as hateful, bigoted, and out of step with social progress.

Technology companies such as Meta (which operates Facebook, WhatsApp, and Instagram), Twitter, Alphabet (which operates YouTube and Google), and Amazon have an increasingly outsized role in the digital public square and have used this influence to shape the public conversation around some of the most important ethical and social issues of our day, often pushing certain ideological agendas and relegating the reach of other ideas in the public square. Many companies are wielding this influence to relegate faith to a private matter and strip the public square of its influence on a significant and virtually unprecedented scale.[2] A university might punish a Christian student for expressing his views, but if the school is public, the student likely has some level of recourse through the courts. Presumably, the student could also choose to join another academic community more welcoming to his religious or ideological convictions. But there are few, if any, parallel protections or alternatives available to those who rely on private internet platforms to acquire information and express their views on pressing issues of the day. This has left many to wonder about the future of faith in the public square if private companies wield such an outsized influence over content and information.[3] The US Supreme Court recently

---

[2] For more on the nature of the public square and digital technologies, see chapter 2, from Bryan Baise.

[3] According to Pew Research Institute, 81 percent of Americans use YouTube and 69 percent use Facebook. Brooke Auxier and Monica Anderson, "Social Media Use in 2021," Pew Research Center, April 7, 2021, https://www.pewresearch.org /internet/2021/04/07/social-media-use-in-2021/. A little under half of Americans get their news on social media, with 68 percent using Facebook for this purpose. See Mason Walker and Katerina Eva Matsa, "News Consumption Across Social Media in 2021," Pew Research Center, September 20, 2021, https://www.pewresearch .org/journalism/2021/09/20/news-consumption-across-social-media-in-2021/. For Christians, churches and ministries' reliance on digital platforms social media spiked because of the COVID-19 pandemic. Ministry Brands reports that "95 percent of church leaders say their reliance on digital tools and church software has

acknowledged this development, noting, "While in the past there may have been difficulty in identifying the most important places . . . for the exchange of views, today the answer is clear. It is cyberspace—the 'vast democratic forums of the Internet' in general, and social media in particular."[4]

Unlike the public forums of old, much of the new digital public square is owned and controlled by private corporations, not governments. This is significant because, unlike governmental entities, private companies are generally not subject to the First Amendment and its protections for free speech of private citizens.[5] Thus, they have a freer hand than the government to impose certain speech and content regulations under the auspice of creating safe environments online. While many speech restrictions in the town square of old could be remedied through civil rights lawsuits filed under the First Amendment, remedies are much harder to come by when a private corporation chooses to moderate content, suppress a post, or remove a message because of its religious or ideological content. Some platforms allow users to appeal content moderation decisions, but even where these processes are in place, they often lack basic due process and transparency.[6]

This danger of not having mechanisms for due process and meaningful appeal is compounded by the reality that the power to regulate speech

---

increased from before the COVID-19 pandemic began. Close to 70 percent of respondents report their usage has increased significantly." See "Ministry Brands Releases Survey Data Revealing the Role of Technology in the Church During the Pandemic and Beyond," Ministry Brands, August 10, 2021, https://www .ministrybrands.com/blog/ministry-brands-releases-survey-data-revealing-the-role -of-technology-in-the-church-during-the-pandemic-and-beyond/.

[4] Packingham v. North Carolina, 137 S. Ct. 1730, 1735 (2017).

[5] For more on this, see chapters 5 and 6, which focus on the nature of religious freedom and the legal complexities of content moderation.

[6] Of note, Meta (Facebook) created the Oversight Board, to which users can appeal content moderation decisions. As of this writing, the board is unable to take up all appeals but has issued numerous opinions overturning Meta's original decisions, often on grounds of free expression and religious freedom both domestically and abroad. For more on the Oversight Board, see https://www.oversightboard.com.

online has become highly centralized.[7] A small handful of companies, including Meta, Twitter, Amazon, and Alphabet, exercise vast control over the beliefs, views, and opinions we can express and are exposed to online. Worse, many of these companies maintain community standards and content moderation policies that overtly suppress certain types of speech and then enforce those policies to stifle the expression of certain social, political, and religious views. Like many universities, private social media platforms frequently label advocating for or promoting a Christian view of sexuality and gender as hate speech.[8] No public or private university exercises this level of direct control over public discourse, and yet there are far more safeguards for speech in the academic context than in the digital public square—the space arguably most crucial for meaningful debate and democratic deliberation.

These developments are of particular importance to Christian individuals and ministries, who often rely on these platforms to share the gospel and advocate for biblical truths on various cultural issues. Deplatforming, moderation, and censorship targeted at those committed to a biblical account of human biology and sexuality is quickly spreading online, carrying with it dire consequences for Christian witness in other areas of public life. This chapter highlights several examples of this concerning trend, explores why it is happening, and offers a road map for restoring free speech and religious expression online. We conclude by providing a framework for how Christians should understand our role and responsibility to advocate for the free expression of religion—especially on gender and sexuality issues—in the digital public square.

---

[7] Biden v. Knight First Amend. Inst. at Columbia Univ., 141 S. Ct. 1220, 1221 (2021) ("Today's digital platforms provide avenues for historically unprecedented amounts of speech. . . . Also unprecedented, however, is the concentrated control of so much speech in the hands of a few private parties.") (Thomas, J., concurring).

[8] For more on the nature of hate speech and violence, see chapter 7 by Brooke Medina.

Content Moderation and Digital Censorship

A small group of private corporations that exercise significant control over the digital public square can silence certain voices and skew national debate on consequential issues. This power poses grave threats to everyone's free speech rights, and especially to the freedom of Christians to express their views on sex, gender, and what it means to be male and female. Amazon, for example, exercises enormous control over the marketplace of ideas because of its effective stranglehold on the book industry. Amazon is the country's dominant book retailer, accounting for over half of all books sold in the US and 80 percent of all e-books.[9] It also exercises significant control over essential conduits for commerce and communications, including infrastructure for purchasing, selling, and transporting books.[10] For this reason, when Amazon deplatforms a book, there are significant consequences. Most significantly, when Amazon pulls a book from its website, it becomes difficult, if not impossible, for large portions of the United States to practically access the book given the market influence and dominance that the company has on the publishing industry.

Second, Amazon's censorship may have long-term negative effects that cause self-censorship across the industry—from authors, to publishers, to distributors. If the bookseller that controls 80 percent of the online book market and over 50 percent of all book sales will not sell a book that expresses a certain viewpoint, then authors, publishers, and distributors will predictably avoid the topic.[11] Amazon's influence can have devastating effects on the free exchange of ideas. This power was especially shown when

---

[9] Jeffrey A. Trachtenberg, "Amazon Publishes Books by Top Authors, and Rivals Fret," *Wall Street Journal*, updated January 12, 2020, https://www.wsj.com/articles/amazon-publishes-books-by-top-authors-and-rivals-fret-11578997802; Greg Ip, "The Antitrust Case Against Facebook, Google and Amazon," *Wall Street Journal*, January 16, 2018, https://www.wsj.com/articles/the-antitrust-case-against-facebook-google-amazon-and-apple-1516121561.

[10] See H. Comm. on the Judiciary, *Investigation of Competition in Digital Markets*, 254 (October 4, 2020), https://judiciary.house.gov/uploadedfiles/competition_in_digital_markets.pdf?utm_campaign=4493-519.

[11] *Investigation of Competition in Digital Markets*, 254.

the company removed scholar and EPPC president Ryan T. Anderson's book *When Harry Became Sally* from its online listings. The book provides a scholarly overview of the human cost of imposing transgender ideology on those struggling with gender dysphoria and argues that the most loving and beneficial therapies focus on helping people live in harmony with their biological sex as male or female.

Anderson is one of today's most respected advocates of orthodox Christian beliefs about marriage, sex, and gender. His credentials are impeccable. Many leading institutions, including Amherst College, Boston College, Harvard College, Columbia University, Princeton University, Stanford University, and Yale University, have hosted Anderson at conferences and seminars. Many leading journals, including the *Harvard Journal of Law and Public Policy* and the *Georgetown Journal of Law and Public Policy*, have published his work. Many leading news outlets, including the *Wall Street Journal*, *New York Times*, and *Washington Post*, have published his op-eds. ABC, CNN, CNBC, Fox News, and other networks often invite him as a guest on their news shows. In 2021, Anderson became president of the Ethics and Public Policy Center, a Washington, DC, think tank that promotes the Judeo-Christian moral tradition.[12] Leading academics hailed the book as compassionate, sensitive, thoughtful, and well researched. Harvard law professor Mary Ann Glendon described *When Harry Became Sally* as "an eminently readable and insightful guide for all who find themselves perplexed by today's debates on gender identity."[13] Paul Vitz, professor emeritus at New York University, called it a "sensitive presentation of gender identity issues."[14] John Finnis, professor emeritus of law and legal philosophy at the University of Oxford, said it was "focused, informative, fair-minded, lucid, and fact-based."[15] And, interestingly, for three years, Amazon sold Anderson's book without incident or issue.

---

[12] "Ryan T. Anderson to Become Next EPPC President," EPPC, January 15, 2021, https://eppc.org/news/ryan-t-anderson-to-become-next-eppc-president/.

[13] Encounter Books, Praise for *When Harry Became Sally*, https://www.encounterbooks.com/books/when-harry-became-sally-paperback/.

[14] Encounter Books, Praise for *When Harry Became Sally*.

[15] Encounter Books, Praise for *When Harry Became Sally*.

Nevertheless, in February 2021, Amazon made the decision to remove Anderson's book from its online marketplace. After an initial silence, Amazon responded to a letter from four prominent Republican senators stating that the company had "chosen not to sell books that frame LGBTQ+ identity as a mental illness," even though Anderson disputes that the book frames the issues in that light.[16] This removal led many to conclude that Amazon was using its outsized influence in the publishing industry to curtail debate on these issues by blocking a divergent understanding of gender and sexuality.

The timing of Amazon's decision to remove Anderson's book is revealing as well. After selling it for three years, Amazon pulled it at the height of the national discussion over whether Congress should pass the Equality Act.[17] Of note, Amazon openly supports the Equality Act, boasts that it was "among the first" to join a coalition of companies supporting the Act, and has urged Congress to "quickly pass the Equality Act."[18] Anderson has publicly opposed the Equality Act for reasons anchored in his Catholic faith. Among other things, he notes his concern that adding "gender identity" to federal nondiscrimination laws would: (1) create unfair playing fields for women and girls in athletics by forcing them to compete against men; (2) violate women's dignity and privacy by forcing them to share private spaces with men; and (3) undermine religious liberty by turning laws meant to shield religious belief and practice into swords used to punish religious institutions and believers who refuse to embrace the government's views

---

[16] For the full letter from Amazon's vice president of public policy, see https://s.wsj.net/public/resources/documents/Amazonletter0311.pdf.

[17] If passed, the Equality Act would add "sexual orientation" and "gender identity" to many existing federal non-discrimination laws. This would negatively impact many areas of life including employment, athletics, housing, public and private schools, businesses, and more. These changes would threaten the religious beliefs of millions of Americans, harm women and girls, and contradict the common good. For analysis of the Equality Act, see "The Equality Act: What You Need to Know, Alliance Defending Freedom," https://adflegal.org/equality-act.

[18] "Congress Should Pass the Equality Act," February 24, 2021, https://www.aboutamazon.com/news/policy-news-views/congress-should-pass-the-equality-act; "Our Positions," https://www.aboutamazon.com/about-us/our-positions, Amazon, February 24, 2021.

on sex and gender.[19] As debate over the Equality Act intensified, Anderson advocated against it. On February 21, 2021, the *New York Post* published his op-ed titled "Biden's Equality Act is a danger to women's and conscience rights."[20] That same day, he learned that Amazon had removed *When Harry Became Sally* from its online marketplace without any notice or explanation to the publisher or author.[21] The US House of Representatives voted to pass the Equality Act just a few days later.[22]

The removal of Anderson's book for his views on sex and gender is not an isolated story. The Heritage Foundation, a conservative think tank and public policy organization, also had its content on gender identity censored. YouTube removed a Heritage video featuring Walt Heyer, a male Christian speaker who at one point in his life identified as a woman. Heyer stated that individuals are "not born transgender," and that gender dysphoria "is a childhood developmental disorder, that adults are perpetrating on our young people today, and our schools are complicit in this."[23] YouTube removed the video, claiming that Heyer's remarks violated its hate speech policy. Even after Heritage appealed the decision, YouTube reaffirmed its initial judgment that Heyer's comments constituted hate speech. Emilie Kao, former director of the DeVos Center for Religion and Society at the

---

[19] See Ryan T. Anderson, "Biden's Equality Act is a danger to women's and conscience rights," *New York Post*, February 21, 2021, https://nypost.com/2021/02/21/bidens-equality-act-is-a-danger-to-womens-and-conscience-rights/.

[20] Anderson, "Biden's Equality Act is a danger to women's and conscience rights."

[21] Ryan T. Anderson (@RyanTAnd), "I hope you've already bought your copy, cause Amazon just removed my book 'When Harry Became Sally: Responding to the Transgender Moment' from their cyber shelves. . . . my other four books are still available (for now). http://tinyurl.com/RTAamazon," February 21, 2021, 2:34 p.m., https://twitter.com/ryantand/status/1363587820565184521?lang=en.

[22] See Gabby Birenbaum, "House Passes the Equality Act in a victory for LGBTQ Americans," Vox, February 26, 2021, https://www.vox.com/2021/2/26/22303053/house-passes-equality-act-lgbtq-senate.

[23] Emily Jashinsky, "Exclusive: Man Tried to Share His Regrets about Transgender Life. YouTube Censored It," The Federalist, June 19, 2020, https://thefederalist.com/2020/06/19/exclusive-man-tried-to-share-his-regrets-about-transgender-life-youtube-censored-it/.

Heritage Foundation, noted that "YouTube . . . decided, under the guise of 'hate speech,' to censor the viewpoint that it doesn't like. This won't help children and families struggling with this disorder who want information from both sides of the debate."[24]

Additionally, Carl Trueman, professor of biblical and religious studies at Grove City College, spoke in August 2021 at the Sacramento Gospel Conference. He delivered a speech on the Christian view of sex and provided a "thoughtful analysis of American cultural attitudes toward sex through the lens of classic Christian thought."[25] Immanuel Baptist Church livestreamed the event on YouTube. YouTube interrupted the live broadcast twice. The second interruption was for a mysterious and ultimately never-specified "content violation."[26] Meta (who operates Facebook) suspended Robert Gagnon, professor of New Testament Theology at Houston Baptist University and renowned expert on biblical sexuality, for twenty-four hours after he criticized the Biden administration's gender-identity executive order for, among other things, violating female military personnel's dignity and privacy by forcing them to shower with males.[27] Facebook claimed that Gagnon's post violated its policy against "violence and incitement."[28] And during the 2021 Summer Olympics, Twitter suspended several conservative commentators for questioning Olympic rules that permit males to compete in women's categories. For example, when New Zealand transgender weight-lifter Laurel Hubbard exited competition after failing all three attempts, Allie Beth Stuckey tweeted that "Laura [sic] Hubbard failing at the event doesn't make his inclusion fair. He's still a man, and men shouldn't compete

---

[24] Jashinsky, "Exclusive: Man Tried to Share His Regrets About Transgender Life. YouTube Censored It."

[25] Salvatore J. Cordileone and Jim Daly, "Social Media's Threat to Religious Freedom," *Wall Street Journal*, August 12, 2021, https://www.wsj.com/articles /social-media-religious-freedom-youtube-first-amendment-section-230-carl -trueman-sacramento-gospel-conference-11628802706.

[26] Cordileone and Daly, "Social Media's Threat to Religious Freedom."

[27] See Rod Dreher, "The Tyranny of Tech and Trans," The American Conservative, January 27, 2021, https://www.theamericanconservative.com/dreher /tyranny-of-tech-and-trans/.

[28] Dreher, "The Tyranny of Tech and Trans."

against women in weightlifting."[29] In response to Stuckey's twelve-hour suspension, Erick Erikson tweeted, "This is absurd. Laurel Hubbard is a man even if Twitter doesn't like it."[30] He also received a twelve-hour suspension. Both times Twitter invoked its hateful conduct policy.[31]

As Christians think about these pressing issues in the digital public square, we must first strive to express our views on sex and gender in respectful ways anchored in the truth that all people are created in the image and likeness of God (Gen 1:26–27). But people of faith must also reckon with the reality that many social media companies, no matter how respectfully you communicate your views, are increasingly restricting the expression of basic religious beliefs about sex and gender, or opinions that align with those beliefs, as "hateful," "violent," "harassing," or "threatening." Unless countered, this trend will threaten Christian witness in other areas of public life as well because the impetus for censorship stretches beyond issues of human sexuality into any area where Christian witness contradicts the current cultural zeitgeist. As Christians, we must advocate for solutions that protect free expression for all our neighbors, including those with whom we disagree, to access the digital public square and express their views.

Why Is Speech Being Censored Online?

The digital public square has become increasingly contentious, and technology companies are suppressing speech—often speech about gender and sexuality—at an alarming rate without substantial repercussions. But why

---

[29] Joseph A. Wulfsohn, "Allie Beth Stuckey Released from 'Twitter Jail' After Referring to Transgender Olympic Athlete as a 'Man,'" Fox News, August 6, 2021, https://www.foxnews.com/media/allie-beth-stuckey-twitter-jail-transgender-olympic-athlete.

[30] Valerie Richardson, "'Laurel Hubbard is a Man' Tweet Lands Erick Erickson in Twitter Jail," *Washington Times*, August 7, 2021, https://www.washingtontimes.com/news/2021/aug/7/erick-erickson-suspended-twitter-laurel-hubbard-ma/.

[31] See Jason Thacker, "Where Do We Draw the Line on Hate Speech?" ERLC, August 9, 2021, https://erlc.com/resource-library/articles/where-do-we-draw-the-line-on-hate-speech/.

is this the case and what can be done about it? We propose that one of the issues at stake in this debate is a judicial *mis*interpretation of Section 230 of the Communications Decency Act. Critics across the political spectrum often pillory Section 230, signed into law in 1996, as the cause of too much or too little content moderation online. The calls to repeal or reform the statute are pervasive and often cut across ideological lines. But it is not the statute itself that created broad immunity for censorship by social media companies. Rather, it is our argument that it was early and misguided judicial interpretations of the statute.[32]

Contrary to popular perception, one of Section 230's primary purposes is to "promote the free exchange of ideas" online.[33] The statute's text recognizes that the internet "offer[s] a forum for a true diversity of political discourse, unique opportunities for cultural development, and myriad avenues for intellectual activity."[34] Congress believed Section 230 was necessary to achieve this objective because, before its enactment, courts were imposing publisher-like responsibility on online services that was hampering innovation for the fledgling medium. Because these companies were engaging in traditional publisher activities (making editorial decisions about what content to allow on their platform), the courts were holding the forerunners of today's social media platforms liable for the defamatory statements of their users. As one court said, "By actively utilizing technology and manpower to delete notes from its computer bulletin boards on the basis of offensiveness and 'bad taste,' . . . [the company] is clearly making decisions as to content, and such decisions constitute editorial control."[35] Put simply, because the company had undertaken the duty to remove content, it could be held legally responsible for *failing to remove* the defamatory statement of a third party.

---

[32] For more on the policy and legal issues in the digital public square, especially Section 230, see chapter 5 from David French.

[33] Carafano v. Metrosplash.com, Inc., 339 F.3d 1119, 1122 (9th Cir. 2003).

[34] 47 U.S.C. § 230(a)(3).

[35] Stratton Oakmont v. Prodigy Services Co., 1995 WL 323710 at *4 (Sup. Ct. N.Y. 1995).

This put companies that provided platforms for the speech of others between a rock and a hard place. They laudably desired to remove obscene, violent, lewd, or similarly objectionable content. But if they did, they would face liability for all content third parties posted on their platform, even if they were unaware of its presence. They had to choose between two bad options: (1) allow obscene and unlawful content to flood their service to avoid liability for third-party posts, or (2) regulate obscene and unlawful content and become liable for all third-party posts. This latter option was even less appealing than the first because of the sheer volume of third-party content on speech-hosting platforms. Congress wisely foresaw how this dilemma would pose an enormous impediment to the promise the internet held as a place for open discourse and the free exchange of ideas, so it enacted Section 230 as a solution. Congress's goal was to permit online services that facilitated the speech of others to enforce some community standards without incurring liability for the content of every message on their services.

The key provisions are Section 230(c)(1) and (c)(2). Section 230(c)(1) says, "No provider or user of an interactive computer service shall be treated as the publisher or speaker of any information provided by another information content provider." The key element of the sentence is found in its second half—"of any information *provided by another* information content provider." This section solves the problem discussed earlier—social media companies being held liable for failing to remove defamatory content posted by third parties. Section 230(c)(1) covers solely acts of omission—a company's failure to remove defamatory content posted by a third party. It does not apply to acts of commission—a company's own speech, editorial judgments, or decisions to censor content or bar users.[36]

Section 230(c)(2), known as the "Good Samaritan" exception, provides limited immunity for a company's acts of commission. It says, "No provider or user of an interactive computer service shall be held liable

---

[36] See National Telecommunications and Information Agency's (NTIA) Petition to the FCC for a Rulemaking to Clarify Provisions of Section 230 of the Communications Act at 27 (July 27, 2020).

on account of—(A) any action voluntarily taken in good faith to restrict access to or availability of material that the provider or user considers to be obscene, lewd, lascivious, filthy, excessively violent, harassing, or otherwise objectionable, whether or not such material is constitutionally protected." This section allows social media companies to remove content that falls into the narrow statutory list so long as the act is "taken in good faith." Some courts have treated the term "otherwise objectionable" as a catch-all that allows companies to restrict content based on their own subjective judgment about what is "objectionable." Other courts, however, have rightly understood that the term "otherwise objectionable" is limited by the terms that precede it and the overarching purpose of the Communications Decency Act, which was to prevent minors from accessing harmful sexual content on the internet. Rightly understood, "otherwise objectionable" is limited to content that is similar to content that is "sexually offensive, violent, or harassing."[37] Taken together, Section 230(c)(1) and 230(c)(2) aimed to solve the conundrum companies faced prior to the statute's enactment—they could now restrict obscene, lewd, lascivious, and other similarly objectionable content without facing liability for the defamatory content provided by third parties. These provisions do not, however, provide blanket immunity for a social media company's every decision that affects content on its platform.

Unfortunately, courts have not honored the targeted nature of the immunity granted by Section 230. Instead, they greatly expanded it to cover any time a social media company is "exercis[ing] . . . a publisher's traditional editorial functions—such as deciding whether to publish, withdraw, postpone or alter content."[38] This dramatically exceeds the scope of the statute's language and immunizes social media companies' own conduct, even when that conduct reaches beyond moderation of obscene third-party content to include takedowns of wholly unobjectionable religious, political, or ideological material. This error has emboldened social media companies

---

[37] Darnaa, LLC v. Google, Inc., 2016 WL 6540452 at *8 (N.D. Cal. 2016).
[38] Zeran v. America Online, Inc., 129 F.3d 327, 330 (4th Cir. 1997).

to engage in increasingly egregious forms of content censorship, including the labeling and removal of Christian views on sexuality and gender.

Legislators, scholars, commentators, and even one Supreme Court justice have proposed remedies to the censorship problem caused by this misguided interpretation of Section 230. But there is no quick fix. Some potential solutions include Justice Clarence Thomas's suggestion that legislatures regulate social media companies as common carriers—similar to telephone companies or package delivery services—or places of public accommodation, and then impose statutory barriers to viewpoint discrimination.[39] Constitutional scholar Phillip Hamburger signaled his support for Justice Thomas's suggestion in a *Wall Street Journal* piece.[40] First Amendment scholar Eugene Volokh has also signaled his openness to certain forms of common-carrier style regulation of social media companies.[41] And the Department of Justice recommended comprehensive reforms to Section 230 that would restore the limited immunity that provision initially intended.[42] While we can and should advocate for sensible legal and legislative solutions to these problems, we should recognize that social media censorship is more a product of cultural changes and advocacy than legal or legislative interventions. Thus, we should also call on social media companies to recognize the purpose of Section 230—to create a robust forum for the exchange of ideas—and advocate for content moderation policies and practices that align with that purpose.

---

[39] *Biden*, 141 S. Ct. at 1221.

[40] See Phillip Hamburger and Clare Morrell, "The First Amendment Doesn't Protect Big Tech's Censorship," *Wall Street Journal*, July 31, 2021, https://www.wsj .com/articles/big-tech-twitter-facebook-google-youtube-sec-230-common-carrier -11627656722.

[41] See Eugene Volokh, "Social Media Platforms as Common Carriers?" Reason, April 20, 2021, https://reason.com/volokh/2021/04/20/social-media-platforms-as -common-carriers/.

[42] See Department of Justice's Review of Section 230 of the Communications Decency Act of 1996, US Department of Justice, https://www.justice.gov/archives /ag/department-justice-s-review-section-230-communications-decency-act-1996.

A Possible Path out of the Censorship Conundrum

Consistent with the purpose of Section 230, the gatekeepers of the digital public square have committed to protecting free expression and creating platforms where people can access and express the broadest range of views.

Consider the following examples:

- **Twitter:** "Twitter's mission is to give everyone the power to create and share ideas and information, and to express their opinions and beliefs without barriers. Free expression is a human right—we believe that everyone has a voice, and the right to use it. Our role is to serve the public conversation, which requires representation of a diverse range of perspectives."[43]

- **Facebook (Meta):** "The goal of our Community Standards is to create a place for expression and give people a voice. Meta wants people to be able to talk openly about the issues that matter to them, even if some may disagree or find them objectionable. . . . Our commitment to expression is paramount."[44]

- **YouTube:** "We believe that everyone deserves to have a voice, and that the world is a better place when we listen, share and build community through our stories. . . . We believe people should be able to speak freely, share opinions, foster open dialogue, and that creative freedom leads to new voices, formats and possibilities."[45]

Unfortunately, these companies have not lived up to these laudable goals. Too often, they are not neutral conduits for others' speech. Rather, they adopt content moderation policies that interfere with the free exchange

---

[43] Hateful Conduct Policy, Twitter, https://help.twitter.com/en/rules-and -policies/hateful-conduct-policy, accessed May 23, 2022.

[44] Facebook Community Standards, Facebook, https://transparency.fb.com /policies/community-standards/.

[45] Our Mission, YouTube, https://www.youtube.com/howyoutubeworks/our -mission/; "We're here to help you become an Impact Creator," YouTube Social Impact, accessed March 19, 2022, https://socialimpact.youtube.com/intl/en-GB /about/.

of ideas and use those policies to suppress certain views on matters of public concern, including the contentious issues of sexuality and gender. As previously discussed, this viewpoint discrimination poses a real threat to the freedom of Christians and other faith groups to express their religious views on sex, gender, what it means to be male and female, and a host of other critical issues.

There is a path forward for these companies to make good on their promises to facilitate free speech and open debate on their platforms. They can model their policies on our nation's free speech tradition, as expressed in First Amendment case law. Social media companies often seem to act as if no one has ever thought about how to deal with unsavory speech in a democratic society. But First Amendment case law is a rich repository of over 230 years of the best thinking on how to protect free speech while retaining the power to restrict obscene, profane, lewd, violent, and similarly objectionable speech. There is nothing "different" or "unique" about regulating content in the digital age that would render past, tried-and-true principles void.

Two cornerstone First Amendment principles bear mentioning at the outset. First, robust debate and free inquiry are essential to sustaining our nation's democratic fabric. As the Supreme Court explained in 1949: "The vitality of civil and political institutions in our society depends on free discussion. . . . [I]t is only through free debate and free exchange of ideas that government remains responsive to the will of the people and peaceful change is affected. The right to speak freely and to promote diversity of ideas and programs is therefore one of the chief distinctions that sets us apart from totalitarian regimes."[46] A commitment to the free exchange of ideas and respect for those with whom we disagree are essential to human flourishing and to fostering a diverse, pluralistic, and tolerant society. As curators of the modern public square, social media companies should treat this commitment as their North Star. It should guide all their content moderation decisions, including policy formulation and enforcement.

Second, it is a "bedrock principle underlying the First Amendment" that ideas cannot be silenced "simply because society finds the idea itself offensive

---

[46] Terminiello v. City of Chicago, 337 U.S. 1, 4 (1949).

or disagreeable."[47] This means that speech cannot be restricted because others consider it "misguided," "hurtful," or "upsetting," or feel that it "arouses contempt" or would "have an adverse emotional impact."[48] Put simply, the First Amendment does not exist to protect popular speech; its primary purpose is to protect speech that is considered unpopular, unorthodox, or as challenging to the status quo. Indeed, the Supreme Court has observed that speech is "often provocative and challenging," frequently "strike[s] at prejudices and preconceptions," and can "have profound unsettling effects."[49] Free speech "best serve[s] its high purpose when it induces a condition of unrest, creates dissatisfaction with conditions as they are, or even stirs people to anger."[50] Any other approach to free speech "would lead to standardization of ideas either by legislatures, courts, or dominant political or community groups."[51]

This principle is probably where social media companies get tripped up most. They understandably desire to create a safe environment for users. But this requires clear definitions. What exactly is "safe" in terms of speech? Problematically, Meta, Twitter, Amazon, and Alphabet's view of "safe" includes protecting people from encountering ideas that make them uncomfortable or that challenge their core beliefs or way of life. That violates the very bedrock of free speech. Federal courts have said that *even K–12 schools* lack the power under the First Amendment to protect students from "criticism of their beliefs or for that matter their way of life."[52] How much more so does this principle apply to the digital public square, which

---

[47] Texas v. Johnson, 491 U.S. 397, 414 (1989).

[48] Hurley v. Irish–American Gay, Lesbian and Bisexual Group of Boston, Inc., 515 U.S. 557, 574 (1995); Snyder v. Phelps, 562 U.S. 443, 458 (2011); Boos v. Barry, 485 U.S. 312, 322 (1988).

[49] *Terminiello*, 337 U.S. at 4.

[50] *Terminiello*, 337 U.S. at 4.

[51] *Terminiello*, 337 U.S. at 4–5.

[52] Nuxoll ex rel. Nuxoll v. Indian Prairie Sch. Dist. 204, 523 F.3d 668, 672 (7th Cir. 2008); Saxe v. State Coll. Area Sch. Dist., 240 F.3d 200, 210 (3d Cir. 2001) ("By prohibiting disparaging speech directed at a person's 'values,' the Policy strikes at the heart of moral and political discourse—the lifeblood of constitutional self-government (and democratic education) and the core concern of the First Amendment. . . . No court or legislature has ever suggested that

is the modern-day equivalent of the traditional public square and mainly facilitates the speech of adults? Social media companies are demonstrating a profound failure to appreciate that a robust marketplace of ideas will be full of speech that makes people uncomfortable, offended, or worse. But this is what is necessary to live in a free society that cherishes free expression. As a majority of Supreme Court justices (including Justices Scalia and Sotomayor) noted in 2011: "Many are those who must endure speech they do not like, but that is a necessary cost of freedom."[53]

To secure the above principles, First Amendment case law places clear limits on the government's ability to regulate speech. Regulations that impact speech must *not* be content-based, viewpoint-based, vague, or overbroad:

- **Content-based:** A regulation is content-based when it targets speech "because of its message, its ideas, its subject matter, or its content."[54]
- **Viewpoint-based:** A regulation is viewpoint-based when it targets speech based on "the specific motivating ideology, or the opinion, or the perspective of the speaker."[55] Viewpoint-based discrimination is a "more blatant" and "egregious" form of content-based discrimination.
- **Vague:** A regulation is vague if it invites arbitrary and discriminatory enforcement due to a lack of objective standards. This discretion is a threat to free speech because it "has the potential for becoming a means of suppressing a particular point of view."[56]
- **Overbroad:** A regulation is overbroad if it is written so broadly that it prohibits a substantial amount of protected speech.[57]

---

unwelcome speech directed at another's 'values' may be prohibited under the rubric of anti-discrimination.")

[53] Sorrell v. IMS Health Inc., 564 U.S. 552, 575 (2011).

[54] Reed v. Town of Gilbert, 576 U.S. 155, 163 (2015).

[55] Rosenberger v. Rector & Visitors of the University of Virginia, 515 U.S. 819, 829 (1995).

[56] Forsyth County v. Nationalist Movement, 505 U.S. 123, 130 (1992).

[57] Broadrick v. Oklahoma, 413 U.S. 601, 611–12 (1973).

Social media companies could go a long way toward protecting free expression on their platforms by aligning their content moderation standards and enforcement decisions with these four guideposts. Unfortunately, their content moderation policies contain many provisions that violate these guideposts, both as written and as applied. Policies purporting to regulate "hate speech," "hateful conduct," "harassment," and "threats" pose the greatest danger to the freedom of all people—especially Christians—to express their views on important topics. In most instances, these policies use the language typically included in anti-discrimination or anti-harassment policies to regulate speech. Decades of First Amendment case law show how these types of regulations threaten free speech and violate the four guideposts identified above.

Courts have long held that government policies that attempt to regulate speech pursuant to characteristics like religion, sex, sexual orientation, and gender identity "impose content-based, viewpoint discriminatory restrictions on speech."[58] In the hands of speech regulators (whether the government or private companies), the list of protected characteristics has the effect of restricting discussion around certain topics (content-based discrimination) or prohibiting the expression of certain views (viewpoint-based discrimination). For example, in *R.A.V. v. City of St. Paul*, the United States Supreme Court reviewed a city anti-bias ordinance, which barred speech that would "arouse . . . anger, alarm or resentment in others on the basis of race, color, creed, religion or gender."[59] The court explained that the ordinance would bar a person from making the forbidden statements about race, religion, gender, and color, but it would allow them to make similar statements about other ideas, like political affiliation or union membership. Thus, the ordinance only applied if the speech was "addressed to one of the specified disfavored topics."[60] In striking down the ordinance, the court ruled that it imposed "special prohibitions on those

---

[58] *Saxe*, 240 F.3d at 206.

[59] R.A.V. v. City of St. Paul, Minn., 505 U.S. 377, 380 (1992).

[60] *R.A.V.*, 505 U.S. at 391.

speakers who express views on disfavored subjects," the very essence of content-based discrimination.[61]

Social media companies' "hate speech" policies are often problematic for similar reasons. Like the ordinance struck down in *R.A.V.* and other anti-discrimination/harassment laws, many private "hate speech" policies purport to restrict certain kinds of speech based on a list of protected characteristics. As written, they directly invite content- and viewpoint-based discrimination; and in practice, that is how these companies enforce them. Twitter deplatformed the *Daily Citizen* (a Christian publication run by Focus on the Family) for four months for a post stating that one of President Biden's nominees was "a transgender woman, that is, a man who believes he is a woman." Twitter said that the post violated its "hateful conduct" policy. Twitter's "hateful conduct" policy states that it bars posts that "promote violence," "directly attack or threaten," or "incit[e] harm" toward others based on "race, ethnicity, national origin, caste, sexual orientation, gender, gender identity, religious affiliation, age, disability, or serious disease."[62] While Twitter understandably desires to restrict violent and threatening speech on its platform, it should do so by adopting policies that (1) bar violent and threatening speech regardless of the idea being communicated, and (2) make clear that they will not be enforced against social, political, and religious views on matters of public concern.

Courts also often strike these policies down for being overbroad. For example, in 2001 in *Saxe v. State College Area School District*, the Third Circuit reviewed a school's anti-harassment policy that barred speech that denigrates, belittles, or offends a person based on their religious traditions, racial customs, sexual orientation, and other personal characteristics.[63] The court found the policy overbroad because it "could conceivably be applied to cover any speech about some enumerated personal characteristics the content of which offends someone."[64] And as the court rightly noted, "The

---

[61] *R.A.V.*, 505 U.S. at 391.

[62] See note 43, above.

[63] *Saxe*, 240 F.3d at 203, 217.

[64] *Saxe*, 240 F.3d at 217.

Supreme Court has held time and again . . . that the mere fact that someone might take offense at the content of speech is not sufficient justification for prohibiting it."[65] Courts have also struck down government policies whose text resemble the language used in social media companies' "hate speech" policies on vagueness grounds. In *Dambrot v. Central Michigan University*, the Sixth Circuit reviewed a public university's "discriminatory harassment" policy, which prohibited "any intentional, unintentional, physical, verbal, or nonverbal behavior that subjects an individual to an intimidating, hostile or offensive educational, employment or living environment" based on "racial or ethnic affiliation."[66] Observing that "different people find different things offensive," the court found the policy vague because its application depended on enforcement officials' subjective judgment about what qualifies as "negative" or "offensive" speech.[67]

Similarly, in *Doe v. University of Michigan*, a court reviewed a policy that prohibited "stigmatizing or victimizing individuals or groups on the basis of race, ethnicity, religion, sex, sexual orientation, creed, national origin, ancestry, age, marital status, handicap or Vietnam-era veteran status."[68] In its opinion, the court noted that it asked the university's lawyer at oral argument "how he would distinguish between speech that was merely 'offensive,' which he conceded was protected, and speech which 'stigmatizes or victimizes'" based on a protected characteristic.[69] His answer? "Very carefully."[70] This candid answer demonstrated the vagueness problem with the policy—the university had never articulated any principled way to distinguish between permissible and sanctionable speech, leaving "[s]tudents of common understanding . . . to guess at whether a comment about a controversial issue would later be found to be sanctionable."[71]

---

[65] *Saxe*, 240 F.3d at 215.

[66] Dambrot v. Central Michigan Univ., 55 F.3d 1177, 1182 (6th Cir. 1995).

[67] *Dambrot*, 55 F.3d at 1184.

[68] Doe v. University of Michigan, 721 F. Supp. 852, 853 (E.D. Mich. 1989).

[69] *Doe*, 721 F. Supp. at 867.

[70] *Doe*, 721 F. Supp. at 867.

[71] *Doe*, 721 F. Supp. at 867.

The same question should be asked about how social media companies distinguish between permissible and impermissible content related to protected characteristics. One such company, Facebook, conceded in an earlier version of their "hate speech" policy that "there is no universally accepted answer for when something crosses the [hate speech] line" and that people have "different levels of tolerance for speech about protected characteristics."[72] This candid concession confirms a disturbing truth— our freedom to express our views is subject to the caprice, whim, and subjective judgments of social media employees and algorithms. We have already seen that social media companies are censoring content expressing views about matters of public concern as "hateful," "violent," "harassing," or "threatening" even when those views cannot fairly be characterized as "obscene, lewd, lascivious, filthy, excessively violent, harassing" or similarly objectionable.

Courts have also routinely found that terms that are the same or similar to those used in social media companies' content moderation policies threaten free speech rights. Courts have found terms such as *threats, insults, epithets, ridicule,* or *personal attacks*;[73] *stigmatize* or *victimize*;[74] *derogatory comments*;[75] *denigrate, belittle,* and *offend*;[76] and *acts of intolerance that demonstrate malicious intent toward others* as deeply problematic and overly broad.[77] Compare that list with a list of terms used by social media companies: *direct attack against people*; *directly attack or threaten*; *targets, insults and abuses*; *incite hatred*; *promote hatred*.[78] There is no meaningful way to distinguish the two lists. Social media companies' policies are littered with vague

---

[72] Richard Allen, "Hard Questions: Who Should Decide What Is Hate Speech in an Online Global Community?" Meta, June 27, 2017, https://about.fb.com /news/2017/06/hard-questions-hate-speech/.

[73] Roberts v. Haragan, 346 F. Supp. 2d 853, 872 (N.D. Tex. 2004).

[74] *Doe*, 721 F. Supp. at 853.

[75] *Nuxoll*, 523 F.3d at 670.

[76] *Saxe*, 240 F.3d at 215.

[77] Bair v. Shippensburg Univ., 280 F. Supp. 2d 357, 370 (M.D. Pa. 2003).

[78] These terms are taken from Twitter, Facebook, and YouTube's "hate speech" policies. See notes 43, 44, and 45, above.

and subjective terms that decades of First Amendment case law say pose real and substantial threats to the freedom of speech.

The First Amendment guideposts discussed above mark the path forward for social media companies. These companies laudably desire to ban violent, threatening, and harassing conduct on their platforms. But they must do so in a manner that does not discriminate based on the content and viewpoint of speech. Social media companies could take an important first step toward this goal by dropping the list of protected characteristics from their hate speech and similar policies. No one should face threats of violence or harassing conduct online. Social media companies should protect *everyone* from this kind of conduct, not just those who fall into certain protected classifications.

Social media companies should seek to avoid vague and overbroad terms that give them and their content moderation teams the ability to discriminate against disfavored views. There are at least two immediate actions available to companies here. First, they should eliminate many of the subjective terms discussed above from their policies. Second, they should specify that the mere expression of personal social, religious, or political views does not constitute harassment, discrimination, hate speech, or threats of violence under their policies. To accomplish this, they should narrow the reach of their policies by focusing them on specific categories of speech that have not traditionally been afforded First Amendment protection.[79] Specifically, the First Amendment does not protect fighting words, incitement, and true threats of violence. Fighting words are "those which by their very utterance inflict injury or tend to incite an immediate breach of the peace."[80] Incitement is speech that is "directed to inciting or producing imminent lawless action and is likely to incite or produce such action."[81] True threats are "those statements where the speaker means to communicate a serious

---

[79] Ultimately, we favor social media companies eliminating the term "hate speech" from their content moderation standards. There is too great a risk that social media companies' employees will enforce this vague term based on their subjective judgments in a manner that suppresses disfavored views.

[80] Chaplinsky v. New Hampshire, 315 U.S. 568, 572 (1942).

[81] Brandenburg v. Ohio, 395 U.S. 444, 447 (1969).

expression of an intent to commit an act of unlawful violence to a particular individual or group of individuals."[82] Modeling policy language or defining existing policy terms based on these unprotected categories of speech (fighting words, incitement, and true threats of violence) would diminish the risk of content moderation policies imperiling the free exchange of ideas in the digital public square.

Finally, the Supreme Court's 1999 decision in *Davis v. Monroe County Board of Education* is a helpful guidepost for the permissible scope of anti-harassment/bullying policies. In *Davis*, the court reviewed a case involving a school district's potential liability for failing to address student-on-student harassment. According to the Supreme Court, to avoid conflict with other constitutional rights, like free speech, schools should only punish harassing conduct that is "so severe, pervasive, and objectively offensive, and that so undermines and detracts from the victims' educational experience, that the victim-students are effectively denied equal access to an institution's resources and opportunities."[83] The *Davis* standard provides a clear road map for social media companies to ensure that their anti-harassment/bullying policies do not interfere with the free exchange of ideas. It is also a far cry from their current practice, which penalizes a single utterance of someone's personal convictions on a matter of public concern as "harassment."

Fortunately, we have some unexpected allies in the cause of restoring free speech online. Nadine Strossen, the former president of the progressive American Civil Liberties Union (ACLU), has spoken out strongly against social media censorship. In her book *Hate: Why We Should Resist It with Free Speech, Not Censorship*, Strossen advocates that internet service providers, search engines, and social media platforms should "respect the free speech rights of others over whom they exercise power."[84] She urges them to "wield their vast power consistent with the core-speech protective viewpoint neutrality" rule and, "except in unusual circumstances, . . . permit all expression

---

[82] Virginia v. Black, 538 U.S. 343, 359 (2003).

[83] Davis v. Monroe County Bd. of Educ., 526 U.S. 629, 651 (1999).

[84] Nadine Strossen, *Hate: Why We Should Resist It with Free Speech, Not Censorship* (Oxford: Oxford University Press, 2018), 30.

that the First Amendment shields from government censorship."[85] In a video for the *Atlantic*, she condemns loose definitions of "hate speech" that permit governments and mega-corporations to censor people and groups.[86] In Strossen's view, with only a few exceptions, rules for conduct on social media need to be left up to social media users.

David Sacks, one of the founders of PayPal, warns that censorship is only the beginning. If tech companies are allowed to choose who gets to speak and who cannot, it is only one more step to choosing who gets to participate in the market and who cannot—in other words, who gets to be in society and who gets left out. He wrote on former *New York Times* reporter Bari Weiss's Substack that PayPal has begun relying on radicalized groups like the Southern Poverty Law Center (SPLC) to decide who to ban from the platform. Sacks writes that "[SPLC'S] ever-increasing list of suspects has grown from unquestionable hate groups, like neo-nazis and the KKK, to organizations who espouse socially conservative views, like the Family Research Council,[87] religious liberty advocates, and even groups concerned with election integrity."[88] He points out that in 2021 White House Press Secretary Jen Psaki indicated that the federal government "is centrally coordinating a blocklist across social media properties."[89] Christians no longer have the luxury of standing by and hoping that someone else fixes this problem for us. We must enter the conversation with social media companies through organized and strategic advocacy alongside free-speech advocates like Strossen and Sacks.[90]

---

[85] Strossen, 32, 31.

[86] See "Why Social Media Shouldn't Censor Hate Speech," *Atlantic*, August 24, 2018, https://www.theatlantic.com/video/index/568498/nadine-strossen/.

[87] Of note in 2012, a shooter entered the FRC headquarters in Washington, DC, injuring one before being detained and arrested. For more on this story, see Carol Cratty and Michael Pearson, "DC shooter wanted to kill as many as possible, prosecutors say," CNN, February 13, 2013, https://www.cnn.com/2013/02/06/justice/dc-family-research-council-shooting/index.html.

[88] David Sacks, "Get Ready for the 'No-Buy' List," Common Sense, July 30, 2021, https://bariweiss.substack.com/p/get-ready-for-the-no-buy-list.

[89] Sacks, "Get Ready for the 'No-Buy' List."

[90] For more on building a public theology for the digital age, including on engaging technology companies similar to how the church has historically engaged state actors, see chapter 1 by Jason Thacker.

Preserving Our Witness in the Digital Public Square

Social media (for all its ills) has emerged as the new public square, and as such, is a crucial medium for preserving and promoting the value of faith in public affairs. Maintaining Christian witness in the digital space is especially important in our present age when internet platforms play such an outsized role in shaping and facilitating public discourse on a myriad of topics. Christians may (and perhaps should) lament this, but the fact remains that the digital space exerts significant influence on our culture and its institutions. This presents both dangers and opportunities for Christians and other people of faith—the danger of being targeted, censored, defunded, and deplatformed for our deeply held beliefs, alongside the opportunity to use internet platforms to share our faith globally and advocate for a religious worldview on matters of public concern.

But what does faithful advocacy in the digital age look like? First and foremost, we as Christians must have the courage to respectfully share our faith with family, friends, neighbors, and colleagues—even when doing so invites dispute and even censorship (or worse). In his 1978 Harvard address, famed writer Aleksandr Solzhenitsyn proclaimed that a "decline in courage may be the most striking feature which an outside observer notices in the West."[91] In an age unsettled about the things that matter most and were once thought to be universal, undisputed facts of existence—namely human nature and the inherent reality of biology—what is most needed is for the church to "value nothing more (highly) than truth" and to have the courage to speak it.[92] This means recognizing that the good of standing on the principles of our faith vastly outweighs whatever social, political, or economic consequences may result.

---

[91] Alexandr Solzhenitsyn, "A World Split Apart" (delivered June 8, 1978, Harvard University), American Rhetoric Online Speech Bank, https://www.americanrhetoric.com/speeches/alexandersolzhenitsynharvard.htm.

[92] Rod Dreher, *Live Not by Lies: A Manual for Christian Dissidents* (New York: Penguin, 2020), 97.

This is not a call for Christians to become "keyboard warriors" and demonize our opponents online. Such an approach is antithetical to true courage, which demands that our engagement with those with whom we disagree—especially on issues of fundamental importance like sexuality, gender, and family—is always characterized by civility, love, prudence, and the pursuit of truth. As Christians, we believe that all people are created in the image and likeness of God (Gen 1:26–27), and therefore they are worthy of love and respect. Because of this foundational belief, we have an outsized responsibility to work against polarization and division online. We should model the kind of discourse we seek to foster in our society—a discourse that recognizes the reality of fundamental differences, but which is ultimately grounded in a deep concern for the other's good—regardless of the nature or depth of the disagreement.

We must also recognize that a genuine care for others does not mean affirming whatever they say or believe. A commitment to truth and our own conscience demands that we charitably advocate against ideas contrary to biblical teaching and which we believe will have negative consequences for individuals and society. This point is particularly apt to discussions on sex, gender, and what it means to be male and female. For example, adding "gender identity" to antidiscrimination laws poses an unprecedented threat to free speech, religious freedom, parental rights, and the progress that women have made toward true equal treatment under the law. Examples of these threats abound. The city of Anchorage, Alaska, attempted to force a faith-based women's shelter to allow men to sleep in the same room as women who had suffered traumatic mistreatment and sexual abuses. (Thankfully, a federal court ruled against the ordinance.)[93] The state of Connecticut adopted a rule that allowed males to compete against female athletes. This resulted in two male athletes who identify as female winning fifteen women's high

---

[93] See "Downtown Hope Center v. Municipality of Anchorage II," Alliance Defending Freedom, December 21, 2021, https://adfmedia.org/case/downtown -hope-center-v-municipality-anchorage-ii.

school track championships that were once held by nine different girls.[94] A college tried to punish a professor for declining on religious grounds to use female pronouns to refer to a male student.[95] Christians must be present in the gender identity debate, advocating for a biblical understanding of human nature and sexuality and against ideas and laws that would have a destructive impact on individuals and society.

While Christians must be courageous and faithful advocates in the digital public square, such efforts will likely falter unless coupled with calls for significant structural reforms, aimed at creating accountability and safeguards to ensure that people of faith maintain the freedom to voice their views online. While Christians may disagree on the specific legislative reforms or policy details, it is incumbent on the church to step into these conversations and stand for free expression and religious freedom for all. Affecting such changes within institutions so overtly hostile to faith is indeed a daunting challenge. Yet such reforms are necessary for the future of Christian witness as well as the preservation of a free society. Given the enormity of the task, where should Christians start?

The first step is to apply the biblical call to "seek the welfare of the city" to our digital spaces as well as our physical ones (Jer 29:7 ESV). Christians have historically played a crucial role in facilitating social reform in Western societies. From ending the gladiatorial contests in Rome and abolishing the

---

[94] See "Athletes Appeal Ruling That Allows CT Athletic Association to Abolish Girls-Only Sports," Alliance Defending Freedom, May 26, 2021, https://adfmedia .org/case/soule-v-connecticut-association-schools.

[95] See "6th Circuit upholds First Amendment rights of Shawnee State professor," Alliance Defending Freedom, March 26, 2021, https://adfmedia.org/press -release/6th-circuit-upholds-first-amendment-rights-shawnee-state-professor. Thankfully, Alliance Defending Freedom (where the authors work) prevailed in this lawsuit. The Sixth Circuit ruled that the college violated the professor's First Amendment rights. The court explained that if "professors lacked free-speech protections when teaching, a university would wield alarming power to compel ideological conformity. A university president could require a pacifist to declare that war is just, a civil rights icon to condemn the Freedom Riders, a believer to deny the existence of God, or a Soviet émigré to address his students as 'comrades.' That cannot be." *Meriwether v. Hartop*, 992 F.3d 492, 506 (6th Cir. 2021).

transatlantic slave trade, to building social institutions (such as hospitals and adoption agencies) and providing for essential human needs, Christians have rightfully seen our biblical mandate to advance human flourishing wherever we find ourselves. It is this fundamental commitment to human flourishing that should inform our approach to digital governance. People of faith ought to engage and seek to influence the structures that govern speech online, not only because such structures impact our witness, but also because the internet has become the new public square where debate and dialogue about consequential social issues and institutions primarily occurs. Our mandate to thoughtfully engage in the realm of digital governance stems both from practical necessity, as well as from a desire to preserve human flourishing by working to ensure a free marketplace of ideas in the digital commons. For individual Christians, this means remaining faithful to our beliefs in the face of adversity and actively "loving our online neighbors as ourselves" (see Mark 12:31). For Christians employed at tech companies, it means being intentional about forming communities of mutual support with fellow believers both in and outside the workplace and then advocating for internal changes that preserve the free exchange of ideas and Christian expression in the digital space. For Christian tech entrepreneurs, it means designing alternative digital spaces and technologies to counter the mass-centralization of Silicon Valley and provide greater opportunities for expression. For pastors, this means teaching and discipling the flock to think wisely and biblically about engaging in the digital public square, marked by conviction and love for one another.

In the present age, marked by moral confusion and the suppression of truth, Christians have a choice. Will we call for reforming the structures and institutions seeking to suppress truth, or will we sit by and watch as our freedoms are erased, and with them, the opportunities to be faithful witnesses to a lost world? The choice is ours, and as this chapter has attempted to argue, the path Christians choose from here will invariably impact the church and the future course of our society. If we hope to faithfully obey the command to "love others" and seek the "city's welfare" in the twenty-first century, we must advocate for the freedom to share our beliefs in the digital public space.

9

Should We Ban Pornography Online?

Navigating the Complexities of Objectionable Content in a Digital Age

Bonnie Kristian

Walking to lunch one day in sixth grade, I overheard some classmates at my tiny Christian school snickering in the gym. They were laughing about something to do with "porn," they told me. I was awkward, a year younger than the rest of my grade, and eager to laugh along. The only problem: I had no idea what "porn" was. I tried to hide my ignorance, asking them to remind me of its meaning, pretending the definition had simply slipped my mind for a moment. Suffice it to say my ploy did not work.

The same story set-up would play out differently now, for the average American child first encounters pornography at age eleven.[1] A sixth grader

---

[1] See "Children and Pornography," Digital Kids Initiative, 2014, https://digitalkidsinitiative.com/wp-content/uploads/2014/08/Children_and_Pornography_Factsheet-Revised-August-2014.pdf.

today is likely not only to know the meaning of "porn" but to have encountered it, even if her parents are as cautious as my mom was.

A Texas mother named Destiny Herndon-De La Rosa told the modern version of my experience in a 2019 op-ed in the *Dallas Morning News*, writing about her eleven-year-old daughter. "At a friend's birthday party, they were playing on the little girl's phone. The girl handed it to my daughter and said, 'Boys are disgusting,'" Herndon-De La Rosa recounted. "My daughter clicked on a male classmate's Snapchat story to find a video of him and a few other boys from her class laughing as they watched rape porn. She said the woman was bound up, saying 'no' as a masked man approached her."[2]

As Herndon-De La Rosa observed, her daughter's experience is not unusual. Many parents give their children unfettered internet access at ever-younger ages, often via smartphones they use without adult supervision, and many schools "not only tolerate phones in the classroom [but] encourage them" as a homework tool.[3] Those devices are also a portal to unlimited pornography, much of it hardcore, available for free, and found easily by inexperienced internet users, like eleven-year-olds.

Intra-family rules about device use and porn access are protective but can only do so much. Herndon-De La Rosa's daughter had no phone of her own and did not seek out explicit content. She still saw it. That reality, to which adults are subject as well, has fueled a renewed interest in and debate among American Christians and political conservatives about the merits of banning (or far more restrictively regulating) online porn.[4] Pornography prohibition is a minority position in the American public—around two in three say porn should be illegal only for those under eighteen—but it's a

---

[2] Destiny Herndon-De La Rosa, "When 6th graders can access rape porn on their smartphones, school becomes toxic," *Dallas Morning News,* December 12, 2019, https://www.dallasnews.com/opinion/commentary/2019/12/12/when-6th-graders-can-access-rape-porn-on-their-smartphones-school-becomes-toxic/.

[3] Herndon-De La Rosa, "When 6th graders can access rape porn on their smartphones, school becomes toxic."

[4] See Jane Coaston, "There's a conservative civil war raging—over porn," Vox, December 12, 2019, https://www.vox.com/policy-and-politics/2019/12/12/21003109/pornography-obscenity-barr-doj-conservatives-libertarians.

robust minority. Roughly a third of the country supports a total ban,[5] a policy that occasionally even finds a national champion, like former Sen. Rick Santorum (R-Pa.) when he ran for the GOP presidential nomination in 2012.[6] Should we do it? Should we ban online porn?

The Case for Banning Online Porn

The rationale for banning online pornography is simple enough and can be advanced in three parts. First: Pornography is evil. It is vile and destructive of relationships. It is degrading and corruptive for producer and consumer alike.[7] It runs blatantly afoul of basic, historic-orthodox Christian convictions about sex and God's will for human flourishing. In the words of the Catechism of the Catholic Church—which on this subject will find wide agreement across denominational lines—porn "offends against chastity" and makes parties involved "an object of base pleasure and illicit profit for others," immersing them in "the illusion of a fantasy world" cut off from God's truth.[8]

Moreover, there is compelling (albeit much-contested) evidence from social science that heavy use of pornography among children tends to follow negative precursors like depression, bullying, trauma, abuse, and poor parental/caregiver relationships.[9] In addition, childhood exposure to porn,

---

[5] See Charles Fain Lehman, "What Do Americans Think About Banning Porn?" Institute for Family Studies, December 18, 2019, https://ifstudies.org/blog/what-do-americans-think-about-banning-porn.

[6] See Elspeth Reeve, "Could You Really Get Rid of Porn on the Internet?" *Atlantic*, March 15, 2012, https://www.theatlantic.com/politics/archive/2012/03/could-you-really-get-rid-porn-internet/330500/.

[7] See Robert P. George and Shaykh Hamza Yusuf, "Pornography, Respect, and Responsibility: A Letter to the Hotel Industry," *Public Discourse*, 2012, https://www.thepublicdiscourse.com/2012/07/5815/.

[8] "Catechism of the Catholic Church," Vatican, 1993, https://www.vatican.va/archive/ENG0015/__P85.HTM.

[9] See Gail Hornor, "Child and Adolescent Pornography Exposure," *Journal of Pediatric Healthcare* 34, no. 2 (March 2020): 191–99, https://www.jpedhc.org/article/S0891-5245(19)30384-0/fulltext.

especially if habitual, can have life-altering consequences. For example, early exposure to pornography is linked to high-risk sexual behavior, sexual aggression, denigration of women, and addictive behavior, including, per a 2020 article in the *Journal of Pediatric Healthcare*, "sexual knowledge beyond what would be expected for the child's age and developmental levels, such as children engaging in sophisticated sexual acts such as intercourse or oral sex."[10] Adult pornography consumption is similarly detrimental to individual users and their marriages alike, insinuating its harm even at a biological level.[11] In short, porn is insidious.

Second, in comparing the internet as a means of porn distribution to older analog options, we find a difference of both degree and kind. In the recent past—and certainly before the mid-twentieth century—pornography was largely available in the form of still images. The limits of the medium acted as something of a constraint on the obscenity of the content. Means of distribution were more limited as well, particularly for children. Anyone wishing to purchase or rent pornographic content had to take the trouble of ordering it by mail or risk the social censure of obtaining it at a brick-and-mortar store.

Online, all those constraints fall away. Some porn sites permit *any* user to upload images or videos of their choosing, allowing porn of every style and subject and ever-more-extreme degrees of depravity and violence to proliferate, while making it impossible to know if the people depicted are consenting adults. (The porn-human trafficking link is much debated, but that some portion of people appearing in pornography are sex-trafficking victims is not in dispute.) The pornography of earlier eras, like the pin-up cards of the World Wars, are so mild by comparison that some demote them to "erotica"—prurient, but not quite pornographic. In the last three decades, aided by the limitlessness of the internet, porn truly has gotten worse and has become monstrously accessible.

---

[10] Hornor, "Child and Adolescent Pornography Exposure."

[11] See Pascal-Emmanuel Gobry, "A Science-Based Case for Ending the Porn Epidemic," American Greatness, December 15, 2019, https://amgreatness.com/2019/12/15/a-science-based-case-for-ending-the-porn-epidemic/.

Thus, the third part of the argument: Based on these two premises, many Christians have concluded, as the Catholic Catechism does, that "civil authorities should prevent the production and distribution of pornographic materials."[12]

The Case against Banning Online Porn

The case for banning online pornography is strong, and one to which I'm sympathetic. The premises are correct: porn *is* evil, and the internet *did* enormously change Americans' porn habits for the worse. Nevertheless, I do not endorse the call for a government ban. As a state policy, it's legally (often constitutionally) fraught, ethically messy, and at risk of grave unintended consequences. Private regulation is more promising, though it comes with some of the same ethical and practical problems. However, for Christians, both state and private regulation can serve as an excuse for abdication of familial and communal responsibilities of discipleship and cultivation of virtue as part of lifelong sanctification in Christ.

State Regulation

Before we go further, let me pause to specify the grounds for discussion: the issue at hand is the prohibition (or regulation moving toward prohibition) of voluntary, private consumption by consenting adults of pornographic content made, to the consumer's best knowledge, exclusively by consenting adults. Child pornography and underage consumption of pornography are already illegal, as they should be. Rape, sexual assault, and other forms of sexual coercion are also illegal. So too are public broadcasts of pornographic content in places where children and nonconsenting adults may encounter them—for example, you cannot put a pornographic billboard on the highway or broadcast porn at primetime on network television.

Of course, the lines I'm drawing are often blurred in the debate over porn bans because they are often blurred in real life. On the production side,

---

[12] "Catechism of the Catholic Church."

it is not always possible to differentiate between simulated and real rape on screen, or to know whether participants are underage or if their involvement was induced under false pretenses. (This ambiguity is what makes calls for "ethically produced porn" impractical even before we come to the moral abhorrence of the concept from a Christian perspective.) On the distribution side, content intended for adults can reach children instead, regardless of whether they seek it out. Still, for all that blurring, there are already laws in place to address these other ills, so my attention here will generally keep to the narrower space defined above.[13]

Prohibition Proposals

Ideas abound for how the government should keep pornography away from the American public. Some, like Matthew Schmitz, literary editor of *First Things*, have called for an outright federal ban. In a *Washington Post* article titled "The case for banning pornography," Schmitz waves away constitutional objections with a brief aside about First Amendment "flexibility." Change public perception of porn's harmfulness, he argues, and the American people will find a way to bend constitutional speech protections around an anti-porn exception.[14]

Other proposals evince greater recognition of the constitutional roadblock but seek ways around it. For instance, a letter to then attorney general William Barr from four lawmakers in 2019 urged more aggressive enforcement of extant obscenity laws as a path to near-prohibition of online porn.[15] The idea was to exploit the leeway in the Miller Test, a three-part metric established by the Supreme Court in *Miller v. California* (1973) to identify

---

[13] See "Obscenity," Department of Justice, March 29, 2021, https://www.justice.gov/criminal-ceos/obscenity.

[14] Matthew Schmitz, "The case for banning pornography," *Washington Post,* May 24, 2016, https://www.washingtonpost.com/news/in-theory/wp/2016/05/24/the-case-for-banning-pornography/.

[15] See Jim Banks, Mark Meadows, Vicky Hartzler, and Brian Babin, "Letter to Attorney General William Barr," December 6, 2019, https://www.nationalreview.com/wp-content/uploads/2019/12/12.6.2019-Obscenity-Letter-to-AG-Barr.pdf.

obscenity (which is illegal) and distinguish it from other content including pornography (which is legal, constitutionally-protected speech).[16] The Miller Test asks:

1. Whether the average person, applying contemporary adult community standards, finds that the matter, taken as a whole, appeals to prurient interests (i.e., an erotic, lascivious, abnormal, unhealthy, degrading, shameful, or morbid interest in nudity, sex, or excretion);

2. Whether the average person, applying contemporary adult community standards, finds that the matter depicts or describes sexual conduct in a patently offensive way (i.e., ultimate sexual acts, normal or perverted, actual or simulated, masturbation, excretory functions, lewd exhibition of the genitals, or sado-masochistic sexual abuse); and

3. Whether a reasonable person finds that the matter, taken as a whole, lacks serious literary, artistic, political, or scientific value.[17]

If the answer to all three questions is yes—and, crucially, the Supreme Court held in *Jacobellis v. Ohio* (1964) that community standards are national, not local—the content is obscenity, and it is prohibited. If any answer is no, it is not.

To the casual reader, the Miller Test might seem to place all porn (or at least all video porn) in the obscenity category, but *legally* that is not the case. Though some hardcore pornography may be targeted by obscenity laws, explains First Amendment expert David L. Hudson Jr. at the Freedom Forum Institute, "many materials dealing with sex, including pornographic magazines, books, and movies, simply do not qualify as legally obscene."[18]

---

[16] See "Citizen's Guide to U.S. Federal Law on Obscenity," Department of Justice, May 28, 2020, https://www.justice.gov/criminal-ceos/citizens-guide-us-federal-law-obscenity.

[17] "Citizen's Guide to U.S. Federal Law on Obscenity."

[18] David L. Hudson Jr., "Pornography and Obscenity," Freedom Forum Institute, July 2009, https://www.freedomforuminstitute.org/first-amendment-center/topics/freedom-of-speech-2/adult-entertainment/pornography-obscenity/.

In *Brown v. Entertainment Merchants Association* (2011), moreover, the Supreme Court specifically held in a majority opinion penned by the conservative Justice Antonin Scalia that "violence is not part of the obscenity that the Constitution permits to be regulated." That case concerned violent video games, which the state of California had attempted to regulate using obscenity laws. By implication, the court's decision means pornography purporting to depict rape or abuse is not automatically deemed obscene in the legal sense.

Suffice it to say, obscenity has long been and continues to be a "confounding" part of First Amendment law and jurisprudence, as Hudson has observed.[19] The use of "community standards" in the obscenity test presents an intriguing opportunity for those campaigning to ban porn: Community standards can shift. Obscenity is not prohibited based on a fixed criterion but a moving sense of public opinion. That's the leeway the letter to Barr sought to exploit, asking him to legally treat substantially more (or even all) online pornography as obscenity.

Other proposals take a more incremental approach. Journalist and law student Anthony Leonardi argues society should seek to ban *free* online porn, forcing porn sites to require users to set up an account and register a payment method. This could screen out younger users and make it less likely that children would encounter pornography accidentally, depending on implementation.[20] Terry Schilling of the American Principles Project makes the case for "adult zones" on the internet, analogous to real estate zoning, as suggested by then-Justices Sandra Day O'Connor and William Rehnquist in a concurring opinion in *Reno v. ACLU* (1997).[21] Porn could be restricted to, say, .xxx domains, Schilling says, with a mandatory access

---

[19] See David L. Hudson Jr., "Obscenity and Pornography," *The First Amendment Encyclopedia*, 2009, https://www.mtsu.edu/first-amendment/article/1004/obscenity-and-pornography.

[20] See Anthony Leonardi, "Why Free Online Porn Should Be Banned," *National Review*, July 21, 2021, https://www.nationalreview.com/2021/07/why-free-online-porn-should-be-banned/.

[21] See Terry Schilling, "How to Regulate Pornography," *First Things*, November 2019, https://www.firstthings.com/article/2019/11/how-to-regulate-pornography.

hurdle (like registering a user account with a government-issued ID) that children will not be able to leap licitly.

Schilling also advocates requiring internet service providers (ISPs) to make a filtered internet service their default offering, asking adults to opt into unfiltered service instead of getting it automatically. ISPs in the UK did this voluntarily amid talk of a legal compulsion,[22] Schilling notes, and Utah has passed a law with a comparable model for smartphones, though it will not take effect until five other states enact substantially similar legislation.[23]

Schilling also proposes making porn aggregation sites legally liable for pornographic user posts to incentivize tougher content moderation so revenge porn and other pornography depicting nonconsenting adults is more swiftly removed and, ideally, prosecuted.[24] Schilling advises doing this by carving out a new exception to the protections of Section 230 of the Communications Decency Act.[25]

---

[22] See Ben Quinn, "Biggest four UK ISPs switching to 'opt-in' system for pornography," *The Guardian*, October 10, 2011, https://www.theguardian.com/society/2011/oct/11/pornography-internet-service-providers.

[23] See "H.B. 72," Utah State Legislature, 2021, https://le.utah.gov/~2021/bills/static/HB0072.html.

[24] See Schilling, "How to Regulate Pornography."

[25] The nature and function of Section 230 is widely misunderstood. Here is a good summary via the *New York Times*: "The federal law, Section 230 of the Communications Decency Act, has helped Facebook, YouTube, Twitter and countless other internet companies flourish. But Section 230's liability protection also extends to fringe sites known for hosting hate speech, anti-Semitic content and racist tropes like 8chan, the internet message board where the suspect in the El Paso shooting massacre posted his manifesto. The First Amendment protects free speech, including hate speech, but Section 230 shields websites from liability for content created by their users. It permits internet companies to moderate their sites without being on the hook legally for everything they host. It does not provide blanket protection from legal responsibility for some criminal acts, like posting child pornography or violations of intellectual property." Daisuke Wakabayashi, "Legal Shield for Social Media Is Targeted by Lawmakers," *New York Times,* May 28, 2020, https://www.nytimes.com/2020/05/28/business/section-230-internet-speech.html.

Legal Problems

The total ban idea, as Schmitz pitched, will not pass constitutional muster. It is—in the words of David French, a constitutional lawyer and conservative Christian (and contributor to this volume)—a "pipe dream." As French explains, "It's been tried. It failed. Miserably."[26] The First Amendment's speech protections are not *that* flexible. If median public opinion shifted dramatically against porn, we could expect more content to be categorized as obscenity but not a total porn ban. That could change, of course, with a different Constitution, a constitutional amendment, or a massive rejection of extensive, longstanding court precedent that treats pornography as protected speech. These dramatic scenarios are not impossible, but they are too fantastic to fall into the purview of this chapter.

The prospects of the obscenity redefinition plan are only marginally better. As French recounts, in the mid-1980s, the city of Indianapolis enacted an ordinance defining and prohibiting pornography on far more stringent terms than those of the Miller Test. The ordinance was challenged, and, according to French, "Indianapolis lost. No, it didn't just lose. It got crushed. First, the trial court rejected the ordinance. The 7th Circuit Court of Appeals affirmed the trial court, [. . . and] the Supreme Court did something unusual—it summarily affirmed the court of appeals decision without argument."[27] The upshot, French says, is that the obscenity standard is clearly and narrowly established: "The consequences of decades of Supreme Court jurisprudence are clear—any attempt to ban pornography is a legal fool's errand. It will not succeed."[28]

Efforts to sneak in a de facto ban under the Miller Test as the 2019 congressional letter proposed are at present legal nonstarters given the capability of national surveys to demonstrate that most of the American public does not want to prohibit porn for adults. That said, if contemporary adult

---

[26] David French, "It's Constitutionally Impossible and Legally Imprudent to Ban Porn," *Dispatch*, February 28, 2020, https://thedispatch.com/p/its-constitutionally-impossible-and.

[27] French, "It's Constitutionally Impossible and Legally Imprudent to Ban Porn."

[28] French, "It's Constitutionally Impossible and Legally Imprudent to Ban Porn."

community standards moved, this approach could become plausible. It would not lead to a total ban—absent significant constitutional changes—but a broadened legal understanding of obscenity could emerge *after* a fundamental cultural transformation on this point—a reversal, essentially, of the sexual revolution.

What about the more incremental options? Default filtering (by ISPs or smartphone makers, as the UK and Utah are pursuing, respectively) could run into First Amendment trouble too. In *Denver Telecommunications v. FCC* (1996), the Supreme Court overturned a law requiring cable providers to confine "patently offensive" sexual content to specific channels, which were blocked from transmission unless customers opted in to receiving them. The law violated the First Amendment's speech protections, the ruling held, though perhaps a more sophisticated filtering method would not.

Schilling's zoning plan and Leonardi's payment plan, both of which turn on mandatory account registration, might be more viable. French thinks the zoning idea could succeed, as it has precedent in the physical world—"the Supreme Court has allowed municipalities to require porn establishments (like adult book stores or strip clubs) to move to specific, designated areas in the community"—and genesis at the Supreme Court itself in the O'Connor-Rehnquist concurrence.[29] However, the justices stipulated that the zoning could not "unduly restrict adult access to the material," which might prove a potent ground for legal challenge depending on the technological approach.

As a practical matter, it is uncertain how reliably pornographic content could be contained to the designated zone. Users with legitimate access could simply copy the content and upload it elsewhere, as commonly happens even with account-locked porn sites today. Once a piece of content is copied, it can be reproduced forever. The game turns into whack-a-mole: take down one illicit site outside the porn zone and five more can pop up in its place.

The one idea unlikely to face constitutional hindrance is the Section 230 carveout. Though Section 230 has been dubbed the "First Amendment of the internet," it is not part of the Constitution and could be altered or repealed

---

[29] French, "It's Constitutionally Impossible and Legally Imprudent to Ban Porn."

by an act of Congress. Indeed, there's interest beyond the porn conversation, on the political left and right alike, in doing exactly that. It's fueled in many cases (I think) by a severe misunderstanding of the probable consequences for free speech online. As *Reason*'s Elizabeth Nolan Brown has written:

> The entire suite of products we think of as the internet—search engines, social media, online publications with comments sections, Wikis, private message boards, matchmaking apps, job search sites, consumer review tools, digital marketplaces, Airbnb, cloud storage companies, podcast distributors, app stores, GIF clearinghouses, crowdsourced funding platforms, chat tools, email newsletters, online classifieds, video sharing venues, and the vast majority of what makes up our day-to-day digital experience—have benefited from the protections offered by Section 230.[30]

She goes on to illustrate that weakening or repealing those protections would impair many innocent activities alongside the illicit.

Schilling's interest, of course, is in the illicit, and specifically in giving "user-submitted pornography aggregation sites—imagine Instagram or YouTube, but for pornography—which make up the majority of free pornography sites" a strong legal reason to make sure they do not host pornography "featuring individuals who did not consent to having their likeness distributed to the public," like revenge porn and other productions of uncertain provenance.[31] This might do some good, forcing aggregators to follow in the footsteps of Pornhub, which after a *New York Times* exposé stopped hosting videos from unverified uploaders, removing millions of clips from its archive.[32] (It should be noted, however, that verified users, at

---

[30] Elizabeth Nolan Brown, "Section 230 Is the Internet's First Amendment. Now Both Republicans and Democrats Want to Take It Away," *Reason,* July 29, 2019, https://reason.com/2019/07/29/section-230-is-the-internets-first-amendment-now -both-republicans-and-democrats-want-to-take-it-away/.

[31] Schilling, "How to Regulate Pornography."

[32] See Samantha Cole, "Pornhub Just Purged All Unverified Content from the Platform," *Vice,* December 14, 2020, https://www.vice.com/en/article/jgqjjy /pornhub-suspended-all-unverified-videos-content.

the time of that announcement, merely consisted of those who had "submitted a selfie of themselves holding a piece of paper with their username and pornhub.com . . . handwritten on it." The site promised a more rigorous process was forthcoming.[33])

Changing Section 230 is one way to achieve this incentive. However, it could also be done by making it a federal crime to share nonconsensual pornography, because Section 230 immunity is already waived for violations of federal criminal law.[34] The chief argument against the Section 230 carveout is that it could begin a pattern of weakening or eventually eliminating an important online speech protection and subjecting sites to the differing criminal codes of all fifty states. The federal criminalization route avoids those outcomes, but it also expands Washington's use of police power, an authority largely reserved for state and local governments in our federalist system.[35]

Moreover, as legal scholars Eric Goldman and Angie Jin argue in an extensive review of nonconsensual pornography dissemination cases for *I/S: A Journal of Law and Policy for the Information Society*, Section 230 in its present state is not an "insurmountable" obstacle to "enforcement actions against intermediaries" (like aggregation sites), and "Section 230 reform may not materially improve the nonconsensual pornography dissemination issues and could substantially harm other essential aspects of the internet."[36] Successful enforcement actions Goldman and Jin reviewed usually turned

---

[33] Cole, "Pornhub Just Purged All Unverified Content from the Platform."

[34] See Ashley Johnson and Daniel Castro, "Fact-Checking the Critiques of Section 230: What Are the Real Problems?" Information Technology and Innovation Foundation, February 22, 2021, https://itif.org/publications/2021/02/22/fact-checking-critiques-section-230-what-are-real-problems.

[35] "The Constitution requires a distinction between what is truly national and what is truly local, [including in assignment] of the police power, which the Founders undeniably left reposed in the States and denied the central Government," the Supreme Court affirmed in *United States v. Morrison* (2000), rejecting federal criminalization of violent crime.

[36] Eric Goldman and Angie Jin, "Judicial Resolution of Nonconsensual Pornography Dissemination Cases," *I/S: A Journal of Law and Policy for the Information Society*, 2018, 283–352.

on broader, long-established laws—like prohibitions of stalking, privacy violation, voyeurism, harassment, identity theft, and the like—rather than *sui generis* revenge porn criminalization or a Section 230 carveout that does not exist. In other words, Schilling's concern that victims get "their day in court" can often be met with extant laws and Section 230 intact.

Furthermore, his proposal could suffer from the same ineffectiveness in preventing dissemination of nonconsensual porn that we see with the current restraints. That's because, as the *Times'* Pornhub report detailed, nonconsensual pornography need only be briefly online to be downloaded, copied, and redistributed *ad infinitum*, including by people who do not know it is nonconsensual. This is a similar weak spot to the zoning plan.[37] This plan might be legally feasible, but it also may improve relatively little.

Conservative porn ban proponents frequently suggest the reason pornography remains legal and easily accessible online is because the conservative movement has inadequate political will. "Conservatives need to overcome their fear of governing the nation that elected them," Schilling says. "We must find the fortitude" to "tackle the online pornography crisis and defend the innocence of children."[38]

However, that explanation misses the mark. Perhaps conservative political will *is* lacking, but the legal and practical barriers are significant, and in many cases the hurdle is constitutional. Spending our energies on futile ideas for protecting ourselves and our children from online pornography is wasteful and evidence of either denial or ignorance of legal reality.

The Problem of the Human Moderator

Should the legal obstacles to these prohibitory proposals be overcome, there is still an important ethical quandary: the problem of the human moderator. If ISPs, domain registrars, web hosts, and/or sites with user-submitted

---

[37] See Nicolas Kristof, "The Children of Pornhub," *New York Times,* December 4, 2020, https://www.nytimes.com/2020/12/04/opinion/sunday/pornhub -rape-trafficking.html.

[38] Schilling, "How to Regulate Pornography."

content are required to screen for pornography—whether to ban it in whole or in part, per the various plans above—someone must do the screening. A lot of this can be handled with artificial intelligence (AI) tools that perform automated moderation. However, because users will object if an overeager AI program repeatedly removes innocent posts or if they have no way to report illicit posts the AI misses, human moderators are hired as back-up for the AI.

Their work is hellish. A 2019 report about Facebook moderators describes "a workplace that is perpetually teetering on the brink of chaos," and "an environment where workers cope by telling dark jokes about committing suicide, then smoke weed during breaks to numb their emotions."[39] The story continues:

> It's a place where, in stark contrast to the perks lavished on [non-contract] Facebook employees, team leaders micromanage content moderators' every bathroom and prayer break; where employees, desperate for a dopamine rush amid the misery, have been found having sex inside stairwells and a room reserved for lactating mothers; where people develop severe anxiety while still in training, and continue to struggle with trauma symptoms long after they leave; and where the counseling [the contracting agency that liaises with Facebook] offers them ends the moment they quit—or are simply let go. The moderators told me it's a place where the conspiracy videos and memes that they see each day gradually lead them to embrace fringe views.[40]

Said one former moderator, who could only stick it out for a year: "We were doing something that was darkening our soul." In 2020, Facebook agreed to a $52 million settlement with former moderators who had been diagnosed with PTSD resulting from the job.[41]

---

[39] Casey Newton, "The Secret Lives of Facebook Moderators in America," The Verge, February 25, 2019, https://www.theverge.com/2019/2/25/18229714/cognizant-facebook-content-moderator-interviews-trauma-working-conditions-arizona.

[40] Newton, "The Secret Lives of Facebook Moderators in America."

[41] Casey Newton, "Facebook Will Pay $52 Million in Settlement with Moderators Who Developed PTSD on the Job," The Verge, May 12, 2020,

Working as a content moderator might, at first glance, seem comparable to law enforcement work that deals with similarly disturbing and/or criminal behavior. But there's a key difference, Minnesota psychology professor Lisa Perez (who has studied traumatic stress among law enforcement investigators of child pornography), told the *Guardian* in 2017. "While [officers] have this emotional exhaustion and burnout, they tend to be very satisfied with their jobs and find them to be meaningful," Perez explains, because they bring consequences to the perpetrators.[42] Moderators churn through deeply disturbing content at a much higher volume with no such resolution. (What is it like to take down the second copy of a grotesque pornographic video you've already removed? Or the third copy? Or the eightieth?)

This is the ethical quandary: If we make the primary locus of constraint on pornographic content the state (or businesses acting at the tip of the legal sword) instead of the consumer, we are in practice requiring more content moderators. We are asking more people to view literally hundreds of pornographic images a day, to risk moral and ideological corruption and PTSD by serving as surrogates for public self-control. This strikes me as a deeply irresponsible form of moral outsourcing, unconscionable for Christians.

There are ways around this problem, but until we can build infallible AI, they would come at a high (and probably politically unacceptable) cost. One option websites and other businesses performing content moderation could choose is AI moderation that errs overwhelmingly on the side of caution. This would mean removing anything with even a suspicion of impropriety, thus eliminating the need for human moderators. The downside would be that it would have many false positives and complaints of censorship would be endless. Frustrated users, perhaps at critical mass, would likely migrate to less-restrictive sites and services were they available.

---

https://www.theverge.com/2020/5/12/21255870/facebook-content-moderator -settlement-scola-ptsd-mental-health.

[42] Olivia Solon, "Facebook is hiring moderators. But is the job too gruesome to handle?" *The Guardian,* May 4, 2017, https://www.theguardian.com/technology /2017/may/04/facebook-content-moderators-ptsd-psychological-dangers.

Another option is something like what Pornhub did, preemptively rejecting all content but that from verified users (with more robust verification than a selfie) and permabanning users with some predetermined number of violations. At scale, this would mean the end of social media as we know it. If implemented at higher levels like domain registration and internet service provision, however, it would also mean the end of the free internet, subjecting every blog and personal website and the like to corporate scrutiny before launch. Plus, as we'll discuss in the next section, once such a verification regime exists for pornography, mission creep is likely to set in. If you've already developed the tools to screen for pornography, why not screen for other objectionable content, even if those objections are much less widely shared?

Unintended Consequences

For the sake of argument, let's suppose all legal hurdles have been overcome, and we've surmounted or declared ourselves unconcerned by the ethical problem of the human moderator. Suppose we've banned pornography on the white-market US internet. What unintended consequences might there be?

One is mission creep. As I've argued at *Week* magazine, if pornography is banned on grounds of public harm (whether in general or specifically to children), that sets a dangerous precedent for less-desirable state content restrictions.[43] Some people, for example, believe passing on the Christian faith (or any religion) to one's own child is morally unacceptable—that it is a form of indoctrination that abuses children's trust in their parents to brainwash them into an archaic and unethical mindset before their full faculties of reason have developed.

This thinking has become markedly more common in the past decade in connection to traditional Christian perspectives on sexuality and

---

[43] See Bonnie Kristian, "Porn is evil. Don't ban it," *Week* magazine, December 18, 2019, https://theweek.com/articles/884676/porn-evil-dont-ban.

gender.[44] It's not a majority view in society today, but neither is it confined to an inconsequential fringe. Prominent new atheist thinker Richard Dawkins, for example, has said teaching a child religion is child abuse and that the damage of sexual abuse of children by Catholic priests "was arguably less than the long-term psychological damage inflicted by bringing the child up Catholic in the first place."[45] Dawkins and his ilk can even marshal some scientific backing for their cause. A study at Boston University in 2014, for instance, found "young children with a religious background are less able to distinguish between fantasy and reality compared with their secular counterparts," per a BBC report on the research.[46] Or they could point to the correlation of higher teenage birth rates with higher religiosity, contending that imparting religious belief to teenagers is harmful because of the adverse experiences teen parents and their children commonly face.[47]

Restrictions on raising children in the faith on grounds of public harm may seem farfetched, I realize. But religiosity is on a steep decline in the United States, and remember the instability built into "contemporary adult community standards."[48] Those standards can move for the better—but also for the worse. Chipping away at the First Amendment to ban pornography would pave the way for other content-specific censorship in the name of

---

[44] For more on thinking through sexuality and gender issues online, see chapter 8 from Christiana Kiefer and Jeremy Tedesco.

[45] Rob Cooper, "Forcing a Religion on Your Children Is as Bad as Child Abuse, Claims Atheist Professor Richard Dawkins," *Daily Mail,* April 22, 2013, https://www.dailymail.co.uk/news/article-2312813/Richard-Dawkins-Forcing-religion-children-child-abuse-claims-atheist-professor.html.

[46] Annie Waldman, "Study: Religious Children Are Less Able to Distinguish Fantasy from Reality," BBC News, July 29, 2014, https://www.bbc.com/news/blogs-echochambers-28537149. Of note, this study has been the subject of considerable debate since its release.

[47] See Spencer Grady-Pawl, "Linking Religion and Teen Pregnancy: There's a Map for That," *The Humanist,* June 28, 2017, https://thehumanist.com/commentary/linking-religion-teen-pregnancy-theres-map.

[48] Bonnie Kristian, "The coming end of Christian America," *The Week,* October 21, 2019, https://theweek.com/articles/872709/coming-end-christian-america.

preventing public harm. This is the perpetual trade-off of civil liberties: the same rules that protect the good protect the bad, and it is naïve, given our political realities, to imagine we can keep the one without the other.

Abusive or overly onerous enforcement is another potential consequence. Arguments for banning pornography, in my observation, do not address or barely address enforcement methods, but this is a crucial matter. What is the enforcement plan? How will law enforcement find out who's consuming porn? What loss of privacy would enforcement entail? What would the punishment be? Would we imprison people caught with porn? We're not talking child pornography or nonconsensual porn, recall, and imprisonment is usually tied to crimes that endanger the public. Does a man watching a pornographic video in the privacy of his home directly endanger his neighbor? There's not even an undisputed case for indirect endangerment, for violent crime rates, including rates of sexual crime, fell dramatically in the same three-decade span during which online porn arose.[49]

Or maybe we would use no carceral punishment for the consumers and reserve prison for the distributors, copying a distinction in some enforcement regimes dealing with vices like prostitution and illicit drugs. But what about repeat offenders, of whom there might be tens of millions in America given pornography's addictive facets? Would there be a three-strikes law for porn consumption? Would a father caught viewing pornography three times be taken out of his home and away from his children? Does that lessen the harm to his family?

---

[49] "Victimization rates for rape in the United States demonstrate an inverse relationship between pornography consumption and rape rates. [. . .] In the United States today rape and sexual assault rates have continued to decrease even as pornography, especially via the internet, has become increasingly and more widely available. [. . .] Rape rates in the United States today are at their lowest levels since 1960 (Bureau of Justice Statistics, 2006). This trend continues even though availability of pornography (number of titles released and number of pornographic websites) increases annually." Christopher J. Ferguson and Richard D. Hartley, "The Pleasure Is Momentary . . . the Expense Damnable?: The Influence of Pornography on Rape and Sexual Assault," *Aggression and Violent Behavior: A Review Journal*, 2009, 323–29.

If we do not like the idea of using our porn ban to expand mass incarceration, what other enforcement mechanism should we use? Fines? Wage garnishment? Probation? Community service? A ban on smartphone ownership or internet use? (This would massively curtail employment and education options.) Registries, like those for sex offenders, that limit where you can live and what jobs you can do?

Or would children be taken away from their parents? Libertarian writer Robby Soave at *Reason* reports children have been taken from their families by Child Protective Services "because of a false accusation from a nosy neighbor or teacher, because perfectly capable children were left alone by themselves for short periods of time, because of injuries that the authorities wrongly attributed to abuse, because doctors' instructions weren't followed to a T, and for a host of other reasons that did not actually necessitate tearing families apart."[50] Pornography use unquestionably harms families, but ban advocates must grapple with whether that harm justifies separating or creating new hardship for those families via incarceration or other enforcement means.

Similarly important to consider is how a ban would affect different populations. A marginal user might stop viewing pornography altogether. Someone with poor tech skills might not be able to get around comprehensive filters and moderation. But absent a truly totalitarian lockdown of the US internet, the predictable outcome of eliminating white-market online porn would be a proliferation of black-market porn, with internet traffic surging into illicit content hubs. These new hubs would likely be hosted outside US jurisdiction and operating totally without moderation. They would place newly illegal porn alongside more grossly abusive, long-since-criminalized content, like child pornography, which many users might never have encountered without the ban.

Porn production would grow more dangerous too, in ways analogous to what we've seen with drug and alcohol prohibition (i.e., involving organized

---

[50] Robby Soave, "Want the Government to 'Defend Families' from Porn? Child Protective Services Should Be a Cautionary Tale," *Reason,* December 13, 2019, https://reason.com/2019/12/13/conservatives-pornography-families-child-services-cps/.

crime and escalating violence toward those in the industry as well as innocent bystanders). This is the hazard of confining to the black market a lucra-
tive, much-desired product that a substantial portion of the public does not
believe is morally objectionable.

What about Private Regulation?

Lest it seem I'm doubtful of all at-scale attempts to curb online pornography
use, let me say a word about voluntary, private regulation. Mainstream social
media sites seeking a broad audience and ad revenue from major brands
already ban porn with a far stricter standard than obscenity law. Some are
more aggressive in their moderation practice than others (e.g., Facebook and
Instagram do more than Twitter), but the policies exist. (Even eBay is crack-
ing down on porn and other sexually explicit items in its marketplace.)[51]
These sites moderate because newer networks, like Parler, that explicitly
reject content moderation are rapidly swamped with porn.[52]

An important recent development on this front was Apple's announcement of several new features to detect child pornography and abuse on
iPhones (including nude photos underage users may take of themselves).
The features that proved controversial involve AI scanning users' photos and
messages, which civil libertarians warned is a powerful tool that could be
co-opted by governments, including authoritarian states, for other surveillance.[53] "[I]t's impossible to build a client-side scanning system that can only
be used for sexually explicit images sent or received by children," explains a

---

[51] See J. Jennings Moss, "EBay to close 'adults-only' section, prohibit the sale
of most sexually oriented items," *Business Journals*, May 17, 2021, https://www
.bizjournals.com/bizwomen/news/latest-news/2021/05/ebay-gets-mostly-out-of
-the-xxx-business.html/.

[52] See Craig Timberg, Drew Harwell, and Rachel Lerman, "Parler's Got a Porn
Problem: Adult Businesses Target Pro-Trump Social Network," *Washington Post,*
December 2, 2020, https://www.washingtonpost.com/technology/2020/12/02/parler
-pornography-problem/.

[53] See Shira Feder, "Apple Has a New Plan to Curb Child Pornography. Here's
Why It's Controversial," *Popular Science,* August 16, 2021, https://www.popsci.com
/technology/apple-fights-to-limit-child-pornography-and-csam/.

critique by the Electronic Frontier Foundation. Apple's new features are not "a slippery slope [but] a fully built system just waiting for external pressure" to obliterate iPhone users' right to privacy.[54] (Apple tweaked the features after public backlash, canceling a function that would have notified parents if their children opted in to viewing an image received via text and identified by AI as sexually explicit.)[55]

These regulations and other private approaches lack the legal barriers faced by state prohibition schemes as well as many of the risks of unintended consequences ("Facebook jail"—a colloquial term for temporary account restrictions—has key differences from a federal penitentiary). Private businesses also may be more responsive than the state to public pressure in the form of market signals and media coverage. Pornhub's policy change happened after credit card giants Visa and Mastercard responded to the *Times* story by declining to process payments to Pornhub going forward, a huge financial blow.[56]

Another advantage of private porn bans, perhaps counterintuitively, is their smaller scale: private actors can only prohibit pornography on sites and services they control and products they produce. That means user privacy violations those bans may occasion are endured voluntarily. No one is required to use Facebook or buy an iPhone (though we should not downplay the extent to which a handful of powerful tech companies, Facebook and Apple included, have infiltrated the rhythms of our daily life; nor should we dismiss how the choice to opt out shrinks if the regulator is, say, the sole

---

[54] India McKinney and Erica Portnoy, "Apple's Plan to 'Think Different' about Encryption Opens a Backdoor to Your Private Life," *Electronic Frontier Foundation,* August 5, 2021, https://www.eff.org/deeplinks/2021/08/apples-plan-think-different -about-encryption-opens-backdoor-your-private-life.

[55] See Jon Porter, "Latest iOS beta blurs nude images for children using Messages app," *The Verge*, November 11, 2021, https://www.theverge.com/2021/11 /11/22776028/ios-15-2-beta-communication-safety-messages-children-sexually -explicit-nudity-scan-notifications.

[56] See Samantha Cole, "Pornhub Just Purged All Unverified Content from the Platform," *Vice,* December 14, 2020, https://www.vice.com/en/article/jgqjjy /pornhub-suspended-all-unverified-videos-content.

local ISP). The smaller scale of private bans also means they do not foster a black market with its attendant violence as state prohibition would.

The one problem private regulation cannot skirt is that of the human moderator. Facebook and Instagram keep their networks PG-13, as most brands and users prefer, by means of moderator misery. I do not know if I bear some responsibility for that misery if I use these sites. I do not post anything moderators have to review, nor does anyone I follow. But however that responsibility shakes out, if we continue to use social media and other online services with human moderators, opponents of pornography should support better working conditions immediately and resource prioritization to phase out moderators' role by improving AI moderation, even if it means false-positive takedowns of our own content from time to time. Losing a Facebook post here or there is a small price to pay to prevent moderators' immiseration and PTSD.

Onward to Virtue

While it's worthwhile to examine legal proposals and pursue private regulation, ultimately, I'm pessimistic about the prospect of eliminating online porn. The question of banning online porn is moot, in practice, unless we institute an authoritarian-type regime to rid the digital public square of this vile and abhorrent content. You can, however, ban it from *your* screen and the screens your children see.

Make no mistake, that is a monumental project. It is a project my family has only begun, because our sons are too small to use screened devices. We're aware we have a long task ahead of us. That task is not porn avoidance, strictly speaking. If, when our twins are eleven, we suddenly say, "We've got to keep them from looking up porn!"—well, then the battle is already lost. "The truth is that if we build our family's technological life around trying to keep porn out," writes Andy Crouch in *The Tech-Wise Family*, "we will fail."[57] The task at hand is sanctification in and through Christ. It is

---

[57] Andy Crouch, *The Tech-Wise Family: Everyday Steps for Putting Technology in Its Proper Place* (Grand Rapids: Baker Books, 2017), 173–74.

development of virtue in imitation of Jesus. It is becoming a person (and raising children) characteristically able to resist the temptation of pornography or become less suspectable to its appeal (1 Cor 10:13).

The standard pushback to this call to virtue is that the problem of online porn is too big and bad for families to address on their own. "You might argue that this is something for parents, and not government, to handle," says pundit Matt Walsh at the *Daily Wire* in a representative pro-ban take:

> But this argument ignores the reality of the situation. Parents cannot possibly shield their children from a porn epidemic that is so ubiquitous and accessible. Even if they restrict all internet access in their own homes, and refuse to allow their children to have phones with internet access (a wise move, to be sure), all it requires is one friend whose parents have not taken that step. And every kid will have at least one friend like that—probably many more than just one. This is a problem that parents *cannot* handle on their own. That's why the state may have a role.[58]

Walsh is not wrong in his diagnosis: families cannot do this on their own. What's wrong is his prescription: though himself Catholic, Walsh mentions no role for Christ or the church, no conception that God may work in us or that in their early formative years, children could live in a community where everyone they know has the same commitment to sanctification, including rejection of porn.

I am not a perfectionist in the Holiness tradition, but Walsh's turn to the state as parents' support suggests an awfully small view of the transformative power of redemption. It seems not to consider that scriptural injunctions to not only "flee" (1 Cor 6:18) but "put to death" sexual immorality (Col 3:5) might be serious expectations for the Christian. It has no apparent room for Paul's insistence that we "rid [ourselves] of all such things," having "taken

---

[58] Matt Walsh, "A Group of Republicans Want the Government to Start Fighting Hardcore Pornography. They're Right. Here's Why," The Daily Wire, December 6, 2019, https://www.dailywire.com/news/walsh-a-group-of-republicans-want-the -government-to-start-fighting-hardcore-pornography-theyre-right-heres-why.

off [the] old self with its practices and hav[ing] put on the new self, which is being renewed in knowledge in the image of its Creator" (Col 3:8–10 NIV). Nor does an impulse to turn to the state to keep porn out of our homes seem informed by passages like 1 Thess 4:3–8, which tells us it's God's will that we "keep away from sexual immorality, that each of you knows how to control his own body in holiness and honor, not with lustful passions, like the Gentiles, who don't know God," and that "anyone who rejects this does not reject man, but God, who gives you his Holy Spirit."

Online pornography's proliferation and extremity do not render these exhortations obsolete. On the contrary, the rising accessibility of porn and falling social opprobrium around sexual immorality gives us much in common with the early church to whom those words were originally written. "There is broad consensus that erotic art was fairly ubiquitous in the public and private spaces of the Roman city," writes historian Thomas A. J. McGinn in *The Economy of Prostitution in the Roman World*, and Romans were "apparent[ly] indifferen[t]" to "women's and children's exposure to erotic art." (Some surviving pots and murals are remarkably explicit given the limits of the media, and lewd ancient poems are *not* the work of a more innocent time.)

Beyond public porn, "prostitution was widespread," and for "the male consumer, sex was both widely available and relatively inexpensive." Roman cities did not zone their brothels into distinct districts, McGinn notes; in fact, "there is no indication that anyone proposed zoning prostitution until the Christians did."[59] The churches (and especially their male congregants) whom Paul told to flee sexual immorality and learn, with God's help, to control their bodies (1 Cor 6:18; 2 Tim 2:22) were surrounded by temptations at least comparable to ours. We cannot plead historically unique hardship here.

Yet even if we could, the remedy of sanctification in community must be the same. The "just one friend" argument is precisely why more than

---

[59] Thomas A. J. McGinn, *The Economy of Prostitution in the Roman World: A Study of Social History and the Brothel* (Ann Arbor: The University of Michigan Press, 2004), 10–11.

external restraints like content filters (which certainly have their place, espe-cially for children and those dealing with addictive behavior) or laws, we need the internal restraint of virtue. And that restraint requires supports: the outworking of our faith in likeminded churches and schools, with inten-tional cultivation of habits, embrace of limits, and absorption of theology concerning sex that help make our eschewal of pornography automatic. As Jesus prayed for his disciples in John 17:15–17, our aim is not to be taken out of the world but to be protected from evil, being sanctified by the truth.

10

Dangers in the Digital Public Square

Navigating Conspiracy Theories and Misinformation in a Post-Truth Age

Jason Thacker

In 2016, Oxford Dictionary named *post-truth* the word of the year after seeing a 2,000 percent spike in the use of the word in 2015.[1] Philosopher Lee McIntyre writes, "As a catch-all phrase, [post-truth] seemed to capture the times."[2] From 2015 to the present, the language of post-truth is often combined with the rise of conspiracy theories and fake news, which have become too common in our homes, communities, and media due in large part to the ubiquity of social media. As truth is routinely called into question, our "communication [with one another] is thwarted, and the possibility of

---

[1] See "Oxford Word of the Year 2016 | Oxford Languages," accessed April 11, 2021, https://languages.oup.com/word-of-the-year/2016/. *Post-truth* is defined as "objective facts are less influential in shaping public opinion than appeals to emotion and personal belief."

[2] Lee C. McIntyre, *Post-Truth*, The MIT Press Essential Knowledge Series (Cambridge, MA: MIT Press, 2018), 1.

rational discourse disappears."[3] Coinciding with the rise of social media as a main form of news and communication in society, there has been a surge in misinformation and conspiracy theories that often revolve around various political and cultural issues, exposing the deep tensions and riffs in society.

Concerns over how to navigate these issues have also become incredibly partisan in nature with one side blaming the other for their presence or persistence in society, rather than examining the nature of these issues and how they are tied to larger movements of truth and morality in society. It is far too convenient and simplistic to merely look at these issues through a partisan lens and pin the blame for society's persistent problems on our ideological foes because of their supposed ignorance or perceived vindictiveness.[4] Rather than simply a partisan issue, the current controversies surrounding the rapid spread of misinformation and propaganda online serve as a symptom of a larger phenomenon centered in the rapid growth of technology and the breakdown of morality as seen in the fact/value dichotomy that began with the rise of empiricism.[5]

Today, society is not only questioning the nature of truth but also learning how to navigate these new digital challenges as it continues to become more divided over the very nature and foundation of truth. Given the ubiquity of misinformation and propaganda in our society, I will first examine the nature of these digital manipulations of truth and their relationship to the rapid growth of technology, then examine the realities of a post-truth society by outlining the breakdown of truth and morality in modern society.

---

[3] D. Stephen Long, *Truth Telling in a Post-Truth World* (Nashville: General Board of Higher Education and Ministry, UMC, 2019), 8.

[4] See McIntyre, *Post-Truth*. Preface. McIntyre himself falls prey to this partisan lumping when he states that the "other side" of the post-truth debate does not consist of people who defend these claims of misinformation or even that think post-truth is a good thing but is primarily made of up those "who deny that a problem even exists." McIntyre goes on to say that he cannot promise that his own assessment of the post-truth society will be balanced, but that he hopes it to be fair. While his candor is appreciated, it is illustrative of the continued breakdown of an engaged and robust public dialogue around these contentious issues.

[5] For more on the fact/value dichotomy through a theological and ethical lens, see Arthur Frank Holmes, *Fact, Value, and God* (Grand Rapids: Eerdmans, 1997).

I will then argue that the rise of misinformation in the digital age is a complex societal issue arising from both technical progress and the rejection of transcendent realities, which many hope to overcome through secular ideals or post-foundationalism. From that foundation, I will articulate a path forward in this digital age through an approach of principled pluralism combined with an awakening to the deleterious effects of technology on society.

While there is no ability to realistically usher in a new period of deep unity on divisive social issues, there is a unique opportunity for Christians to model principles of grace and human dignity. By seeking toleration and compromise in public discourse, we might still overcome the worst effects of misinformation in society, all the while exposing the gross effects of technology in public life. A Christian vision for the digital public square must include a wide range of participants, including the church, government, and private sector working as tolerant partners, not combatants, to obtain a more stable and thriving democracy in this technological age.

The Nature and Appeal of Misinformation

In the United States, tensions flared after the 2016 election and the inauguration of President Donald J. Trump, who often claimed that all the mainstream media was "fake news," especially when he disliked the often-partisan coverage of his actions or that of his administration. Soon after Trump's inauguration in 2016, press secretary Sean Spicer vehemently disputed the reported crowd size at the president's inauguration in a White House press conference, which soon left White House advisor Kellyanne Conway to defend those statements on *Meet the Press* by saying that Spicer had intended to present "alternative facts."[6] But the language of "alternative facts" or conspiratorial thinking is not relegated to one party in the American political system as some in media studies and politics today want to claim. Conservatives often likewise decry a post-truth

---

[6] "Conway: Press Secretary Gave 'Alternative Facts,'" NBC News, January 22, 2017, https://www.nbcnews.com/meet-the-press/video/conway-press-secretary-gave-alternative-facts-860142147643.

understanding of reality by progressives on many consequential topics in American society, such as sexuality issues and the ability to change one's gender based on personal beliefs about human anthropology and the rejection of scientific evidence.[7]

While one party's post-truth claims are derided on late-night comedy shows as backward and ignorant, the other is widely celebrated on social media and throughout mainstream society as progressive and future oriented. As post-truth language became more common, it soon became clear to astute observers that this concept was deeply embedded in society. This is evident not only in the fracturing public trust and discourse, but also in our national psyche as the warring political parties debated how to navigate this new phenomenon where "objective facts are less influential in shaping public opinion than appeals to emotion and personal belief."[8] Christians, in particular, must step back from the political and partisan rancor of the moment to examine not only *what* is going on in the digital public square but also *why* it is taking place and *what* is the best path forward for the church in these divided times.

But to grasp the nature and rise of misinformation in society, one must start by seeking to define the terms used in the debate. Misinformation refers to a broad category of false or misleading information that often spreads *unintentionally*, while disinformation refers to the *intentional* dissemination of false information by moral actors.[9] There is also a significant semantic overlap between disinformation and propaganda, which is defined as the intentional reordering of facts or even spreading disinformation for a particular purpose—often to direct the actions or alter the beliefs of a

---

[7] For more on the rejection of biological realities of sexuality by those who affirm transgenderism, see Anderson, *When Harry Became Sally*.

[8] Oxford University Press, "Word of the Year 2016," Oxford Languages," accessed March 21, 2022, https://languages.oup.com/word-of-the-year/2016/.

[9] Information scholar Peter Pomerantsev defines misinformation as "content that misleads by accident" and disinformation as "content designed to mislead." See Peter Pomerantsev, *This Is Not Propaganda: Adventures in the War against Reality* (New York: PublicAffairs, 2019), 186.

given group or set of individuals.[10] Philosopher Brian L. Keeley defines a conspiracy theory as "a proposed explanation of some historical event (or events) in terms of the significant causal agency of a relatively small group of persons—the conspirators—acting in secret."[11] Conspiracy theories often take the form of disinformation or propaganda, given how they are designed to distort reality and the nature of truth.

Disinformation, or propaganda as a broader category, has historically been seen merely as a political tool used to sway the support of the public toward a particular end by shifting facts or reinterpreting them toward a desired outcome. It is increasingly being used throughout society to alter public opinion.[12] Misinformation is not a new phenomenon, as many today tend to believe. However, in years past it was employed mostly by leading social institutions, government leaders, or prominent cultural figures. But now, with the rise of social media and the further democratization of information sharing through technological means, misinformation has gone mainstream. Anyone with access to a smartphone, including malicious actors intending to manipulate large segments of society, now has these tools at their disposal.

Some of the most horrifying historical examples of propaganda and disinformation are described in striking details by Adolf Hitler in his book *Mein Kampf.*[13] Hitler and his Nazi regime were masters of propaganda, which allowed them to grossly influence the German people and wield significant

---

[10] For more on the sociological aspects of disinformation and propaganda, see Jacques Ellul, *The Technological Society* (New York: Alfred A. Knopf, 1964), 363–75. An extended discussion of propaganda can be found in Jacques Ellul, *Propaganda: The Formation of Men's Attitudes* (New York: Vintage Books, 1973).

[11] Brian L. Keeley, "Of Conspiracy Theories," *Journal of Philosophy* 96, no. 3 (March 1999): 109–26. The term *conspiracy theory* often carries significant negative connotations, which is used to combat their spread and discredit them in the public square. For more on the connotations of the term, see Andrew McKenzie-McHarg, *Conceptional History and Conspiracy Theories* in Michael Butter, ed., *Routledge Handbook of Conspiracy Theories* (Abingdon, UK: Routledge, 2020), 16–17.

[12] See Ellul, *The Technological Society*, 363.

[13] I am indebted to Dr. John Dyer of Dallas Theological Seminary for the initial connection of misinformation and conspiracy theories to Hitler's propaganda.

power over much of Europe for a time. Despite Hitler's sinister intentions, he aptly described that the goal of propaganda "is to influence a whole people" by "understanding the emotional ideas of the great masses and finding . . . the way to the attention and thence to the heart of the broad masses."[14] Hitler argued that effective propaganda must "follow a simple line" of argumentation that consists of "a very few points and must harp on these slogans until the last member of the public understands what you want him to understand," thus deceiving them to accomplish a particular end.[15] The goal is to overly simplify an idea and adjust the message to those with the lowest level of intelligence, because any complexity or nuance will backfire and work against the stated goal of changing the thinking and behavior of the masses. He went on to say that the "the function of propaganda is not to weigh and ponder the rights of different people, but exclusively to emphasize the one right which it has set out to argue for. Its task is not to make an objective study of the truth, in so far as it favors the enemy, and then set it before the masses with academic fairness; its task is to serve our own right, always and unflinchingly."[16]

For Hitler, the goal of disinformation and propaganda is to persuade others by manipulating their emotions and not through reason or honest discourse. While many modern-day digital manipulations of the truth may not be as dehumanizing and evil as the atrocities Hitler engaged in, he nevertheless isolates the core truth behind these methods of deception, which is to distort reality to gain power and position over another. With the ubiquity of digital misinformation and technical progress in this post-truth society, one might not even need to be as covert as Hitler to deceive the masses and control the public narrative.

One of the most prescient figures in the twentieth century writing about the influence of technology on society was the French sociologist Jacques Ellul, who wrote in 1954 of propaganda as a form of technique.[17]

---

[14] Adolf Hitler, *Mein Kampf* (Boston: Houghton Mifflin, 2001), 180.

[15] Hitler, 180.

[16] Hitler, 182.

[17] See Ellul, *The Technological Society*, 363–75. For Ellul, technique referred to "the *totality of methods rationally arrived at and having absolute efficiency* (for a given stage of development) in *every* field of human activity," (xxv, emphasis in original).

While Ellul notes that propaganda has been around since the beginning of human civilization with the use of language, he describes a marked shift in how propaganda was taking hold in his day to shape all aspects of civic life as a particular form of technical development. For Ellul, modern propaganda was the convergence of two different techniques. First, it is made up of *mechanical techniques* like radio, press, and motion pictures—which today would also include television and social media—that allow for large-scale communication to the masses, while simultaneously addressing each individual in a group. Second, it also contains a *psychological technique*, which give access to the knowledge of the human psyche, allowing a propagandist to shape the nature of truth and how one views the world.[18] Ellul rightly points out that this latter technique has the profound ability to allow propaganda to "become as natural as air or food" in a society where "the individual is able to declare in all honesty that no such thing as propaganda exists." But this is true only because humanity has become "so absorbed by [this technique] that he is literally no longer able to see the truth."[19] The blinding nature of propaganda—and by extension misinformation—allows it to operate below the consciousness of humanity that leads to a loss of reality, a confusion of motives, an identification of opposites, and an interplay of accusations.[20]

A similar concept of modern technology as a form of propaganda or disinformation is picked up on by media theorist Neil Postman in his classic work *Amusing Ourselves to Death*. He describes the influence of technological advances—namely the television of his day—by using the phrase "the medium is the metaphor."[21] He writes how the medium through which

---

Ellul did not simply see technology as a simple tool, but rather a more complex and dominant force that encompassed all human existence, as discussed in chapter 1. Propaganda was one such technique whereby humans are brought into new world order based on technical efficiency alone, rather than reason and morality.

[18] See Ellul, 363–64.

[19] Ellul, 366.

[20] See Ellul, 367.

[21] Postman picks up a version of this phrase "the medium is the message" from sociologist and media theorist Marshall McLuhan. See Marshall McLuhan,

something is communicated has significant bearing on the content itself and how one receives that message.[22] Postman describes this phenomenon by saying, "Major new medium changes the structure of discourse; it does so by encouraging certain uses of the intellect, and by demanding a certain form of content—in a phrase, by creating new forms of truth telling."[23] Postman describes television—and by extension other forms of modern technology—as "altering the meaning of 'being informed' by creating a species of information that might be properly be called *disinformation*."[24] Postman goes on to argue that disinformation is "misleading information," which is "misplaced, irrelevant, fragmented or superficial—information that creates the illusion of knowing something but which in fact leads one away from knowing."[25] What Postman describes here is better labeled as mis-information in this age of social media, though, given that disinformation is the intentional distribution of falsifiable information.[26] Postman argues that society is "losing our sense of what it means to be well informed" given how technology shapes humanity and their understanding of the world itself. He

---

Understanding Media: The Extensions of Man, ed. W. Terrence Gordon, Critical Edition (Corte Madera, CA: Gingko Press, 2003).

[22] See Neil Postman, *Amusing Ourselves to Death: Public Discourse in the Age of Show Business*, 20th Anniversary Edition (New York: Penguin Books, 2006), 3–15.

[23] Postman, 27.

[24] Postman, 107 (emphasis original).

[25] Postman, 107.

[26] Postman argues that he does not mean to "imply that television news deliberately aims to deprive Americans of a coherent, contextual understanding of their world," but that when the news is packaged as simply entertainment—which is the exact case with modern day social media even more so than television—then deception and misinformation are the inevitable results because society is trained to not dwell too long on any bit of information. He later states that "it has been demonstrated multiple times that a culture can survive misinformation and false opinion," but "it has not yet been demonstrated whether a culture can survive if it takes the measure of the world in twenty-two minutes. Or if the value of its news is determined by the number of laughs it provides." Little did Postman know how much society would benefit from just twenty minutes of prolonged attention given the milliseconds of attention that social media demands from humanity before changing the topic at hand. Postman, 107–8, 113.

goes on to say that "ignorance is always correctable . . . but what shall we do if we take ignorance to be knowledge?"[27] Technology, especially social media, can elevate misinformation and bring about widespread acceptance of it in ways that Postman could only imagine in his day.

Misinformation, disinformation, propaganda, and conspiracy theories can engender such rampant confusion and subconscious delusion in society that humanity naturally begins to treat everything with suspicion as evil. As a result they transfer all of disillusionment onto the "official enemy," which with today's increased polarization easily becomes "them."[28] Cass Sunstein defined this tribalization and labeling of "them" in his infamous 1999 article "The Law of Group Polarization," where he describes the process of how this law "helps to explain extremism, 'radicalization,' cultural shifts, and the behavior of political parties and religious organizations; it is closely connected to current concerns about the consequences of the Internet; it also helps account for feuds, ethnic antagonism, and tribalism."[29] This phenomenon of tribalism and deep polarization in public society can easily be seen in attitudes toward the failures of the opposing political party, scapegoating various ethnic groups for social issues, or even the caricaturing of faith traditions themselves as sheer ignorance. If one buys into the idea that their "enemies" are really distorting truth to fit a particular agenda and that feeling is reciprocated, it can naturally degenerate into a situation where the very nature of truth begins to erode or where people start to claim their own "alternative facts" or understanding of truth. This post-truth understanding of the world is based on the pursuit of power, self-aggrandizement, and control.

---

[27] Postman, 107–8.

[28] For more on the concept of "them" and how it applies to the current cultural and political moment, see Benjamin E. Sasse, *Them: Why We Hate Each Other and How to Heal* (New York: St. Martin's Press, 2018); and David French, *Divided We Fall: America's Secession Threat and How to Restore Our Nation* (New York: St. Martin's Press, 2020).

[29] Cass R. Sunstein, "The Law of Group Polarization," *Chicago Unbound*, John M. Olin Program in Law and Economics Working Paper No. 91, 1999, 39.

Realities of a Post-Truth Society

Propaganda and disinformation are not new phenomena but are exacerbated in a technologically driven society. These derivations of truth are not simply relegated to one voting bloc or even a particular political ideology. According to Ellul, they are pervasive throughout all of society and often outside of public awareness. But these concepts have taken on a particular relevance given the rise of social media platforms and the ease of sharing unverified information to the masses. In the age of social media, a single individual without any real authority or standing in society can falsely claim something is fake news or share a conspiracy theory widely without any real recourse or accountability. What once was the exclusive domain of government and various institutions in society with access to technological tools—like that of the radio, press, and motion pictures—is now available to anyone with a smartphone and rhetorical savviness. This marked shift in the democratization of communication techniques paired with the breakdown of traditional gatekeepers in society helped to usher in a new era of post-truth.

Historically, the breakdown of traditional forms of truth and morality began with the rise of empiricism during the Enlightenment and the perceived failures of traditional religious belief and medieval philosophy to bring about order and peace in an increasingly pluralistic society.[30] There was an intentional push toward the pursuit of technological and scientific innovation in nearly every area of life, which kicked off a surge of cultural, political, and social changes that society is still grappling with today. Throughout the Enlightenment, modern scientific pursuits began to take root as humanity sought to understand the biological and cultural underpinnings of our world and why things work the way they do. But an unfortunate stream of Enlightenment thinking was the rejection of religion and faith as a moral and epistemological foundation for a society.

---

[30] See James Davison Hunter and Paul Nedelisky, *Science and the Good: The Tragic Quest for the Foundations of Morality*, Foundational Questions in Science (New Haven, CT: Yale University Press, 2018), xiii–xv.

Neil Postman argues that this drive toward empiricism and rationalism ultimately led to the subsequent rejection of many traditional control mechanisms of truth and a breakdown of trust in institutions like the church, government, and press.[31] Society no longer had a shared understanding of truth unless it could be empirically verified through science. Not surprisingly, this development had a chilling and disorienting effect on many people trying to perceive the fullness of reality outside the physical world. One of the most tragic losses for civilization was the wholesale rejection by many of the prior foundations for morality and truth. This shift to empiricism also brought about a new stream of thinkers who sought an empirical basis for morality in the "new moral science," which James Davidson Hunter and Paul Nedelisky aptly show in their work *Science and the Good*. They conclude that this shift in our culture has in many ways led to an embracing of a nihilistic utilitarianism today because there is no real moral epistemological foundation for judging between what is right and wrong.[32]

As communications scholars Johan Farkas and Jannick Schou describe, echoing Postman, "the traditional gatekeepers of truth, such as editors, journalists, and public intellectuals, have lost their monopoly on public issues, and in this process, so-called malicious actors and misinformed citizens have started to spread their own lies, deception, hate, propaganda and fake information on a previously unseen scale" due in large part to the rise of the public's use of social media.[33] They go on to argue that "Truth and Reason have been superseded by alternative facts and individual gut feelings," which

---

[31] See Neil Postman, *Technopoly: The Surrender of Culture to Technology* (New York: Vintage Books, 1993), 71–91. Postman builds up the work of Beniger and his discussion of the various control mechanisms that helped to build our information society. See James Ralph Beniger, *The Control Revolution: Technological and Economic Origins of the Information Society* (Cambridge, MA: Harvard University Press, 1997).

[32] See Hunter and Nedelisky, *Science and the Good*, 168. For more on how technology and nihilism can be intertwined, see Nolen Gertz, *Nihilism and Technology* (Lanham, MD: Rowman & Littlefield International, 2018).

[33] Johan Farkas and Jannick Schou, *Post-Truth, Fake News and Democracy: Mapping the Politics of Falsehood*, Routledge Studies in Global Information, Politics and Society 19 (New York: Routledge, 2019), 2.

in turn leads some to claim that the very fabric of democracy is rupturing.[34] Public theologian Russell Moore describes this post-truth understanding of individual gut feelings as the basis for truth as a "secular Azusa Street" revival, where personal feelings of morality and truth are prized as more influential than traditional sources.[35] This rise of expressive individualism paired with the bifurcation of truth and morality gives way to a post-truth society, where gut feelings and personal desires override the sense of reality and truth in society. This phenomenon combined with the rise of disruptive technologies— such as television, the internet, social media—function as a perfect recipe for the current climate of dis/misinformation, conspiracy theories, and propaganda that society is experiencing today. But what is society to do about these technological derivations of truth and the nature of a post-truth society?

Proposals for Navigating a Post-Truth Society

Considering the nature of misinformation and propaganda paired with the deep sociological tensions of a technologically rich post-truth society, it is natural to question what might serve as the best path forward to restore the trust in institutions that has been lost over the years. While there are countless proposals and immense complexity in these debates, three proposals encapsulate the main ideas put forth to restore the tenets of democracy and take back control from wild conspiracy theories and claims of alternative facts in this post-truth society.

Secular Foundationalism

In 2018, French president Emmanuel Macron spoke to a joint session of Congress about the growing threats of fake news and misinformation in

---

[34] Farkas and Schou, 2.

[35] Personal correspondence with Dr. Russell Moore, public theologian at *Christianity Today* and former president of the Ethics and Religious Liberty Commission of the Southern Baptist Convention. Moore is referencing the famous Azusa Street Pentecostal revival that occurred in Los Angeles, California, between 1906 and 1915.

a post-truth society. In his speech titled "To Protect Our Democracies," Macron argued that our society must "fight against the ever-growing virus of fake news, which exposes our people to irrational fear and imaginary risk. . . . Without reason, without truth, there is no real democracy because democracy is about *true choices and rational decisions*."[36] In the speech, Macron echoed an approach that has been put forth over the last decade by many scholars and academics described as a secular foundationalist approach to politics and culture. Macron defines democracy as the "cause of freedom and human rights," which is intentionally devoid of any religious connections, undertones, and especially any transcendent moral foundation. Like many proponents of this view, Macron sees that misinformation and propaganda can and will be used to undermine democracy as well as Western values, but he argues that these issues must be dealt with on purely secular terms.

It has already been noted that these issues precede the rise of social media technologies and became widespread in society alongside the rise of the secular state. As Jacques Ellul points out, "propagandistic manipulations take place under all forms of government and in all walks of life."[37] Thus, it is ironic that world leaders and scholars would seek to counter the dangers facing today's digital public square through a strictly secular approach to truth as if secularism did not help to usher in this breakdown of truth under the auspice of expressive individualism and complete moral autonomy.[38] Political philosopher Michael J. Sandel describes this secular form of

---

[36] Emmanuel Macron, "French President Macron Addresses U.S. Congress," April 25, 2018, http://transcripts.cnn.com/TRANSCRIPTS/1804/25/ctw.01 .html; emphasis added. This sentiment is not limited to a European context, as many politicians in the United States have also warned of dire consequences to democracy due to rise of disinformation. Referencing Facebook's decision to indefinitely suspend President Donald Trump from Facebook, Senator Elizabeth Warren (D-MA) tweeted, "We still need to rein in disinformation and protect our democracy." Elizabeth Warren (@ewarren), Twitter, May 5, 2021, 5:22 p.m., https:// twitter.com/ewarren/status/1390069300707348486.

[37] Ellul, *The Technological Society*, 368.

[38] For more on the rise of expressive individualism, see Charles Taylor, *A Secular Age* (Cambridge, MA: Belknap Press, 2007), 473–95. Taylor describes expressive

governing morality as "non-judgmental toleration," meaning it "permits some practice on grounds that take no account of the moral worth of the practice in question."[39] He goes on to say, "liberal toleration is non-judgmental toleration in the sense that it seeks to bracket substantive moral and religious controversies; it seeks to avoid passing moral judgement on the practices it permits."[40] Though, a secular approach to these issues often takes an intolerant position against certain moral claims and practices that are deemed unworthy for public discourse.[41] For example, this was seen in how religious adherents were scapegoated as promoting or contributing to misinformation and terroristic activities as described by Macron.

In February 2021, France's National Assembly passed a controversial "non-separatism" bill that supporters argued would help protect the country from "Islamist separatism." The bill was controversial given the country's lay tradition of discouraging behavior that sought to impose religious viewpoints in the public square.[42] The bill sought to expand the "neutrality principle," which forbids all civil servants and private contracts or public services from sharing political views publicly or from wearing physical representations of their religion, which many, including Muslims, took as a direct assault on their beliefs.[43] Muslims were not alone in this fear, though, because the French minister of the interior, Gèrald Darmanin, said,

---

individualism as reflective of "the age of authenticity" seen in the period of the 1960s in the West.

[39] Michael J. Sandel, "Judgmental Toleration" in Robert P. George, ed., *Natural Law, Liberalism, and Morality: Contemporary Essays* (Oxford, UK: Oxford University Press, 1996), 107.

[40] Sandel, 107.

[41] This is especially seen in the debate over hate speech in our digital age. For more on this topic, see chapter 7 by Brooke Medina.

[42] See Cailey Griffin, "Why Has France's Islamist Separatism Bill Caused Such Controversy?" *Foreign Policy* (blog), February 23, 2021, https://foreignpolicy.com/2021/02/23/why-france-islamist-separatism-bill-controversy-extremism/.

[43] See Peter Yeung, "France's Controversial 'Separatism' Bill: Seven Things to Know," Al Jazeera, February 15, 2021, https://www.aljazeera.com/news/2021/2/15/frances-controversial-separatism-bill-explained.

"Evangelicals are a very important problem."[44] In a separate interview he added that "we cannot discuss with people who refuse to write on paper that the law of the Republic is superior to the law of God."[45] While he later apologized for these remarks, this illustrative tone and method of secular governance nevertheless shows how a secular foundationalism seeks to subjugate and overtake religion to form a purely rational approach devoid of transcendent values to governance.[46]

Part of the motivation behind these types of proposals was, in the words of President Macron, "to fight against the terrorist propaganda that spreads out its fanaticism on the internet,"[47] which seems in line with the way that others such as Lee McIntyre approach these complex and controversial issues—which is to shift the blame and refuse to see how we all share in these issues in the digital public square. While combating radical terrorism is commendable and in line with the approach that will be advocated for later, many worried at the time France passed this bill—and are still worried—that a purely secular approach to the problems of the day concerning misinformation and propaganda will fail at the outset.[48]

Published in 1984, *The Naked Public Square* by Richard John Neuhaus offers a deep critique of a purely secular vision and models an understanding of the public square that reveals the constant interplay of religion and politics that cannot be ultimately avoided or kept separate, regardless of what

---

[44] Joel Forster, "French Minister of Interior Says 'Evangelicals Are a Very Important Problem,'" Evangelical Focus, February 4, 2021, https://evangelicalfocus .com/europe/10061/french-minister-of-interior-says-evangelicals-are-a-very -important-problem.

[45] Forster, "French Minister of Interior Says 'Evangelicals Are a Very Important Problem.'"

[46] See "French Minister of Interior Apologises for 'Unfortunate' Remarks against Evangelicals," Evangelical Focus, February 16, 2021, https://evangelicalfocus.com /europe/10236/french-minister-of-interior-apologises-for-unfortunate-remarks -against-evangelicals.

[47] Macron, "French President Macron Addresses U.S. Congress."

[48] For more on the role of liberalism and technology in society, see Patrick J. Deneen, *Why Liberalism Failed* (New Haven, CT: Yale University Press, 2018), 91–109.

some proponents of a "naked" or purely secular public square want to claim. Neuhaus defines this vision of a secular foundationalism through the image of the naked public square, explaining the goal is to "exclude religion and religiously grounded values from the conduct of public business."[49] As Dutch theologian—and one-time prime minister—Abraham Kuyper has explained, secular liberalism "only means that in their opinion religion belongs to the realm of the inner life and that the state as political power must avoid as much as possible all contact with this inner life."[50] Kuyper shows that the main error in this system centers around the "claim that one cannot really know if there is a God, hence that nothing objective can be established in regard to religion, and that this whole feature of the inner life of human beings belongs to the subjective, personal, at most domestic and ecclesiastical domain."[51] Neuhaus rightly shows that many of the secular approaches to the public square—and the rise of digital governance by extension that arose after his death in 2009—simply look down upon religion given the rise of empiricism and rationalism with the Enlightenment. "In principle," Neuhaus explains, "we should be suspicious of explanations for other people's beliefs and behavior when those explanations imply that they would believe and behave as we do, if only they were as mature and enlightened as we are."[52] He goes on to argue that religion is not a purely private matter as many secularists argue, but that religious dogma cannot go unchecked in the democratic experiment to the ire of many in the religious community.

If he were alive today, Neuhaus may argue that the French approach to combating misinformation and propaganda is ill-conceived on two fronts: secularism cannot provide a stable ground for a digital democracy because it lives under the illusion that it is devoid of religious-like undertones and dogmas itself, and the reality that faith cannot simply be a private matter if

---

[49] Richard John Neuhaus, *The Naked Public Square: Religion and Democracy in America* (Grand Rapids: Eerdmans, 1997), ix.

[50] Abraham Kuyper, *Our Program: A Christian Political Manifesto*, trans. Harry Van Dyke, Abraham Kuyper Collected Works in Public Theology (Bellingham, WA: Lexham, 2015), 58.

[51] Kuyper, 58–59.

[52] Neuhaus, *The Naked Public Square*, 16.

understood properly. Secular foundationalism may seem like a tenable position in pluralistic society, but as Neuhaus and others have shown, it lacks a cohesive and transcendent moral foundation upon which to judge decisions as right or wrong.

Post-Foundationalism

Juxtaposed to the secular foundationalist approach advocated by Macron and others, Farkas and Schou argue for a post-foundationalist approach to truth. They believe this can reinvigorate public discourse and help society navigate the rise of misinformation and propaganda based on how this approach allows for a diversity in the foundations of truth and seeks to champion everyone's right to operate in society as they see fit without anyone able to claim superiority over another's view.[53] Post-foundationalism is based on the understanding that "social relationships are always operating based on multiple, contingent grounds," meaning that "we cannot reduce the world to the unfolding of any singular order, principle, or foundation."[54] Without a singular order, principles, or foundation to society, humanity is able to chart their own course in the pursuit of truth and morality. Their articulation of post-foundationalism is undergirded by the ideas of postmodernism and its leading figures such as Jacques Derrida and Marxist scholars Ernesto Laclau and Chantal Mouffe.[55] Sociologist Oliver Marchart describes what is at stake in political post-foundationalism as "not the impossibility of *any* ground, but the impossibility of a *final* ground."[56] Farkas and Schou

---

[53] For more on post-foundationalism, see *The Demise of Foundationalism and the Retention of Truth: What Evangelicals Can Learn from C. S. Peirce* in Amos Yong, *The Dialogical Spirit: Christian Reason and Theological Method in the Third Millennium* (Cambridge, UK: Lutterworth, 2014), 19–46. Yong describes the two main outworkings of this view as post-liberalism and post-modernism.

[54] Farkas and Schou, *Post-Truth, Fake News and Democracy*, 17.

[55] For more on the relationship of democracy and post-foundationalism, see Oliver Marchart, *Post-Foundational Theories of Democracy* (Edinburgh: Edinburgh University Press, 2016).

[56] Oliver Marchart, *Post-Foundational Political Thought: Political Difference in Nancy, Lefort, Bafiou and Laclau* (Edinburgh: Edinburgh Univ. Press, 2008), 155.

point out that it is important to note that "post-foundationalism does not just claim that certain parts of social reality are more or less contingent. It claims that everything is necessarily contingent."[57] Thus, the only thing that is not contingent is contingency itself, which is logically incoherent and self-authenticating.

Farkas and Schou state in their book *Post-Truth, Fake News, and Democracy* that applying post-foundationalism to the current political debates over misinformation and conspiracy theories can yield a more political and less truth-oriented public square. They argue "that a way of saving democracy and the democratic tradition might be to create, nurture, and assemble genuine spaces for the enactment of politics proper. Democracy does not need more truth but more politics and popular rule."[58] Their proposal seems to indicate that society should not focus on facts as much but rely on majoritarian rule, which ironically has been shown to exacerbate these political tensions and the breakdown of society under secularism in the first place. This approach has come under heavy criticism, not only because of these "rule by majority" perspectives, but by many philosophers who argue that post-foundationalism and post-modernism are not really new eras in political theory or epistemology at all.

According to Alasdair MacIntyre, the phrase "post-Enlightenment" better describes this understanding of reality because it recognizes that post-modernism is simply a variant of modern thought itself.[59] Philosopher Harold Netland similarly pushes back on post-foundationalism as a new epoch in truth-telling by saying that many of the leading figures, including Derrida, "share an epistemological skepticism and critique of metaphysics

---

[57] Farkas and Schou, *Post-Truth, Fake News and Democracy*, 18.

[58] Farkas and Schou, 154.

[59] See Alasdair C. MacIntyre, *Three Rival Versions of Moral Inquiry: Encyclopedia, Genealogy, and Tradition* (Notre Dame, IN: Univ. of Notre Dame Press, 2006), 215. Worldview scholar and apologist James Sire notes that "postmodernism is not 'post' anything; it is the last move of the modern, the result of the modern taking its own commitments seriously and seeing that they fail to stand the test of analysis." James W. Sire, *The Universe Next Door: A Basic Worldview Catalog*, sixth edition (Downers Grove, IL: IVP Academic, 2020), 204.

that has dominated Western philosophy since the time of Immanuel Kant."[60] While it may be valuable to take into account the perspectives of these post-modern thinkers, many of the same criticisms of secular foundationalism and its rejection of moral validity in religious claims hold true here as well.

Principled Pluralism

As previously argued, a purely secular approach to the public square is untenable because it negates the public aspects of faith and stands without a robust transcendent understanding of truth. While post-foundationalism seeks to allow more diversity in the public square, it does so by denying a final ground in the pursuit of truth as it argues for a multiplicity to truth claims. It may seem that these two approaches are the best options available to a society suffering from the delusion of misinformation, but what if there was an approach to the public square that allowed for true diversity of thought while acknowledging everyone's inability to know truth exhaustively? Principled pluralism is an approach to civic society that seeks to allow for a true diversity of thought by encouraging the toleration of ideas and some notion of compromise on societal decisions, but also one that allow members of the community to operate from a foundation of truth grounded in a transcendent reality.[61] This approach has been advocated in various forms by leading figures such as Richard John Neuhaus, John Inazu, David VanDrunen, and others.[62]

---

[60] Harold A. Netland, *Encountering Religious Pluralism: The Challenge to Christian Faith & Mission* (Downers Grove, IL: InterVarsity Press, 2001), 65.

[61] It should be noted that this approach also allows for some things deemed as conspiracy theories or misinformation that are later proven to be true or contain an element of truth, all of which adds to the psychological appeal and complexities in dealing with social media. Social medial promotes immediate declarations and gut-level feelings rather than virtuous depth. Principled pluralism seeks to allow more speech, not less, and promotes a less reactionary spirit as we seek to navigate these issues in the digital public square. For more on these issues, see chapter 2 from Bryan Baise on the nature of the public square and principled pluralism.

[62] Inazu argues for a "confident pluralism," while David VanDrunen argues for "conservative liberalism." See John D. Inazu, *Confident Pluralism: Surviving and*

Neuhaus was one of the founders of the modern public theology movement that sought to apply the timeless truths of Christianity to issues of public life in a pluralistic society. He rightly recognized that the moral foundation of society must be grounded in a transcendent reality and that people should be able to publicly operate out of their understandings of truth in all aspects of life. Written prior to the rise of post-foundationalism, Neuhaus's vision for the public square drew criticisms from all sides of the debate over the public square. To the ire of secularism, he refused to grant that religion is simply a private matter that should not be allowed in the public square in the pursuit of some secular ideal. However, he also argued that religious dogma cannot simply go unchecked in the democratic experiment. Neuhaus argued for a form of pluralism that did not deny realities, but also did not seek to subjugate religion or allow the government to "act as a theological referee amid religious diversity," as ethicist Andrew T. Walker writes.[63]

Walker explains that "pluralism does not treat truth claims as relative but equal in their opportunity to be made without fear of reprisal."[64] This concept of pluralism is at odds with a purely secular approach that forbids religion any influence in the public square. It allows for varying and often contradictory truth claims to be put forth in the public square, renewing an open and free society that can champion free expression and a marketplace of ideas. Philosopher Robert P. George explains, "the avoidance . . . of unjust or otherwise immoral policies by people of goodwill is powerfully served by permitting, indeed encouraging, vigorous debate, criticism, and dissent."[65]

Thriving through Deep Difference (Chicago: University of Chicago Press, 2016), 83–92; and David VanDrunen, *Politics after Christendom: Political Theology in a Fractured World* (Grand Rapids: Zondervan Academic, 2020), 358–83.

[63] Andrew T. Walker, *Liberty for All: Defending Everyone's Religious Freedom in a Pluralistic Age* (Grand Rapids: Brazos Press, 2021), 178.

[64] Walker, 178. See also Michael J. Sandel, "Judgmental Toleration" in George, *Natural Law, Liberalism, and Morality*, 107. Sandel argues for a "judgmental toleration," meaning a form of toleration that "assesses the moral worth or permissibility of the practice at issue and permits or restricts it according to the weight of those moral considerations in relation to competing moral and practical considerations."

[65] Robert P. George, *Making Men Moral: Civil Liberties and Public Morality* (Oxford: Clarendon Press, 2001), 202.

The free exchange of ideas in a principled pluralistic approach to governance and in the public square allows for more robust dialogue, rather than simply forbidding any religious claims in public discourse.

This principle goes both ways—allowing freedom of conscience and expression for all people, religious and non-religious alike. Kuyper explains that Christians above all "must not shrink from allowing freedom for believer and unbeliever alike, or else the strength on which we want to lean will appear to be another than the strength of faith."[66] As theologian and ethicist Carl F. H. Henry states from a societal standpoint, "it is not the role of government to judge between rival systems of metaphysics and to legislate one among other. Government's role is to protect and preserve a free course for its constitutional guarantees."[67] Henry's idea of freedom of conscience may also be extended to say that it also is not the role of other powerful private institutions, like technology companies themselves, to judge between these rival systems, even though they currently also have a freedom of expression to moderate their platforms as they choose. This is currently a highly debated idea within both conservative and progressive circles in the United States.

Neuhaus articulates a twofold vision of compromise and tolerance for the public square that seeks to understand both religion and democracy in their proper forms—a vision that is much more robust than critics often ascribe to him. For Neuhaus, compromise does not equate with weakness or giving up on deeply held beliefs but rather engaging in a robust dialogue over important issues and seeking a workable solution for as many parties as possible. He states, "Compromise and forgiveness arise from the acknowledgment that we are imperfect creatures in an imperfect world. Democracy is the product not of a vision of perfection but of the knowledge of imperfection."[68] He goes on to argue that compromise is also "not an immoral act, nor is it an amoral act" because "the person who makes a

---

[66] Kuyper, *Our Program*, 68.

[67] Carl F. H. Henry, *The Christian Mindset in a Secular Society: Promoting Evangelical Renewal & National Righteousness* (Portland, OR: Multnomah Press, 1984), 80.

[68] Neuhaus, *The Naked Public Square*, 114.

compromise is making a moral judgment about what is to be done when moral judgments are in conflict."[69] He critiques the popular two-kingdoms view of public theology and proposes a "twofold rule of God" that "underscores that it is the one God who rules over all reality, and his will is not divided."[70] This ensures that the public square is not devoid of a transcendent grounding for morality. Though, some on both sides of the divide will argue that Neuhaus gives away too much in the debate to the other side and that his middle-ground approach is ultimately untenable in the increasingly hostile public square.

Neuhaus's vision of compromise picks up on the idea of true toleration that has been popularized by some today as a path forward in these divisive times of polarization and tribalism.[71] VanDrunen states, "Tolerance is a proper feature of justice in our fallen but preserved world: acting justly may require us to tolerate people we do not like and modes of conduct we disapprove."[72] Compromise in Neuhaus's view is not about compromising truth or abandoning principle but recognizing that there are multiple moral actors present in any given decision and the need for humility in a workable vision of democracy. It means that "having set aside the sectarian and triumphalist alternatives, one acts with moral responsibility in an arena that requires compromise."[73] He later describes this project as one true democracy that understands that there "will always be another inning, another election, another appeal, another case to be tested."[74] It is understandable

---

[69] Neuhaus, 114.

[70] Neuhaus, 115.

[71] David VanDrunen argues for a robust pluralism and toleration in civic affairs from a framework based in the Noahic covenant. VanDrunen sees the Noahic covenant as a covenant that God made with society that is not directly fulfilled in Christ like the other covenants God made with his people (e.g., Abrahamic, Davidic, etc.). In his political theology, he proposes a way to navigate the deep tensions of the day using a framework of natural law spawning from the Noahic covenant, which involves a limited government, robust civic engagement, and an informed citizenry. See VanDrunen, *Politics after Christendom*, 181–213.

[72] VanDrunen, 185.

[73] Neuhaus, *The Naked Public Square*, 124.

[74] Neuhaus, 181.

why this particular vision would be unsettling to those who hold other views of the public square. It means not only recognizing other truth claims that are superior to the state itself, but also seeing the humanity of your supposed "enemies" and working toward a common future together without coercing one another to abandon their understanding of truth. A principled pluralism is focused on solving the issues at hand in a diverse society, rather than simply arguing about the nature of truth and seeking to coerce belief.[75]

While this principled pluralism approach can serve society by allowing for a level of diversity and respecting of persons even with their disparate visions of truth, a line must still be drawn by society as to what level of diversity will be allowed. As David VanDrunen argues, "Every human community and institution must reckon with the degree of diversity it will embrace, or at least tolerate. No institution can stand completely open."[76] This boundary of acceptable pluralism is difficult at times to obtain and will likely shift over time. One such line that is drawn focuses on the idea of the common good, but even a sense of a common good seems to necessitate some shared moral vision among the members of even the most tolerant society. This tension leads VanDrunen and others to question if a common good is even obtainable in this type of society.[77] Despite some of these tensions and questions surrounding any type of a shared moral consensus, a principled pluralism-type approach can still serve society well. It can remind Christians that this world is not their home and that their understanding of morality will not always be accepted by the wider culture.

---

[75] For an extended discussion on pluralism and Christian mission, see Walker, *Liberty for All*, 175–212. Walker rightly articulates that this view of pluralism "invites outward reasoned deliberation based on internalized religious premises. A commitment to public discourse that is publicly accessible does not negate the possibility of a distinctly Christian argument in the public square" (198). While Walker is directly speaking about the nature of religious freedom, his argument may be extended to the current debates over online governance and content moderation considering the pressing challenges described here with misinformation and propaganda as well.

[76] VanDrunen, *Politics after Christendom*, 181.

[77] See VanDrunen, 187.

VanDrunen rightly states that "a modest, rights-based justice may be the appropriate foundation for political coexistence, but it is a poor philosophy of life."[78] While Christians may advocate for these principles in the public square, it does not mean they will gain a wide hearing or that society will ultimately follow the created order as ordained by God. But this does not stop the church from respecting the diversity of thought in the public square and tolerating ideas that may be contradictory to the Christian moral tradition in the times between Christ's advents for the sake of political coexistence. It simply allows for a more diverse civil society and seeks to uphold the dignity of all people in hopes that the same level of respect is reciprocated.

Christian Engagement in the Digital Public Square

As illustrated, the lack of a shared moral consensus combined with an explosive tribalism has helped give rise to the culture of misinformation and conspiracy theories that society experiences today. This paired with a technological imperative as described by Ellul and others shows that the rise of these dangers in the digital public square are not isolated to one particular voting bloc or ideology. A way of navigating these tensions and restoring some semblance of a diverse, yet stable society is a civic understanding of principled pluralism as the best path forward in line with Christian moral tradition, as well as highlighting the church's unique role in public discourse. Two main principles arise from this study that can be applied to the church's engagement with the rest of society in this age of social media. First, Christians must recognize the widespread influence of technology on society and the ways that technology alters how one sees or interacts within society. As philosopher Nolen Gertz describes, "Technologies go beyond providing us with goals and shaping our activities, they can also influence our values and shape our judgements."[79] Technology constantly shapes the moral imagination of humanity, and recognizing how technology changes

---

[78] VanDrunen, 372.
[79] Gertz, *Nihilism and Technology*, 3.

all of society can allow the church to engage these pressing issues with openness and hope.[80]

Second, Christians can engage the public debates of the day from a principled position that allows for true diversity of thought without compromising the nature of truth. Grounded in an understanding of the dignity of all people, Christians can model for society how to have these debates from a convictional, yet grace-filled perspective. In a society that prizes efficiency, speed, and at times public contempt for one's "enemies," believers can prioritize the dignity of all people, including those who disagree with us on these important issues. By advocating for a pluralism in the digital public square, society might be able to stave off some of today's conspiracy theories and misinformation because these aberrations of truth often flow from feelings of rejection and/or the inability to authentically live out deeply held beliefs. Truth is often twisted to show the evil of another to regain what feels lost in a society that seeks to subjugate religion or other beliefs under the heavy hand of the state or society. When everything in society is deemed a battle or uses war-like language, it is natural for all forms of communication to take on a similar paradigm and for groups to use whatever means available—namely social media and communication platforms—to sound the alarm bells of an overreaching government or a public square that is devoid of any real diversity. Christians can model an open marketplace of ideas without compromising truth by recognizing that our battle in this life is not against flesh and blood, but against the cosmic powers of darkness (Eph 6:12).

Even as the raging winds of secularism and the shifting sands of postfoundationalism collide with Christian thought in the digital age, the

---

[80] For more on how technology shapes the moral imagination, see Jason Thacker, *The Age of AI: Artificial Intelligence and the Future of Humanity* (Grand Rapids: Zondervan, 2020) and Jason Thacker, "How Social Media Has Aided the Disintegration of Our Public Discourse," ERLC, January 8, 2021, https://erlc.com /resource-library/articles/how-social-media-has-aided-the-disintegration-of-our -public-discourse/. Also see Nicholas Carr's work on how the internet is changing the physiological makeup of the human brain. Nicholas G. Carr, *The Shallows: What the Internet Is Doing to Our Brains* (New York: W. W. Norton, 2011).

church can be reminded that she engages these issues from a place of stead-fast hope and peace, grounded in the transcendent reality of God's created order but also with an anticipation of eschatological harmony.[81] Christians have a steady hope, even in the midst of an uncertain future, because we know that God is, above all, sovereign over history and all of humanity, and that nothing will ever supplant the image of God in which human beings are created.

---

[81] See VanDrunen, *Politics after Christendom*, 187.

11

Centralizing Power and the Heavy Hand of the Regime

The International Challenges of Technology and Human Rights

Olivia Enos

On January 31, 2020, after the World Health Organization declared COVID-19 a global emergency, Sun Feng, a Christian in Shandong province, China, sent an urgent message to his WeChat group urging them to begin nine days of prayer and fasting for victims of the virus and their families. On the seventh day of the fast, local police from the Public Security Bureau detained Mr. Sun for twenty-four hours. They ordered him to stop so-called unauthorized prayers. Instead, he announced an additional day of fasting and prayer as a form of nonviolent protest. As a consequence, police confiscated his cell phone and computers.[1]

---

[1] See "China Harasses Citizens for Reporting on Coronavirus," ChinaAid, March 4, 2020, https://www.chinaaid.org/2020/03/china-harasses-citizens-for -reporting.html.

The situation Mr. Sun faced during the COVID-19 pandemic is emblematic of the great lengths to which the Chinese government will go to suppress activities that do not comply with the Chinese Communist Party's (CCP) precepts. In most countries, Mr. Sun's actions would be considered commonplace—an everyday means of living out his most closely held beliefs in concert with other members of his same faith. In China, however, his actions are illegal.

The enforcement of these restrictive measures is made possible by the CCP's draconian surveillance efforts that cover even simple phone applications like WeChat. Mr. Sun's situation is but one example of the ways the CCP—and many governments around the globe—curtail fundamental freedoms and human rights through digital means.

To understand government repression in the digital realm, it is important to understand the nature of digital authoritarianism. The first part of this chapter will define digital authoritarianism and explain why it matters. Then, we will examine what motivates the digital authoritarian. We will continue our deep dive into this subject by identifying emerging trends in how autocratic nations are repressing disfavored and minority viewpoints as well as survey some of the most flagrant perpetrators such as Burma, Belarus, North Korea, Russia, and China. Finally, we will conclude the chapter by presenting some options for governments and citizens to respond to the challenges created by digital authoritarianism.

What Is Digital Authoritarianism and Why Does It Matter?

There is a battle raging worldwide over values. While historically these battles have been won and lost on physical battlefields, today's battles are also being conducted in the digital realm.[2] Nowhere is this clearer than online.

---

[2] See Kara Frederick, "Democracy by Design: An Affirmative Response to the Illiberal Use of Technology for 2021," Center for a New American Security, December 15, 2020, https://www.cnas.org/publications/reports/democracy-by-design.

In their annual *Freedom of the Net* report, Freedom House, a nonprofit devoted to promoting good governance worldwide, reports that 40 percent of the sixty-five countries surveyed in 2020 saw an overall decline in internet freedom.[3] To make matters worse, only nineteen of the sixty-five countries surveyed saw improvements in internet freedom during the same reporting period. This means that most countries are witnessing either stagnations or deteriorations in their internet freedom, leading some to conclude that digital authoritarianism is on the rise.

Downward trends in internet freedom are happening amidst the backdrop of the global coronavirus pandemic, where many people are experiencing increases in violations of their right to privacy. Democratic and authoritarian governments alike increasingly used surveillance technology to track people's movements as a means of contact tracing during the COVID-19 outbreak, for example.[4] And authoritarian actors like China have used the distractions of the pandemic to continue to refine their use and abuse of surveillance technology to collectivize between 1.8 million and 3 million Uyghurs in political reeducation camps. This is to say nothing of rising restrictions on access to information, such as the Burmese military systematically cutting off access to the internet at politically sensitive moments during the February 2021 coup,[5] Russian authorities

---

[3] See Adrian Shahbaz, "Freedom on the Net 2018: The Rise of Digital Authoritarianism," Freedom House, https://freedomhouse.org/report/freedom-net/2018/rise-digital-authoritarianism.

[4] See Victor Cha, "Asia's COVID-19 Lessons for the West: Public Goods, Privacy, and Social Tagging," *Washington Quarterly* 43, no. 2 (June 16, 2020), https://cpb-us-e1.wpmucdn.com/blogs.gwu.edu/dist/1/2181/files/2020/06/Cha_TWQ_43-2.pdf; Olivia Enos, "Responding to COVID–19 in Southeast Asia," The Heritage Foundation, April 14, 2020, https://www.heritage.org/asia/report/responding-covid-19-southeast-asia.

[5] See Andrea Januta and Minami Funakoshi, "Myanmar's Internet Suppression: In Myanmar, the Junta's Intensifying Crackdowns on Protesters in the Street Are Mirrored by Its Rising Restrictions Online," Reuters, April 7, 2021, https://graphics.reuters.com/MYANMAR-POLITICS/INTERNET-RESTRICTION/rlgpdbreepo/.

launching disinformation campaigns,[6] or China's Great Firewall and its mass censorship.[7]

Experts say that many of these actions are typical of digital authoritarians. There is some debate over the definition of digital authoritarianism, but for the purposes of this chapter, we will use the following from Steven Feldstein, a non-resident fellow at the Carnegie Endowment's Democracy, Conflict, and Governance Program. According to Feldstein,

> A common definition entails "the use of digital information technology by authoritarian regimes to surveil, repress, and manipulate domestic and foreign populations." This is a sensible starting point, but disaggregating digital authoritarianism by technology and tactic offers more insights.
>
> Digital repression comprises six techniques: (1) surveillance, (2) censorship, (3) social manipulation and harassment, (4) cyberattacks, (5) internet shutdowns, and (6) targeted persecution against online users. These six techniques are not mutually exclusive. Intrusive spyware, for example, implanted by government security services on a user's computer, is both a form of surveillance as well as a cyberattack. But each technique offers a specific set of objectives and draws from a unique set of tools to fulfill its function.[8]

———————

[6] See Alina Polyakova and Chris Meserole, "Exporting digital authoritarianism," Brookings Institution, https://www.brookings.edu/wp-content/uploads/2019/08/FP_20190826_digital_authoritarianism_polyakova_meserole.pdf.

[7] See Conrad Chan et al., "Free speech vs Maintaining Social Cohesion: A Closer Look at Different Policies," Stanford University, https://cs.stanford.edu/people/eroberts/cs181/projects/2010-11/FreeExpressionVsSocialCohesion/china_policy.html. For more on China's Great Firewall, which is China's attempt to completely isolate the Chinese internet from the rest of the world, see Elizabeth C. Economy, *The Third Revolution: Xi Jinping and the New Chinese State* (New York: Oxford University Press, 2018), 55–90.

[8] Steven Feldstein, "When It Comes to Digital Authoritarianism, China Is a Challenge—but Not the Only Challenge," War on the Rocks, February 12, 2020, https://warontherocks.com/2020/02/when-it-comes-to-digital-authoritarianism-china-is-a-challenge-but-not-the-only-challenge/.

Feldstein's definition of digital authoritarianism puts meat on the bones of a somewhat vague concept. Digital authoritarianism draws on our traditional understandings of a specific regime type—an authoritarian—and his definition provides specific examples of the tools and methods digital authoritarians have at their disposal.

This concept of a digital authoritarian is a helpful one, because it enables policymakers to draw upon traditional policy tools, or to refashion them, for a new context. It also enables policymakers to draw on some of the theoretical and practical concepts that have already been teased out in the real world and apply them to the digital realm.

Why Do Digital Authoritarians Engage in Repression?

Like all authoritarians, digital authoritarians are engaged in the business of repression. The first—and principal—motivation of a digital authoritarian is to maintain power. Second, and to that end, they repress and sideline opposition. Finally, they use technology to acquire, distort, and restrict access to information—whether for innocuous or pernicious ends—because, at root, many forms of digital repression bely a fundamental assumption: namely, that information is power.

Power Politics in the Digital Realm

Digital authoritarians engage in digital repression to maintain their grip on power. To an authoritarian, any threat—real or imagined—to their power must be neutralized, because regime stability and security are paramount.[9]

---

[9] See Sheena Chestnut Greitens, "Internal Security and Grand Strategy: China's Approach to National Security Under Xi Jinping," Testimony before the U.S.-China Economic and Security Review Commission, January 28, 2021, https://www.uscc.gov/sites/default/files/2021-01/Sheena_Chestnut_Greitens_Testimony.pdf. And Sheena Chestnut Greitens, "The United States' Strategic Competition with China," Testimony before the Senate Armed Services Committee, June 8, 2021, https://www.armed-services.senate.gov/imo/media/doc/06.08%20Greitens%20Testimony.pdf.

Therefore, a range of otherwise inexcusable options are justified at the altar of retaining power and legitimacy.

Victor Cha, renowned scholar of North Korea, notes that three generations of the Kim regime have sought to maintain power principally through *juche* ideology, or self-reliance.[10] Over time this morphed into *neo-juche* ideology, which meant self-reliance through nuclear weapons. For North Korea, self-reliance has also been achieved through human rights violations—like sending three generations of individuals to a political prison camp or publicly executing people for defying the regime. In other words, North Korea will threaten international security and the rights of its own citizens in pursuit of power.

Jung Pak, deputy assistant secretary of state for East Asia and Pacific Affairs, put a finer point on it in her book *Becoming Kim Jong-un*: "Repression and the nuclear weapons program thus form the two pillars of his regime's survival: the denial of human rights and the country's status as a nuclear weapons power are mutually reinforcing."[11]

North Korea acts similarly in the digital public square. When Sony Pictures was about to release the satirical film *The Interview* in 2014, North Korean cyberattackers sprang into action and hacked Sony.[12] The hack resulted in the release of sensitive and confidential employee data that revealed vulnerabilities in Sony's cybersecurity.[13] The North Koreans carried out the cyberattack because the movie portrayed Pyongyang in an unflattering light. To those leading the regime, this was impermissible and a sufficient cause to attack the movie company. When power and

---

[10] See Victor Cha, *The Impossible State: North Korea, Past and Future* (New York: HarperCollins, 2013).

[11] Jung Pak, *Becoming Kim Jong Un: A Former CIA Officer's Insights into North Korea's Enigmatic Young Dictator* (New York: Ballantine Books, 2020), 126.

[12] See Bruce Klingner, "North Korean Cyberattacks: A Dangerous and Evolving Threat," The Heritage Foundation, September 2, 2021, https://www.heritage.org /asia/report/north-korean-cyberattacks-dangerous-and-evolving-threat.

[13] See Andrea Peterson, "The Sony Pictures Hack Explained," *Washington Post*, December 18, 2014, https://www.washingtonpost.com/news/the-switch/wp/2014 /12/18/the-sony-pictures-hack-explained/.

legitimacy are at stake, no action, however big, is too much to safeguard it. North Korea has also carried out cyber hacks to pilfer large sums of money from several banks worldwide. It is believed that North Korea has stolen as much as $2 billion from cyber hacks—all money that can line the coffers of the regime and may even go toward its weapons development programs.[14] In 2021, three North Korean cyber hackers were charged by the US Department of Justice for attempting to steal and extort $1.3 billion in cash and cryptocurrency.[15] One of the North Korean hackers, Park Jin Hyok, was also charged for the role he played in the Sony hack.[16]

In addition to its various hacking exploits, the Kim regime restricts internet access and cell phone access inside the country to ensure that its people do not have access to information that contradicts what the regime tells them about the outside world. All of the actions outlined above are variations of a tool in the digital authoritarian's toolbox. Some affect security and some affect human rights. All actions are justified by the claim that they safeguard regime legitimacy and power.

The North Korean case highlights the integrated relationship between issues of national security and human rights in the digital realm—and the reinforcing ways that violations of national security and human rights are used to maintain power. Countering digital authoritarianism, therefore, may require policy tools that address challenges posed to both national security and human rights, rather than pursuing policies that address either issue in isolation from the other.

---

[14] See Bruce Klingner and Luke Kim, "North Korean Cyberattacks Pose Threat to U.S.," The Heritage Foundation, June 3, 2021, https://www.heritage.org /cybersecurity/commentary/north-korean-cyberattacks-pose-threat-us.

[15] See Ellen Nakashima, "U.S. Accuses Three North Koreans of Conspiring to Steal More Than $1.3 Billion in Cash and Cryptocurrency," *Washington Post*, February 17, 2021, https://www.washingtonpost.com/national-security/north -korea-hackers-banks-theft/2021/02/17/3dccf0dc-7129-11eb-93be-c10813e3 58a2_story.html.

[16] See Nakashima, "U.S. Accuses Three North Koreans."

Sidelining Opposition

Since digital authoritarians are often motivated by power, they seek to neutralize specific groups they see as especially threatening to their power base. Governments are especially eager to target their opposition, or to target forces they see as at odds with their own interests. Unfortunately, this often puts minority groups—especially religious or ethnic minorities—in the crosshairs. Let's consider a few examples:

Political Opposition and Religious Minorities in Burma

The Burmese military, also known as the Tatmadaw, has a long history of suppression. On February 1, 2021, this suppression reached its pinnacle when the military carried out a coup, ignoring the will of the Burmese people who granted the National League for Democracy (NLD) a landslide victory in the November 2020 elections. In response to the coup, hundreds of thousands of Burmese, as part of a massive civil disobedience movement, took to the streets to protest. The Burmese military was quick to clamp down through digital means.

First, as reported by Reuters, on the night before the coup, the military visited internet providers and put guns to operators' heads to cut wires that provided internet connectivity.[17] Second, as protests began in response to the coup, the military began cutting off access to the internet for brief, unpredictable periods—for example, the military cut access for approximately thirty hours on February 6.[18] The military then restricted access to critical social media platforms often used for organizing, including Facebook, Messenger, and WhatsApp.[19] Third, the military cut off

---

[17] See Andrea Januta and Minami Funakoshi, "Myanmar's Internet Suppression," Reuters, April 7, 2021, https://graphics.reuters.com/MYANMAR-POLITICS /INTERNET-RESTRICTION/rlgpdbreepo/.

[18] See Januta and Funakoshi, "Myanmar's Internet Suppression."

[19] See Christopher Giles, "Myanmar coup: How the military disrupted the internet," BBC News, February 4, 2021, https://www.bbc.com/news/world-asia -55889565.

cell phone connectivity, further complicating the Burmese people's ability to organize.[20]

This is hardly the first time that the Burmese government has restricted internet or cell phone coverage. In 2020, Linda Lakhdir, Asia legal advisor for Human Rights Watch, called on the Burmese government to "immediately end what is now the world's longest government-enforced internet shutdown."[21] She was referring to the situation in the Rakhine and Chin states, both areas where religious and ethnic minorities reside. There have been ongoing skirmishes between ethnic armed groups in Chin state and long-term persecution of Muslim Rohingya who reside in Rakhine state. Given that many internet providers in Burma are wholly or partially state-owned, the government can flex its muscle to restrict access and hamstring access for minorities who are often viewed as opposition.

Uyghurs in China

Few countries have targeted their religious minorities more ardently than China. The persecution of the Uyghur Muslims will go down in the annals of history as genocide and crimes against humanity.[22] Their persecution is aided, in no small part, by the draconian deployment of surveillance technology that is used to identify and collectivize millions of Uyghurs in political reeducation camps.

The Chinese government has deployed what China scholar Adrian Zenz of the Victims of Communism Memorial Foundation identifies as

---

[20] See "Myanmar Junta Orders Shutdown of Internet, Providers Say," VOA News, April 2, 2021, https://www.voanews.com/east-asia-pacific/myanmar-junta -orders-shutdown-internet-providers-say.

[21] "Myanmar: End World's Longest Internet Shutdown," Human Rights Watch, June 19, 2020, https://www.hrw.org/news/2020/06/19/myanmar-end-worlds-longest -internet-shutdown#.

[22] See Michael R. Pompeo, "Determination of the Secretary of State on Atrocities in Xinjiang," U.S. Department of State, January 19, 2021, https://2017 -2021.state.gov/determination-of-the-secretary-of-state-on-atrocities-in-xinjiang /index.html.

"grid-style social management."[23] According to the Jamestown Foundation, this system "segments urban communities into geometric zones so that security staff can systematically observe all activities with the aid of new technologies."[24] The system combines rapid deployment of surveillance technology and the use of an application called the IJOP to identify "suspicious behaviors" monitored by China's vast network of law enforcement.[25] "Suspicious behaviors" can be as innocuous as a decision to exit out the back door of your home as opposed to the front.[26] Zenz describes the vast web of law enforcement as "convenience police stations," suggesting that police stations in China are now as commonplace as convenience stores.

It is fair to assert that apart from the surveillance technology, the CCP could not have collectivized and interned Uyghurs at such a rapid pace. As of 2022, there are between 1.8 and 3 million Uyghurs in over 260 known political reeducation camps in China.[27] In July 2021, the Biden administration expanded the scope of the national emergency declared under the Trump administration noting "that the use of Chinese surveillance technology outside the PRC, as well as the development or use of Chinese surveillance technology to facilitate repression or serious human rights abuses,

---

[23] Adrian Zenz and James Leibold, "Chen Quanguo: The Strongman Behind Beijing's Securitization Strategy in Tibet and Xinjiang," The Jamestown Foundation, September 21, 2017, https://jamestown.org/program/chen-quanguo-the-strongman-behind-beijings-securitization-strategy-in-tibet-and-xinjiang/.

[24] Zenz and Leibold, "Chen Quanguo."

[25] Maya Wang, "China's Algorithms of Repression: Reverse Engineering a Xinjiang Police Mass Surveillance App," Human Rights Watch, May 1, 2019, https://www.hrw.org/report/2019/05/01/chinas-algorithms-repression/reverse-engineering-xinjiang-police-mass; Nazish Doklia and Maya Wang, "Interviewing China's Big Brother App," Human Rights Watch, May 1, 2019, https://www.hrw.org/news/2019/05/01/interview-chinas-big-brother-app#.

[26] Doklia and Wang, "Interviewing China's Big Brother App."

[27] See Megha Rajagopalan et al., "Built to Last," BuzzFeed News, August 27, 2020, https://www.buzzfeednews.com/article/meghara/china-new-internment-camps-xinjiang-uighurs-muslims.

constitute unusual and extraordinary threats. This executive order allows the United States to prohibit—in a targeted and scoped manner—US investments in Chinese companies that undermine the security or democratic values of the United States and our allies."[28] The president's executive order specifically prohibits US investment in the notorious Chinese company Hikvision, which is believed to have produced much of the surveillance technology used to collectivize Uyghurs in camps.[29]

China targets Uyghurs because the CCP has defined all religious practice as extremist, and Uyghurs in particular as separatist (since the Turkic minority has at times called for independence). In China's view, if something is perceived as extremist, then it is a threat to the country's core goals of maintaining internal stability and sovereignty. In the CCP's mind, because Uyghurs threaten the Party's core interests, few options are off the table—even galvanizing new and emerging technologies to be repurposed as tools of repression.

Opposition in Belarus

In 2021, Freedom House documented a significant decline in freedom of the internet in Belarus, a small eastern European country that borders Russia and Ukraine.[30] The reporting period overlapped with a tainted presidential election that saw the then twenty-six-year reigning dictator Alyaksandr Lukashenka win reelection—a victory essentially guaranteed by Russian

---

[28] "FACT SHEET: Executive Order Addressing the Threat from Securities Investments that Finance Certain Companies of the People's Republic of China," The White House, June 3, 2021, https://www.whitehouse.gov/briefing-room /statements-releases/2021/06/03/fact-sheet-executive-order-addressing-the-threat -from-securities-investments-that-finance-certain-companies-of-the-peoples -republic-of-china/.

[29] See "Executive Order on Addressing the Threat from Securities Investments that Finance Certain Companies of the People's Republic of China."

[30] See "Freedom on the Net 2021: Belarus," Freedom House, https://freedom house.org/country/belarus/freedom-net/2021.

backing.[31] Pro-democracy protests began in August 2020 amid a resurgence in the opposition party's popularity in the country.[32]

Taking a typical play out of the Russian information restriction playbook, Lukashenka and his government carried out internet shutdowns, restricted access to high-traffic Belarusian news websites including TUT.by and NN.by, and arrested popular opposition journalists, civil society activists, and other opposition forces.[33] There are estimated to be approximately 550 individuals currently being held as political prisoners in Belarus for their role in the protests.[34]

Belarus's seventy-two-hour internet shutdown in August 2020 was aided by "deep packet inspection" (DPI) technology, which enables rogue governments to monitor internet traffic and censor sensitive information for political purposes.[35] DPI is not always used for nefarious purposes. In fact, the original application of DPI technology was to identify spam, malware, or potential sources of viruses, not for censorship. Nevertheless, DPI has been repurposed by other authoritarian actors, including China and Russia.[36]

---

[31] See Peter Dickinson, "Dictator vs democracy: Belarus one year on," Atlantic Council, August 9, 2021, https://www.atlanticcouncil.org/blogs/ukrainealert /dictator-vs-democracy-belarus-one-year-on/.

[32] See Alexis Mrachek, "She Defied 'the Last Dictator in Europe.' Now, She Is Asking the U.S. to Support the People of Belarus to Secure Freedom," The Heritage Foundation, July 21, 2021, https://www.heritage.org/europe/commentary/she -defied-the-last-dictator-europe-now-she-asking-the-us-support-the-people.

[33] See Freedom House, "Belarus."

[34] See Mrachek, "The Last Dictator."

[35] See Aliide Naylor, "Belarus Turned Off the Internet. Its Citizens Hot-Wired It," Gizmodo, August 26, 2020, https://gizmodo.com/belarus-turned-off-the-internet-its -citizens-hot-wired-1844853575; Chris Brook, "What Is Deep Packet Inspection? How It Works, Use Cases for DPI, and More," Digital Guardian, December 5, 2018, https://digitalguardian.com/blog/what-deep-packet-inspection-how-it-works -use-cases-dpi-and-more; Ryan Gallagher, "Belarusian Officials Shut Down Internet with Technology Made by U.S. Firm," Business & Human Rights Resource Centre, August 28, 2020, https://www.business-humanrights.org/en/latest-news/belarus -officials-shut-down-internet-with-technology-allegedly-made-by-us-firm/.

[36] See Duncan Geere, "How deep packet inspection works," Wired, April 27, 2012, https://www.wired.co.uk/article/how-deep-packet-inspection-works; Alena

Lukashenka faced a real threat of losing an election. Belarus is already a rights-abusing regime, and the Belarusian leader used whatever tools necessary to sideline the opposition and its supporters. This was, in effect, a powerplay by the dictator, which in this instance was successful.

Information as Power

If information is power, and power is the chief end of a digital authoritarian, then using digital means to restrict access to information, acquire personal or other forms of information, and distort information is imperative.

Digital authoritarians use a variety of tools not only to glean information but also to manipulate it. Over the past several years, the rise of disinformation, and various actors seeking to manipulate information in the digital context has received significant attention.[37] While many digital authoritarians have undertaken disinformation campaigns, the two major players remain Russia and China.

The Internet Research Agency and Russian Disinformation Campaigns

Russia has several reasons for engaging in disinformation efforts. Most, ultimately, boil down to power politics.

As one RAND study put it, Russia has a special interest in targeting former communist countries because,

> first, effectively influencing the political outcomes of these countries helps establish a cushion against what it considers malign Western influence. Second, some of these countries, including the Baltics and Ukraine, have minority populations of Russian speakers who are former Soviet citizens and their descendants. It is a matter of established Russian policy—specifically, what is called the

---

Epifanova, "Subjugating RuNet: The Kremlin's New Levers of Control over Elections and Society," Wilson Center, September 20, 2021, https://www.wilsoncenter.org/blog-post/subjugating-runet-kremlins-new-levers-control-over-elections-and-society.

[37] For more on disinformation and the manipulation of information, see chapter 10 by Jason Thacker.

compatriot policy—to protect the interests of this population and, more importantly, influence the population to support pro-Russia causes and effectively influence the politics of its neighbors.[38]

Russia views the internet as a by-product of US influence and maintains an abiding interest in subverting the norms and structure of the internet's functionality.[39] That is why disinformation campaigns form a pivotal role in their overarching efforts to undermine the internet's liberalization potential. Russia has long played a pivotal role in propagating disinformation, but recent actions have put their disinformation efforts squarely in the spotlight.[40]

As the use of bots came to the fore, there were reports of a "troll factory"—or, as NATO defines it "an entity conducting disinformation propaganda on the Internet"—that employed somewhere between 300 and 1,000 people in St. Petersburg.[41] It is now believed that this troll factory—which likely played a critical role in promoting disinformation during the annexation of Crimea and during US elections in 2016—was operated by Russia's Internet Research Agency (IRA) led by Yevgeny Prigozhin.[42] Prigozhin is an associate of Russian president Vladimir Putin who does the

---

[38] Todd C. Helmus et al., *Russian Social Media Influence: Understanding Russian Propaganda in Eastern Europe* (Santa Monica: Rand Corporation, 2018), 3, https://www.rand.org/content/dam/rand/pubs/research_reports/RR2200/RR2237/RAND_RR2237.pdf

[39] See Robert Morgus, "The Spread of Russia's Digital Authoritarianism," in *AI, China, Russia, and the Global Order: Technological, Political, Global, and Creative Perspectives*, ed. Nicholas D. Wright (Washington, DC: U.S. Department of Defense, 2018), 86, https://apps.dtic.mil/sti/pdfs/AD1066673.pdf#page=100.

[40] Russia's use of disinformation was on full display during the unjust invasion of neighboring Ukraine in 2022 as well.

[41] "Media—(Dis)information—Security," NATO Defence Education Enhancement Programme, https://www.nato.int/nato_static_fl2014/assets/pdf/2020/5/pdf/2005-deepportal2-troll-factories.pdf; Samantha Bradshaw et al., "Country Case Studies Industrialized Disinformation: 2020 Global Inventory of Organized Social Media Manipulation," Oxford Internet Institute, 326, https://demtech.oii.ox.ac.uk/wp-content/uploads/sites/127/2021/03/Case-Studies_FINAL.pdf.

[42] Neil MacFarquhar, "Inside the Russian Troll Factory: Zombies and a Breakneck Pace," *New York Times*, February 18, 2018, https://www.nytimes.com/2018/02/18/world/europe/russia-troll-factory.html.

president's bidding on a range of unsavory tasks.[43] He was later indicted by a federal grand jury for interfering in US elections and is now on the FBI's most wanted list with a reward of up to $250,000 for anyone with information leading to his arrest.[44]

The troll factory has been described as functioning similarly to a marketing agency, "with departments focused on graphics, data analysis, and search engine optimization, as well as IT and financing. . . . Initially, the IRA was used as a tool of domestic political manipulation, but it increasingly turned to foreign interference operations—first in Ukraine and later around the world."[45] Most of the IRA's function is to make false information appear legitimate, thereby misleading consumers of the information it produces.

If Russia can influence or alter the outcome in a foreign election, or even reshape domestic opinions about a politically sensitive priority of the Russian state, it advances its geopolitical power and objectives. While its efforts, in this instance, do not focus on collecting personal information to expand its power, Russia uses tools of manipulation to achieve the same outcome.

China's Social Credit System, Surveillance, and Invasions of Privacy

Few countries collect more information about their (and other countries') citizens than China. China certainly engages in disinformation, but to understand the full range of a digital authoritarian's options, it is important to understand China's social credit system.

We already have some understanding of the great lengths to which the CCP has gone to collectivize Uyghurs. Xinjiang is, in fact, a testing ground for an eventual nationwide deployment of the Chinese government's so-called social credit system—a system instituted to measure the Chinese

---

[43] See Neil MacFarquhar, "Yevgeny Prigozhin, Russian Oligarch Indicted by U.S., Is Known as 'Putin's Cook,'" *New York Times*, February 16, 2018, https://www.nytimes.com/2018/02/16/world/europe/prigozhin-russia-indictment-mueller.html.

[44] See MacFarquhar, "Yevgeny Prigozhin"; "Wanted by the FBI: Yevgeniy Viktorovich Prigozhin," FBI, https://www.fbi.gov/wanted/counterintelligence/yevgeniy-viktorovich-prigozhin/yevgeniy-vicktorovich-prigozhin3.pdf.

[45] Bradshaw et al., "2020 Global Inventory," 326.

people's adherence to the values espoused by the CCP.[46] Each person is assigned a numeric value: 1,000 points. Any deviation from acceptable social norms results in a demerit. The demerit affects an individual's ability to purchase travel tickets (train, bus, and plane) and can affect whether he or she can qualify for a loan from the bank. It is doled out by government officials and has been piloted in numerous Chinese provinces, both as publicly and privately managed policies.[47] The system is described by many as Orwellian and may partially explain how individuals in Xinjiang were selected and destined for political reeducation facilities. The social credit system relies on surveillance technology as well as on citizen-based reporting to identify misbehavior and determine subsequent demerits. As a Human Rights Watch report in 2019 stated, the app IJOP was able to be reverse engineered, showing the Chinese government used it to monitor and select individuals from the population in Xinjiang for internment in the political reeducation facilities.[48]

The IJOP technology enables the Chinese government to collect information on an individual's car, blood type, day-to-day habits (such as whether he exited his home from the front or back door), and summarily deems behavior suspicious (or not) through this highly invasive system of monitoring. It's not entirely clear how or even where all the personal data is stored, but it is collected via surveillance technology and enforced through China's rigorous application of grid-style social management.

The CCP's social credit system demonstrates that even public morality can be monitored and enforced by the state. The CCP's chosen method

---

[46] See Simina Mistreanu, "Fears About China's Social-Credit System Are Probably Overblown, But It Will Still Be Chilling," *Washington Post*, March 8, 2019, https://www.washingtonpost.com/opinions/2019/03/08/fears-about-chinas -social-credit-system-are-probably-overblown-it-will-still-be-chilling/?utm_term= .4a12e0945aee.

[47] See Jamie Horsley, "China's Orwellian Social Credit Score Isn't Real," *Foreign Policy*, November 16, 2018, https://foreignpolicy.com/2018/11/16/chinas -orwellian-social-credit-score-isnt-real/.

[48] See News release, "China's Algorithms of Repression," Human Rights Watch, May 1, 2019, https://www.hrw.org/report/2019/05/01/chinas-algorithms -repression/reverse-engineering-xinjiang-police-mass-surveillance.

relies heavily on access to as much information about a person as is humanly possible to collect. This reveals an underlying assumption about the CCP: the more information the government has on a person, the easier it is to control them. The easier it is to control a person, the more power the CCP ultimately possesses.

Merging the Digital with the Physical World

In addition to undertaking disinformation campaigns and collecting personal information, many digital authoritarians actively seek to merge the digital world with the real one.

One example of this, highlighted by Paul Mozur in the *New York Times*, is how China has sought to question people in real time for digital content the CCP deems questionable.[49] The rapid response times to shutting down dissent on the internet has a ripple effect in the real world. As Mozur argues, if China looks at its successes in establishing the Great Firewall, or other means of control, it may use the internet as a perfect landscape for refining techniques of repression applied offline.[50]

This desire to merge the digital with reality may ultimately evolve into an eventual goal of replacing the physical with the digital wherever possible. This is, in part, because it is far easier to control and manipulate thought in the digital realm than it is to stamp out dissent in the physical world.

---

[49] See Paul Mozur and Aaron Krolik, "A Surveillance Net Blankets China's Cities, Giving Police Vast Powers," *New York Times*, December 17, 2019, https://www.nytimes.com/2019/12/17/technology/china-surveillance.html; Paul Mozur, "Paul Mozur on How China is Using Tech Against its Own People," interview by Christiane Amanpour, PBS, May 7, 2019, https://www.pbs.org/video/paul-mozur-how-china-using-tech-against-its-own-people-fjfol/.

[50] Paul Mozur, "Inside China's Dystopian Dreams: A.I., Shame, and Lots of Cameras," *New York Times,* July 8, 2018, https://www.nytimes.com/2018/07/08/business/china-surveillance-technology.html; Paul Mozur, "One Month, 500,000 Face Scans: How China Is Using A.I. to Profile a Minority," *New York Times*, April 14, 2019, https://www.nytimes.com/2019/04/14/technology/china-surveillance-artificial-intelligence-racial-profiling.html.

Trends to Watch in Digital Authoritarianism

As we explored the motivations of digital authoritarians, a few themes emerged that help us understand the landscape of digital authoritarianism. These themes are likely to continue to challenge policymakers far into the future and therefore merit additional attention before we turn to some potential solutions to mounting challenges in the digital sphere.

Three particular trends are worth noting:

1. Digital authoritarians almost universally restrict access to information to maintain power and control.
2. Some actors are exporting their models of authoritarianism.
3. Some actors are promoting an alternate model in the digital sphere that hinges on a faulty notion of so-called digital sovereignty.

These three trends are important for policymakers to understand, as they encompass many of the issues policymakers will need to proactively prepare for and tackle in the years ahead.

Trend #1: Restricting Access to Information

As we explored the motivations of digital authoritarians, a pattern emerged: a vast majority of digital authoritarians restrict access to information. This is because information restriction is a pervasive tool of control and does not necessarily require advanced digital prowess to accomplish. The difference between Russian and Chinese tools of information restriction are especially salient examples of how differing levels of cyber sophistication and tools do not change the outcome. Both models can achieve censorship and exert control over their populations despite Russia's less-sophisticated models of censorship vis-à-vis China.[51]

---

[51] See Matthew Cebul and Jonathan Pinckney, "Digital Authoritarianism and Nonviolent Action: Challenging the Digital Counterrevolution," United States Institute of Peace, 12, https://www.usip.org/sites/default/files/2021-07/sr_499-digital_authoritarianism_and_nonviolent_action_challenging_the_digital_counterrevolution.pdf.

There are a range of models used by various governments to limit their citizens' access to information. Some do not even require digital means, like North Korea, where the regime attempts to put in place an airtight seal along its border to ensure prohibited information does not get in. But even in North Korea (where access to the internet, computers, and cell phones is relatively limited) the regime restricts internet access, tracks cell phone usage, and deploys draconian methods to ensure that its people only receive and consume the information the regime wants them to. Others, like China, have innovated and used technology to further deepen its control over its population. China's "Great Firewall" limits the aperture of information people can access on their computer or smartphone.[52] And while not every country restricts or controls information all the time, many countries clamp down on internet access and shut down cell towers at politically opportune moments, such as the Burmese government did in the lead-up to the 2021 coup.

North Korea, perhaps, is one of the most comprehensive examples of information restriction in the world. Few countries are more cut off from the outside world as North Korea, and few governments have as tight a grip on information access as the Kim regime. Fortified and refined over three generations of the Kim dynasty, access to unapproved information is near-impossible to come by in the Democratic People's Republic of Korea (DPRK). Yet, as many have noted, North Koreans still manage to gain access to information because they are hungry for it.[53]

Tenacious North Koreans often seek out information by listening to foreign radio broadcasts, through information smuggled into the country on USBs, and by watching Korean dramas and Western media, listening to K-pop, and even using cell phones. According to a report by the Center for Strategic and International Studies, approximately 16 percent of North Koreans, or roughly 4 million people, have a cell phone.[54] While there are

---

[52] See Cebul and Pinckney, "Digital Authoritarianism and Nonviolent Action," 8.

[53] See Olivia Enos, "Improving Information Access in North Korea," The Heritage Foundation, December 7, 2016, https://www.heritage.org/asia/report/improving-information-access-north-korea.

[54] See Robert R. King, "North Koreans Want External Information, But Kim Jong-Un Seeks to Limit Access," Center for Strategic & International Studies, May

no definitive studies on the percentage of North Koreans with access to more advanced forms of technology, a 2019 survey of 200 recent North Korean defectors conducted by Unification Media Group (UMG) found that 91 percent of North Korean refugees had watched foreign media.[55] And of that same group of respondents, "76.5% of respondents used DVD players, 20% used notebook computers, and 11% used desktop computers to view foreign media."[56]

For many North Koreans, access to information is a literal lifeline. Their access to information, in fact, helps them decide whether to stay behind and facilitate change from within or to flee to freedom beyond North Korea's borders.[57] One defector, Yeonmi Park, said that watching the movie *Titanic* caused her to question what the regime told her about the outside world. She claims that watching the movie contributed to her decision to defect.[58]

But just as outside information can serve as a lifeline, it also often requires North Koreans to put their lives on the line merely to access it. The same study that documented the prevalence of access to technology in North Korea, also found that of the 200 defectors surveyed, at least 75 percent said they witnessed someone in North Korea being punished for watching foreign media.[59] Punishment can range anywhere from interro-

---

15, 2019, https://www.csis.org/analysis/north-koreans-want-external-information -kim-jong-un-seeks-limit-access.

[55] See Mun Dong Hui, "UMG Releases 200-Person Survey on North Korea's Shifting Media Landscape," *Daily NK*, June 25, 2019, https://www.dailynk .com/english/75-of-defectors-in-survey-witnessed-someone-being-punished-for -watching-foreign-media-in-north-korea/.

[56] Hui, "UMG 200-Person Survey."

[57] See Jonathan Corrado and Rachel Minyoung Lee, "Getting Outside Information Past Big Brother in North Korea," War on the Rocks, August 2, 2021, https://warontherocks.com/2021/08/getting-outside-information-past-big-brother -in-north-korea/.

[58] See Nathan Thompson, "'Watching Titanic Made Me Realise Something Was Wrong in My Country,' Says North Korean Defector," *The Guardian*, August 26, 2014, https://www.theguardian.com/world/2014/aug/26/north-korea-defector -titanic.

[59] See Hui, "UMG 200-Person Survey."

gation at the police station, to a public beating, to public execution. Even worse, some are sent to brutal political prison camps where death is a near certainty, but it is far slower, and usually death by starvation. Limiting access to information in North Korea is literal dogma. For people of faith, the Kim regime's commitment to information restriction is incredibly costly. Consider this story about North Korean Christian Ms. Hyeona Ji.

In 2014, the United Nations (UN) released the Commission of Inquiry Report (COI), which determined the Kim regime had committed crimes against humanity in North Korea. Justice Michael Kirby, the lead investigator for the COI, concluded that one of the most overlooked findings of the report was the persecution of religious minorities, especially Christians.[60] Christians in North Korea can literally be killed for the mere possession of a Bible.[61] And when North Korean refugees are repatriated by the Chinese government back to North Korea, they are asked whether they had contact with Christian missionaries.[62] If their answer is yes, they are often sent to political prison camps.

North Korean Christian Hyeona Ji escaped North Korea four times. Every time, she was asked whether she was a Christian, and she recounted how, like Peter, she denied her Christian faith three times.[63] When she was living in North Korea, she had experienced previous interrogations over the

---

[60] See "North Korean Human Rights: The Road Ahead, Commemorating the One Year Anniversary of the UN Commission of Inquiry Report," Center for Strategic and International Studies, February 17, 2015, http://csis.org/event/north -korean-human-rights-road-ahead.

[61] See Olivia Enos, "North Korea Is the World's Worst Persecutor of Christians," *Forbes*, January 25, 2017, https://www.forbes.com/sites/oliviaenos/2017/01/25 /north-korea-is-the-worlds-worst-persecutor-of-christians/?sh=476b3948318e.

[62] See "Report of the Commission of Inquiry on Human Rights in the Democratic People's Republic of Korea," United Nations Human Rights Council, February 7, 2014, 9, https://documents-dds-ny.un.org/doc/UNDOC/GEN/G14 /108/66/PDF/G1410866.pdf?OpenElement.

[63] See Samuel Smith, "N. Korean Defector Recalls Denying Christ 3 Times Like Apostle Peter Amid Regime Torture," *Christian Post*, July 27, 2018, https:// www.christianpost.com/news/n-korean-defector-recalls-denying-christ-3-times -like-apostle-peter-amid-regime-torture.html.

Bible her mom had smuggled home inside a bag of rice (and as a result of being caught had been beaten by authorities). Ms. Ji knows the consequences firsthand of being a Christian in North Korea, so she has dedicated her life to promoting freedom in this closed-off, hostile country. While the situation in North Korea represents an extreme form of despotic behavior, it is a case study in the logical results of instituting a comprehensive digital authoritarian model. The North Korean case also demonstrates the high costs of failing to address digital authoritarianism. As is evidenced by the North Korean situation, such draconian policies—left unchallenged—literally cost lives.

Trend #2: Exporting Surveillance and Digital Authoritarian Norms

Few countries have built out their surveillance state or have exerted greater influence over the development of surveillance states in other nations than China. China's social credit system, as well as the surveillance system that ensures its success, is ripe for exportation. In fact, China's exportation of surveillance technology is not merely hypothetical. It is increasingly a reality in many places around the world.

According to Freedom House's "2018 Freedom of the Net" report, eighteen of the sixty-five countries surveyed in the report were "provided high-tech tools of surveillance that lack respect for human rights."[64] Each of these countries received this technology from China, including many in Africa and South America.

Africa

Under Xi Jinping's leadership, China's engagement with Africa continues to grow.[65] With continued engagement comes increasing efforts to thwart

---

[64] Shahbaz, "The Rise of Digital Authoritarianism."

[65] See Joshua Meservey, "Implications of China's Presence and Investment in Africa," testimony before the Subcommittee on Emerging Threats and Capabilities,

democracy and promote authoritarianism.[66] China is using surveillance technology for its own intelligence-gathering purposes, as well as equipping African governments with the tools needed to spy on and regulate their own populations in an invasive manner.

In 2018, the African Union (AU) levied accusations that the Chinese government hacked into computer systems at the AU headquarters in Addis Ababa, Ethiopia. Beijing footed the $200 million bill for the development of the AU headquarters, which was built by a Chinese state-owned enterprise (SOE).[67] The Chinese government allegedly lined the walls with microphones and rigged the system so that they received downloads from AU servers nightly between 2012 and 2017.[68]

China is also exporting surveillance technology to African governments to equip them with the tools necessary to spy on local populations. According to one Council on Foreign Relations report, China is exporting its artificial intelligence (AI) technology to Zimbabwe, Angola, and Ethiopia—where they are now using facial recognition software to spy on their populations, ostensibly for law enforcement purposes.[69]

According to Freedom House, in addition to permitting the deployment of facial recognition AI surveillance technology, the government of Zimbabwe is permitting the exportation of data on millions of Zimbabweans

---

U.S. Senate, December 12, 2018, https://www.armed-services.senate.gov/imo/media/doc/Meservey_12-12-181.pdf.

[66] See Meservey, "Implications of China's Presence and Investment in Africa."

[67] See John Aglionby, Emily Feng, and Yuan Yang, "African Union Accuses China of Hacking Headquarters," *Financial Times*, January 29, 2018, https://www.ft.com/content/c26a9214-04f2-11e8-9650-9c0ad2d7c5b5.

[68] See Viola Rothschild, "China's Heavy Hand in Africa," Council on Foreign Relations, February 15, 2018, https://www.cfr.org/blog/chinas-heavy-hand-africa; Mailyn Fidler, "African Union Bugged by China: Cyber Espionage as Evidence of Strategic Shifts," Council on Foreign Relations, March 7, 2018, https://www.cfr.org/blog/african-union-bugged-china-cyber-espionage-evidence-strategic-shifts.

[69] See Arthur Gwagwa, "Exporting Repression? China's Artificial Intelligence Push into Africa," Council on Foreign Relations, December 17, 2018, https://www.cfr.org/blog/exporting-repression-chinas-artificial-intelligence-push-africa.

to the Chinese company CloudWalk so that they can "recognize faces with darker skin tones."[70]

As the report notes, this agreement was made without the consent of the citizens whose data is being collected and shared. All of these tools are being used to monitor for political insubordination or behavior the government deems suspicious.

South America

A chilling 2019 *New York Times* exposé revealed China's deployment of ECU-911, a vast system of 4,300 surveillance cameras, across Ecuador with the help of the Chinese government.[71] The system Ecuador deployed was produced by Chinese state-owned enterprise (SEO) C.E.I.E.C. (China National Electronics Import & Export Corporation) and Huawei. While Ecuadorian authorities sold the deployment of the technology as a "tough-on-crime" measure, in reality, few limits are placed on the scope and scale of the technology's application and use. Given Ecuador's long history of suppressing political activists and freedom, the likelihood of it being used for authoritarian purposes is high.[72] Bolivia also deployed a similar system created by the Chinese known as BOL-110.[73] Under the same guise as systems deployed in Ecuador, the system was put in place allegedly for law enforcement monitoring purposes. Curbing crime is a justification that resonates strongly with populations in Latin America, who have long endured the consequences of cartel crime, drug trafficking, and other illicit activities.

---

[70] Shahbaz, "The Rise of Digital Authoritarianism."

[71] See Paul Mozur, Jonah M. Kessel, and Melissa Chan, "Made in China, Exported to the World: The Surveillance State," *New York Times*, April 24, 2019, https://www.nytimes.com/2019/04/24/technology/ecuador-surveillance-cameras -police-government.html.

[72] To learn more, see Freedom House, "Ecuador: Freedom in the World 2021 Country Report," accessed February 14, 2022, https://freedomhouse.org/country /ecuador/freedom-world/2021.

[73] See R. Evan Ellis, "The Future of Latin America and the Caribbean in the Context of the Rise of China," Center for Strategic and International Studies, November 2018, https://csis-prod.s3.amazonaws.com/s3fs-public/publication /181119_FutureofLatinAmerica.pdf.

However, the deployment of advanced surveillance technology does not address the root cause of these many problems—a lack of rule of law and the failures of a legal and judicial system that fail to protect vulnerable populations. Instead, new technologies give broken systems of justice increased opportunities for exploitation.

While China may not ultimately seek to export its entire system and model of governance abroad,[74] it is indisputable that it has exported elements of its surveillance state into other countries. This is a trend to watch as this is likely to erode respect for the rule of law and in particular respect for privacy and freedom of expression worldwide. There can be no question that the surveillance state in China has contributed to significant deteriorations in human rights and freedom in China. Should other governments implement those same models, we are likely to see a steady decline in respect for human rights in those locales as well.

Trend #3: Digital Authoritarian's Quest for "Cyber Sovereignty"

Over the last several years, actors like Russia and China have become increasingly committed to the idea of so-called cyber sovereignty. One Chatham House report describes Russia's quest for cyber sovereignty, noting that "in accordance with its views on the international system and law, Moscow upholds the traditional understanding of sovereignty and the principle of non-intervention at the core of its policy toward global internet matters. As a result, it conceives of cyberspace as a territory with virtual borders corresponding to physical state borders, and wishes to see the remit of international laws extended to the internet space, thereby reaffirming the principles of sovereignty and non-intervention as it understands them."[75]

---

[74] See "China's Development Finance," AidData, https://www.aiddata.org /china-development-finance.

[75] Julien Nocetti, "Contest and Conquest: Russia and Global Internet Governance," *International Affairs* 91, no. 1 (2015): 112, https://www.chathamhouse .org/sites/default/files/field/field_publication_docs/INTA91_1_07_Nocetti.pdf.

More specifically, China seeks to establish an alternate model to the US model of a free and open internet. It envisions an internet where the Chinese government has sovereign authority over its jurisdictional internet that would correspond with Chinese borders. In practice, this is manifested through the Great Firewall where the Chinese government controls what Chinese citizens see on Chinese internet. This also means that what the Chinese government does to restrict the internet is the CCP's business and no one else's. This is also where requests for data localization come from. (For example, one of the reasons why Meta does not operate in China is because the Chinese government would require that all data from Meta servers be stored locally and therefore would be ripe for retaliatory use by the Chinese government against citizens who post objectionable content).[76] Here is a succinct summary of China's aims on the internet:

> China has promoted "cybersovereignty" as an organizing principle of internet governance, in direct opposition to U.S. support for a global, open, and secure internet. China envisions a world of national internets, with government control justified by the sovereign rights. Beijing also wants to weaken the bottom-up, private-sector-led model of internet governance, known as the multistakeholder approach championed by the United States and its allies.[77]

Both Russia and China view the internet as a Western invention and therefore see the quest for control over the internet as a battle against the rules-based order.[78] The idea of "non-intervention" is heavily emphasized in

---

[76] See Josh Constine, "Zuckerberg warns of authoritarian data localization trend," TechCrunch, April 26, 2019, https://techcrunch.com/2019/04/26/facebook-data-localization/.

[77] Adam Segal, "China's Alternative Cyber Governance Regime," testimony before the US China Economic Security Review Commission, US Senate, March 13, 2020, 3, https://www.uscc.gov/sites/default/files/testimonies/March%2013%20Hearing_Panel%203_Adam%20Segal%20CFR.pdf.

[78] See Shanthi Kalathil, "The Evolution of Authoritarian Digital Influence: Grappling with the New Normal," Prism 9, no. 1 (October 2020): 34, https://

Chinese foreign policy and is often invoked whenever the US (or any other nation) raises concerns over China's own human rights record. Russia and China, therefore, are engaged in a form of lawfare against the West over who sets the rules of the road in the digital sphere.

There are other actors across the globe—perhaps with less-authoritarian aims—who are also peddling in ideas over sovereignty in the digital realm. India and the European Union both employ notions of data sovereignty, which has some important distinctions from China and Russia's broader notions of cyber sovereignty. Take India's Personal Data Protection law (DPB), for example. The DPB "control[s] the collection, processing, storage, usage, transfer, protection, and disclosure of personal data of Indian residents."[79] Unlike China, the Indian government believes in its citizens' right to personal privacy; however, it views individual data as a "national asset" to be used by the government.[80]

While many of India's actions look similar to China's—for example, pressing for sovereignty through data localization and using personal data in cases where it serves India's national interest—Indian citizens are given the ability to opt in, or consent to sharing their data with the government.[81] These consent provisions are quite similar to those enshrined in the European Union's General Data Protection Regulation (GDPR).[82] While there is a fine line between India and the EU's notions of cyber sovereignty and those of more authoritarian regimes like China and Russia, it is a line nonetheless. This distinction of consent is meaningful, even if the Indian and EU models are not as solid as those with a more free and open data

---

ndupress.ndu.edu/Portals/68/Documents/prism/prism_9-1/prism_9-1_33-50 _Kalathil-2.pdf?ver=DJRX5DRHKfqeXbyt6et98w%3D%3D.

[79] Vijay Govindarajan, Anup Srivastava, and Luminita Enache, "How India Plans to Protect Consumer Data," *Harvard Business Review*, December 18, 2019, https://hbr.org/2019/12/how-india-plans-to-protect-consumer-data.

[80] Govindarajan et al., "How India Plans to Protect Consumer Data."

[81] See Arindrajit Basu and Justin Sherman, "Key Global Takeaways From India's Revised Personal Data Protection Bill," Lawfare, January 23, 2020, https://www .lawfareblog.com/key-global-takeaways-indias-revised-personal-data-protection-bill.

[82] See Basu and Sherman, "Key Global Takeaways."

landscape. It is unlikely that either Russia or China—and any other actors that share their viewpoint—will quickly relent in their quest for cyber sovereignty. This represents an important line in the debate over a free versus unfree digital sphere. It is a trend that should be not only closely monitored but also carefully and purposefully countered. A decision to ignore these arguments and not address them will result in a fundamentally different internet landscape in the future.

A Way Forward

There can be no question that digital authoritarians pose a significant threat worldwide. They are systematically eroding the space for a free and open digital realm. Their activities in the digital realm are leading to violations of human rights and limiting freedom in the physical world. The challenge for policymakers will be devising a strategy that goes beyond mere opposition to rising digital authoritarianism. As Kara Frederick, a Research Fellow for Tech Policy at The Heritage Foundation, aptly notes, a "strategy aimed only at staunching the illiberal use of technology will fail in the long term. Instead, the U.S. government and tech companies alike must recruit democratic allies to purvey an affirmative agenda that promotes digital freedom across the globe."[83] So how exactly do policymakers chart a successful course that safeguards freedom and liberties on the internet?

I would hearken back to a subject we discussed at the beginning of this chapter—namely that a positive agenda to tackle threats to freedom in the digital realm requires: (1) a clear-eyed view of the problem, (2) an understanding of the motivations of those who would seek to subvert freedom in the digital realm, and (3) the application of concepts and tools used in US foreign policy to counter authoritarianism refashioned to combat digital authoritarianism.

US policymakers must redouble their commitment to protecting universal human rights—including the right to life, the right to free expression, free speech, and freedom of religion. These rights are not Western rights—as

---

[83] Frederick, "Democracy by Design."

opponents like Russia and China are so quick to disparagingly label them—rather, they are inherent to every human by God's design, no matter their ethnicity, nationality, or background. The US has at times been less than clear about its commitment to protecting human rights abroad—even sending mixed signals about how human rights priorities rank vis-à-vis other policy priorities. There needs to be a clear commitment to promoting a free and open world and to protecting the rights of citizens across the globe, especially when their governments refuse to do so. And importantly, we must view human rights policy as complementary to, rather than competing with, national security goals.

One component of a positive agenda could be better coordinating with US allies and partners in preserving a free and open digital realm. There have been times where US allies—even those who ostensibly share our values—have impeded efforts at promoting information access (e.g., South Korea's anti-leaflet law).[84] Better coordination and communication of shared priorities could go a long way toward building a coalition to tackle these challenges.

An area where allies and partners committed to preserving freedom and human rights could coordinate is on the institution of sanctions against violators of human rights and freedom in the digital sphere. The US has tools, like the Global Magnitsky Act, that enables the US Treasury to target individuals and entities committing human rights violations and engaging in corruption. For example, the United States, the United Kingdom, Canada, and the European Union (EU) all sanctioned key Chinese government officials responsible for committing atrocities against Uyghurs.[85] This type of coordinated effort is powerful and had meaningful policy implications (like Europe temporarily suspending negotiations over a planned

---

[84] See Olivia Enos, "Anti-Leaflet Law Poses Threat to Freedom in North and South Korea," *Forbes*, December 17, 2020, https://www.forbes.com/sites/oliviaenos/2020/12/17/anti-leaflet-law-poses-threat-to-freedom-in-north-and-south-korea/.

[85] See Emily Rauhala, "U.S., E.U., Canada and Britain Announce Sanctions on China over the Abuse of Uyghurs," *Washington Post*, March 22, 2021, https://www.washingtonpost.com/world/xinjiang-sanctions-european-union/2021/03/22/1b0d69aa-8b0a-11eb-a33e-da28941cb9ac_story.html.

investment agreement between the EU and China).[86] But these tools are not being used aggressively enough to target violators of human rights online and through digital means. More regularized targeting of individuals for the human rights violations they commit online or through digital means may discourage future bad behavior and stem the tide of future erosion of liberty in the digital sphere.

Another potential area of multilateral coordination is on investment in sensitive technologies. Chinese dual-use technology firms like Hikvision, for example, should not continue to receive foreign funding if funders are aware that those technologies are going toward carrying out atrocities in Xinjiang. Another component of a positive agenda to tackle digital authoritarianism involves promoting access to information for all peoples. US policy has long emphasized improving information access for people—especially those in hard-to-reach places where their governments actively restrict access to information. The North Korean Human Rights Act and the grants provided to nongovernmental organizations (NGOs) to improve information access are one example of such a policy.[87] Critical to the success of these grants are civil society actors including NGOs, missionaries, and even well-placed individuals to speak to the information environment on the ground. The US government is not omniscient and often relies on non-government eyes and ears on the ground to ensure information gets into the hands of the people who need it most.

As with many things in the US government, their information promotion efforts have not kept pace with new and emerging technologies. The US should continue to invest in private sector innovations—without picking winners and losers—to penetrate digital markets gone dark due to authoritarian repression and seek new and creative ways of doing so. There are many more detailed options—both high tech and low tech—for combating

---

[86] See "MEPs Refuse Any Agreement with China Whilst Sanctions Are in Place," European Parliament, May 20, 2021, https://www.europarl.europa.eu/news /en/press-room/20210517IPR04123/meps-refuse-any-agreement-with-china -whilst-sanctions-are-in-place.

[87] See Enos, "Improving Information Access."

digital authoritarianism, but these are good themes or places to start as the US considers how to put forth and build on a pro-freedom agenda.

There can be no doubt of the severe challenges and threat posed by digital authoritarianism. These challenges necessitate a response not only from governments but also from individuals. As Christians, we believe that every person is endowed with certain unalienable rights by our Creator and that the possession of those rights extends to every individual in both the physical and digital realms. Believers should press their governments to safeguard these rights and we should do our part in ensuring that people across the globe have free and open access to the gospel.[88] Closed internets and closed societies do not threaten the gospel and its liberating effects. But so many believers and nonbelievers alike struggle to access the Bible or get accurate information about Christianity and the truths of the gospel. Christians should be at the forefront of defending access to information because of how interconnected these issues in the digital public square are, not only for our brothers and sisters in Christ but for all people. The challenge for countries that champion free expression and religious freedom will be to construct a positive agenda that takes into consideration the wide-ranging issues of technology policy and the potential abuses of these tools as part of a robust international human rights agenda for this digital age.

---

[88] For more on the missiological implications of free expression and religious freedom, see chapter 6 by Joshua B. Wester.

PART III
The Church

12

Following @Jesus

Discipleship in the Twenty-First Century

Jacob Shatzer

Having grown up in the church, I cannot remember a time that I did not know who Jesus's disciples were. At Immanuel Baptist Church in Coeur d'Alene, Idaho, I learned as a child about these twelve men who followed Jesus around. Frankly, I was a bit envious of the exciting things they got to see. As I grew older, I came to know that people who trusted Jesus today should also follow him. We could be disciples too—though I secretly suspected that it must have been easier back in Jesus's time, when you could watch Jesus heal people and perform miracles.

By my teenage years, I had begun to understand better what a life of discipleship might look like. I was taught by others—discipled, in fact—in spiritual practices and corporate worship, and I was blessed with many people who nurtured in me a deep love for Jesus and the Bible. I began to learn that as a follower of Jesus, I also should be making disciples. In youth group at Calvary Baptist Church in Cedar Rapids, Iowa, I learned an important element of this idea of making disciples. In one lesson, my youth pastor read us the following verses: "Jesus came near and said to them, 'All authority has been given to me in heaven and on earth. Go, therefore, and make disciples of all nations, baptizing them in the name of the Father and of the Son and of the Holy Spirit, teaching them to observe everything I have commanded you. And remember, I am with you always, to the end of the age'" (Matt 28:18–20).

He then went on to explain that while we read two commands in verse 19—"Go" and "make disciples"—there is in fact only one command in the Greek text: "Make disciples." The "go" part is not a command at all; the word describes the circumstances telling us *when* we should make disciples: "as we are going." In other words, for the first time I began to realize that disciple-making is not something we set off to the side, but it is something that should intertwine with all aspects of a believer's life.

My point here is not to debate points of Greek grammar, syntax, or Bible translation, but to bring out a point that serves as a foundation for our understanding of discipleship. We do not get to decide to pursue disciple-making in perfect conditions, in the ideal world, or in the ideal setup. We make disciples as we are going. Today, for Christians in most of the world, that means making disciples in a digital age: an age when famine and disease still run rampant, but smartphones are in the hands of billions. What does it mean to make disciples as we inhabit this world? In this chapter, we will examine the nature of discipleship, new methods of discipleship to be evaluated through the lens of wisdom, and the opportunities and challenges of following Jesus in an increasingly digital world. In our technological age, it might seem impossible to resist some of these forces that are changing how we think about ourselves, our identities, how we relate to others, and what we value most. But we must if we are to answer the calling to make disciples in the digital public square.

What Is Discipleship?

Discipleship is a simple concept. In ancient Israel, disciples would follow rabbis, learning from both their teaching and from how they lived their lives. When we read about Jesus's ministry and see him selecting twelve disciples, that's one basic element of what is going on. Jesus chose twelve to point to his ministry as the fulfillment of God's promises to Israel, and he did not choose the people you would expect. If these men had been the type of men who became disciples of rabbis, they would have been following other rabbis already, not fishing or collecting taxes. In other words, Jesus selected less-than-likely men to be his first disciples. Not only that, Jesus charged these less-than-likely disciples with making more disciples. We see a bit of what that includes in Matthew 28, where Jesus told his disciples to teach future disciples to obey, which would encompass behavior and not just belief.

But why should Christians care about obedience? According to New Testament professor Jonathan Lunde, "The answer to this question turns on the nature of the covenantal relationship we have with God through Jesus. What we discover is that grace has always grounded God's relationships with his people, but that same grace persistently brings the demand of righteousness."[1] In other words, obedient discipleship is part of being a Christian.

But if we are saved by faith, is not discipleship an optional extra? Lunde helps here again, explaining, "Although this covenant is a grant covenant, such that the absolute righteousness demanded by God is received by faith in Jesus's representative obedience, we have learned that God's righteous demand never diminishes in the wake of his grace." And because "Jesus is the messianic King who articulates this demand, his genuine disciples will hear his summons and follow."[2] When we properly understand the salvation that Jesus offers, we realize that we are saved *to be* disciples, to be made more like Christ in the place where he has placed us.

Sometimes we misunderstand the purpose of discipleship. It is certainly not to earn God's favor, which believers already have by virtue of being united with Christ (Rom 8:1). Rather, discipleship centers on God's promises and mission: "We have also learned that central to the promises God made with Abraham is his overarching desire to bless all nations by filling the earth with the knowledge of himself. Not surprisingly, then, to speak of

---

[1] Jonathan Lunde, *Following Jesus, the Servant King: A Biblical Theology of Covenantal Discipleship* (Grand Rapids: Zondervan, 2010), 35.

[2] Lunde, 115.

discipleship necessarily includes the language of 'mission.'"[3] Discipleship is not only about our own personal lives and relationships with Jesus; instead, it is also about helping advance God's mission of bringing light and salvation to the world.

Jesus does not excuse us from keeping God's commands as disciples. Lunde argues that Jesus serves as a filter, a lens, and a prism for understanding God's law. Jesus is the filter because "he fulfills elements of the law in such a way as to render their ongoing observance obsolete."[4] He is the lens because he "recovers and preserves the law's commands by bringing their original intent back into focus and interpreting them in the greater scope of their entirety."[5] Finally, Jesus is a prism for God's law, because he "refracts" the law to new levels.[6] Jesus does not do away with the law, but he enables us to engage and obey the law in a fuller sense.

Discipleship to Jesus aims at righteousness. Jesus's relation to the law is to fulfill it on our behalf, but then also through the work of the Holy Spirit to transform us into righteous followers. Righteous living is not the opposite of grace, but the outgrowth of grace. In fact, as Lunde explains, "Grace foils legalism. But grace fuels righteousness."[7] Discipleship is the path to righteousness, aimed at and fueled by grace in Christ.

Although discipleship transforms individuals, it does not transform us only for our own sake. Following Christ in discipleship means following Christ on his mission. As Lunde explains:

> The longer you look at Jesus, the more you will want to serve him in his world. That is, of course, if it's the real Jesus you're looking at. Plenty of people in the church and outside it have made up a "Jesus" for themselves, and have found that this invented character makes few real demands on them. He makes them feel happy from time to time but doesn't challenge them, doesn't suggest they get

---

[3] Lunde, 115.
[4] Lunde, 181–82.
[5] Lunde, 182.
[6] Lunde, 182.
[7] Lunde, 274.

up and do something about the plight of the world. Which is, of course, what the real Jesus had an uncomfortable habit of doing.[8]

Our discipleship, then, results in following Jesus on mission into the world, for the sake of the world. As we consider discipleship in a technological age, we must evaluate opportunities and challenges not only in light of personal growth, but also with the mission of God in mind.

New Methods of Discipleship in the Twenty-First Century

If discipleship means following Jesus in our own world, Christians today face the opportunities and challenges of following Jesus in an increasingly digital environment. Some believers primarily see the opportunities that our technology provides for us. Others primarily see the challenges. We'll try to explore both, starting with the opportunities.

Digital Community

Our digital technologies provide new opportunities for connection. Meta (Facebook), for instance, ran a series of commercials in 2021 highlighting its groups feature, showing how it enables people with common backgrounds or interests to find community: "Dance Accepts Everyone" and "DeafHoops" are two examples of Facebook groups, each of which emphasizes the community that is facilitated by digital technology. In these two examples, something very embodied and physical is in view, but the digital technology provides the opportunity to share video or join together virtually for an activity. Social media not only provides the platform for pre-existing groups to connect, but the algorithms are also working behind the scenes, recruiting new people to the community. These systems essentially decided that "those who like ＿＿ also like ＿＿" as it invited people into new groups.

---

[8] N. T. Wright, *Following Jesus: Biblical Reflections on Discipleship*, with a new preface by the author (Grand Rapids: Eerdmans, 2014), xiv.

This opportunity is not without challenges, which we'll get into below. However, two challenges merit highlighting here. First, the opportunity of digital community forces us to ask, "What is a community?" To what degree is a group communicating via text chat or video a *community*? Second, what makes a *good* community? Facebook not only makes it easier for DeafHoops to recruit and connect, it also has facilitated the growth of hate groups and recruitment. While Facebook works to limit this sort of usage, it hasn't been very successful so far.[9]

During the COVID-19 pandemic, Christians saw another way that digital technology can help with Christian community. Many churches, Bible studies, and small groups met online for various lengths of time during the pandemic. For example, my grandmother was able to continue a longtime Bible study throughout the pandemic. Whatever you think about in-person church versus digital opportunities for gathering, the opportunity for people to maintain some sort of connection to others while unable to gather in person, is something to be thankful for. At the same time, we recognize with the rise of terms like "Zoom fatigue" that there is something different about relationships mediated between screens. Again, we see that this opportunity for connection comes with challenges as well.

Digital Education

Opportunities for education online burst onto the scene with innovations like the massive open online course (MOOC), the exponential growth of schools such as Liberty University, and partnerships between privately held education startups and public universities.[10] While online education has not proven to be the magic solution that some were proclaiming it would be a decade ago, technology does provide access to educational resources at

---

[9] See Charles Arthur, *Social Warming: The Dangerous and Polarising Effects of Social Media* (London: Oneworld, 2021), 55–60.

[10] For instance, see the partnership between Udacity and San Jose State University. Ry Rivard, "Udacity Project on 'Pause,'" Inside Higher Ed, July 18, 2013, https://www.insidehighered.com/news/2013/07/18/citing-disappointing-student-outcomes-san-jose-state-pauses-work-udacity.

previously unknown levels. On one hand, the digital as a distribution channel has made it possible for books, educational videos, and other resources to be provided to people around the globe. This has extended the reach of many ministries, as they are able to provide material to Christians around the world.

As digital education continues to expand, we will come to learn more about what sorts of situations this opportunity works well for, as well as what limitations it brings with it. Every form of education comes with limitations, and this form will continue to be no exception. But even as we might recognize some limitations, we should also acknowledge that this is a wonderful opportunity for discipleship, especially as Bible teaching becomes more widely available to train people to know God in order to love and serve God.

Challenges of Discipleship in the Twenty-First Century

Discipleship in the twenty-first century not only provides some unique opportunities but also brings various challenges. These challenges can be difficult to notice given the ubiquity of technology today, which is why we'll spend more time discussing these concerns than on the opportunities. One commentator on digital life, Andrew Keen, argues that while we see many of the positive opportunities the internet makes possible, we are less adept at noticing its negative effects.[11] This might vary depending on your general stance toward technology, but it is significant to note: just because you do not immediately notice any drawbacks to digital life, it does not mean they are not there.[12] You might just need help noticing them. We could engage these challenges in various ways. While some argue that problems are so inherent in certain forms of technology that we should simply reject them, others fall on the other end of the spectrum and argue that the

---

[11] See Andrew Keen, *The Internet Is Not the Answer* (New York: Grove, 2015).

[12] For a brief overview of a Christian philosophy of technology, see chapter 1, by Jason Thacker.

challenges are not a big deal and that they are simply the latest version of humanity's struggle.

I find myself somewhere in the middle. As I've argued elsewhere, the technological age poses serious challenges to our understanding of what it means to be human, and what we value in life.[13] At the same time, many of these challenges are similar to temptations that humans have always faced in a broken world. In what follows, I will not attempt to strike a balance, as though that were possible, but I want to keep two truths in mind. First, there really is nothing new under the sun, and we should recognize that many technological challenges are new forms of old problems. But second, we should also recognize that most of us are so enmeshed in a digital lifestyle that our exposure to these challenges and temptations is much more serious and difficult to discern. As we seek to faithfully follow Christ in a digital age, we should be confident that Jesus is Lord of all things—including technological advance—while at the same time recognizing that our sinful hearts are adept at twisting absolutely everything.

As we explore these challenges, I'm going to frame each one in fairly mundane terms and then explain them in a way that indicates what's new and particularly dangerous about the digital versions of these challenges. Also, we must remember that the hope of the gospel extends even to the technological challenges we face today. In other words, each of these challenges is an opportunity for the proclamation of the gospel's transforming power. We'll look for this chance as we go along.

We Are Lonely

In *When the Sparrow Falls*, Neil Sharpson paints a picture of a future world in which the vast majority of countries come to be ruled by artificial intelligences that provide "guidance" to the human governments—guidance they always accept.[14] This is true for all nations except the small Caspian

---

[13] See Jacob Shatzer, *Transhumanism and the Image of God: Today's Technology and the Future of Christian Discipleship* (Downers Grove, IL: IVP Academic, 2019).

[14] See Neil Sharpson, *When the Sparrow Falls* (New York: Tor, 2021).

Republic, where AIs have been outlawed. The entire plot of the novel circles around something that shakes the citizens of the Caspian Republic to their core: an AI manages to live among them for about twenty years, even rising to serve in leadership positions, completely undetected in human-looking skin. One of the greatest writers has not only bought into the ruse, but he actually falls in love with this very convincing robot. His realization that the person is actually a robot sets off a chain of events that destroys many involved.

With this story, Sharpson attempts to suggest not only that AI is advancing at such a rate that it will be able to provide expert political and economic advice, but that self-generating algorithms might one day be worthy companions. The entire tone of the novel is that the people of the Caspian Republic are foolishly resisting the inevitable—the merging of the human with various forms of artificial intelligence. Sharpson is nudging us toward a sense that relationships with artificially intelligent robots or "beings" of some sort is not only possible, but in many ways superior to the frustrations we experience with our embodied selves and embodied companions. Seems far-fetched, right? But is it? Do we trust ourselves not to want that option if or when it comes?

We already see a significant openness to relationships with robots because we are so lonely. As Sherry Turkle reminds us, "Online, we preached authenticity but practiced self-curation. We were constantly in touch yet lonelier than before."[15] Elderly people who are isolated, without family visiting, increasingly find solace in robot pets. Robot dogs are now available for purchase, and some feel the same sense of companionship and care as they do with living dogs.[16] And companies are competing in the production of

---

[15] Sherry Turkle, *The Empathy Diaries: A Memoir* (New York: Penguin, 2021), 335.

[16] For more on this, see Meghan O'Gieblyn, "A Dog's Inner Life: What a Robot Pet Taught Me about Consciousness," *The Guardian*, August 10, 2021, https://www.theguardian.com/science/2021/aug/10/dogs-inner-life-what-robot-pet-taught-me-about-consciousness-artificial-intelligence. This article is drawn from her recently published book, *God, Human, Animal, Machine: Technology, Metaphor, and the Search for Meaning* (New York: Doubleday, 2021).

sex robots, which can be programmed to be just the sort of companion a person desires. We are lonely, and many of us seek to heal that loneliness by turning to artificial forms of companionship. The problem is we should not seek devices that wean us from our dependence on one another, because that relationality is not worth giving up.[17]

The gospel, of course, speaks to this temptation to think of oneself in an isolated fashion. The church in the New Testament is spoken of as a body, with many parts that need each other (1 Corinthians 12). As we pursue discipleship in a digital age, we should recognize that technologies that claim to connect people can actually leave people feeling even more isolated. We must recognize the problems with loneliness and seek to be communities of faith that reflect the "many parts, one body" picture that the New Testament provides (Rom 12:4–5; 1 Cor 12:12–31; Eph 4:16).

We Are Never Alone and Never Forgiven

While social media provides helpful opportunities for communication and connection between people near and far, and the internet itself offers the chance to encounter and learn from vast amounts of information, all of this activity comes at a cost. A short and somewhat dramatic way to put it is: we're never alone, and what we do never really goes away.

Information and communications technologies are widespread, and they engulf us. We need them, or at least think we do. By 2014, 87 percent of Americans were using the internet, the vast majority seeing it as good for society and good for themselves as individuals. We've grown so connected to our networks that people actually call 911 when Facebook is down.[18] As researcher Shoshana Zuboff puts it, any rights to privacy, the knowledge gained from our online activity, and even the application of that knowledge "have been usurped by a bold market venture powered by unilateral claims

---

[17] See Turkle, *Empathy Diaries*, 346.

[18] See Shoshana Zuboff, *The Age of Surveillance Capitalism: The Fight for a Human Future at the New Frontier of Power* (New York: Public Affairs, 2019), 537n2.

to others' experience and the knowledge that flows from it." She goes on to say, the digital dream has "darkened," and "mutated," "into a voracious and utterly novel commercial project."[19] Not only is our information being kept, but it is also being used, and its use is big business.

The fact that we're never alone shapes our behavior. This impact happens in a couple of ways: on social media, everything we are doing is meant to be seen by and reacted to by others. It's a performance of sorts. Channeling some insights from twentieth-century French philosopher Michel Foucault, sociologist Sherry Turkle observes that "Online, we perform a self because we always imagine ourselves seen."[20] Just as Foucault could argue that the prospect of being watched in a prison changed the behavior of inmates, the idea that people might see what we post, how we frame our profiles, or how we interact with someone else's post impacts the way we act. When we are online—especially if we are on social media—we're always on the stage, and this impacts the way we behave.

Not only is everything a sort of performance, we also cannot really escape our previous performances. In reflecting on her own life journey, Turkle felt that, growing up, she had lived in fear of everything "counting." As she recounts, "I'd been allowed my dreams, certainly, but I'd had a life without a moratorium. Instead, I had been terrorized by the idea of a permanent record."[21] While Turkle thought that "life online" provided young people with the opportunity to try out a range of different identities and roles, without things being counted against them, this view does not take into account that many people struggle to escape what they've done online. Whether it means not getting a job, or losing a job based on what one previously shared or posted,[22] or just never being able to "live down" something done or said, our mistakes can emerge again (sometimes much later at very inopportune times). (This issue is, of course, complicated, because some

---

[19] Zuboff, 7.

[20] Turkle, *Empathy Diaries*, 196.

[21] Turkle, 53.

[22] See, for example, Sarah McDermott, "I Lost My Job over a Facebook Post—Was That Fair?" BBC Online, November 6, 2017, https://www.bbc.com/news/stories-41851771.

online behavior does demonstrate patterns of sin, or lack of discernment, that should indeed have "real life" consequences. More on that later.)

The gospel speaks to this issue, not by denying that real sin happens online and may be documented, but by promising that in Christ we are indeed offered forgiveness. In fact, we worship a God who promises to separate our sins from us "as far as the east is from the west" (Ps 103:12). As we follow Jesus in a digital world, this truth is part of the good news that the world around us is hoping for and desperately needs. This challenge of not being alone, and of our online activity being documented and stored impacts the way we interact with one another and the way we seek to overcome past sins and mistakes. But it goes even further. In fact, some believe that the way we are watched and how our actions are recorded and used may eventually cost us our humanity.[23] Even if not, it certainly changes the way we think about what it means to be human.

We Are Reduced to Our Data

As computers become more advanced, and as we interact more with artificial intelligence, we cannot help but begin to think of ourselves in terms of computing and data. For instance, as Sherry Turkle saw in her work with children interacting with computers and robots, "Since the computer's programming made it seem 'sort of alive,' they wondered if people were programmed as well? How exactly, asked the children, were people different from machines?"[24] In some ways, we've begun to reduce ourselves to this parallel. We are machines; we can capture all that we are in data.

This change emerges when we think about the analogies we make when we think of humans and our brains. Many in the transhumanist movement, for instance, reduce our humanity to what goes on in our brains, and they further reduce that to what can be rendered by data. The promise of digital immortality—upload "you" into the cloud!—is built on this reduction of

---

[23] See Zuboff, *Surveillance Capitalism*, 12.
[24] Turkle, *Empathy Diaries*, 292.

humans to data. Just because some of what we do can be represented by data, it does not follow that all that we are can be reduced to data.

Even science fiction wrestles with this notion. In *Fall; or, Dodge in Hell*,[25] Neal Stephenson crafts a story of the digital afterlife, built around his main character, Dodge, who is the first to have his consciousness "uploaded" after death. As the narrative goes forward and more people seek digital immortality, the practice morphs from scanning the brain to scanning the whole body, because the scientists come to realize that human life is embodied and uploading only the brain is incomplete. Here we see characters playing with an idea—we are more than our brains—but at the same time still reducing humans to our data. Even our bodies, in this imaginative model, can be "digitized" and transferred into a digital afterlife.

We might think that we do not buy into this reduction, but we can notice this change if we look for it. Part of the drive to post experiences—and meals—on social media comes from a sometimes-under-the-radar sense that if we do not post it, it "does not count" as an experience, or at least not in the same way. We can easily buy into an "I post, therefore I am" reduction of our lives and experiences. We feel this draw to take who we are, what we do, what we experience, and to reduce it to data that can be shared. Or, as Turkle puts it from her extensive research, "We are treated as objects when we are swept up as data to be bought and sold on an international market."[26] Further, "Social media and artificial intelligence insert themselves into every aspect of our lives [and turn us] into commodities, data that is bought and sold on the marketplace."[27] In our drive to put our lives online, we're reducing our lives to the data we produce.

This reduction does not only impact the way we think about our bodies or the lives we live. As Meghan O'Gieblyn argues, our interaction with artificial intelligence is changing the way we think about spirituality and the soul as well. She is worth quoting at length here:

---

[25] Neal Stephenson, *Fall; or, Dodge in Hell* (New York: HarperCollins, 2019).
[26] Turkle, *Empathy Diaries*, 341.
[27] Turkle, 347.

It is meaningless to speak of the soul in the 21st century (it is treacherous even to speak of the self). It has become a dead metaphor, one of those words that survive in language long after a culture has lost faith in the concept. The soul is something you can sell, if you are willing to demean yourself in some way for profit or fame, or bare by disclosing an intimate facet of your life. It can be crushed by tedious jobs, depressing landscapes and awful music. All of this is voiced unthinkingly by people who believe, if pressed, that human life is animated by nothing more mystical or supernatural than the firing of neurons.[28]

Not only has our increasingly digital environment posed challenges to how our culture thinks about the soul—or lack of a soul—but it also impacts the way we process life's deepest questions. Again, O'Gieblyn:

Today, artificial intelligence and information technologies have absorbed many of the questions that were once taken up by theologians and philosophers: the mind's relationship to the body, the question of free will, the possibility of immortality. These are old problems, and although they now appear in different guises and go by different names, they persist in conversations about digital technologies much like those dead metaphors that still lurk in the syntax of contemporary speech. All the eternal questions have become engineering problems.[29]

Yuval Noah Harari puts it this bluntly as well, noting that it impacts what we think not only about the soul but also about God: "Every technical problem has a technical solution. We do not need to wait for the Second Coming to overcome death. A couple of geeks in a lab can do it. If traditionally death was the specialty of priests and theologians, now the engineers are taking over."[30] At least they claim to be.

---

[28] O'Gieblyn, "A Dog's Inner Life."

[29] O'Gieblyn.

[30] Yuval Noah Harari, *Homo Deus: A Brief History of Tomorrow* (New York: HarperCollins, 2017), 22–23.

This challenge invites a gospel response as well. Just as our digital environment can tempt us to think of ourselves as disembodied data, early heresies such as Gnosticism saw the human body as disgusting and irredeemable; true salvation came through secret knowledge and escape from the material world. Reducing all that it means to be human to data, and painting a future picture divorced from the materiality of our bodies, sounds eerily similar. But the gospel promises a different salvation, one that affirms our embodiedness. The Second Person of the Trinity became fully human, taking on all that it means to be human, including embodiedness. While Jesus's resurrection body was different in mysterious ways, it was still a recognizable human body. Moreover, in his ascended glory, Jesus remains incarnate King. The Christian hope of resurrection and eternal life is an embodied hope, a hope that rejects the notion that we can be reduced to data, or that the eternal existence of some copy of part of us would count as "eternal life."[31]

We Envy and Worship Idols

Our digital age tempts us with plenty of opportunities to envy and even worship our own modern-day idols. Not only do we envy the technology others have that we might not, but we are immersed in social environments that bombard us with what other people are enjoying. We not only craft our own personal profiles and curate a version of our life as we post updates, but we are constantly reading and interpreting what others post, and this regular immersion in the lives of others can spur envy. We want what others have. Certainly not a new temptation, but one we encounter in a new way.

This experience extends beyond envying what others have; it is also about what others do. There's even an acronym for this problem: FOMO, or "fear of missing out." When we constantly see what others are doing, we are left wondering if what we're doing is the best choice, or if we're in fact missing out on something better. For some people, this leads to decision paralysis: there are so many options that we're aware of, we cannot choose;

---

[31] For more on this problem and potential ways to navigate this faulty understanding of humanity, see Shatzer, *Transhumanism and the Image of God*, 120–24.

or once we do choose, we cannot enjoy our choice because we're constantly running a calculus on what we might be missing out on. Even worse, this process is being refreshed repeatedly via social media throughout our day.

Envy is always closely related to idolatry. We can easily slip from *wanting* what others have to *worshiping* what others have. Theologian Craig Detweiler extends this insight, pointing out that we can even seek to make ourselves into gods of sorts: "[We are tempted] by Google and Facebook and Twitter to build our digital brand, to become iGods of our making. An iGod can be a technology, a technologist, or a person bewitched by the power promised by the gadget."[32] We can easily begin to worship devices, powerful people in the technological world, or even ourselves. We should not be surprised by this, as idolatry has been a constant temptation for humans, who are quick to build gods in our own image, or in the image of something we value. We even create things and claim that they do what God did or what God has promised he will do.[33] We then proclaim that these idols can save us.

Again, the gospel provides a response to this perennial temptation, presented as it is to us in all its flashy technological garb. Dealing with envy and idolatry are a key aspect of what discipleship needs to look like in our age. As Detweiler notes, "As we consider how to be the church in the twenty-first century, let us identify the prevailing assumptions that undergird a technocracy and that compete for our loyalty. What kind of faith are the iGods selling?"[34] Following Christ is an exclusive path; there is no room for other gods. Part of discipleship in the age of technology is learning to recognize when the love we have for technology, and the expectations we hold for what it can do, expands beyond simple appreciation for an aspect of God's creation and into making a created thing into a god.

---

[32] Craig Detweiler, *iGods: How Technology Shapes Our Spiritual and Social Lives* (Grand Rapids: Brazos, 2013), 2.

[33] See Christopher J. H. Wright, *"Here Are Your Gods": Faithful Discipleship in Idolatrous Times* (Downers Grove, IL: IVP Academic, 2020), 68.

[34] Detweiler, *iGods*, 203.

We Are Distracted

Paying attention has always been a challenge, but being immersed in digital technology has taken this challenge to a new level. This issue first emerged in popular culture with Nicholas Carr's brilliantly titled "Is Google Making Us Stupid?,"[35] which he published in 2008 and followed with a book-length argument to the same effect.[36] Basically, his argument is that we've become accustomed to dealing with smaller and shorter bits of information, and this change has limited our ability to pay attention to larger and longer sources of information. We like tweets; we cannot read *War and Peace*. Think what you will about the impact of that on our enjoyment of Russian literature, but the simple fact is that we're becoming more scattered and distracted. While there might be advantages to the ability to process different types of information, our distraction and our inability to focus and pay attention have negative impacts on our ability to pay attention to one another and to God.

Our attention has become a commodity in this digital age, and one that we struggle to focus and control. In his book on news consumption, English scholar Jeffrey Bilbro provides a helpful metaphor, drawn from Henry David Thoreau. In the eighteenth century, Scottish engineer John McAdam created a new method for road building. Instead of building roads on large stones, McAdam used small stones, often broken by hand, to surface roads. As Bilbro explains, "The angular edges of these rocks would bind together and form a smooth, long-lasting surface for traffic."[37] Thoreau had this picture in mind when he explained that paying attention to trivial things has a negative impact on our attention. It "macadamizes" our intellect, breaking

---

[35] Nicholas Carr, "Is Google Making Us Stupid? What the Internet Is Doing to Our Brains," *Atlantic* (July/August 2008, https://www.theatlantic.com/magazine/archive/2008/07/is-google-making-us-stupid/306868/.

[36] Carr, *The Shallows*. Carr published an expanded and updated version in 2020. In its introduction he notes, "The year 2020 has arrived. We're not smarter. We're not making better choices."

[37] Jeffrey Bilbro, *Reading the Times: A Literary and Theological Inquiry into the News* (Downers Grove, IL: IVP Academic, 2021), 16.

it into fragments that can be more easily shaped and formed into other uses. This metaphor certainly extends to today and invites a bit of an update. Imagine your mind as a gravel road, smashed to pieces and serving as a thoroughfare—think of how many times your mind feels completely "run over"! Instead of meditating on Scripture or thinking about bigger ideas, our attention flits from headlines to tweets to short videos to text messages. Those fractured bits of distraction meld together and form us. We are distracted, and this distraction impacts our discipleship.

The gospel responds to this problem too because the problem is not a new one. Paul knew that Christians would struggle to think about and focus on the right things. His charge in Col 3:2 to "set your minds on things above" surely contributes to how we think about being distracted. Part of discipleship and pursuing spiritual maturity is developing the ability to pray, to read God's Word, and to *attend* to our relationship with God and our relationships with one another. When our technological environment makes it harder for us to pay attention to anything for very long, we must recognize that one part of discipleship is correcting that. In practical terms, we need to call one another to attend to God's Word, plumbing its depths, and paying attention to more than just tweetable verses each morning.

Our technologies certainly vie for our attention and keep us busy. This busyness wasn't something that everyone saw coming. As Sherry Turkle reflects on the beginning of her career working as a sociologist at MIT (the 1970s and 1980s), she notes that she was surrounded by cutting-edge technologists who were not sure how people would keep computers busy. Think about that! They were not sure we would be able to think of enough things to do on computers. But as Turkle puts it, "Now it is clear that they keep us busy. We are their killer app."[38] Discipleship requires that we reclaim our attention and focus it on Christ.

---

[38] Turkle, *Empathy Diaries*, 282.

We Cannot Relate

While our social media can make us feel more connected, and while companies are now marketing robotic pets to help us cope with our isolation, these technologies also seem to be having a negative effect on our ability to relate to one another. Sherry Turkle's decades-long work on the social impact of technology highlights this well. As she reflects:

> Over the years at MIT, I have been able to see how easy it is for a fascination with technology to take well-intentioned people away from empathy and its simple human truths. So technologists become invested in the promise of electronic medical records and forget how important it is for physicians to make eye contact with patients during their meetings. . . . These days, our technology treats us as though we were objects and we get in the habit of objectifying one another as bits of data, profiles viewed. But only shared vulnerability and human empathy allow us to truly understand one another.[39]

Put another way in an earlier book, "We are being silenced by our technologies—in a way, 'cured of talking.' These silences—often in the presence of our children—have led to a crisis of empathy that has diminished us at home, at work, and in public life."[40] She is more specific, too, relating the effects of technology to friendship, stating, "The computer offered the illusion of companionship without the demands of friendship. You could interact but never feel vulnerable to another person."[41] Or, as she wondered in an earlier book, "Does virtual intimacy degrade our experience of the other kind and, indeed, of all encounters, of any kind?"[42] All of this while

---

[39] Turkle, xix.

[40] Sherry Turkle, *Reclaiming Conversation: The Power of Talk in a Digital Age* (New York: Penguin, 2015), 9.

[41] Turkle, *Empathy Diaries*, 334.

[42] Sherry Turkle, *Alone Together: Why We Expect More from Technology and Less from Each Other* (New York: Basic, 2011), 12.

"Relationships with robots are ramping up; relationships with people are ramping down."[43]

These changes will certainly impact what discipleship looks like. Will we follow robot pastors?[44] Will we settle for online discipleship rather than embodied communities of faith with local leaders, Bible studies, fellowship, and other connections? While it is not likely that all of this will change at once, we must consider how our broader understanding of friendships and human relationships in a technological age will impact our discipleship relationships and pathways. Surely if Jesus took on flesh and dwelt among us, we should not outsource discipleship to robot pastors. If discipleship were merely about getting information, then perhaps an artificial intelligence is all we need to interact with. But if faith is transformative and embodied, as well as involving information, then robot pastors will always be limited.[45]

We Are Not Accountable: Church Discipline in a Digital Age?

Increasingly we observe that online interactions seem to encourage behavior that people would not engage in if they were face-to-face with other people. Studies have shown that this can work in a positive way, as people create online personas with strengths they lack in real life, and eventually they begin to improve in those areas in their real lives.[46] But what happens when the online personalities or the online behavior conflicts with the character a person displays the rest of the time in real life? What happens when their

---

[43] Turkle, 19.

[44] Other religions have started down this road: "Since 2019, Kodaiji, a 400-year-old Buddhist temple in Kyoto, Japan, has had a robot priest called Mindar. Mindar is narrow AI; that is, it has one job—delivering a sermon—and that's what it repeats all day. The plan is to update this million-dollar avatar of the deity of Mercy, with machine-learning capabilities, so that it can respond directly to seekers." Jeanette Winterson, *12 Bytes: How We Got Here, Where We Might Go Next* (London: Jonathan Cape, 2021), 102.

[45] See Jason Thacker, "How the Dreams of Robot Pastors Reveal a Deficiency in the Church," ERLC, February 17, 2020, https://erlc.com/resource-library/articles/how-the-dreams-of-robot-pastors-reveal-a-deficiency-in-the-church--2/.

[46] See Turkle, *Empathy Diaries*, 163.

weaknesses show more? Jarod Lanier notes this well in his caution about social media: "Social media is biased, not to the Left or the Right, but downward. The relative ease of using negative emotions for the purposes of addiction and manipulation makes it relatively easier to achieve undignified results."[47]

More specifically, what happens when clear patterns of sin and abuse emerge online, patterns that if in "real life," in front of real people, a church might hold someone accountable for? Discipleship in the twenty-first century, in an increasingly digital and technological world, will require churches to make clearer the relationship between online behavior and real-life discipleship and church membership. The New Testament addresses the guiding principle at issue here, insisting that churches hold Christians accountable and exercise church discipline for unrepentant sin (for example, Matt 18:11–14; 1 Cor 5–7; Heb 12:5–12). Pastors and other church leaders will need to begin to articulate better that online behavior is not immune to this accountability. This is true not only for sins committed privately, but also for some of the "downward" bias that Lanier mentions: the verbal abuse, lies, unfair treatment, and general hostility that sometimes characterizes communication in online public forums. If a church would not tolerate sinful speech in the "real life" public, why would it tolerate it in digital public forums?

Conclusion

Discipleship is not optional: Jesus calls us to make disciples wherever we find ourselves. We are in the midst of profound technological change, the effects of which are only beginning to show. While some technologies provide genuine opportunities for discipleship and the advancing of God's mission, there are even more significant challenges. The challenges are more significant, in my mind, because they are more difficult to notice, easier to gloss over, and damaging to the witness of the church and the path of discipleship.

---

[47] Jaron Lanier, *Ten Arguments for Deleting Your Social Media Accounts Right Now* (New York: Henry Holt, 2018), 20.

Social media, for instance, seems to have more negative effects the longer we engage with and study it. Jarod Lanier puts the issue bluntly: "Some have compared social media to the tobacco industry, but I will not. The better analogy is paint that contains lead. When it became undeniable that lead was harmful, no one declared that houses should never be painted again. Instead, after pressure and legislation, lead-free paints became the new standard. Smart people simply waited to buy paint until there was a safe version on sale. Similarly, smart people should delete their accounts until nontoxic varieties are available."[48] In discipleship, we must be willing to be honest about this, and to encourage ourselves and those in our churches to choose a wiser path.

At the same time, we cannot successfully go back to a time before this technological age, at least not without some sort of terrible global upheaval that destroys or limits our technology. Part of what we must do is remember what is significant to the formative life of discipleship amid Christian communities. In her reflections on technological changes, Sherry Turkle encourages us to simply remember when it was different—before these "normal" things were so normal. Because maybe, just maybe, there is something important that we've lost. As she puts it:

> The amazing thing about living through dramatic change is you are right there when something that once seemed odd begins to seem natural. The trick is to remember why it once seemed odd, because that might be a reason worth remembering. We must remember when it felt most natural to communicate by text or Zoom or online instead of having face-to-face conversations. Even when sharing intimate sentiments. Or condolences.[49]

Some things we can resist; some things we must simply remember, and hope for again.

In our technological age, it might seem impossible to resist some of these forces that are changing how we think about ourselves, our identities,

---

[48] Lanier, 27.
[49] Turkle, *Empathy Diaries*, 338.

how we relate to others, and what we value most. I would compare it to being caught in a riptide. I lived in Florida for about a year, and while there I was told what to do if caught in a riptide. You do not swim directly back to shore against the riptide. Instead, you swim parallel to the shore, keeping the shore in sight, until you no longer feel the tide pushing you out. Then you swim back toward shore. In Turkle's advice to remember what has changed, and to hold on to what is good that we're beginning to lose, I think we see something like this. Keeping an eye on the shore, swimming alongside the current, in hopes that we will not be swept out to sea with the spirit of the age or the gods of the age. That's the challenge of every age that Christians live in, and it remains the challenge today.

13

The World Is Watching

Proclaiming Truth and Maintaining Our Witness in the Digital Age

Keith Plummer

I am indebted to the late Francis Schaeffer. Humanly speaking, I stumbled across his writing at a dark time in my early Christian life when I felt that I was at a point of having to decide between pursuing the life of the mind and abandoning it for the sake of cultivating a vibrant faith. In Schaeffer, I found someone who exemplified, though imperfectly to be sure, the possibility of the two peaceably and powerfully coexisting. I found in him someone who took seriously the kinds of questions that had caused me such emotional and intellectual upheaval. Through his writings I learned that the Christian faith has intellectually and existentially satisfying answers. I have frequently described Schaeffer as a stream in my spiritual desert, and so he was. His impact on me has been profound. Repeatedly I have returned to a work of his that I had not read for some time and thought to myself, "Oh, *that's* where I got that!" It should come as no surprise, then, that my thinking about the church's witness in the digital public square would also bear Schaeffer's marks.

The integrity and credibility of the church's witness was a constant concern of Schaeffer's, as is evidenced by the title of one of his books—*The Church Before the Watching World*[1]—and the content of several others, such as *The Mark of the Christian*. The publisher's foreword to the latter work opens with an observation that holds as true today as it did when it was first published in 1970: "Christians have not always presented a pretty picture to the world. Too often they have failed to show the beauty of love, the beauty of Christ, the holiness of God. And the world has turned away."[2] While in one sense opportunities for non-Christians to observe Christians living in community have decreased, the opportunity for the unbelieving world to behold Christians interacting virtually is at an all-time high, which, unfortunately, is not all good news.

Though Schaeffer predated the internet, I'm persuaded that he offers much for Christians desirous of faithfully bearing witness in the digital age to seriously consider. This is particularly true of one of his lesser-known works, *Two Contents, Two Realities*.[3] In it, Schaeffer noted four things he considered "absolutely necessary" if Christians were to meet the evangelistic need and challenges of the last quarter of the twentieth century. Two of these he called contents, by which he meant revealed truth that could be propositionally articulated and cognitively embraced. The other two essentials Schaeffer had in mind he called realities, by which he meant the living out or practice of the professed contents. In this chapter, we will examine the two contents required for engaging the culture and then how the way we communicate to the world around us may in fact distract from or even contradict our message. While the church should avail itself of new technologies to commend and defend the greatest message the world has known

---

[1] Francis A. Schaeffer, *The Complete Works of Francis A. Schaeffer: A Christian Worldview*, 2nd ed., vol. 4, *A Christian View of the Church* (Westchester: Crossway, 1982), 113–79.

[2] Francis Schaeffer, *The Mark of the Christian* (Downers Grove, IL: InterVarsity Press, 1970), 5.

[3] See Schaeffer, *The Complete Works*, 3:407–22.

or ever will know, we also must not allow pragmatism or efficiency to eclipse biblically informed thinking and living.[4]

Absolute Necessities for Engaging Culture

The first of the two contents was sound doctrine. Schaeffer was insistent that "Christianity is a specific body of truth" that had to be communicated and trusted if one was to be saved.[5] Thus, Christian preaching, whether to intellectuals or to those lacking formal education, must be rich in content. Those we seek to win to Christ must understand that we are not calling them to exercise a blind, emotional leap of faith but to trust a message that is true to the way things are and for which there is ample reason. Christians, said Schaeffer, must avoid the error of "evangelical existentialism" that implores people not to ask questions but to just believe. As Schaeffer put it, "It must be the whole man who comes to understand that the gospel is truth and believes because he is convinced on the basis of good and sufficient reason that it is truth."[6] Christian evangelism necessitates strong doctrinal content and a demonstrable commitment to the truth professed.

In addition to doctrinal content, Christian evangelism requires that Christians provide honest answers to unbelievers' honest questions; this was the second content Schaeffer named. Since God has revealed truth about himself and the world in the Scriptures, the church must patiently listen to and respond to the questions non-Christians are asking, to show them that the Bible really does address the issues of life, not just those deemed spiritual or religious. Biblical revelation, while not exhaustive, is comprehensive, having implications for the totality of life.[7]

---

[4] For more on this theme of efficiency and technology, see the discussion of Jacques Ellul in chapter 1.

[5] See Schaeffer, *The Complete Works*, 407.

[6] Schaeffer, 408.

[7] Schaeffer, 413.

Schaeffer pointed to the apostle Paul as an example of answering questions in the course of evangelizing. In his ministry to both Jews and Greeks, Paul not only preached the message about Christ but also entertained the questions of his hearers.[8] But the primary example of answering questions was Jesus himself. As Schaeffer explained, "He was constantly answering questions. Of course they were different kinds of questions from those which arose in the Greek and Roman world, and therefore His discussion was different. But as far as His practice was concerned, He was a man who answered questions, this Jesus Christ, this Son of God, this second person of the Trinity, our Savior and our Lord."[9]

By referring to offering honest answers to honest questions, Schaeffer was not naively suggesting that all questions concerning Christianity are innocent. He recognized that fallen people suppress God's revelation in unrighteousness, as Paul explained in Rom 1:18–32. Nevertheless, "It is not true that every intellectual question is a moral dodge. There are honest intellectual questions, and somebody must be able to answer them."[10] Part of the love Christians are to display toward our non-Christian neighbors is having "enough compassion to learn the questions of our generation."[11] This imperative runs throughout Schaeffer's works, and it is particularly important—albeit perhaps more difficult—to accomplish in our information-saturated day. Learning the questions people are asking requires making time to attentively listen to them, a skill that the practices and paces to which we've become habituated, severely diminish and degrade.

At the time of his writing, Schaeffer lamented that too many Christians did not have the patience and perseverance needed to answer the questions of their contemporaries. They wanted to be able to offer instant answers, "as though we could take a funnel, put it in one ear and pour in the facts, and then go out and regurgitate them and win all the discussions." This would

---

[8] See Schaeffer, 413.
[9] Schaeffer, 413–14.
[10] Schaeffer, 414–15.
[11] Schaeffer, 414.

not suffice, however, because "Answering questions is hard work."[12] What is required is that believers begin to listen with compassion to the non-Christians in their lives, seek to understand what their questions really are, and read and study to find answers to those questions. The provision of such answers was necessary but not sufficient to bring people to salvation because "Answers are not salvation."[13] The work of the Holy Spirit is essential to anyone "bowing and accepting God as Creator and Christ as Savior."[14] But this work is not mutually exclusive of Christians' apologetic efforts. Schaeffer wrote, "Nonetheless, what I am talking about is our responsibility to have enough compassion to pray and do the hard work which is necessary to answer the honest questions. Of course, we are not to study only cultural and intellectual issues. We ought to study them and the Bible and in both ask for the help of the Holy Spirit."[15]

By realities, Schaeffer had in mind the embodiment and living out, individually and corporately, of the content professed and proclaimed. Yes, Christianity has propositional content that one must believe in order to be a true Christian. However, Christian faith is more than mere subscription to a system of doctrines. As Schaeffer succinctly noted, "The end of Christianity is not the repetition of mere propositions."[16] Rather, it is a practicing of the confessed content on both individual and corporate levels, an essential part of the church's defense and commendation of the gospel to the world.

Schaeffer called the first of the two realities true spirituality. He shared a spiritual crisis he had in 1951 and 1952 when he questioned the lack of spiritual reality both in his own life and in that of the Christian group with which he was affiliated at the time that professed a high regard for the Bible and a commitment to historic Christian orthodoxy. His own spiritual fervor was not what it had been in his nascent Christian life. These factors led him to take a pause from ministry during which he seriously reconsidered the

---

[12] Schaeffer, 414.
[13] Schaeffer, 414.
[14] Schaeffer, 414.
[15] Schaeffer, 414.
[16] Schaeffer, 416.

truthfulness of the faith. "I thought and wrestled and prayed, and I went all the way back to my agnosticism. I asked myself whether I had been right to stop being an agnostic and to become a Christian. I told my wife, if it didn't turn out right I was going to be honest and go back to America and put it all aside and do some other work."[17]

The outcome of that period of soul-searching was a renewed confidence in the truth of Christianity and a newfound realization of a truth that he had not been previously taught—the ongoing experience of what he called true spirituality.[18] This reality of true spirituality consisted of the believer living in a moment-by-moment dependence on the indwelling Spirit to manifest spiritual fruit. As he described it, "There must be something real of the work of Christ in the moment-by-moment life, something real of the forgiveness of specific sin brought under the blood of Christ, something real in Christ's bearing His fruit through me through the indwelling of the Holy Spirit. These things must be there. There is nothing more ugly in all the world, nothing which more turns people aside, than a dead orthodoxy."[19]

The beauty of human relationships was the second necessary reality. Because Christians understand who man is as the image of the infinite, personal, and holy God, their relationships are to bear witness to humanity's dignity, and they must refuse to treat fellow image-bearers as either animals or machines. This beauty is to be demonstrated in how Christians treat non-Christians as well as each other. Jesus's command to love our neighbor as ourselves entails "treating every man we meet well, every man whether he is in our social stratum or not, every man whether he speaks our language or not, every man whether he has the color of our skin or not."[20] Regardless of how brief or long our encounter with another human is, love requires that we treat him or her with honor and respect on account of his or her being a reflection of God. According to Schaeffer, "Every man is to be treated on

---

[17] Schaeffer, 416.

[18] It was this period of wrestling that gave rise to the book *True Spirituality*. See Schaeffer, *The Complete Works*, 3:193–378.

[19] Schaeffer, 3:417.

[20] Schaeffer, 418.

the level of truly being made in the image of God, and thus there is to be a beauty of human relationships."[21]

The reality of beauty in human relationships is especially to be displayed in the interaction of Christians with each other. As Schaeffer observed, "Now, if we are called upon to love our neighbor as ourselves when he is not a Christian, how much more—ten thousand times ten thousand times more—should there be beauty in the relationships between true Bible-believing Christians, something so beautiful that the world would be brought up short!"[22] The evangelistic and apologetic power of Christian love is an emphasis throughout Schaeffer's work but is perhaps nowhere more concentrated than in *The Mark of the Christian*.[23] Here, on the basis of Jesus's high priestly prayer for the unity of his followers so that the world would believe that the Father had sent him (John 17:23), Schaeffer concluded that love is the final or ultimate apologetic. Schaeffer did not suggest this as a substitute for offering an intellectual defense and commendation of the faith. However, he maintained, on the basis of Jesus's words, that the world could not be expected to give the gospel a hearing apart from Christians practicing demonstrable love between themselves. This observable love Schaeffer referred to as "the final apologetic."[24]

As committed as he was to engaging the intellects of unbelievers, Schaeffer knew that doing so was not enough to turn people from spiritual darkness to light, from sinful rebellion to humble repentance and faith. As we have seen, this requires the work of the Spirit opening spiritually blind eyes. It also requires his work in Christ's people, producing the fruit of observable love that testifies to the truth that Christ is the Son of God who came into the world to offer himself for the salvation of sinners. In Schaeffer's words, "People will not believe only on the basis of proper answers. The two should not be placed in antithesis. The world must have the proper answers

---

[21] Schaeffer, 418.

[22] Schaeffer, 419.

[23] When Schaeffer wrote of "beauty," he did so intending to mean "love." On this he wrote, "I would call it *love*, but we have so demoted the word that it is often meaningless. So, I use the word *beauty*." Schaeffer, 3:419–20.

[24] Schaeffer, *Mark of the Christian*, 17.

to their honest questions, but at the same time there must be a oneness in love between all Christians."[25]

Schaeffer concluded *Two Contents, Two Realities* claiming that if the gospel is to progress in the world, what is needed are two orthodoxies: an orthodoxy of doctrine and one of community. The presence of both is what accounts for the rapid spread of the Christian movement in its first few centuries of existence. Concerning community, Schaeffer noted that from reading the book of Acts and the New Testament epistles, "We realize that one of the marks of the early church was a real community, a community that reached down all the way to their care for each other in their material needs."[26] To the question of whether modern evangelical churches have exhibited that kind of community, Schaeffer answered negatively and said that on the contrary, they have often been "preaching points and activity generators."[27] He continued: "When a person really has desperate needs in the area of race, or economic matters, or psychological matters, does he naturally expect to find a supporting community in our evangelical churches? We must say with tears, many times no!"[28] Schaeffer's categories of contents and realities in concert with the insights of media ecology can prove helpful in thinking about the benefits and limitations of the internet as a tool for bearing Christian witness to the world.

Content and Reality in the Digital Age

If the internet does anything well, it's transfer content. Since its inception, believers have been enthusiastic about the capacity information technologies have for transmitting biblical and theological content around the world with great speed. Thanks to the internet, the gospel can reach people in regions closed to traditional missionaries. The web is a cornucopia of sound biblical and theological content produced by churches, parachurch ministries, and

---

[25] Schaeffer, 18.
[26] Schaeffer, *The Complete Works*, 3:420.
[27] Schaeffer, 420.
[28] Schaeffer, 420.

individuals. Evangelistic and apologetic content abounds in varied forms such as podcasts, websites, apps, and social media platforms. As we think about the first orthodoxy Schaeffer called for, that of doctrine, the internet seems well-suited as a vehicle for its communication. Daily the internet proves to be a valuable source for those inquisitive about the faith to explore and for those wishing to give answers to skeptics and opponents to the faith to find answers. As we think about the first of Schaeffer's two orthodoxies, consisting of the two contents of sound doctrine and honest answers to honest questions, it is not difficult to see the asset that information technologies are to facilitating their advancing. For this, we should thank God.

Yet, even with the capabilities that exist for making use of digital technologies, we must not neglect considering how the vehicles we employ are impacting the content we wish to deliver. Perhaps, for the sake of this discussion, it would be more appropriate to speak of the media employed as containers for the content as opposed to vehicles. Christians cannot be so enamored with the speed, scope, and efficiency with which information technology allows us to transfer sound doctrine and apologetic answers, that we fail to consider how the packaging by which the content is delivered might be shaping and, in some cases, even distorting it, those consuming it, and those communicating it. It will not do to argue that technologies are neutral and all that matters is how we use them.[29] Though there are promising signs of change, Christians have for too long assessed digital technologies solely based on what they were used to communicate and/or consume. However, this is a reductionistic approach that fails to consider the formative power of our tools. If we are serious about not only making converts but also becoming more like Christ in every way, then understanding media ecology is no longer optional in our high-tech world but necessary.[30]

---

[29] For more on a Christian philosophy of technology and how technology is shaping humanity, see chapter 1 by Jason Thacker. See also John Dyer, *From the Garden to the City: The Place of Technology in the Story of God* (Grand Rapids: Kregel, 2022).

[30] Two excellent Christian explorations of the formative powers of social media are Chris Martin, *Terms of Service: The Real Cost of Social Media* (Nashville: B&H,

In 1998, Neil Postman, perhaps best known for his book *Amusing Ourselves to Death: Public Discourse in the Age of Show Business*,[31] addressed a gathering of theologians and religious leaders in Denver, Colorado. The title of his lecture was "Five Things We Need to Know about Technological Change." Postman said the ideas he was to present were based on his thirty years of studying technological change and claimed they were "the sort of things everyone who is concerned with cultural stability and balance should know."[32] His hope was that his reflections would help his audience understand the effects of technological change on religious faith. Among the things Postman thought necessary to know about technology and technological change was that there is no such thing as a neutral technology. In denying that technology is neutral, Postman was speaking in philosophical rather than moral terms. Christians can be quick to point out that tools in themselves are neither good nor evil and thereby put an end to all assessment on those grounds. However, this is premature.

Here's how he explained what he meant: "Embedded in every technology there is a powerful idea, sometimes two or three powerful ideas. These ideas are often hidden from our view because they are of a somewhat abstract nature. But this should not be taken to mean that they do not have practical consequences."[33] Tools have a formative power in that they incline us to see the world in particular ways. They prioritize some of our senses and neglect or diminish others. They foster habits of mind that lead us to form certain expectations and desires. As Postman went on to explain: "Every technology has a philosophy which is given expression in how the technology makes people use their minds, in what it makes us do with our bodies, in how it codifies the world, in which of our senses it amplifies, in which of our

---

2022) and Felicia Wu Song, *Restless Devices: Recovering Personhood, Presence, and Place in the Digital Age* (Downers Grove, IL: InterVarsity Press, 2021).

[31] See Neil Postman, *Amusing Ourselves to Death: Public Discourse in the Age of Show Business* (New York: Penguin, 1985).

[32] Neil Postman, "Five Things We Need to Know about Technological Change," delivered on March 28, 1998, https://web.cs.ucdavis.edu/~rogaway/classes/188/materials/postman.pdf.

[33] Postman, "Five Things We Need to Know about Technological Change."

emotional and intellectual tendencies it disregards. This idea is the sum and substance of what the great Catholic prophet, Marshall McLuhan meant when he coined the famous sentence, 'The medium is the message.'"[34]

In his *Technopoly*, Postman writes that "embedded in every tool is an ideological bias, a predisposition to construct the world as one thing rather than another, to value one thing over another, to amplify one sense or skill or attitude more loudly than another."[35] Nicholas Carr, author of *The Shallows: What the Internet Is Doing to Our Brains*, issues a warning that we would do well to heed in all our technology use: "We shouldn't allow the glories of technology to blind our inner watchdog to the possibility that we've numbed an essential part of our self."[36]

When we come to the second of Schaeffer's orthodoxies focusing on community, the internet does not serve well as a medium that cultivates and communicates the spiritual realities that he deemed essential to the church's witness. Christians cannot afford to neglect this consideration. We cannot afford to allow our lives in the digital public square to alienate, distract, or detach us from our local communities of faith or the communities in which they are situated. The desire to prioritize virtual interaction over embodied presence is ever present.[37]

We must think seriously about the nature of place and what community is. Throughout the Scriptures we see that God has always intended that the corporate life of his people, living in obedience to his commands, would be a testimony to his reality to those who did not acknowledge him. We read in Deuteronomy 4:5–6, for example: "See, I have taught you statutes and rules, as the LORD my God commanded me, that you should do them in the land that you are entering to take possession of it. Keep them and do

---

[34] Postman, "Five Things."

[35] Neil Postman, *Technopoly: The Surrender of Culture to Technology* (New York: Vintage, 1993), 13.

[36] Nicholas Carr, *The Shallows: What the Internet Is Doing to Our Brains* (New York: W. W. Norton, 2010), 212.

[37] For more on the nature and importance of embodiment, see Gregg R. Allison, *Embodied: Living as Whole People in a Fractured World* (Grand Rapids: Baker Books, 2021).

them, for that will be your wisdom and your understanding in the sight of the peoples, who, when they hear all these statutes, will say, 'Surely this great nation is a wise and understanding people'" (ESV).

Israel was to be a society that showed what life under Yahweh's rule looked like. Moses instructed them that their obedience to the commandments in the land would be a demonstration and display of God's wisdom embodied in their life together. When we turn to the New Testament, we see the importance of Christian community to the church's witness to its unbelieving neighbors. For example, in his letter to Titus, Paul took great pains to instruct him on how he was to teach the believers in Crete to live among each other. Verses 1–10 of chapter 2 are instructions about how believers in various stages of life are to live with and relate to each other:

> But as for you, teach what accords with sound doctrine. Older men are to be sober-minded, dignified, self-controlled, sound in faith, in love, and in steadfastness. Older women likewise are to be reverent in behavior, not slanderers or slaves to much wine. They are to teach what is good, and so train the young women to love their husbands and children, to be self-controlled, pure, working at home, kind, and submissive to their own husbands, that the word of God may not be reviled. Likewise, urge the younger men to be self-controlled. Show yourself in all respects to be a model of good works, and in your teaching show integrity, dignity, and sound speech that cannot be condemned, so that an opponent may be put to shame, having nothing evil to say about us. Bondservants are to be submissive to their own masters in everything; they are to be well-pleasing, not argumentative, not pilfering, but showing all good faith, so that in everything they may adorn the doctrine of God our Savior. (ESV)

That the apostle had in mind how Christian relations contribute to the commendation of the gospel to unbelievers is evident by several purpose clauses indicating the reason for the instruction given: "that the word of God may not be reviled" (v. 5), "so that an opponent may be put to shame, having nothing evil to say about us" (v. 8), and "so that in everything [bondservants] may adorn the doctrine of God our Savior" (v. 10). In *Evangelism in the Early Church*, Michael Green notes how essential observable Christian love was to the church's evangelistic effort, citing this connection as a primary reason the apostles took dissension among believers so seriously:

> Greed and arrogance about spiritual gifts threatened this fellowship at Corinth; disunity at Philippi and Rome, immorality in the churches to which 2 Peter and Jude were directed, snobbery among the recipients of James. But the speed and earnestness with which these failures in fellowship were unmasked and reproved by the Christian leaders is eloquent proof of the universal conviction that the extent and power of the Christian outreach depended on the unity and fellowship of the brotherhood.[38]

Recall that in describing the reality of beauty in human relationships, Schaeffer said that the church should be a display of such beauty that the world would be brought up short. Loyalty and love grounded in affinity and similarity in social status, ethnicity, education, and so on is in no way befuddling to non-Christians. It's sociologically explainable, and what people expect. Such was also the case in the early centuries of the Christian church. Green describes how Christian associations for fellowship were qualitatively different from their non-Christian counterparts, and how this was integrally related to the church's witness and outreach:

> Here were societies in which aristocrats and slaves, Roman citizens and provincials, rich and poor, mixed on equal terms and without distinction: societies which possessed a quality of caring and love which were unique. Herein lay its attraction. *Here was something that must be guarded at all costs if the Christian mission was to go ahead.* It is for this reason, among others, that we find Christian unity such a crucial matter not only to the New Testament writers, but to Ignatius, Clement, and the second century authors in general. It was, as Paul told the Corinthians, only a church which

---

[38] Michael Green, *Evangelism in the Early Church* (Grand Rapids: Eerdmans, 1970), 181.

was manifestly united, where each member could and did speak as the Holy Spirit possessed him, that would convince the visiting outsider that God was among them.[39]

The vital interdependence of Christian witness and Christian love should lead us to do some serious thinking about what it means to witness to the truth of Christ in the digital public square.

Witness in a Technological Society

First, a corporate witness presupposes a shared location in which Christians live together, and in which their life together is capable of being observed by non-Christians. I contend that Christian witness is best practiced in the context of Christian community where community is understood in terms of embodied locality. Before the advent of digital ecology, it would have been unnecessary to make such a clarification; a shared location was assumed for most of the church's history. However, that has changed dramatically with our acclimation to life online. We have become quite comfortable speaking of cyber*space*, online *gatherings*, and even of a digital *public square*, all of which use terminology originally associated with bodily presence in a shared location. I confess to being uncomfortable using such language. Yes, I know language changes over time and meaning changes with usage. However, I fear these changes reflect a depreciation of the goodness of being embodied creatures and an attitude cultivated by our immersion in digital technology that regards presence and place as being immaterial to fulfilling relationships. I throw my hat in with that of Carl Trueman who laments, "The loss of commercial town centers and the rise of the internet have detached people from real communities. Now bizarre phrases such as 'online community' and 'he pledged allegiance to Isis online' actually make sense because we know how the very idea of community has been evacuated of the notion of bodily proximity and presence."[40]

---

[39] Green, 182 (emphasis in original).

[40] Carl Trueman, *The Rise and Triumph of the Modern Self: Cultural Amnesia, Expressive Individualism, and the Road to Sexual Revolution* (Wheaton, IL: Crossway, 2020), 404–5.

In the fall of 2021, Facebook CEO Mark Zuckerberg announced that the corporation was changing its name to Meta. This included great promises about plans to offer hardware and services that would enable people to immerse themselves in augmented and virtual reality experiences. During his announcement, Zuckerberg spoke excitedly about going "beyond the physical world" and "being present" to each other as avatars. Not long before this, I listened in amazement to a podcast featuring a pastor trying to make the case that virtual reality church is just as legitimate as meeting in person.[41] How is it that people who confess that Jesus of Nazareth is God incarnate, who believe his body was broken and raised again for our salvation, and who look forward to the resurrection and glorification of our own bodies and the restoration of the earth, can treat presence and place so peripherally? While there are likely several factors contributing to this, I believe a large part of the answer is that the digital tools with which we have become so accustomed, do not value either physical presence or place.

Jacob Shatzer notes that "[t]echnology encourages us to think of ourselves as isolated individuals who can choose to associate in various ways. It downplays the importance of the local place and therefore affects the way we think and feel about our local places."[42] While recognizing that bearing witness to the gospel can take multiple forms, Shatzer does not think that place and presence can be substituted by digital mediation:

> However, bearing witness requires presence; it requires being somewhere. Christians can certainly bear a form of witness in virtual places, and as those virtual experiences provide more and more of a

---

[41] Jason Daye, "DJ Soto: Why Virtual Reality Church Is Just as Legitimate as Gathering in Person," ChurchLeaders, July 28, 2021, https://churchleaders.com/podcast/402303-dj-soto-virtual-reality-church-legitimate.html. For a thoughtful biblical/theological perspective on the importance of presence and place for the life of the church and a warning about allowing the values of digital technology to shape our thinking about ecclesiology and discipleship, see Jay Kim, *Analog Church: Why We Need Real People, Places, and Things in the Digital Age* (Downers Grove, IL: IVP Academic, 2020).

[42] Jacob Shatzer, *Transhumanism and the Image of God: Today's Technology and the Future of Christian Discipleship* (Downers Grove, IL: IVP Academic, 2019), 133–34.

sense of presence, that will become more common. Yet the virtual will never be the same as physical presence. We cannot shed the metaphor of the church as the body of Christ—the analogy being to the physical body of Christ, not Jesus' Second Life avatar.[43]

As we think about being Christ's witnesses in the hyper-connected age, Christians must be on guard against the subtle yet potent ways in which our digital habits entice us to diminish the goodness of being embodied and perhaps to conceive of some alternative form of existence as superior. Ian Harber and Patrick Miller offer sound counsel concerning what may be necessary to accomplish this: "Followers of Jesus must resist constant digital connection, forming communities where people intentionally disconnect from virtual reality to be present with others: look them in the eye, give them a hug, and simply *be* with them. This will be countercultural in the best way."[44]

As those who testify to the redemptive miracle of the Word having become flesh, Christians must assess technological usage by more than the criteria employed by those who do not know Christ. Professors of the goodness of creation and the wonder of the incarnation should never fall prey to the thought that digitally mediated interaction is equivalent to or even better than face-to-face engagement in shared physical space. Of course, there are times when distance, health concerns (e.g., a global pandemic), or other extenuating circumstances will prevent face-to-face interaction with those we are seeking to reach with the gospel. However, because we are testifying to the goodness of creation and the redeeming of that creation by Immanuel, God with us, the church should strive to use technologies in ways consistent with those truths. Craig M. Gay poses the question that should be more forward in our thoughts as we seek to commend the gospel to the world and make disciples:

---

[43] Shatzer, 139.

[44] Ian Harber and Patrick Miller, "How to Prepare for the Metaverse," The Gospel Coalition, November 2, 2021, https://www.thegospelcoalition.org/article/prepare-metaverse.

And so we must ask, Are our technologies enhancing ordinary embodied face-to-face relations, for example, by creating and/or protecting time and space for them? Are our devices making these relations more vivid and meaningful? If they are, then we ought to use them with deep gratitude. If, for example, we find that our use of social media makes us more attentive to the needs of others, then wonderful! We should use it gratefully. Yet if we find, instead, that our technologies are . . . undermining our ordinary, embodied, face-to-face relations with each other, then this should give us pause. It may be that technology is interposing itself between us, making our communication less fluid and our interaction less meaningful.[45]

Prioritizing Locality in the Digital Public Square

The prioritizing of physical community is important to the church's witness in a digital age in another way related to the second of Schaeffer's contents—giving honest answers to honest questions. As noted, according to Schaeffer, Christians are to have enough compassion to learn the questions of their non-Christian neighbors. The constant and immediate access we have to happenings around the nation and around the world can easily distort our perception of what is going on in our immediate communities and distract us from the cares, concerns, questions, and needs of those with whom we are in close proximity. My wife and I occasionally turn on cable news while having dinner to see what's going on in the nation and the world. At some point, usually after we've tired of seeing "breaking news" for the umpteenth time, one of us will say, "Hey, let's watch some local news." Trevin Wax notes how difficult it is to stay focused on one's own locale on account of the media around us:

Paying attention to the people closest to you is challenging in a media environment that tempts us to paint in broad strokes and

[45] Craig M. Gay, *Modern Technology and the Human Future: A Christian Appraisal* (Downers Grove, IL: InterVarsity Press, 2018), 177.

fixate on omnipresent problems. As a result, "we tend to confuse what is most depicted with what is most real," Samuel James observes. "Our concern is disproportionately directed toward things that loom large in the media hive, because that's where our awareness of The World comes from."[46]

Of course, since so many of us are connected to the "hive," attention to global matters will certainly intersect with the concerns of the individuals we encounter in our local regions. Nevertheless, we must take time to explore the specific questions and objections that the non-Christians we rub shoulders with on a daily basis actually have.

Though true spirituality and human relationships require shared physical space and embodied presence to be fully manifested, this does not absolve Christians of the responsibility to practice them to the best of our ability in our digital encounters. Here too, though, we must be cognizant of the ways our tools form us, and thus there is much to gain from the observations of media ecology. To speak about the formative powers of our communication technologies is not to suggest in any way that they divest us of agency. We are responsible for the choices we make in our digitally mediated communication. Our technology cannot make us act in particular ways, but it can and does present us with numerous temptations. To be ignorant of these temptations is to be ill-prepared to combat our sin and represent Christ well. We must be aware of how the values and priorities of a world that does not acknowledge God are embedded in the digital tools in which we immerse ourselves. Shatzer points the way between the extremes of an unrealistic option of avoiding technology all together and adopting a mindset that as long as we use them wisely, we do not need to think about the formative powers of our tools because they cannot tell us what to do:

> Rather, part of responsible, wise, faithful use of tools is analyzing the ways that certain tools shape us to see the world in certain ways, and then to ask whether those ways are consistent with the life of a

---

[46] Trevin Wax, *The Multi-Directional Leader: Responding Wisely to Challenges from Every Side* (Austin: The Gospel Coalition, 2021), Kindle.

disciple of Christ. If they aren't, then the answer could be to reject certain tools. Or it could be to limit tools in a certain way or to commit to other forms of life that can strengthen us in our resolve to pursue holiness in light of the many ways our world tempts us off that path.[47]

We must know not only our tools but ourselves. In the same manner that we must be painfully honest about what situations and relationships we must avoid because of their powerful downward pull on us, so too we must seriously consider what online activity lures us into sinful attitudes and actions. For some of us, deactivating or deleting a favored social media account may be the eye or hand we must cut off to follow Jesus more faithfully and shine more brightly in a dark world (Matt 5:29–30).

Truth and Beauty in the Digital Age

As we have seen, Schaeffer was insistent on the necessity of truth (content) and beauty (spiritual reality) coexisting for the sake of the church's witness. When it comes to our use of the internet, we concentrate much on it as a vehicle of communicating and defending truth. Yet anyone who has spent any time online can hardly say that believers in Christ on the whole place a high premium on practicing the truth with respect to each other or, for that matter, to the world. Blaise Pascal wrote, "It is false piety to preserve peace at the expense of truth. It is also false zeal to preserve truth at the expense of charity."[48] How readily we can deceive ourselves that ugliness does not matter as long as it's for the sake of the truth. This is a lie we must consistently reject.

John Newton, the former slave ship captain and writer of the beloved hymn "Amazing Grace," is another saint whose works have left their mark on me. If I could recommend only one of his works for Christians in the digital public square, it would be his letter to a friend preparing to publish an article critical of a fellow minister's theological position of substantial

---

[47] Shatzer, *Transhumanism*, 6–7.

[48] Blaise Pascal, "The Pensees: Rearranged and Selected as a Christian Apologetic," in *The Mind on Fire: An Anthology of the Writings of Blaise Pascal Including "The Pensees,"* ed. James Houston (Portland: Multnomah, 1989), 230.

error. In what has come to be known as "A Guide to Godly Disposition," Newton wrote, "The Scriptural maxim that 'man's anger does not bring about the righteous life that God desires,' is verified by daily observation. If our zeal is embittered by expressions of anger, invective, or scorn—we may think we are doing service of the cause of truth, when in reality we shall only bring it into discredit!"[49] Regardless of how loudly we might profess that we are committed to extending and defending the message of Christ, our lack of love toward one another in digital "spaces" betrays our profession. Treating either non-Christians or fellow believers with derision, contempt, and incivility is exactly the opposite of what we are commanded concerning adorning the teaching of our great God and Savior (Titus 2:10).

I recently asked students in a course I teach called Technology and Christian Discipleship to assess the idea of virtual reality church biblically and theologically. I wanted them to think how key Christian doctrines should inform our online practices. When I voiced some of the concerns I've written about here, a few students took a defensive posture and said that Christians are called to reach people. They rightly noted that we should not abandon opportunities that exist to take the gospel to people who might never think to enter a church. They saw only two options—either virtual reality church or forsake the "mission field" of cyberspace. I tried to persuade them that there are more options and that I wasn't suggesting that Christians wipe the dust of the internet off our feet. The church should avail itself of new technologies to commend and defend the greatest message the world has known or ever will know. Yet we must always ask whether and how the ways we seek to reach people with that message in fact undermine the content we wish to persuade people of. We dare not allow pragmatism or efficiency to eclipse biblically informed thinking and living.

---

[49] John Newton, *The Works of John Newton*, vol. 1 (Edinburgh: Banner of Truth, 2015), 188.

AFTERWORD

One of the great difficulties (and opportunities) of writing on ethics and technology is that technology is always changing. Each day there are new technologies being developed, new ideas being put forth in the public square, and new ethical challenges arising that can overwhelm even the most seasoned among us. About the time that you finish a project like this and get it in the hands of an editor, the pace of technological progress can make one feel that it will quickly be outdated even before publication date. While there are obviously some truths to that assertion since not every single example or news story used in this volume will be up-to-date whenever you read it, projects like this book are not designed or written to be relevant only in the immediacy of the latest controversy on Twitter, tirade on Facebook, viral video on TikTok, or breaking news alert that declares how everything is going to change due to the immediacy of whatever happened five minutes ago. Our use of technology has conditioned us to believe that only the immediate truly matters and that the shelf life for information is only as long as it takes us to scroll to the next controversy, news story, or opportunity for outrage.

But the allure of immediacy is not just limited to social media or our contemporary digital technologies. Media theorist and cultural critic Neil Postman described this idea in 1985 as the "now . . . this" culture, where we are only given approximately forty-five seconds to dwell on an issue or idea before being interrupted by a newscaster who is diverting our attention to another story. He writes, "The newscaster means that you have thought long enough on the previous matter, that you must not be morbidly preoccupied with it, and that you must now give your attention to another fragment of news or a commercial."[1] Postman was prescient in his evaluation of how the information medium conditions how we see and understand the gravity of the latest happenings. But given the rise of social media and other digital technologies, many of us long for the day when our attention spans were forty-five seconds given how quickly we can swipe up on our feeds, spending less than a second or two to think deeply on a given issue and form a public opinion about it.

While much of our society (including you and me) are routinely given to seeing the world as bite-size chunks of entertainment as we give in to the sense of immediacy, reading a volume like this will challenge and press us to consider these ethical issues of technology in a much deeper way than we are accustomed to in the digital public square of today. That type of depth naturally comes at a cost, as not everything we read is written in response to what just came across your social media feed or that breaking news alert you just missed on your phone, which is likely sitting right next to you as you read these words. That is the beauty of reading, though, in the age of immediacy, since it causes us to slow down, think deeply, and reflect on what truly matters.

The allure of the immediate is one of the most challenging aspects of digital culture and one that Christians must counteract. We must reprogram ourselves to navigate in light of timeless truths and steadfast ethical principles. The Christian ethic is not developed in response to immediate challenges but is rather derived from how the eternal God has made the world and how he has spoken to his people from eternity past about how they are to love him and love their neighbors in light of what he has accomplished in Christ (Matt 22:37–39). In truth, by the time you read this book, there very well may be a broken URL or two, updates to a company's content moderation policies, or even a major new player on the tech scene. But none of those things alter the nature of the Christian ethic even if the application of

---

[1] Neil Postman, *Amusing Ourselves to Death: Public Discourse in the Age of Show Business*, 20th ann. ed. (New York: Penguin Books, 2006), 99–100.

some of these principles might shift as the technology evolves and opinion in the public square shifts.

For example, one such development took place in the spring of 2022, just as final edits were being made to this collection of essays. Though there have been countless twists and turns since the original announcement, Tesla CEO and technologist Elon Musk made waves in the news by making a bid to purchase Twitter and take the company private. Musk had long been a fan of Twitter, amassing nearly 100 million followers on the platform. The announcement of this purchase in April 2022 was met with both cheers and lament from across the ideological perspective given Musk's stated commitment to free expression and less content moderation on the platform. He said that his goal was to make Twitter a truly free speech–oriented platform given how many have pointed out how ideological bias has affected the company's content moderation policies and the information that is promoted by the platform.

Musk tweeted in March 2022, "Given that Twitter serves as the de facto public town square, failing to adhere to free speech principles fundamentally undermines democracy."[2] By April, Twitter's board announced that they had agreed to allow Musk to purchase the platform for $44 billion with a plan to take the company private amid a litany of changes to how the company operates. But as the deal was progressing, it seemed that the complex realities and problems of content moderation we have discussed in this volume were being realized and that fixing these types of problems may not be as simple as one might initially think.

Just as fast as the deal came together, Musk announced that the deal had been put on a temporary hold on May 13, and subsequently the deal fell apart, as there were major questions regarding the number of fake/bot accounts on the platform.[3] Limiting these types of accounts was a major

---

[2] Elon Musk (@elonmusk), "Given that Twitter serves as the de facto public town square, failing to adhere to free speech principles fundamentally undermines democracy," Twitter, March 26, 2022, 12:51 p.m., https://twitter.com/elonmusk/status/1507777261654605828

[3] Elon Musk (@elonmusk), "Twitter deal temporarily on hold pending details supporting calculation that spam/fake accounts do indeed represent less than 5% of

pillar of Musk's proposed clean-up effort for Twitter along with a host of other proposed reforms. At the time of writing, there is a legal battle over the original deal, and it seems likely that Twitter will not ultimately be purchased by Musk. One thing is clear even amid the ever-evolving news cycle: whether we like it or not, we live in an increasingly technological society centered around the digital public square, and technology has a profound effect on us as individuals and on how we imagine our society to function.[4]

As we began working on this project, I knew as editor that a volume like this would be a challenge given how complex the issues are before society today and how quickly things seem to change. Whether it be the proposed acquisition and reform of a major social media platform; the rise of a new medium, such as the metaverse and its unique challenges for content moderation; or even the emergence of new data showing the effects of social media on our brains,[5] Christians must be ready to engage the world as it is, not as how we want it to be.

The contributions contained in this volume are not meant to be knee-jerk emotional reactions to meet the moment, but rather thoughtful reflections on how Christians might navigate the challenges before us, rooted and shaped by the richness of the Christian ethic that is not timebound, nor simply convenient in the moment. In this age of distraction and immediacy, may we take the time to slow down, ask the hard questions, and reflect deeply on how the Christian ethic applies to all of life, including the digital public square of our day.

---

users," May 13, 2022, 4:44 p.m., Twitter, https://twitter.com/elonmusk/status/152 5049369552048129?s=20&t=3WiQLDLD8cSdMLzztQuIxg

[4] For more on this concept of a social imaginary, see Charles Taylor, *Modern Social Imaginaries* (Durham, NC: Duke University Press, 2004).

[5] Julie Jargon, "TikTok Brain Explained: Why Some Kids Seem Hooked on Social Video Feeds," *Wall Street Journal,* April 2, 2022, https://www.wsj.com /articles/tiktok-brain-explained-why-some-kids-seem-hooked-on-social-video -feeds-11648866192?mod=e2tw.

CONTRIBUTORS

Bryan Baise serves as associate professor of philosophy and apologetics at Boyce College, where he also directs the Augustine Honors Collegium and the Philosophy, Politics, and Economics degree program. He has contributed to edited academic volumes and writes popular-level essays for several Christian outlets. Bryan is a graduate of the University of Kentucky and The Southern Baptist Theological Seminary. He resides in Louisville, Kentucky, with his wife and three children and is probably too emotionally invested in college sports.

Olivia Enos is a policy analyst, writer, and researcher focusing on human rights and national security issues in Asia. Her research spans a wide range of subjects, including democracy and governance challenges, human trafficking and human smuggling, religious freedom, refugee issues, and other social challenges in the region. Enos has a regular column with *Forbes*. She graduated with a bachelor's degree in government from Patrick Henry College and a master's in Asian studies from Georgetown University.

David French is a senior editor at the *Dispatch* and a contributing writer for the *Atlantic*. He is a graduate of Harvard Law School, a former lecturer at Cornell Law School, and a past president of the Foundation for Individual Rights in Education. David is a New York Times bestselling author, and his most recent book is *Divided We Fall: America's Secession Threat and How to Restore Our Nation*. He is a former major in the United States Army Reserve and is a veteran of Operation Iraqi Freedom, where he earned a Bronze Star.

Christiana Kiefer serves as senior counsel for the Alliance Defending Freedom. Since joining ADF, Kiefer has defended the constitutionally protected freedom of churches and Christian ministries to exercise their faith without government interference and worked to ensure that women and girls are protected from harmful gender-identity policies. She is a graduate of Liberty University and Oak Brook College of Law and Government Policy.

Bonnie Kristian is a journalist and author of *Untrustworthy: The Knowledge Crisis Breaking Our Brains, Polluting Our Politics, and Corrupting Christian Community* (2022) and *A Flexible Faith: Rethinking What It Means to Follow Jesus Today* (2018). She is a columnist at *Christianity Today* and a fellow at Defense Priorities, a foreign policy think tank. Her work has been widely published at outlets including the *New York Times, The Week, USA Today*, CNN, and Politico. A graduate of Bethel Seminary, she lives in Pittsburgh with her husband and twin sons.

Nathan Leamer is vice president of public affairs at Targeted Victory. Previously, he served as policy advisor to FCC chairman Ajit Pai. Before working at the commission, he was a senior fellow at the R Street Institute, where he managed the institute's government relations and wrote extensively on emerging technology, intellectual property, and privacy. Before these roles, he worked as a legislative aide on Capitol Hill. He is a graduate of Calvin University.

Brooke Medina serves as vice president of communications for the John Locke Foundation. She has completed numerous programs with the Charles Koch Institute, including the Koch Leaders Program and Koch Communications Fellowship, focusing on the philosophical underpinnings of market-based management and classical liberalism. She also sits on the board of directors for ReCity Network. Her writing has been published in numerous outlets, such as *The Hill*, the *Washington Examiner*, the *Daily Signal*, and FEE. She is a graduate of Regent University, holding a BA in government and a minor in English.

Keith Plummer serves as professor of theology and dean of the School of Divinity at Cairn University. He previously served as a pastor in the Evangelical Free Church of America. Keith is a contributing author to *Before You Lose Your Faith: Deconstructing Doubt in the Church*. He earned his PhD from Trinity Evangelical Divinity School.

Jacob Shatzer serves as associate dean in the School of Theology & Missions, associate professor of theological studies, and assistant provost at Union University in Jackson, Tennessee. He is also associate professor of Christian ethics at Southwestern Baptist Theological Seminary in Fort Worth, Texas. He is a graduate of Union University, Southern Seminary, and Marquette University.

Patricia Shaw LLB (Hons), LLM, FRSA, is CEO of Beyond Reach Consulting Limited and is based in the UK but advises internationally on AI and data ethics, policy, governance, and corporate digital responsibility. Patricia has twenty years' experience as a lawyer in data, technology, and regulatory/government affairs and is a qualified solicitor in England and the Republic of Ireland. She has authored and edited numerous works on law and regulation, policy, ethics, and AI.

Jeremy D. Tedesco serves as senior counsel and senior vice president of corporate engagement for the Alliance Defending Freedom. In this role, Tedesco leads ADF's efforts to combat corporate cancel culture and to build a business ethic that respects free speech, religious freedom, and human dignity. Tedesco was also part of the legal teams that successfully litigated *Masterpiece Cakeshop v. Colorado Civil Rights Commission*, *Reed v. Town of Gilbert*, and *Arizona Christian School Tuition Organization v. Winn*, before the United States Supreme Court. He is a graduate of Regent University School of Law.

Jason Thacker serves as chair of research in technology ethics and director of the research institute at the Ethics and Religious Liberty Commission of the Southern Baptist Convention. He also serves as an adjunct instructor of philosophy, ethics, and worldview at Boyce College in Louisville, Kentucky. He is the author and editor of several books on Christian ethics, including *Following Jesus in a Digital Age* and *The Age of AI: Artificial Intelligence and the Future of Humanity*. He is a graduate of the University of Tennessee and The Southern Baptist Theological Seminary.

Joshua B. Wester is an associate research fellow of the Ethics and Religious Liberty Commission, focusing on issues of public theology, political philosophy, and religious freedom. He holds a ThM in public theology from Southeastern Baptist Theological Seminary. He is currently pursuing a PhD in Christian ethics at The Southern Baptist Theological Seminary.

AUTHOR INDEX

SUBJECT INDEX

RELATED RESOURCES

The digital age promised deep connections, rich communication, and more access to information than we could ever imagine. But while technology has brought incredible benefits and conveniences into our lives, it also has led to countless unintended consequences and deep ethical challenges that push us to consider how to live out our faith in a technological society. This volume is part of a larger research project led by the The Ethics and Religious Liberty Commission. The project is designed to provide resources to help believers navigate this digital age and think through complex and crucial ethical challenges with biblical wisdom and insight.

**To learn more,
visit ERLC.com/digital and check out
these other recent titles from B&H and Lifeway Adults.**

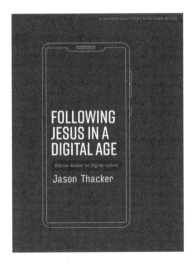